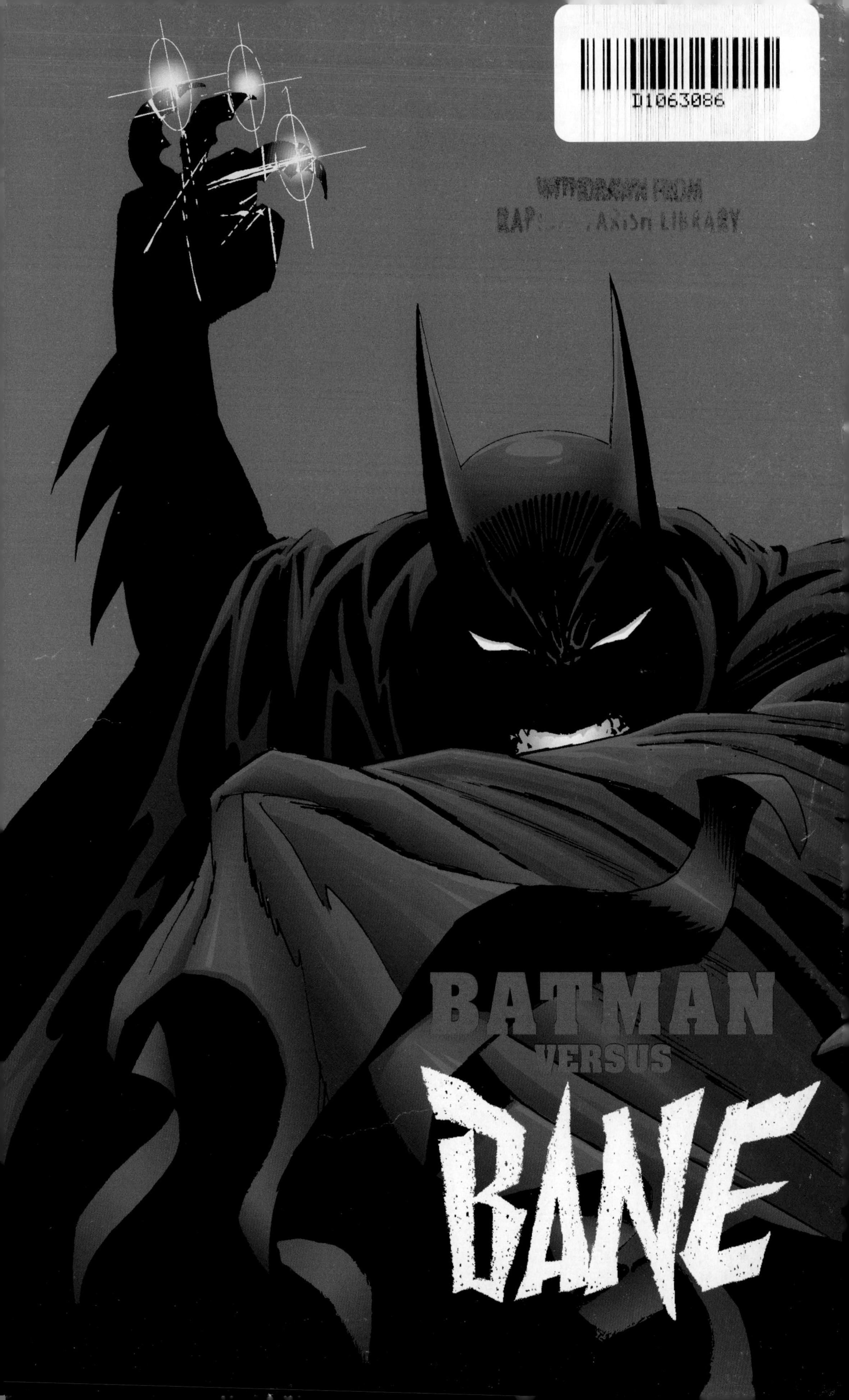
BATMAN
VERSUS
BANE

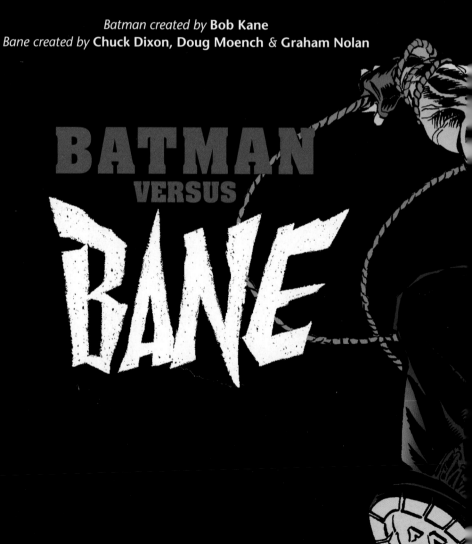

Chuck Dixon *Writer*
Graham Nolan *Penciller*
Tom Palmer Eduardo Barreto   Bill Sienkiewicz *Inkers*
Noelle Giddings Adrienne Roy *Colorists*
Android Images *Separator*
Bill Oakley *Letterer*
Glenn Fabry *Collection Cover*

Batman created by **Bob Kane**
Bane created by **Chuck Dixon, Doug Moench** & **Graham Nolan**

BATMAN
VERSUS
BANE

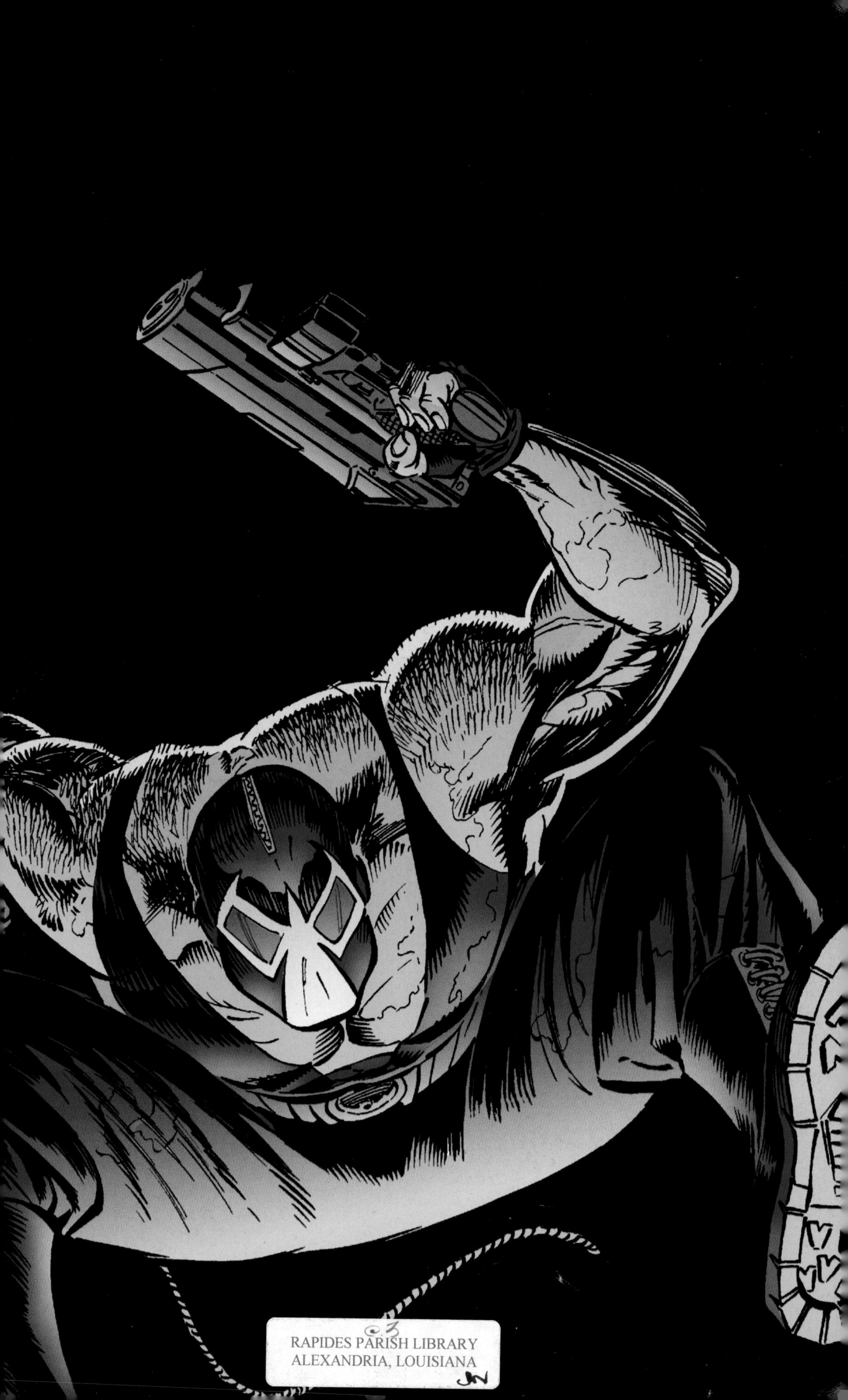

BATMAN VERSUS BANE

Published by DC Comics. Cover and compilation Copyright © 2012
DC Comics. All Rights Reserved.
Originally published in single magazine form in BATMAN: VENGEANCE
OF BANE #1, BATMAN: BANE OF THE DEMON #1-4, 52 #46,
COUNTDOWN #4, 7 Copyright © 1993, 1998, 2007, 2008
DC Comics. All Rights Reserved. All characters, their distinctive
likenesses and related elements featured in this publication are
trademarks of DC Comics. The stories, characters and incidents
featured in this publication are entirely fictional. DC Comics does
not read or accept unsolicited ideas, stories or artwork.

DC Comics, 1700 Broadway, New York, NY 10019
A Warner Bros. Entertainment Company.
Printed by RR Donnelley, Salem, VA, USA. 1/20/12. First Printing.

ISBN: 978-1-4012-3377-8

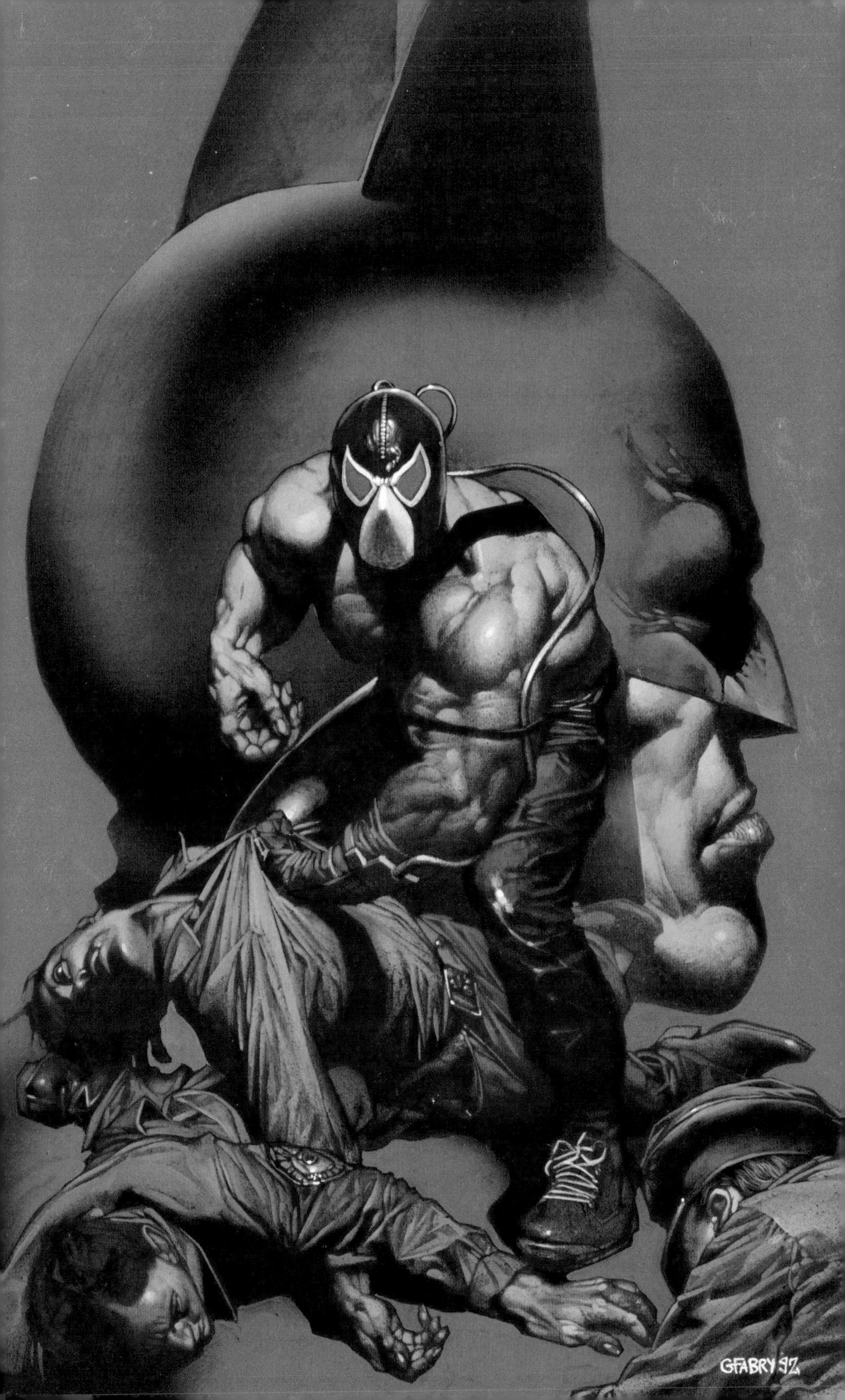
GFABRY 92

VENGEANCE OF BANE

CHUCK DIXON · WRITER
GRAHAM NOLAN · PENCILLER
EDUARDO BARRETO · INKER
ADRIENNE ROY · COLORIST
BILL OAKLEY · LETTERER
SCOTT PETERSON · ASSISTANT EDITOR
DENNIS O'NEIL · EDITOR

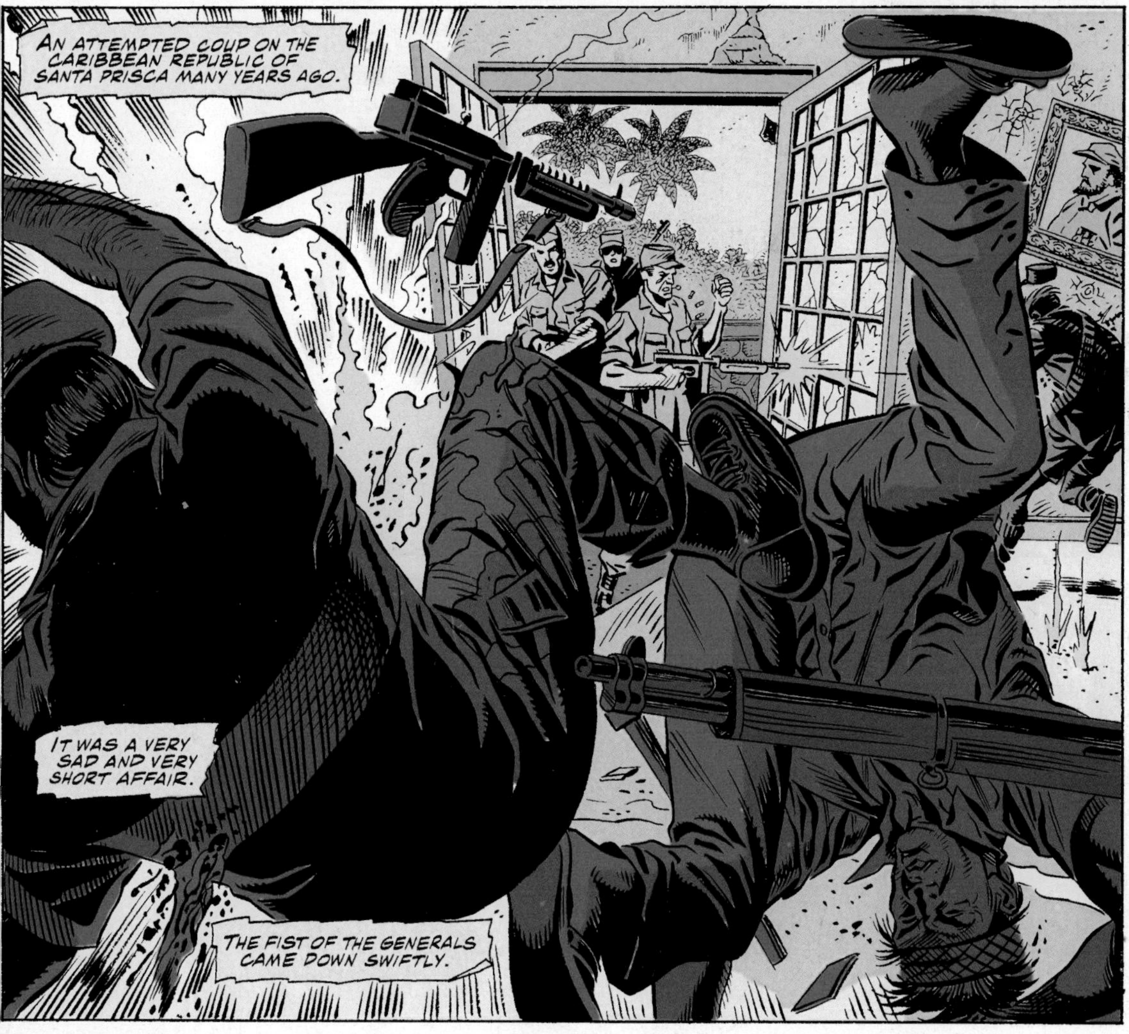
AN ATTEMPTED COUP ON THE CARIBBEAN REPUBLIC OF SANTA PRISCA MANY YEARS AGO.
IT WAS A VERY SAD AND VERY SHORT AFFAIR.
THE FIST OF THE GENERALS CAME DOWN SWIFTLY.

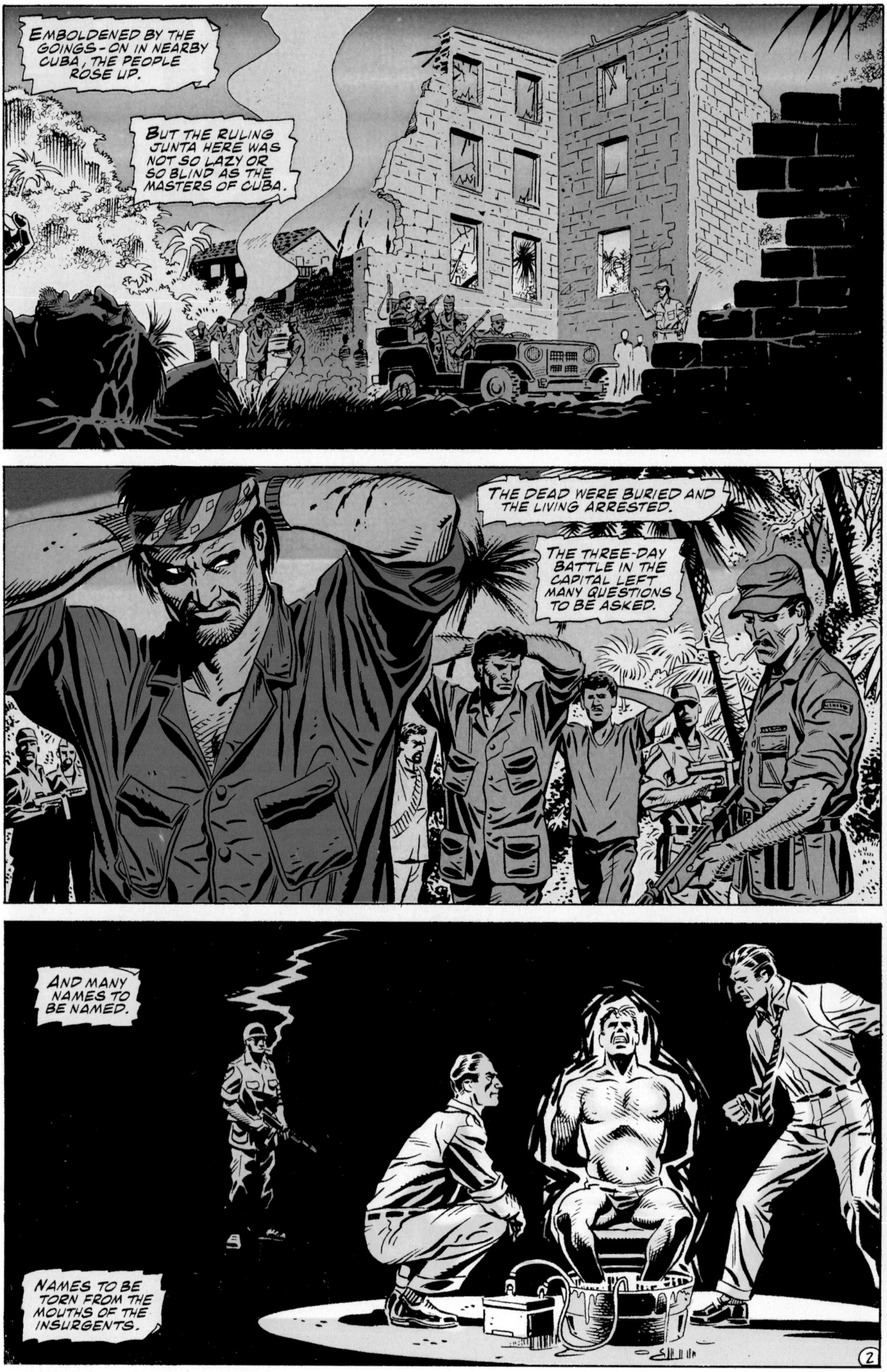
EMBOLDENED BY THE GOINGS-ON IN NEARBY CUBA, THE PEOPLE ROSE UP.
BUT THE RULING JUNTA HERE WAS NOT SO LAZY OR SO BLIND AS THE MASTERS OF CUBA.
THE DEAD WERE BURIED AND THE LIVING ARRESTED.
THE THREE-DAY BATTLE IN THE CAPITAL LEFT MANY QUESTIONS TO BE ASKED.
AND MANY NAMES TO BE NAMED.
NAMES TO BE TORN FROM THE MOUTHS OF THE INSURGENTS.

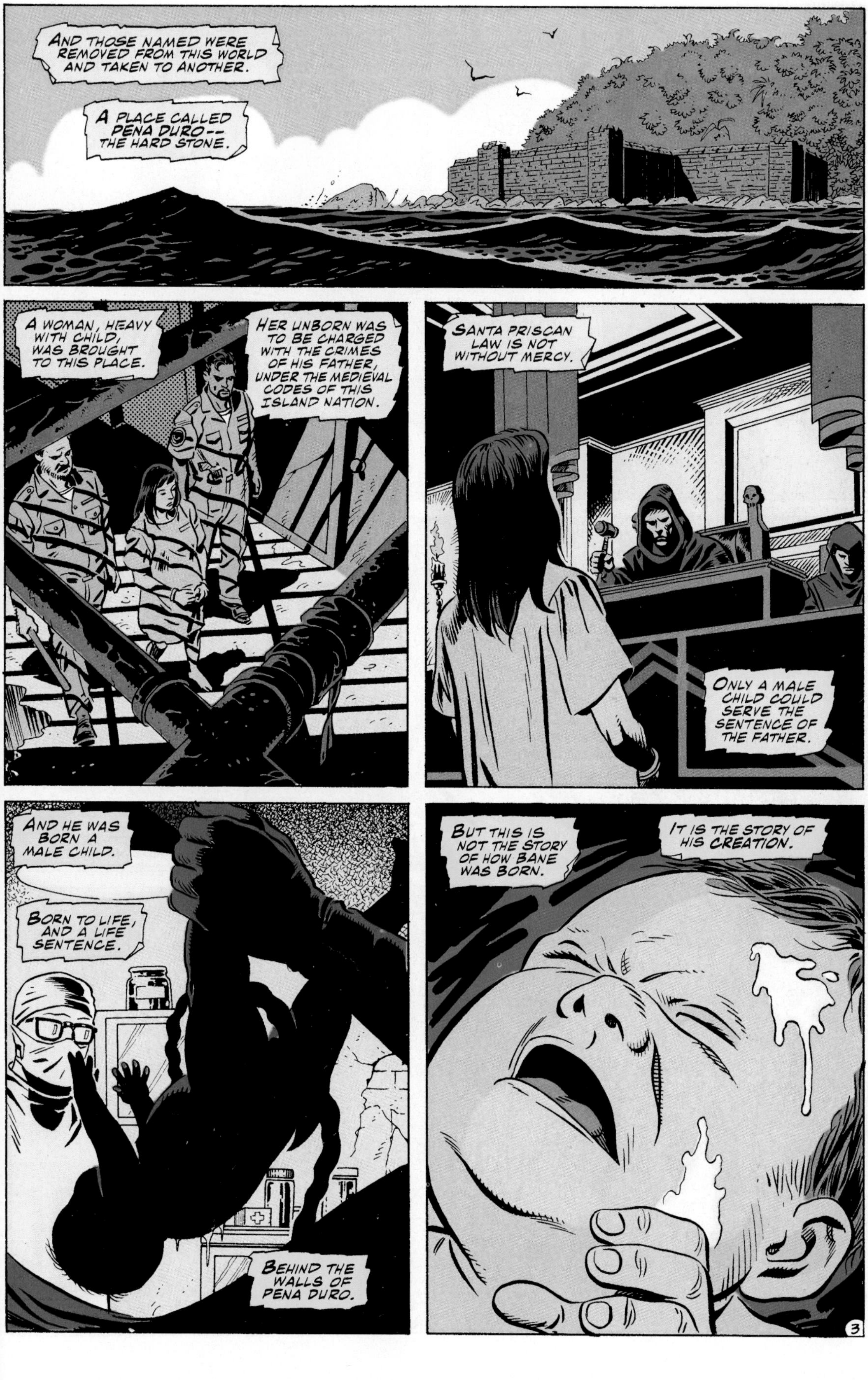
AND THOSE NAMED WERE REMOVED FROM THIS WORLD AND TAKEN TO ANOTHER.
A PLACE CALLED PENA DURO-- THE HARD STONE.
A WOMAN, HEAVY WITH CHILD, WAS BROUGHT TO THIS PLACE.
HER UNBORN WAS TO BE CHARGED WITH THE CRIMES OF HIS FATHER, UNDER THE MEDIEVAL CODES OF THIS ISLAND NATION.
SANTA PRISCAN LAW IS NOT WITHOUT MERCY.
ONLY A MALE CHILD COULD SERVE THE SENTENCE OF THE FATHER.
AND HE WAS BORN A MALE CHILD.
BORN TO LIFE, AND A LIFE SENTENCE.
BEHIND THE WALLS OF PENA DURO.
BUT THIS IS NOT THE STORY OF HOW BANE WAS BORN.
IT IS THE STORY OF HIS CREATION.
3

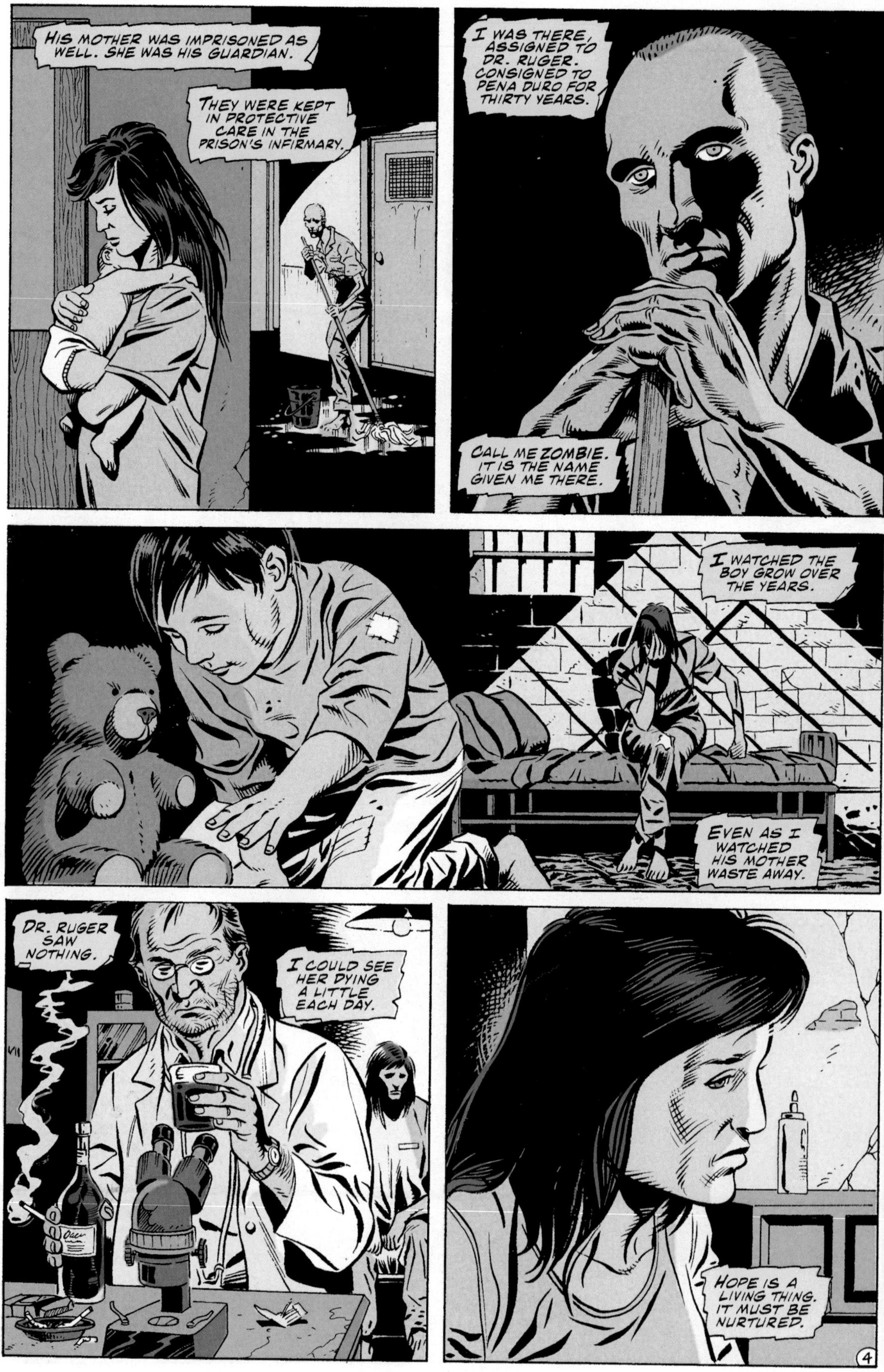
HIS MOTHER WAS IMPRISONED AS WELL. SHE WAS HIS GUARDIAN.
THEY WERE KEPT IN PROTECTIVE CARE IN THE PRISON'S INFIRMARY.
I WAS THERE, ASSIGNED TO DR. RUGER. CONSIGNED TO PENA DURO FOR THIRTY YEARS.
CALL ME ZOMBIE. IT IS THE NAME GIVEN ME THERE.
I WATCHED THE BOY GROW OVER THE YEARS.
EVEN AS I WATCHED HIS MOTHER WASTE AWAY.
DR. RUGER SAW NOTHING.
I COULD SEE HER DYING A LITTLE EACH DAY.
HOPE IS A LIVING THING. IT MUST BE NURTURED.

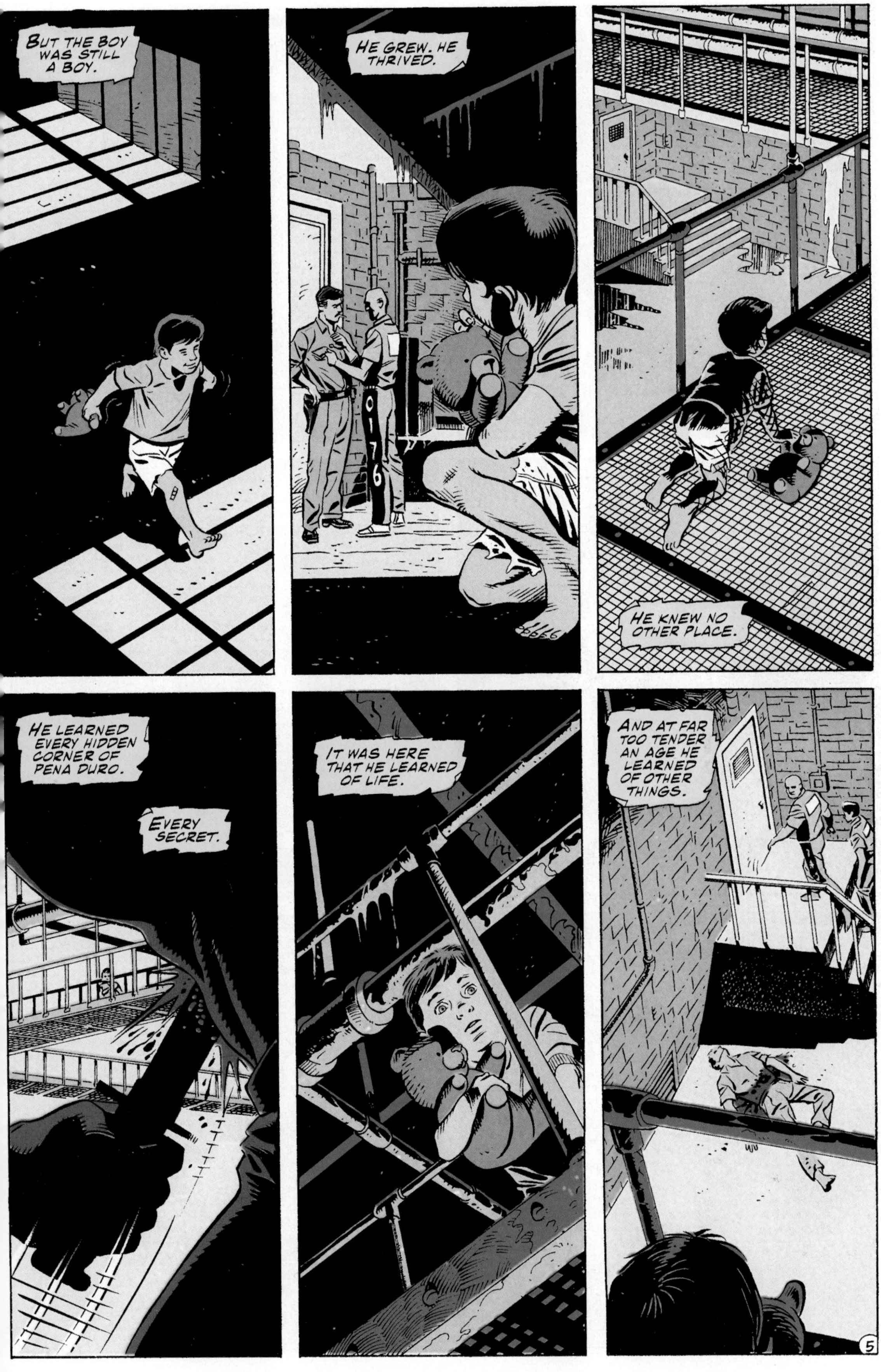

BUT THE BOY WAS STILL A BOY.
HE GREW. HE THRIVED.
0176
HE KNEW NO OTHER PLACE.
HE LEARNED EVERY HIDDEN CORNER OF PENA DURO.
EVERY SECRET.
IT WAS HERE THAT HE LEARNED OF LIFE.
AND AT FAR TOO TENDER AN AGE HE LEARNED OF OTHER THINGS.

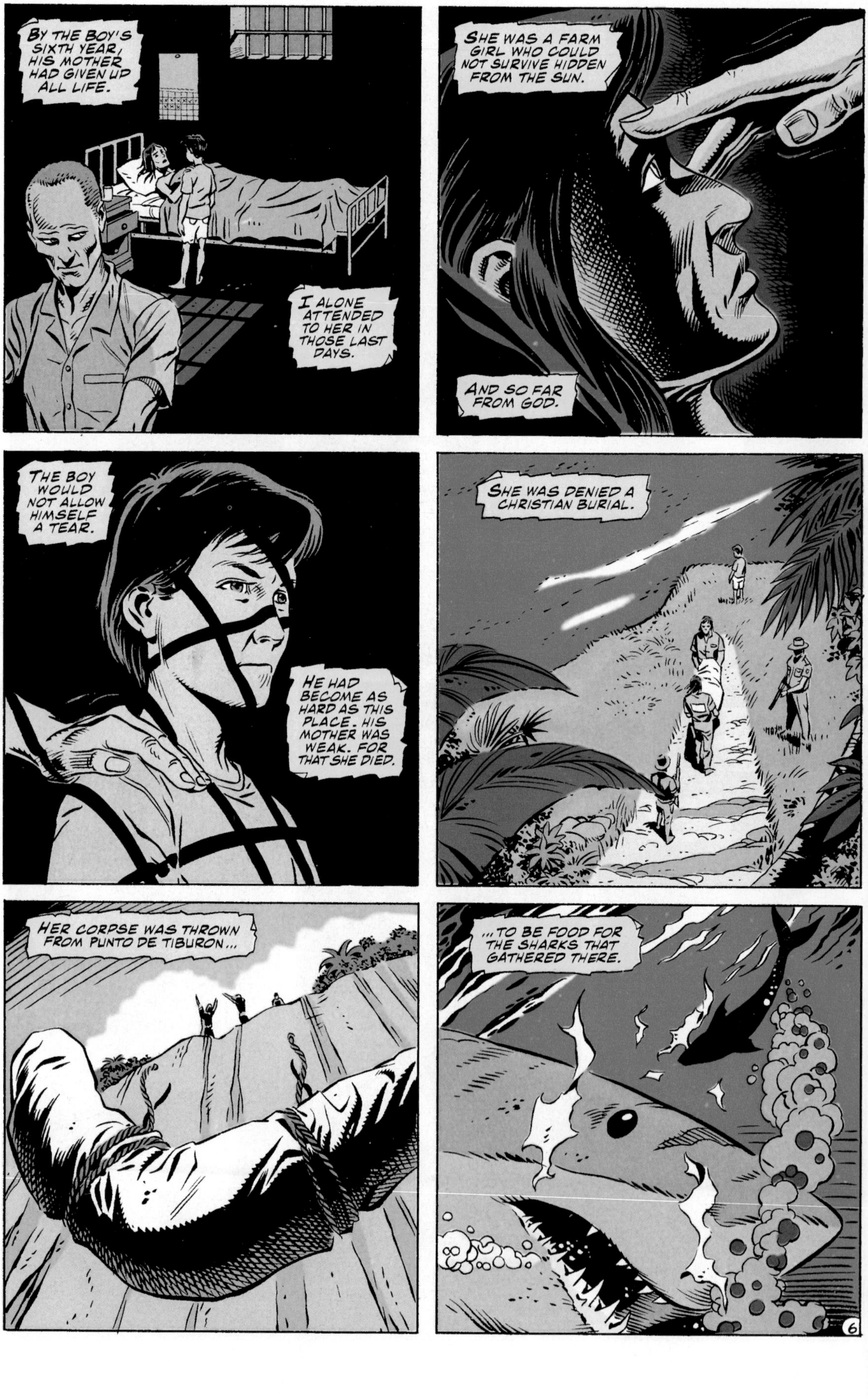
BY THE BOY'S SIXTH YEAR, HIS MOTHER HAD GIVEN UP ALL LIFE.
I ALONE ATTENDED TO HER IN THOSE LAST DAYS.
SHE WAS A FARM GIRL WHO COULD NOT SURVIVE HIDDEN FROM THE SUN.
AND SO FAR FROM GOD.
THE BOY WOULD NOT ALLOW HIMSELF A TEAR.
HE HAD BECOME AS HARD AS THIS PLACE. HIS MOTHER WAS WEAK. FOR THAT SHE DIED.
SHE WAS DENIED A CHRISTIAN BURIAL.
HER CORPSE WAS THROWN FROM PUNTO DE TIBURON...
...TO BE FOOD FOR THE SHARKS THAT GATHERED THERE.

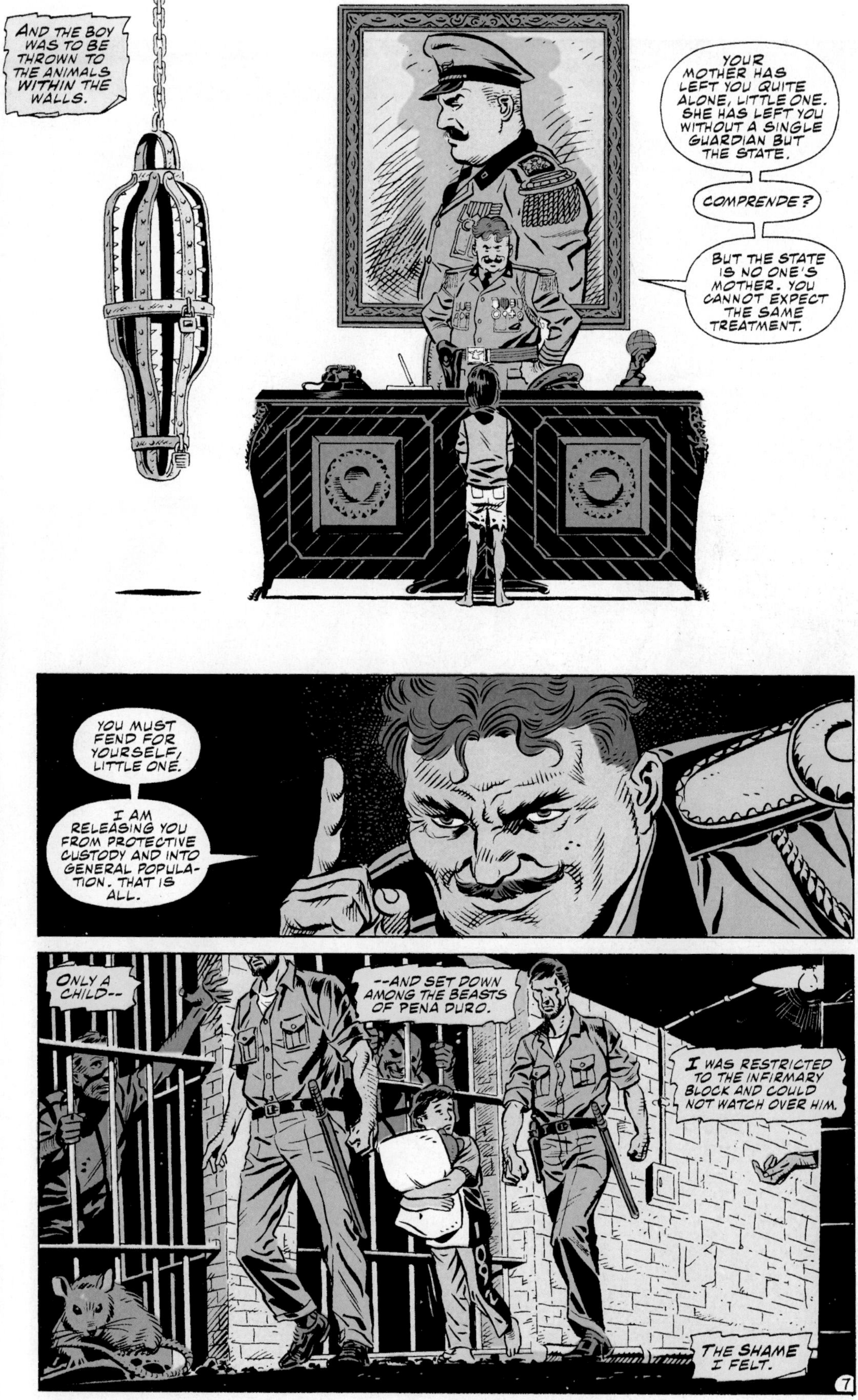
AND THE BOY WAS TO BE THROWN TO THE ANIMALS WITHIN THE WALLS.
YOUR MOTHER HAS LEFT YOU QUITE ALONE, LITTLE ONE. SHE HAS LEFT YOU WITHOUT A SINGLE GUARDIAN BUT THE STATE.
COMPRENDE?
BUT THE STATE IS NO ONE'S MOTHER. YOU CANNOT EXPECT THE SAME TREATMENT.
YOU MUST FEND FOR YOURSELF, LITTLE ONE.
I AM RELEASING YOU FROM PROTECTIVE CUSTODY AND INTO GENERAL POPULATION. THAT IS ALL.
ONLY A CHILD--
--AND SET DOWN AMONG THE BEASTS OF PENA DURO.
I WAS RESTRICTED TO THE INFIRMARY BLOCK AND COULD NOT WATCH OVER HIM.
THE SHAME I FELT.

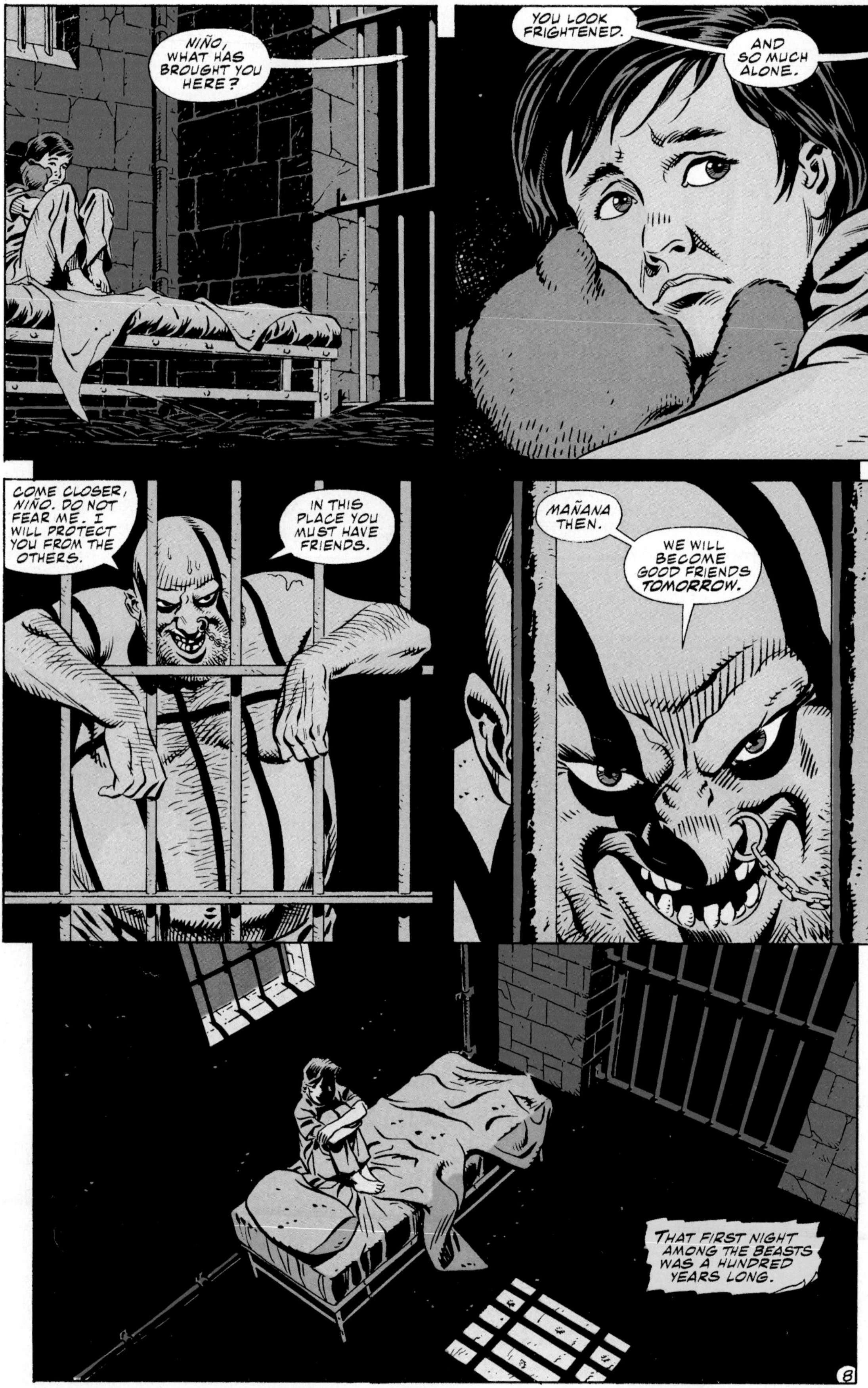
NIÑO, WHAT HAS BROUGHT YOU HERE?
YOU LOOK FRIGHTENED.
AND SO MUCH ALONE.
COME CLOSER, NIÑO. DO NOT FEAR ME. I WILL PROTECT YOU FROM THE OTHERS.
IN THIS PLACE YOU MUST HAVE FRIENDS.
MAÑANA THEN.
WE WILL BECOME GOOD FRIENDS TOMORROW.
THAT FIRST NIGHT AMONG THE BEASTS WAS A HUNDRED YEARS LONG.
8

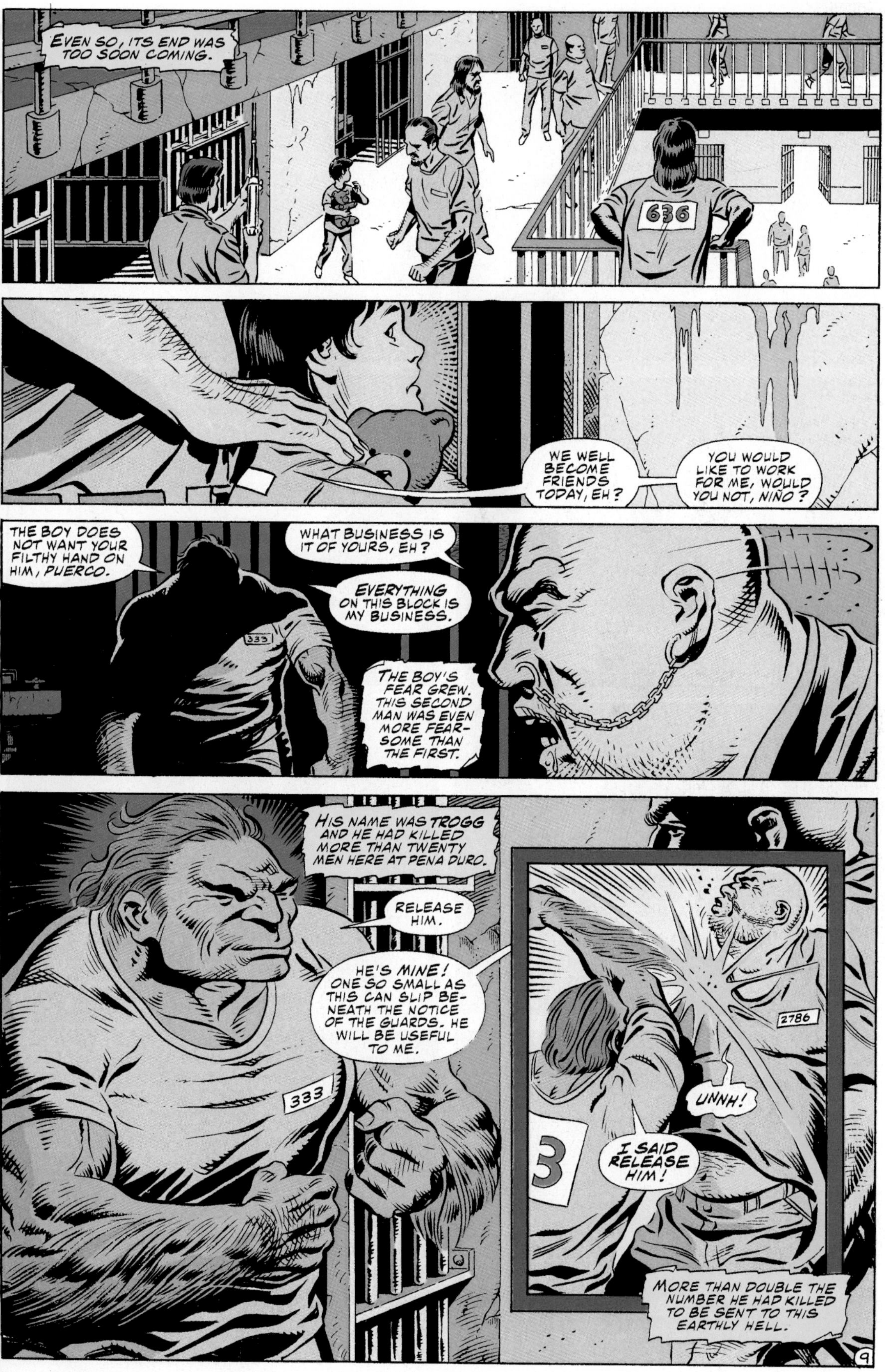
EVEN SO, ITS END WAS TOO SOON COMING.
636
WE WELL BECOME FRIENDS TODAY, EH?
YOU WOULD LIKE TO WORK FOR ME, WOULD YOU NOT, NIÑO?
THE BOY DOES NOT WANT YOUR FILTHY HAND ON HIM, PUERCO.
WHAT BUSINESS IS IT OF YOURS, EH?
EVERYTHING ON THIS BLOCK IS MY BUSINESS.
333
THE BOY'S FEAR GREW. THIS SECOND MAN WAS EVEN MORE FEARSOME THAN THE FIRST.
HIS NAME WAS TROGG AND HE HAD KILLED MORE THAN TWENTY MEN HERE AT PENA DURO.
RELEASE HIM.
HE'S MINE! ONE SO SMALL AS THIS CAN SLIP BENEATH THE NOTICE OF THE GUARDS. HE WILL BE USEFUL TO ME.
333
2786
UNNH!
I SAID RELEASE HIM!
MORE THAN DOUBLE THE NUMBER HE HAD KILLED TO BE SENT TO THIS EARTHLY HELL.

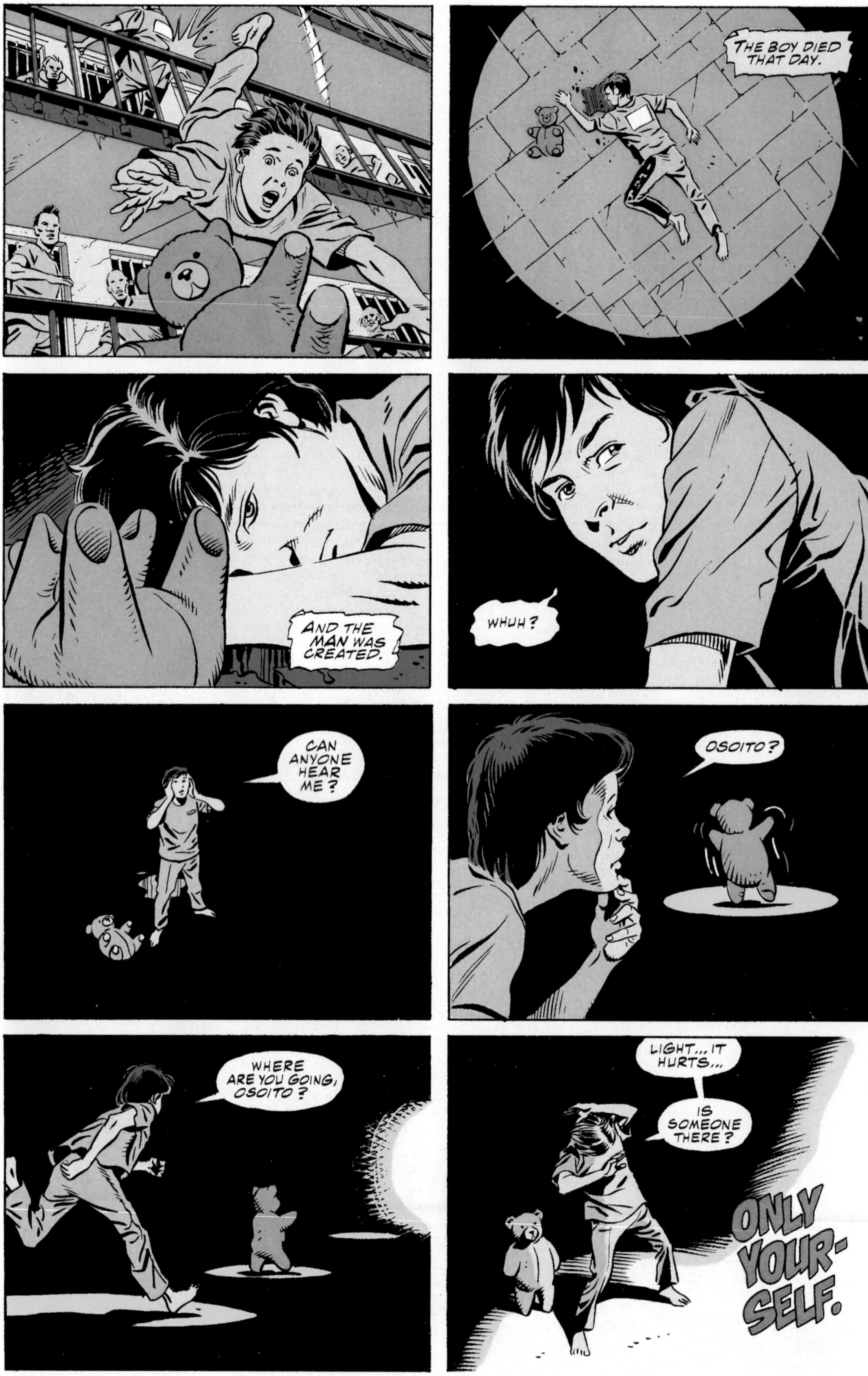
THE BOY DIED THAT DAY.
AND THE MAN WAS CREATED.
WHUH?
CAN ANYONE HEAR ME?
OSOITO?
WHERE ARE YOU GOING, OSOITO?
LIGHT... IT HURTS...
IS SOMEONE THERE?
ONLY YOUR-SELF.

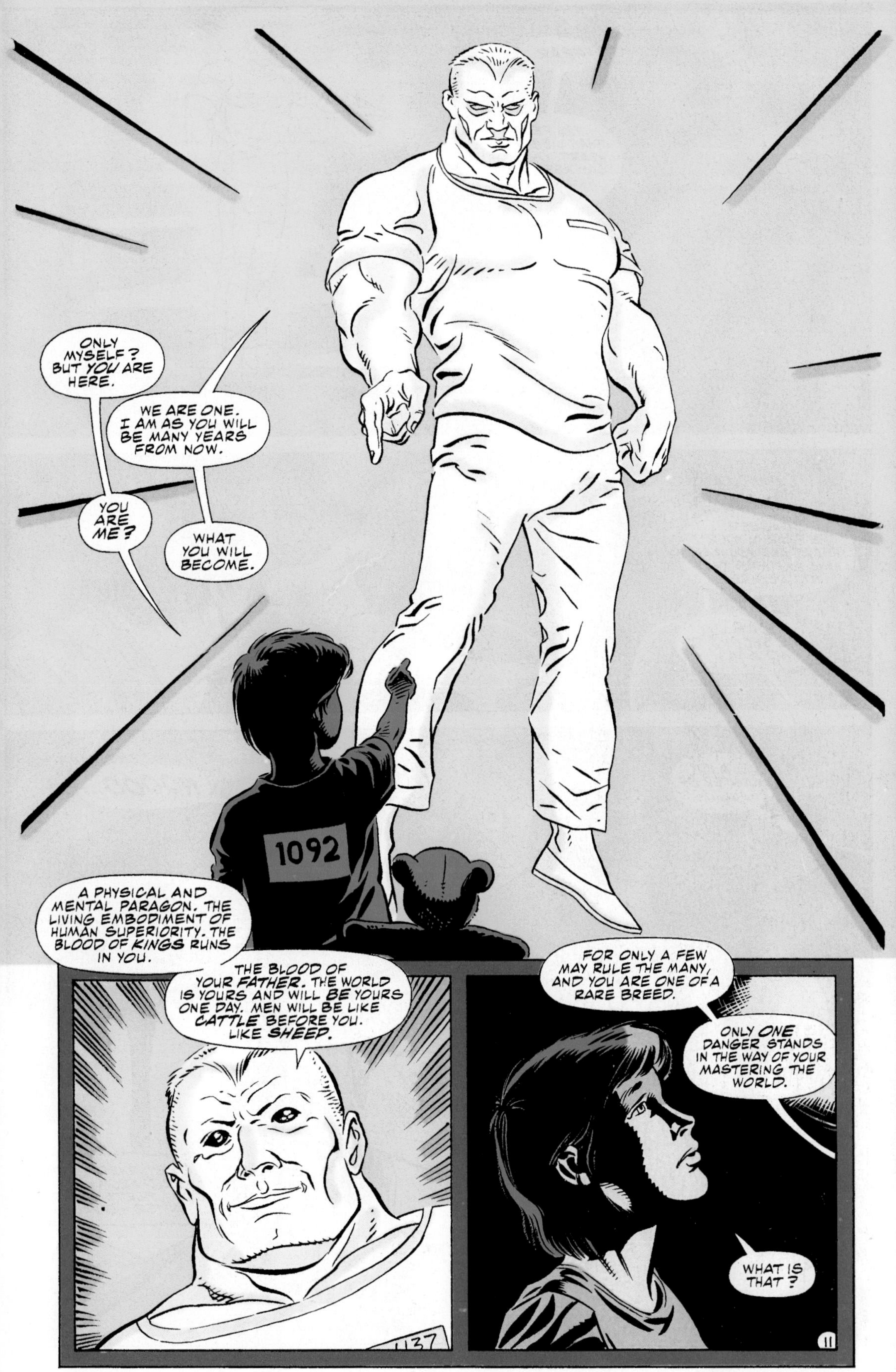
ONLY MYSELF? BUT YOU ARE HERE.
WE ARE ONE. I AM AS YOU WILL BE MANY YEARS FROM NOW.
YOU ARE ME?
WHAT YOU WILL BECOME.
1092
A PHYSICAL AND MENTAL PARAGON. THE LIVING EMBODIMENT OF HUMAN SUPERIORITY. THE BLOOD OF KINGS RUNS IN YOU.
THE BLOOD OF YOUR FATHER. THE WORLD IS YOURS AND WILL BE YOURS ONE DAY. MEN WILL BE LIKE CATTLE BEFORE YOU. LIKE SHEEP.
FOR ONLY A FEW MAY RULE THE MANY, AND YOU ARE ONE OF A RARE BREED.
ONLY ONE DANGER STANDS IN THE WAY OF YOUR MASTERING THE WORLD.
WHAT IS THAT?

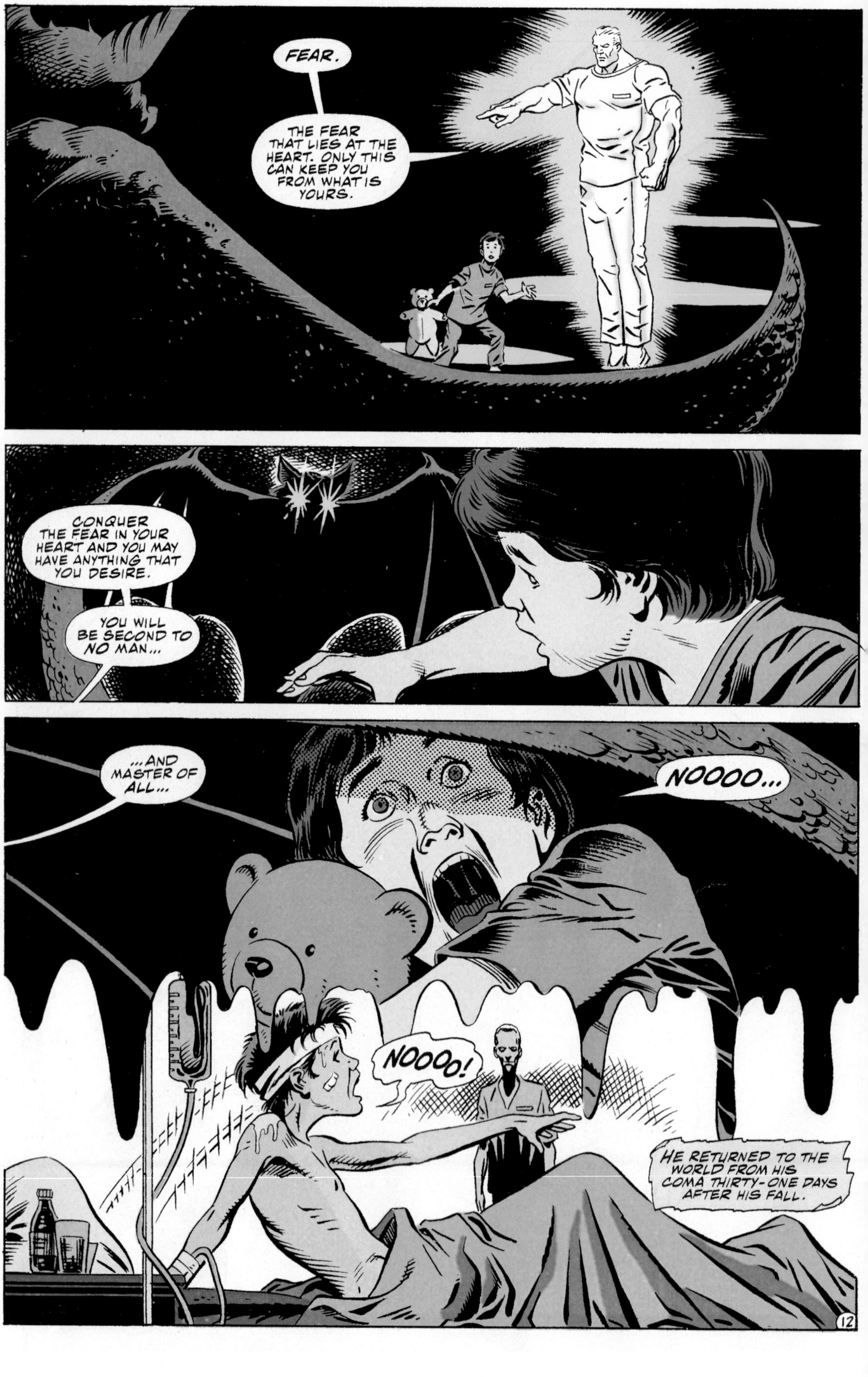
FEAR.
THE FEAR THAT LIES AT THE HEART. ONLY THIS CAN KEEP YOU FROM WHAT IS YOURS.
CONQUER THE FEAR IN YOUR HEART AND YOU MAY HAVE ANYTHING THAT YOU DESIRE.
YOU WILL BE SECOND TO NO MAN...
...AND MASTER OF ALL...
NOOOO...
NOOOO!
HE RETURNED TO THE WORLD FROM HIS COMA THIRTY-ONE DAYS AFTER HIS FALL.
12

HE RETURNED NO LONGER A CHILD.

ARE YOU SLEEPING?

QUE...?

NIÑO? I THOUGHT YOU HAD DIED...

THE NIÑO IS DEAD, PUERCO.

BUT I AM HERE.

DO YOU STILL WANT ME TO WORK FOR YOU?

NO....

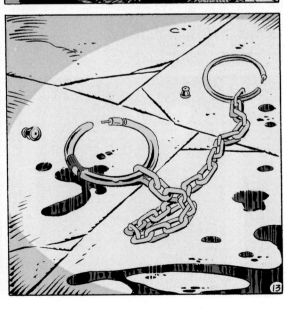

13

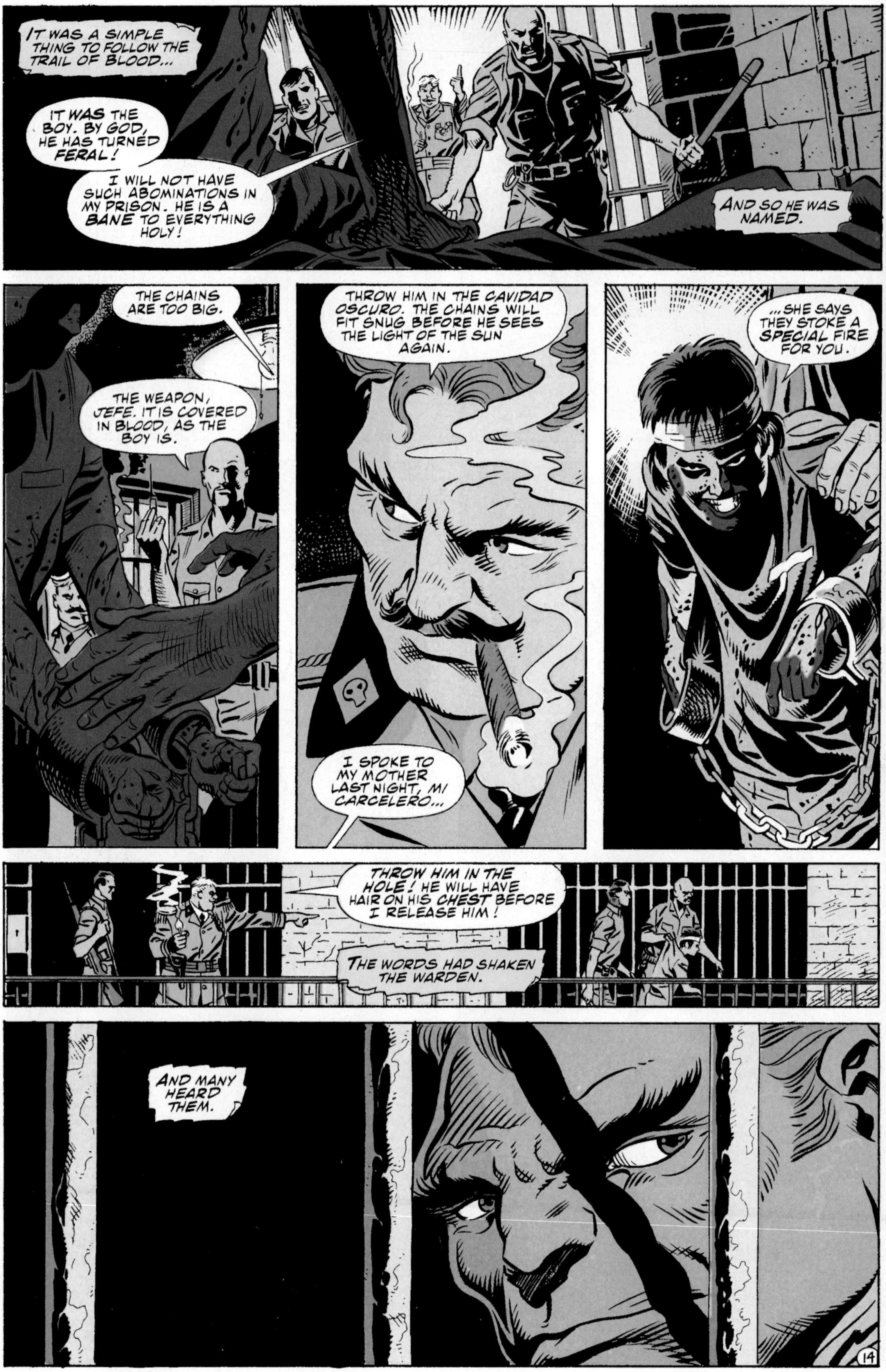
IT WAS A SIMPLE THING TO FOLLOW THE TRAIL OF BLOOD...
IT WAS THE BOY. BY GOD, HE HAS TURNED FERAL!
I WILL NOT HAVE SUCH ABOMINATIONS IN MY PRISON. HE IS A BANE TO EVERYTHING HOLY!
AND SO HE WAS NAMED.
THE CHAINS ARE TOO BIG.
THE WEAPON, JEFE. IT IS COVERED IN BLOOD, AS THE BOY IS.
THROW HIM IN THE CAVIDAD OSCURO. THE CHAINS WILL FIT SNUG BEFORE HE SEES THE LIGHT OF THE SUN AGAIN.
I SPOKE TO MY MOTHER LAST NIGHT, MI CARCELERO...
...SHE SAYS THEY STOKE A SPECIAL FIRE FOR YOU.
THROW HIM IN THE HOLE! HE WILL HAVE HAIR ON HIS CHEST BEFORE I RELEASE HIM!
THE WORDS HAD SHAKEN THE WARDEN.
AND MANY HEARD THEM.
14

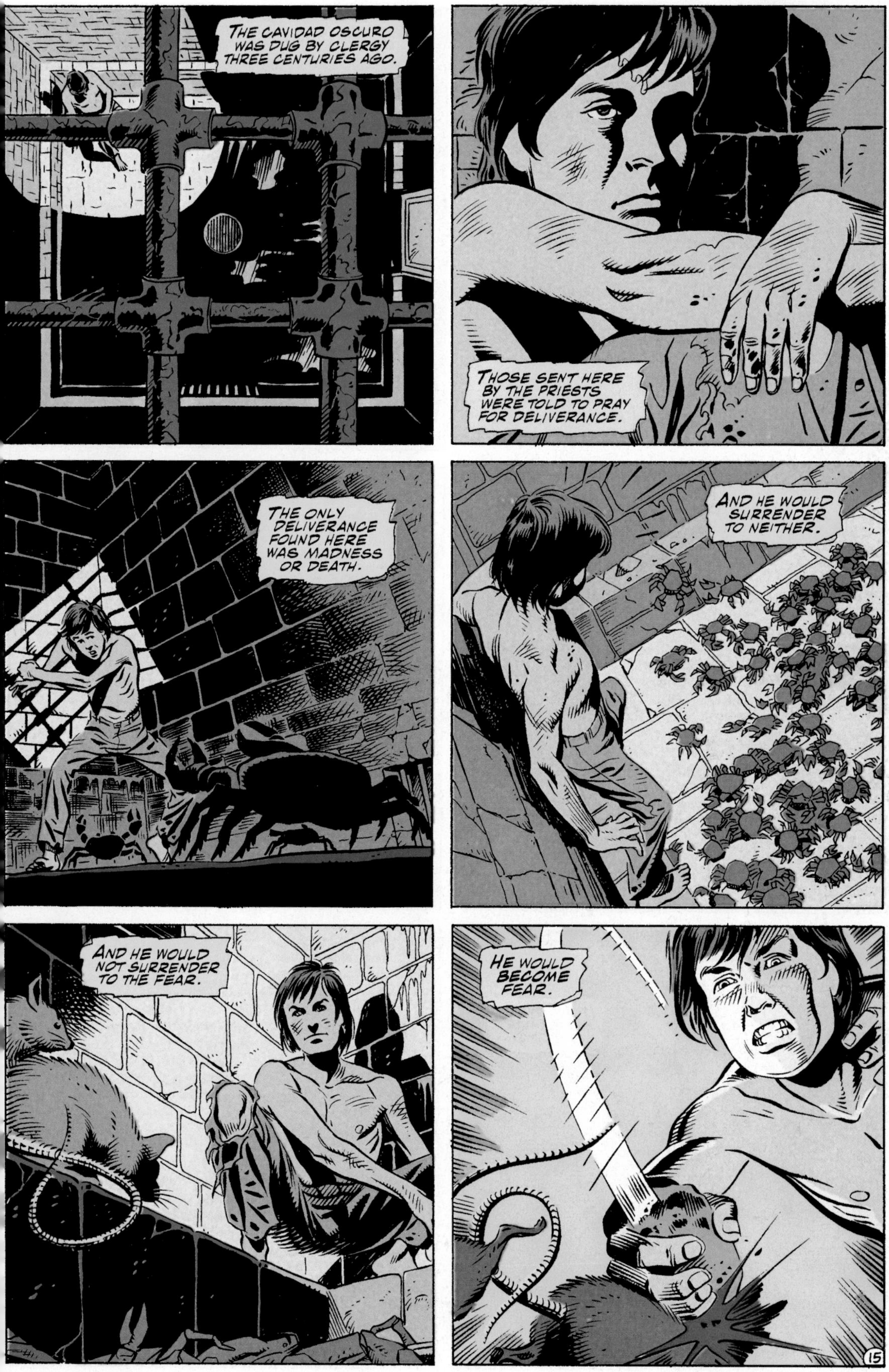
THE CAVIDAD OSCURO WAS DUG BY CLERGY THREE CENTURIES AGO.
THOSE SENT HERE BY THE PRIESTS WERE TOLD TO PRAY FOR DELIVERANCE.
THE ONLY DELIVERANCE FOUND HERE WAS MADNESS OR DEATH.
AND HE WOULD SURRENDER TO NEITHER.
AND HE WOULD NOT SURRENDER TO THE FEAR.
HE WOULD BECOME FEAR.

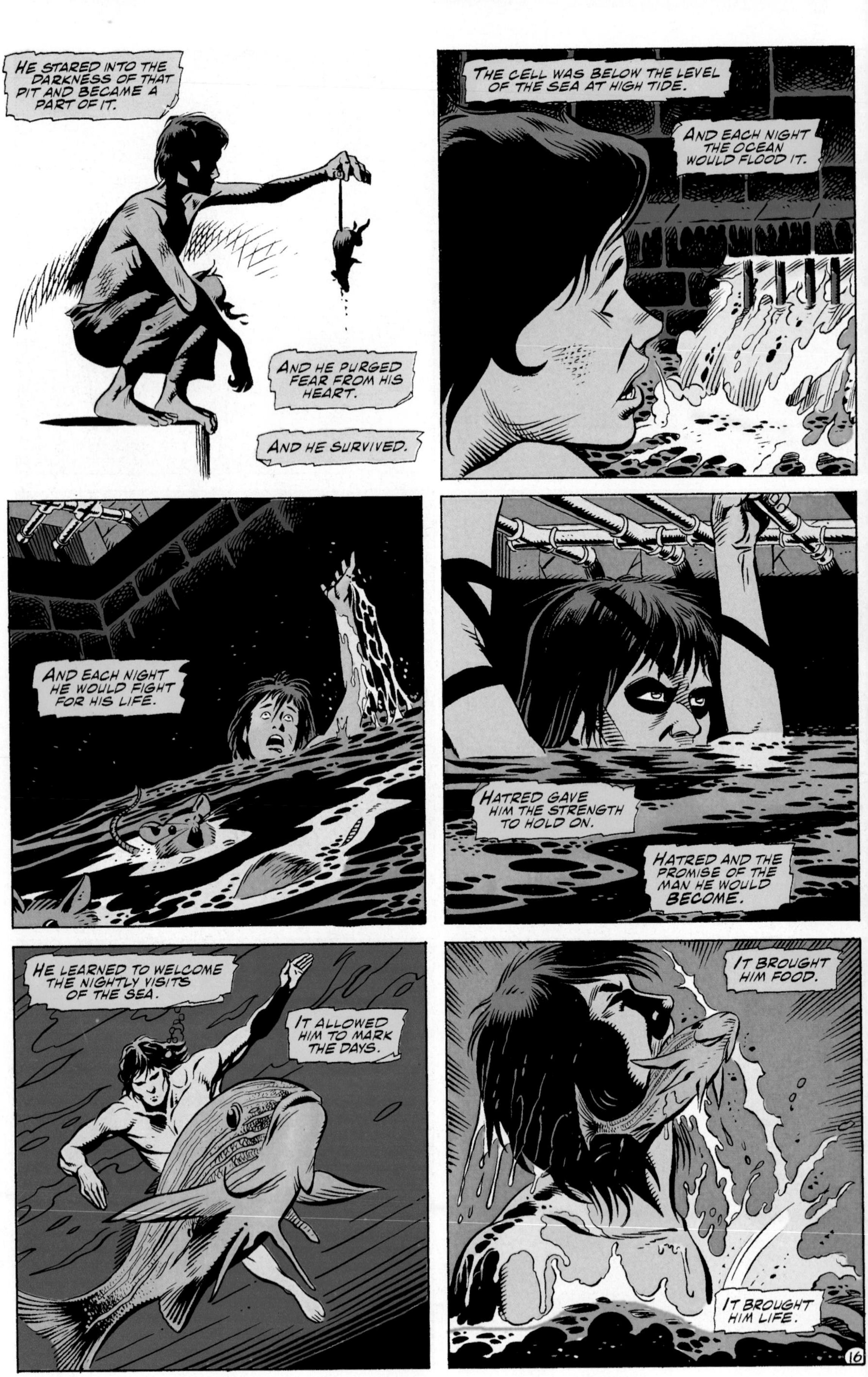
HE STARED INTO THE DARKNESS OF THAT PIT AND BECAME A PART OF IT.
AND HE PURGED FEAR FROM HIS HEART.
AND HE SURVIVED.
THE CELL WAS BELOW THE LEVEL OF THE SEA AT HIGH TIDE.
AND EACH NIGHT THE OCEAN WOULD FLOOD IT.
AND EACH NIGHT HE WOULD FIGHT FOR HIS LIFE.
HATRED GAVE HIM THE STRENGTH TO HOLD ON.
HATRED AND THE PROMISE OF THE MAN HE WOULD BECOME.
HE LEARNED TO WELCOME THE NIGHTLY VISITS OF THE SEA.
IT ALLOWED HIM TO MARK THE DAYS.
IT BROUGHT HIM FOOD.
IT BROUGHT HIM LIFE.
16

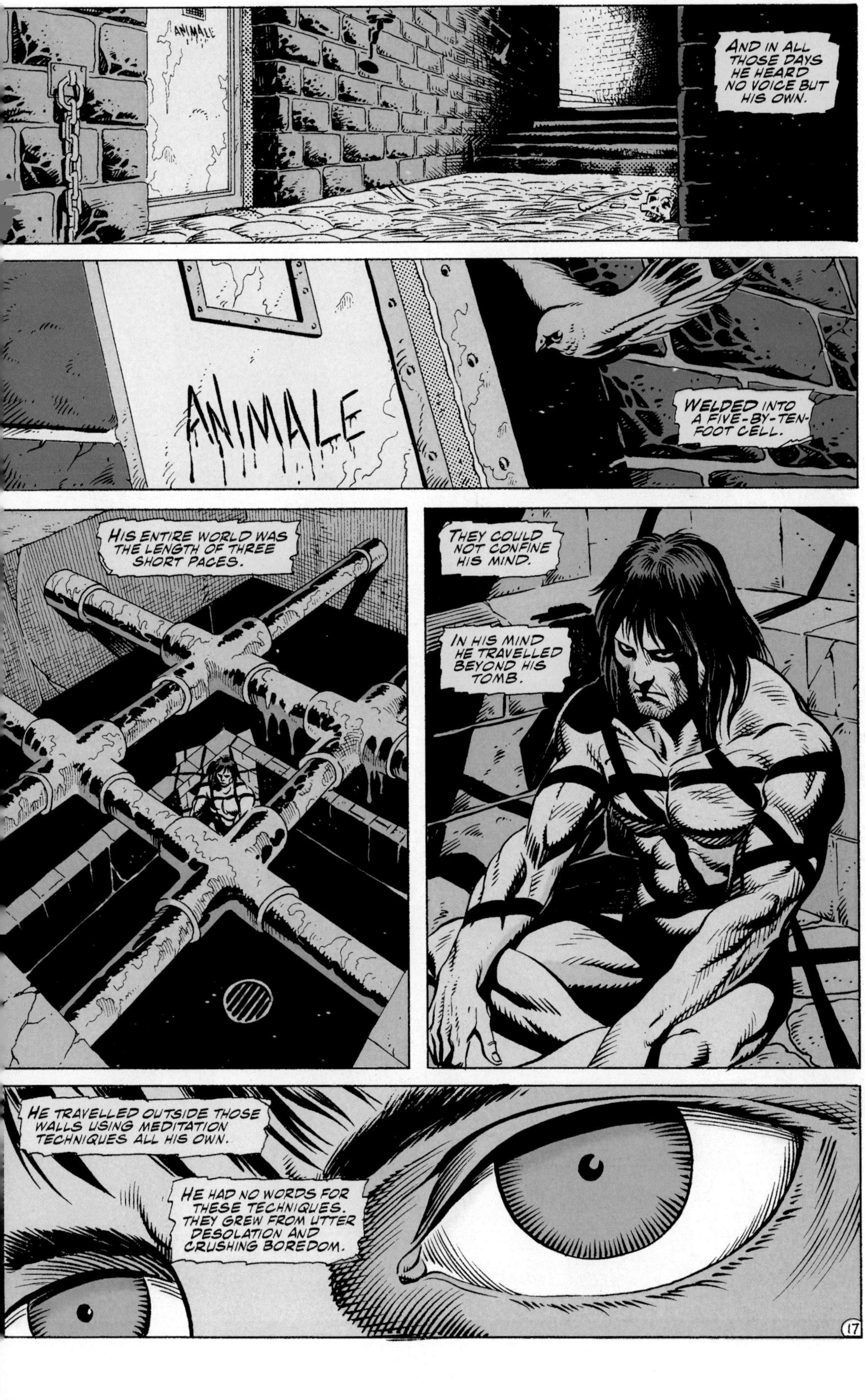
AND IN ALL THOSE DAYS HE HEARD NO VOICE BUT HIS OWN.
ANIMALE
ANIMALE
WELDED INTO A FIVE-BY-TEN-FOOT CELL.
HIS ENTIRE WORLD WAS THE LENGTH OF THREE SHORT PACES.
THEY COULD NOT CONFINE HIS MIND.
IN HIS MIND HE TRAVELLED BEYOND HIS TOMB.
HE TRAVELLED OUTSIDE THOSE WALLS USING MEDITATION TECHNIQUES ALL HIS OWN.
HE HAD NO WORDS FOR THESE TECHNIQUES. THEY GREW FROM UTTER DESOLATION AND CRUSHING BOREDOM.

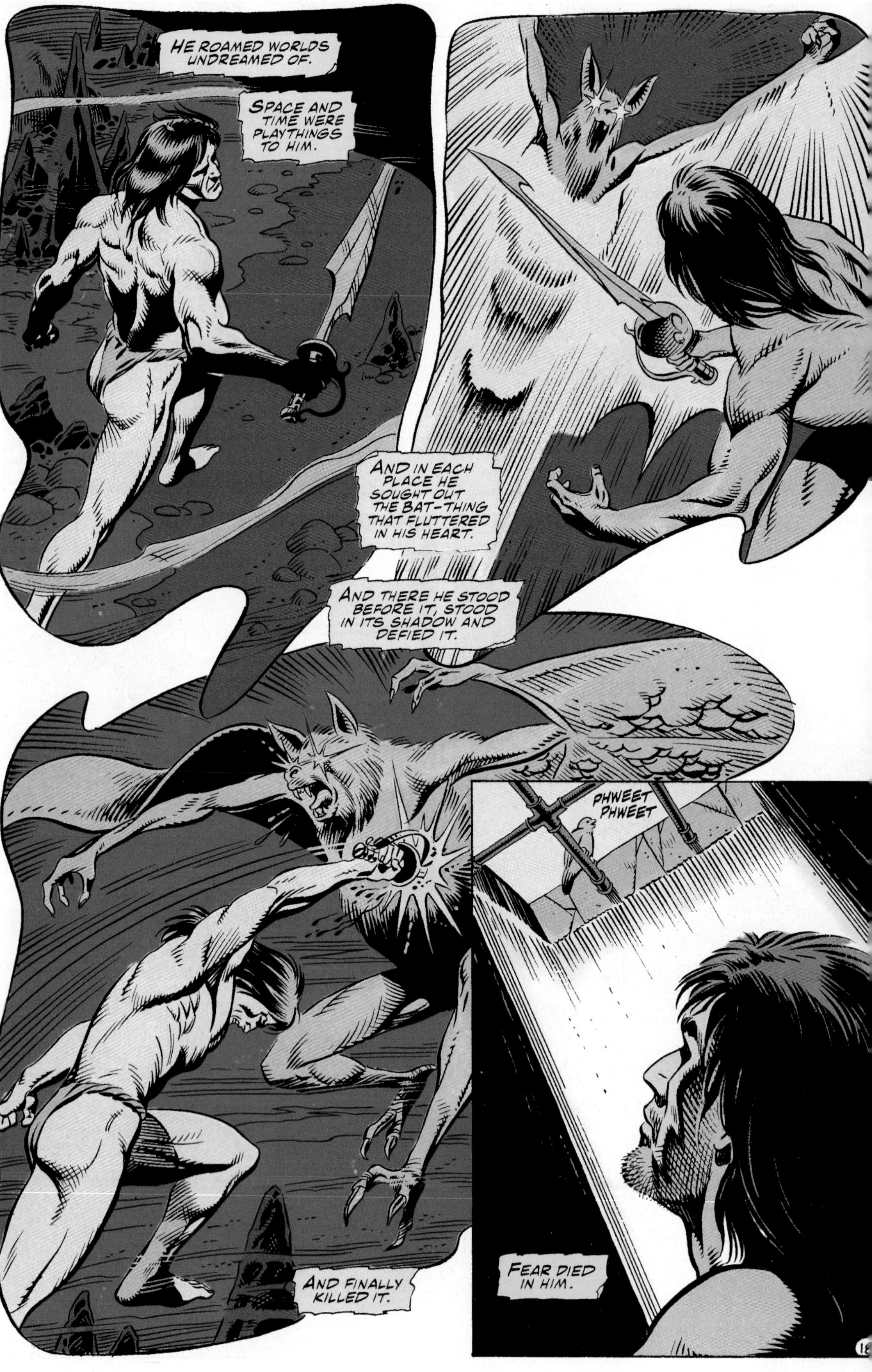
HE ROAMED WORLDS UNDREAMED OF.
SPACE AND TIME WERE PLAYTHINGS TO HIM.
AND IN EACH PLACE HE SOUGHT OUT THE BAT-THING THAT FLUTTERED IN HIS HEART.
AND THERE HE STOOD BEFORE IT, STOOD IN ITS SHADOW AND DEFIED IT.
AND FINALLY KILLED IT.
PHWEET PHWEET
FEAR DIED IN HIM.

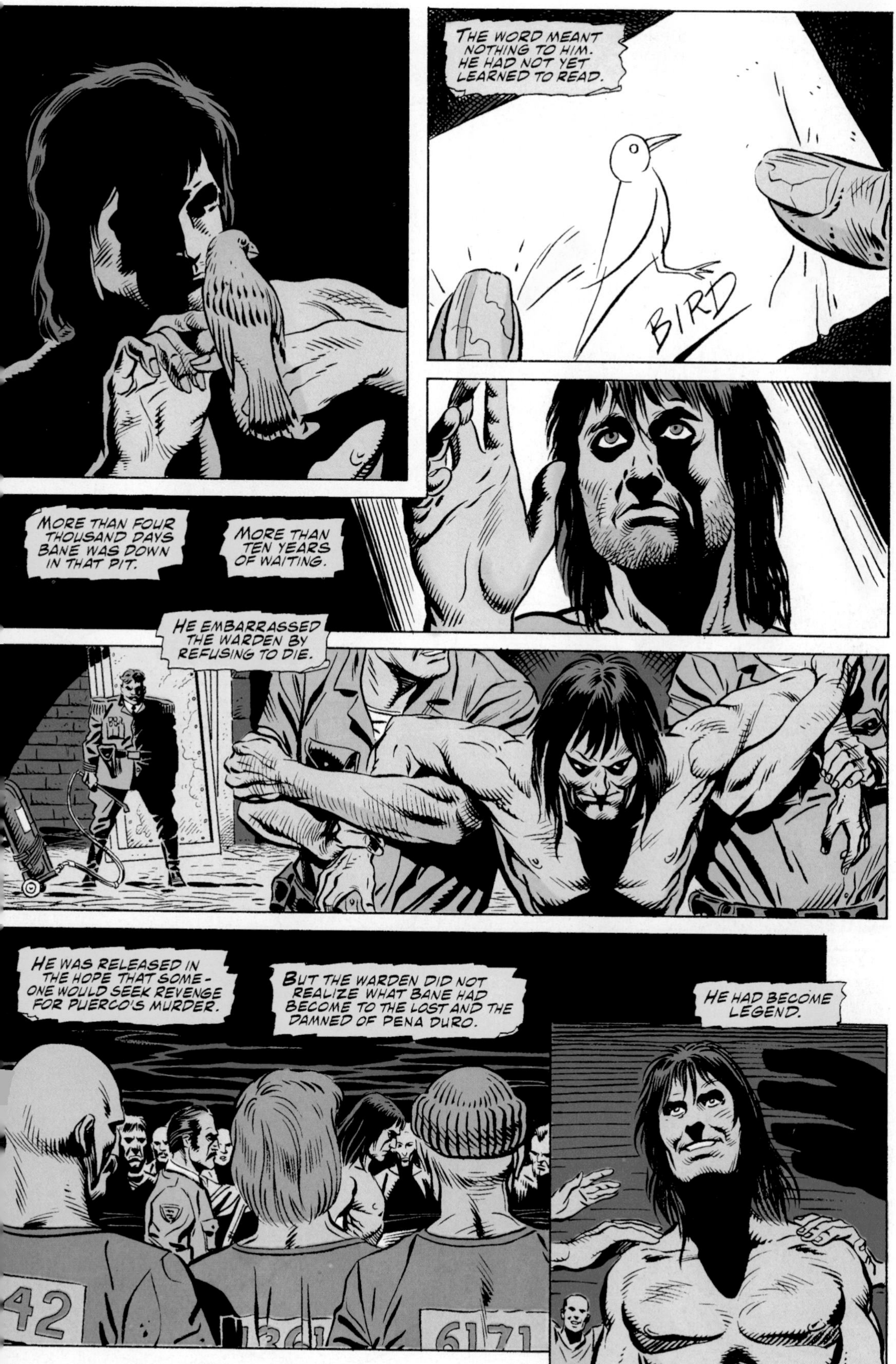
THE WORD MEANT NOTHING TO HIM. HE HAD NOT YET LEARNED TO READ.
BIRD
MORE THAN FOUR THOUSAND DAYS BANE WAS DOWN IN THAT PIT.
MORE THAN TEN YEARS OF WAITING.
HE EMBARRASSED THE WARDEN BY REFUSING TO DIE.
HE WAS RELEASED IN THE HOPE THAT SOME-ONE WOULD SEEK REVENGE FOR PUERCO'S MURDER.
BUT THE WARDEN DID NOT REALIZE WHAT BANE HAD BECOME TO THE LOST AND THE DAMNED OF PENA DURO.
HE HAD BECOME LEGEND.
42
6171

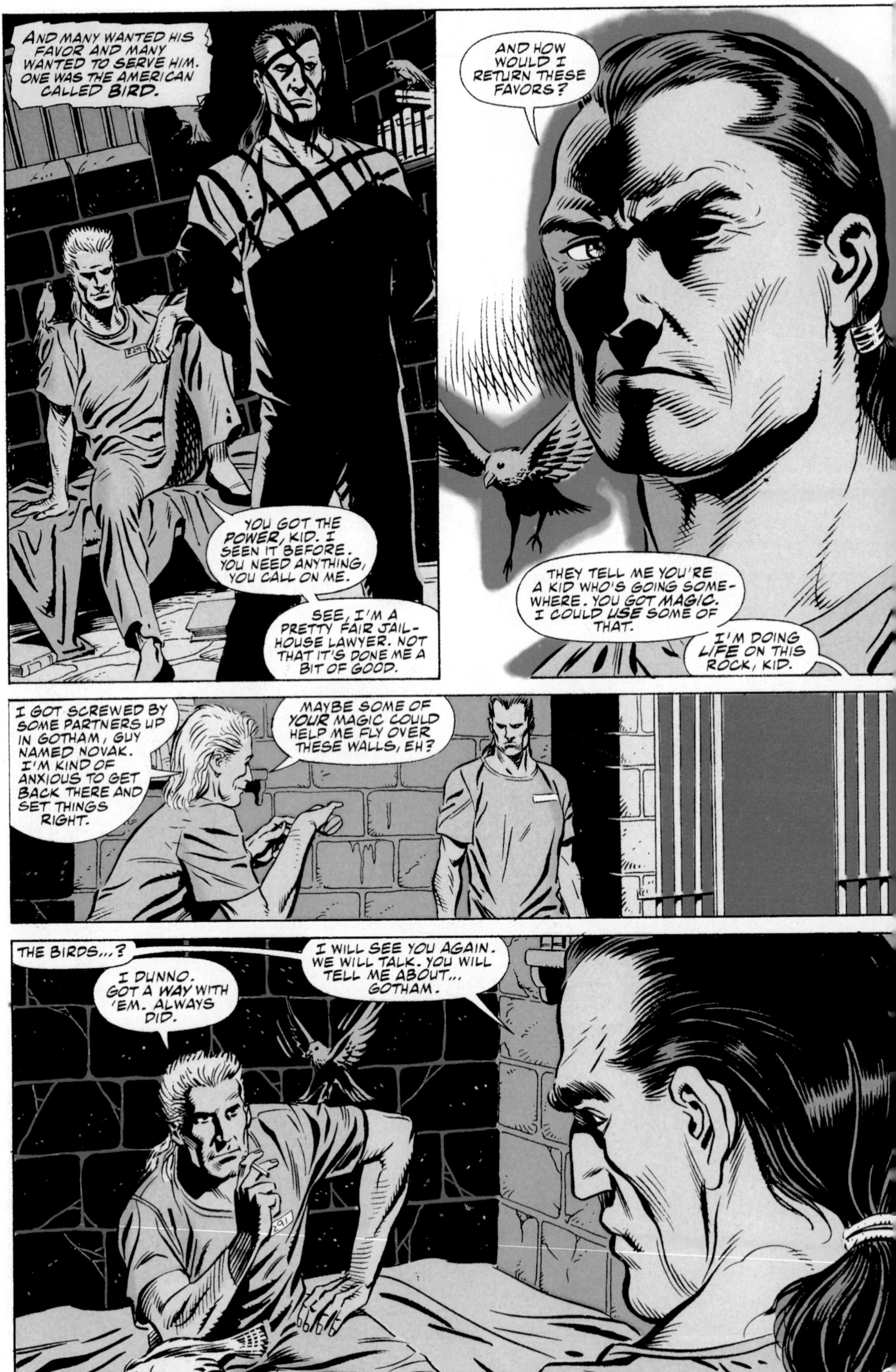
AND MANY WANTED HIS FAVOR AND MANY WANTED TO SERVE HIM. ONE WAS THE AMERICAN CALLED BIRD.
AND HOW WOULD I RETURN THESE FAVORS?
YOU GOT THE POWER, KID. I SEEN IT BEFORE. YOU NEED ANYTHING, YOU CALL ON ME.
SEE, I'M A PRETTY FAIR JAIL-HOUSE LAWYER. NOT THAT IT'S DONE ME A BIT OF GOOD.
THEY TELL ME YOU'RE A KID WHO'S GOING SOME-WHERE. YOU GOT MAGIC. I COULD USE SOME OF THAT.
I'M DOING LIFE ON THIS ROCK, KID.
I GOT SCREWED BY SOME PARTNERS UP IN GOTHAM, GUY NAMED NOVAK. I'M KIND OF ANXIOUS TO GET BACK THERE AND SET THINGS RIGHT.
MAYBE SOME OF YOUR MAGIC COULD HELP ME FLY OVER THESE WALLS, EH?
THE BIRDS...?
I DUNNO. GOT A WAY WITH 'EM. ALWAYS DID.
I WILL SEE YOU AGAIN. WE WILL TALK. YOU WILL TELL ME ABOUT... GOTHAM.

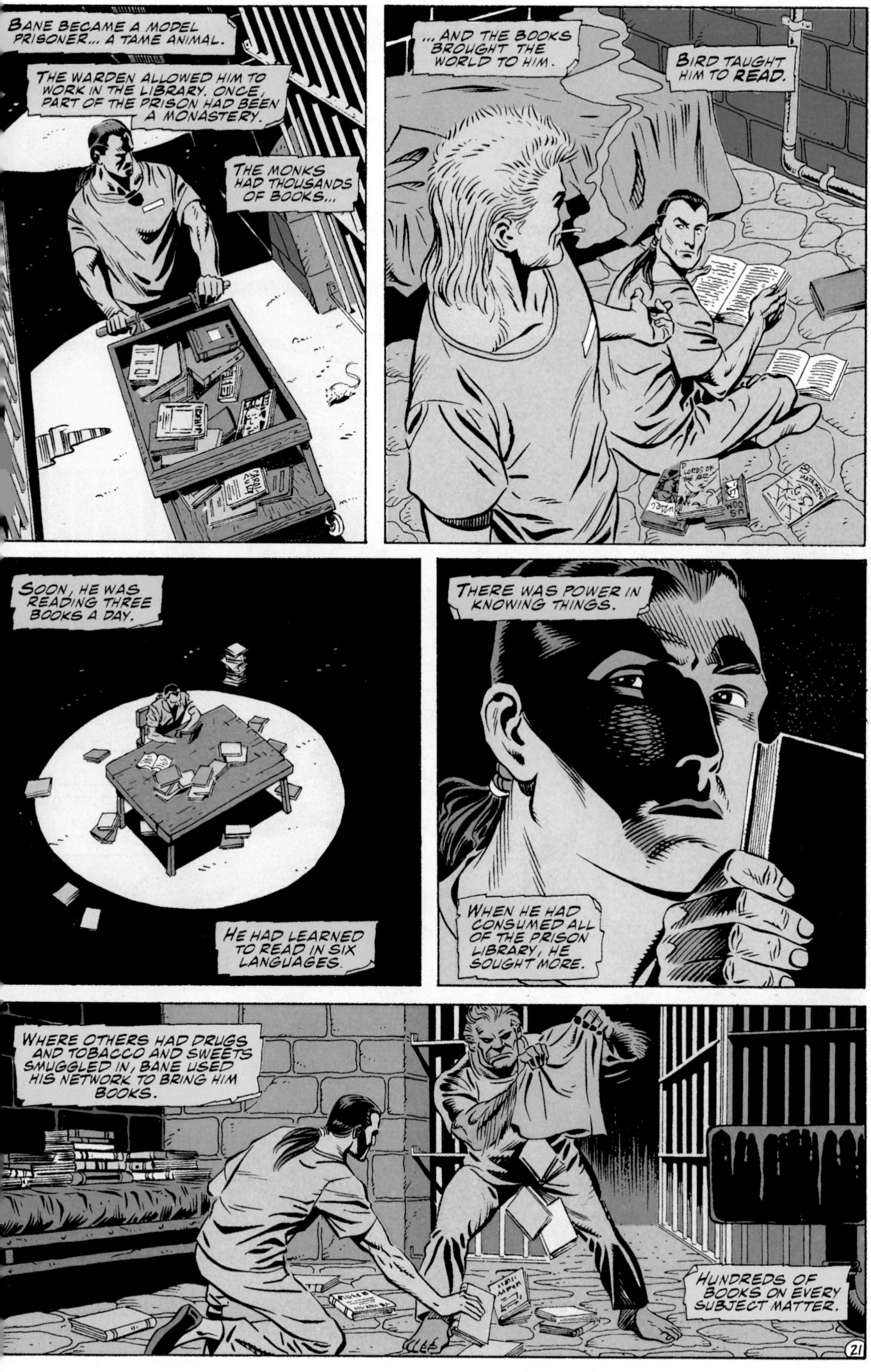

BANE BECAME A MODEL PRISONER... A TAME ANIMAL.
THE WARDEN ALLOWED HIM TO WORK IN THE LIBRARY. ONCE, PART OF THE PRISON HAD BEEN A MONASTERY.
THE MONKS HAD THOUSANDS OF BOOKS...
...AND THE BOOKS BROUGHT THE WORLD TO HIM.
BIRD TAUGHT HIM TO READ.
SOON, HE WAS READING THREE BOOKS A DAY.
HE HAD LEARNED TO READ IN SIX LANGUAGES.
THERE WAS POWER IN KNOWING THINGS.
WHEN HE HAD CONSUMED ALL OF THE PRISON LIBRARY, HE SOUGHT MORE.
WHERE OTHERS HAD DRUGS AND TOBACCO AND SWEETS SMUGGLED IN, BANE USED HIS NETWORK TO BRING HIM BOOKS.
HUNDREDS OF BOOKS ON EVERY SUBJECT MATTER.

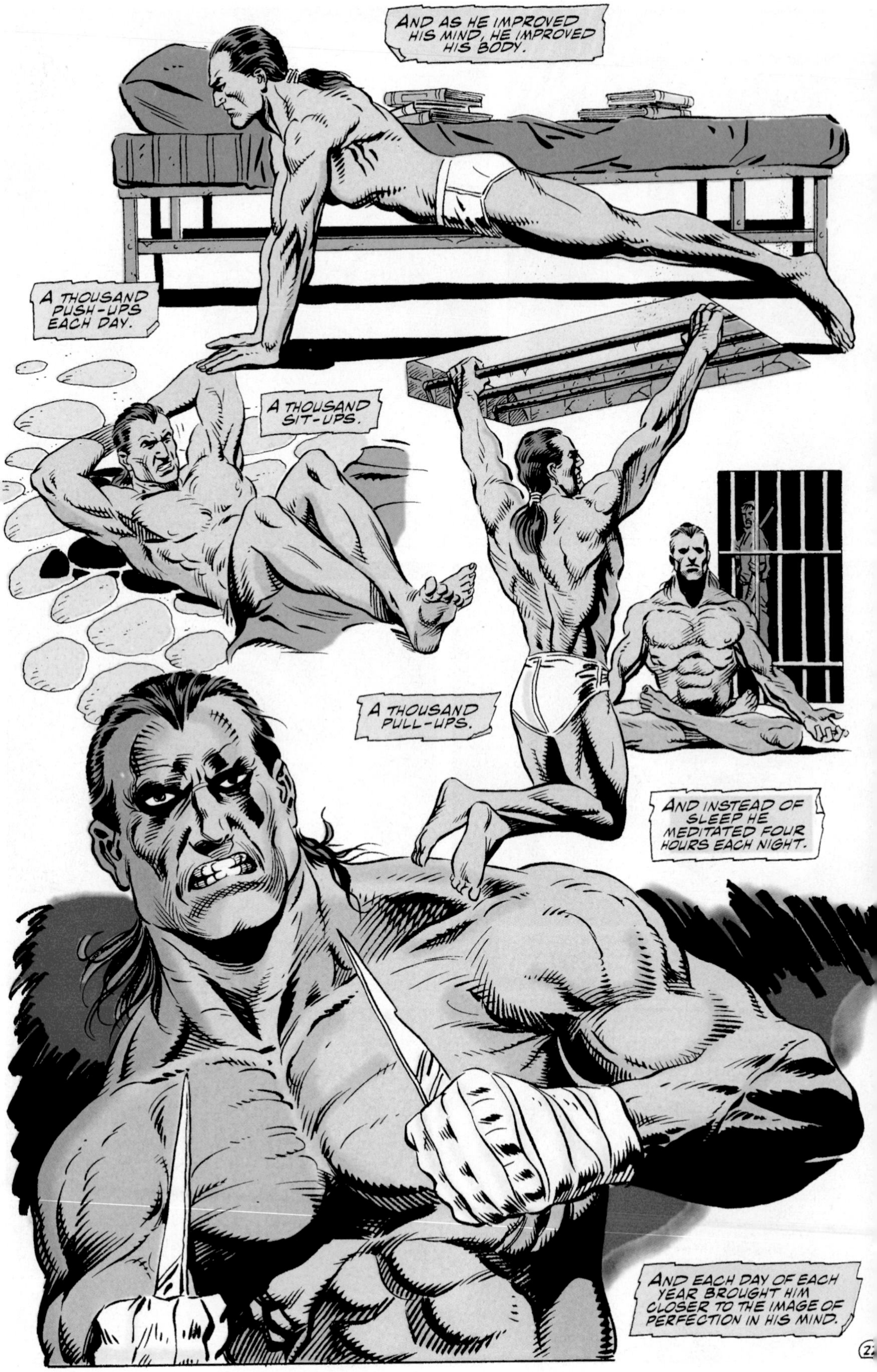
AND AS HE IMPROVED HIS MIND, HE IMPROVED HIS BODY.
A THOUSAND PUSH-UPS EACH DAY.
A THOUSAND SIT-UPS.
A THOUSAND PULL-UPS.
AND INSTEAD OF SLEEP HE MEDITATED FOUR HOURS EACH NIGHT.
AND EACH DAY OF EACH YEAR BROUGHT HIM CLOSER TO THE IMAGE OF PERFECTION IN HIS MIND.

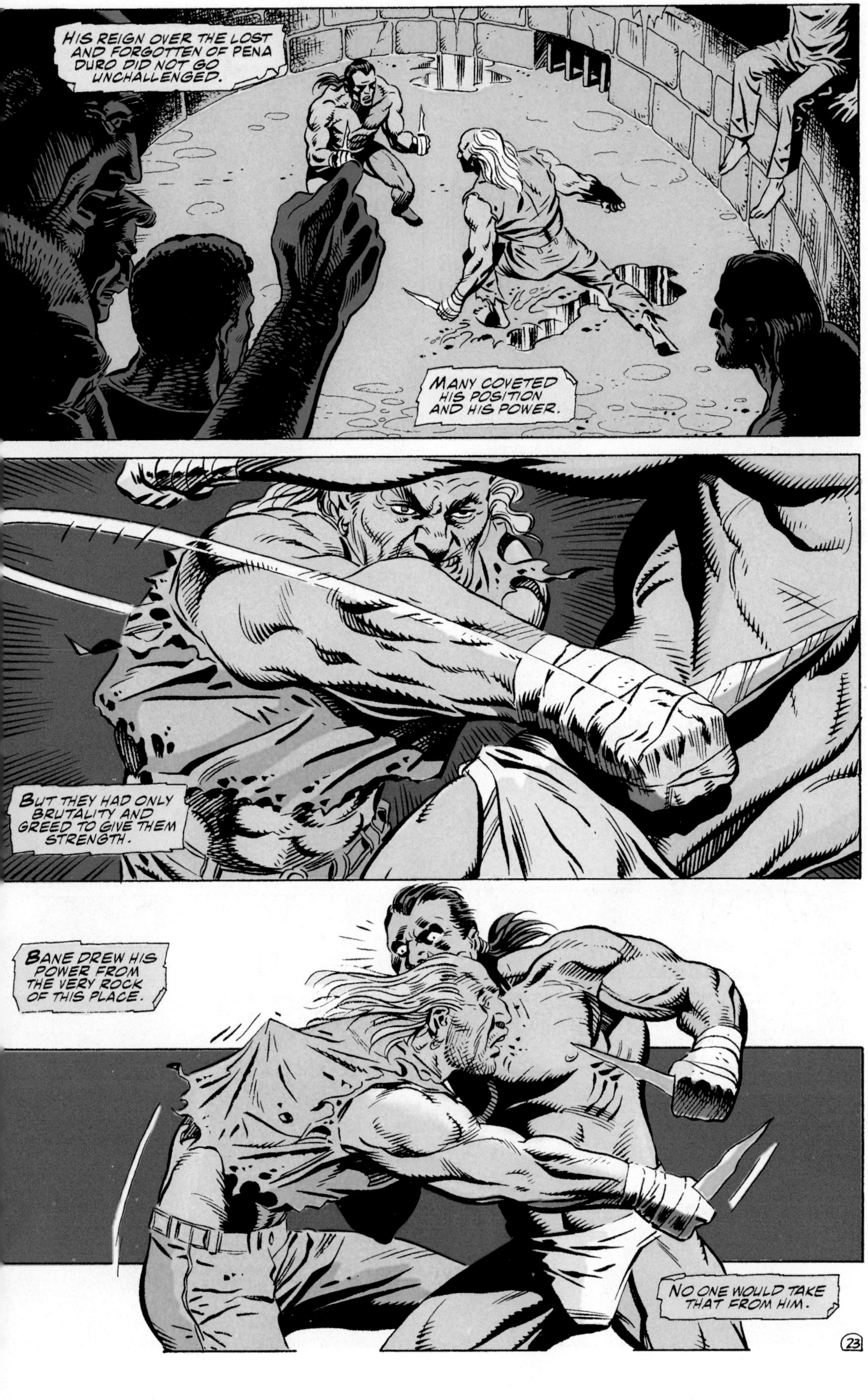
HIS REIGN OVER THE LOST AND FORGOTTEN OF PENA DURO DID NOT GO UNCHALLENGED.
MANY COVETED HIS POSITION AND HIS POWER.
BUT THEY HAD ONLY BRUTALITY AND GREED TO GIVE THEM STRENGTH.
BANE DREW HIS POWER FROM THE VERY ROCK OF THIS PLACE.
NO ONE WOULD TAKE THAT FROM HIM.

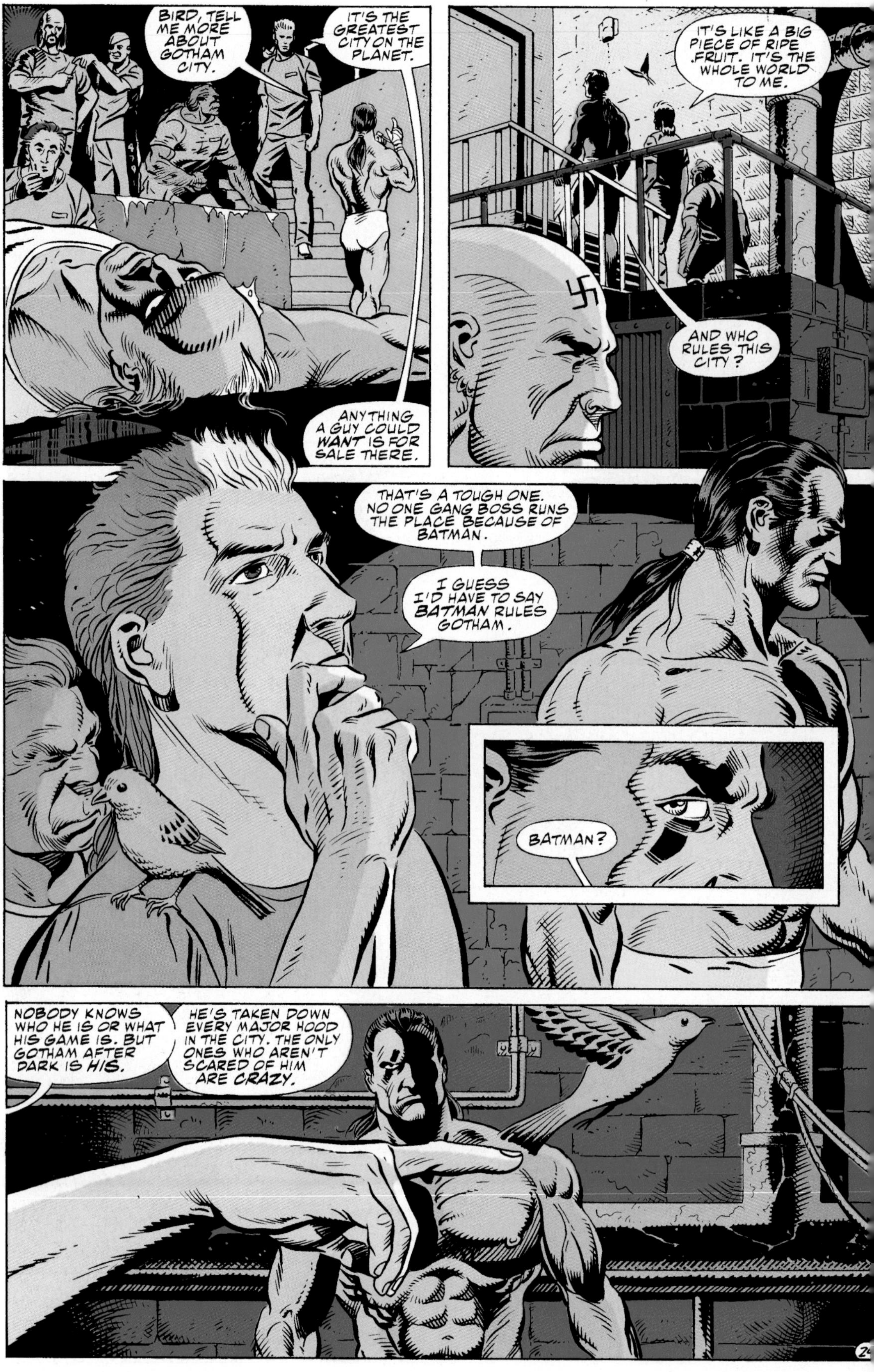
BIRD, TELL ME MORE ABOUT GOTHAM CITY.
IT'S THE GREATEST CITY ON THE PLANET.
ANYTHING A GUY COULD WANT IS FOR SALE THERE.
IT'S LIKE A BIG PIECE OF RIPE FRUIT. IT'S THE WHOLE WORLD TO ME.
AND WHO RULES THIS CITY?
THAT'S A TOUGH ONE. NO ONE GANG BOSS RUNS THE PLACE BECAUSE OF BATMAN.
I GUESS I'D HAVE TO SAY BATMAN RULES GOTHAM.
BATMAN?
NOBODY KNOWS WHO HE IS OR WHAT HIS GAME IS. BUT GOTHAM AFTER DARK IS HIS.
HE'S TAKEN DOWN EVERY MAJOR HOOD IN THE CITY. THE ONLY ONES WHO AREN'T SCARED OF HIM ARE CRAZY.

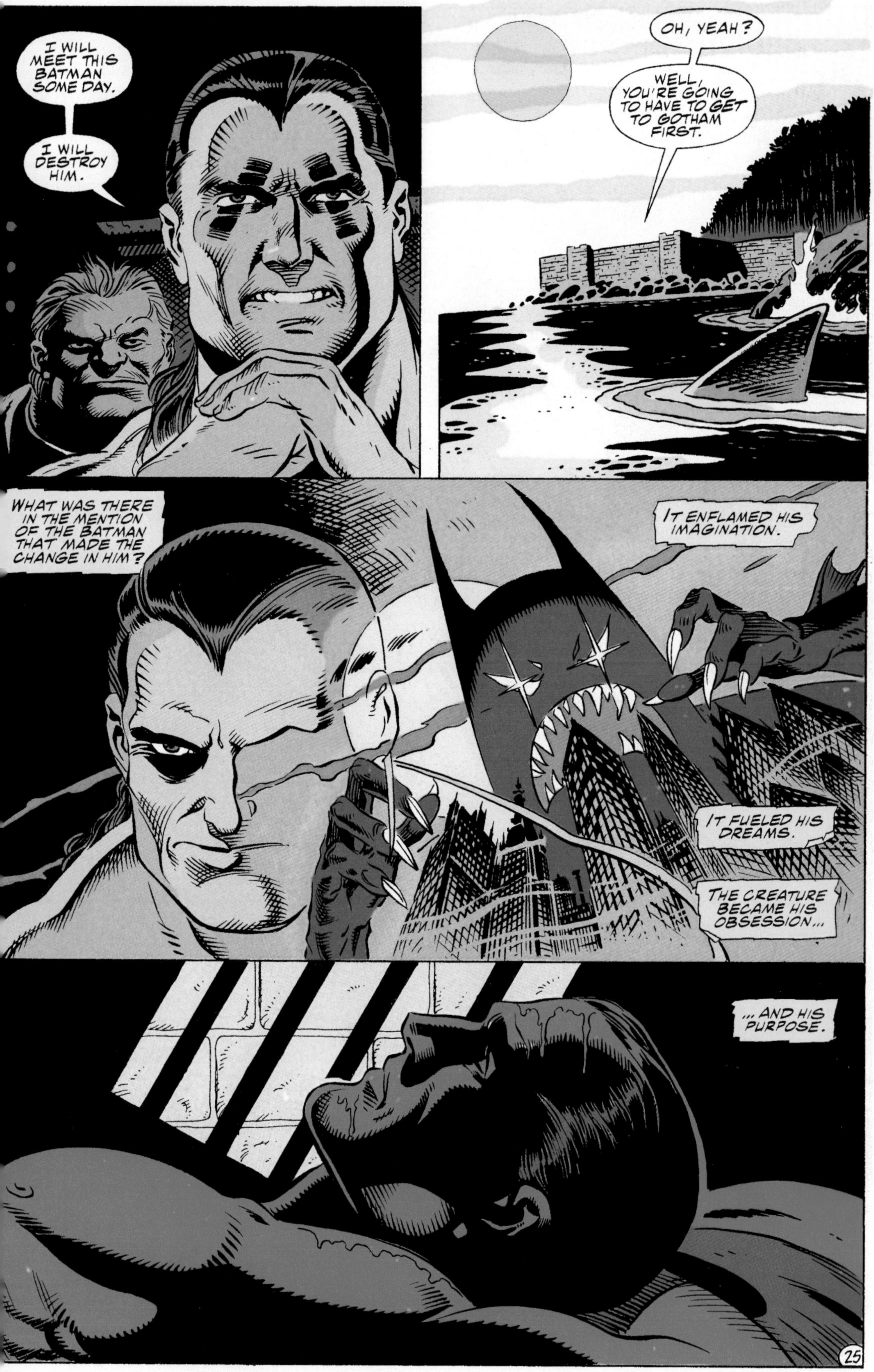

I WILL MEET THIS BATMAN SOME DAY.
I WILL DESTROY HIM.
OH, YEAH?
WELL, YOU'RE GOING TO HAVE TO GET TO GOTHAM FIRST.
WHAT WAS THERE IN THE MENTION OF THE BATMAN THAT MADE THE CHANGE IN HIM?
IT ENFLAMED HIS IMAGINATION.
IT FUELED HIS DREAMS.
THE CREATURE BECAME HIS OBSESSION...
...AND HIS PURPOSE.

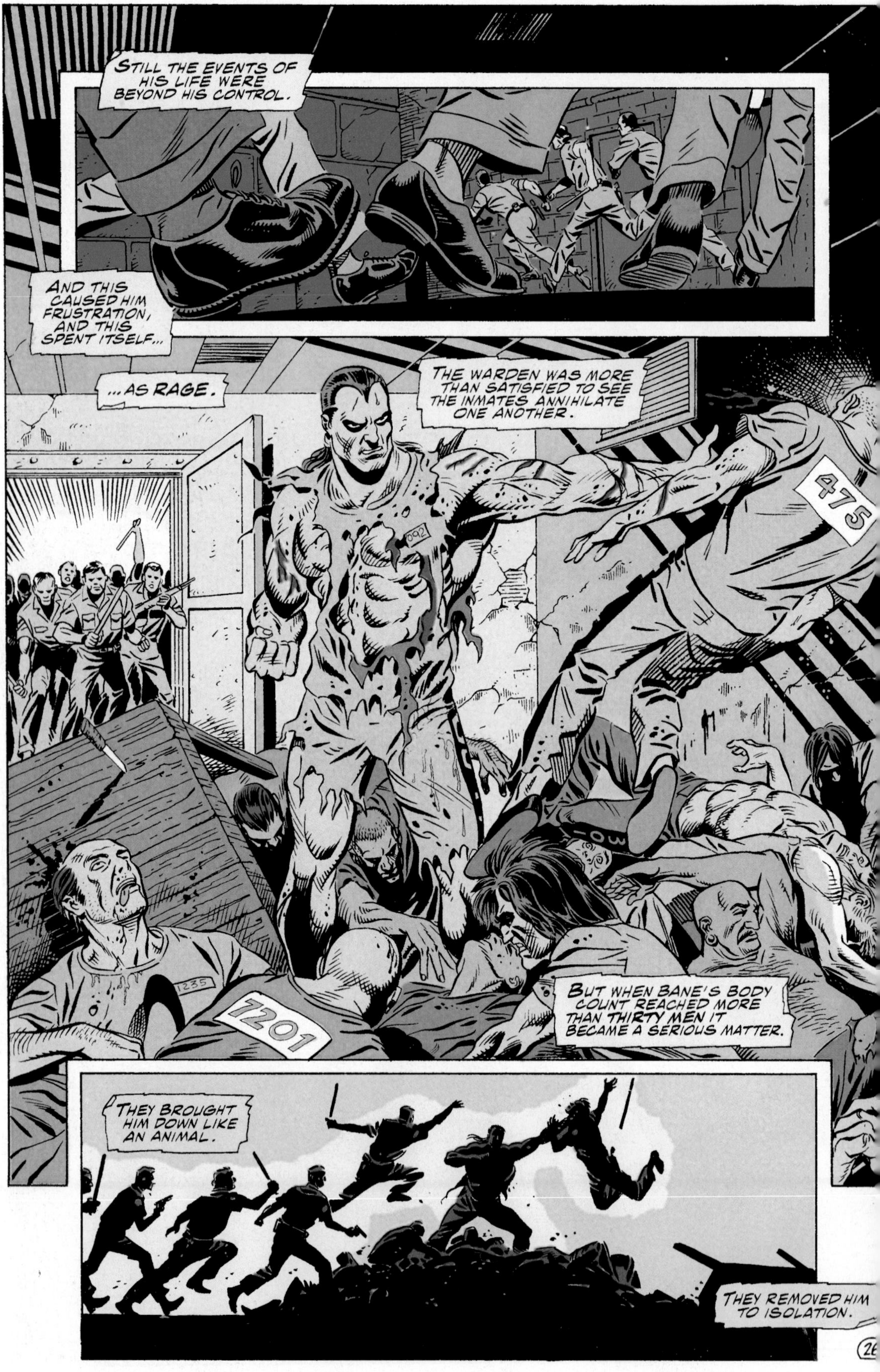
STILL THE EVENTS OF HIS LIFE WERE BEYOND HIS CONTROL.
AND THIS CAUSED HIM FRUSTRATION, AND THIS SPENT ITSELF...
...AS RAGE.
THE WARDEN WAS MORE THAN SATISFIED TO SEE THE INMATES ANNIHILATE ONE ANOTHER.
475
092
1235
7201
BUT WHEN BANE'S BODY COUNT REACHED MORE THAN THIRTY MEN IT BECAME A SERIOUS MATTER.
THEY BROUGHT HIM DOWN LIKE AN ANIMAL.
THEY REMOVED HIM TO ISOLATION.

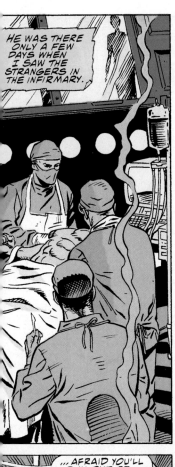

HE WAS THERE ONLY A FEW DAYS WHEN I SAW THE STRANGERS IN THE INFIRMARY.

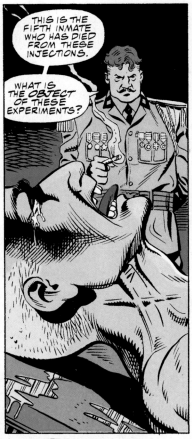

THIS IS THE FIFTH INMATE WHO HAS DIED FROM THESE INJECTIONS.

WHAT IS THE *OBJECT* OF THESE EXPERIMENTS?

A NEW NERVE TOXIN? THE FORMULA FOR A SUPER SOLDIER? SOME MILITARY APPLICATION, I'M CERTAIN.

WHAT IS *YOUR* CONCERN...

...AFRAID YOU'LL RUN OUT OF PRISONERS?

DEAD. THE CRETIN'S HEART EXPLODED.

I'LL NEED ANOTHER SUBJECT IMMEDIATELY. CAN YOU GET ME A *STRONG* ONE THIS TIME, WARDEN? ONE THAT WILL LAST *MORE* THAN THREE DAYS?

I HAVE JUST SUCH A MAN IN ISOLATION AT THE MOMENT.

27

I COULD NOT GET TO BANE TO WARN HIM.

WHAT COULD HE HAVE DONE IN ANY CASE?

THE LAB BUILDING WAS NEW, BUILT BY THE ARMY TO HOUSE THIS EXPERIMENT.

THEY HAD ALREADY KILLED FIVE MEN WITH THEIR DRUGS.

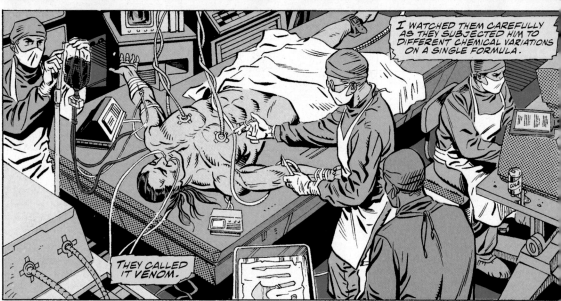

I WATCHED THEM CAREFULLY AS THEY SUBJECTED HIM TO DIFFERENT CHEMICAL VARIATIONS ON A SINGLE FORMULA.

THEY CALLED IT VENOM.

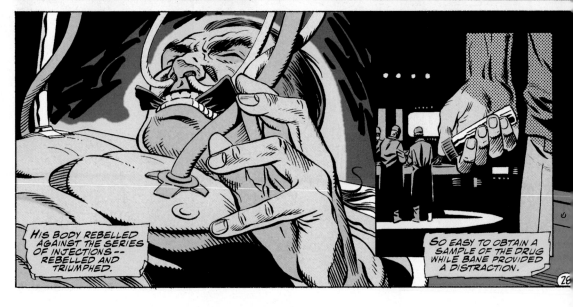

HIS BODY REBELLED AGAINST THE SERIES OF INJECTIONS-- REBELLED AND TRIUMPHED.

SO EASY TO OBTAIN A SAMPLE OF THE DRUG WHILE BANE PROVIDED A DISTRACTION.

26

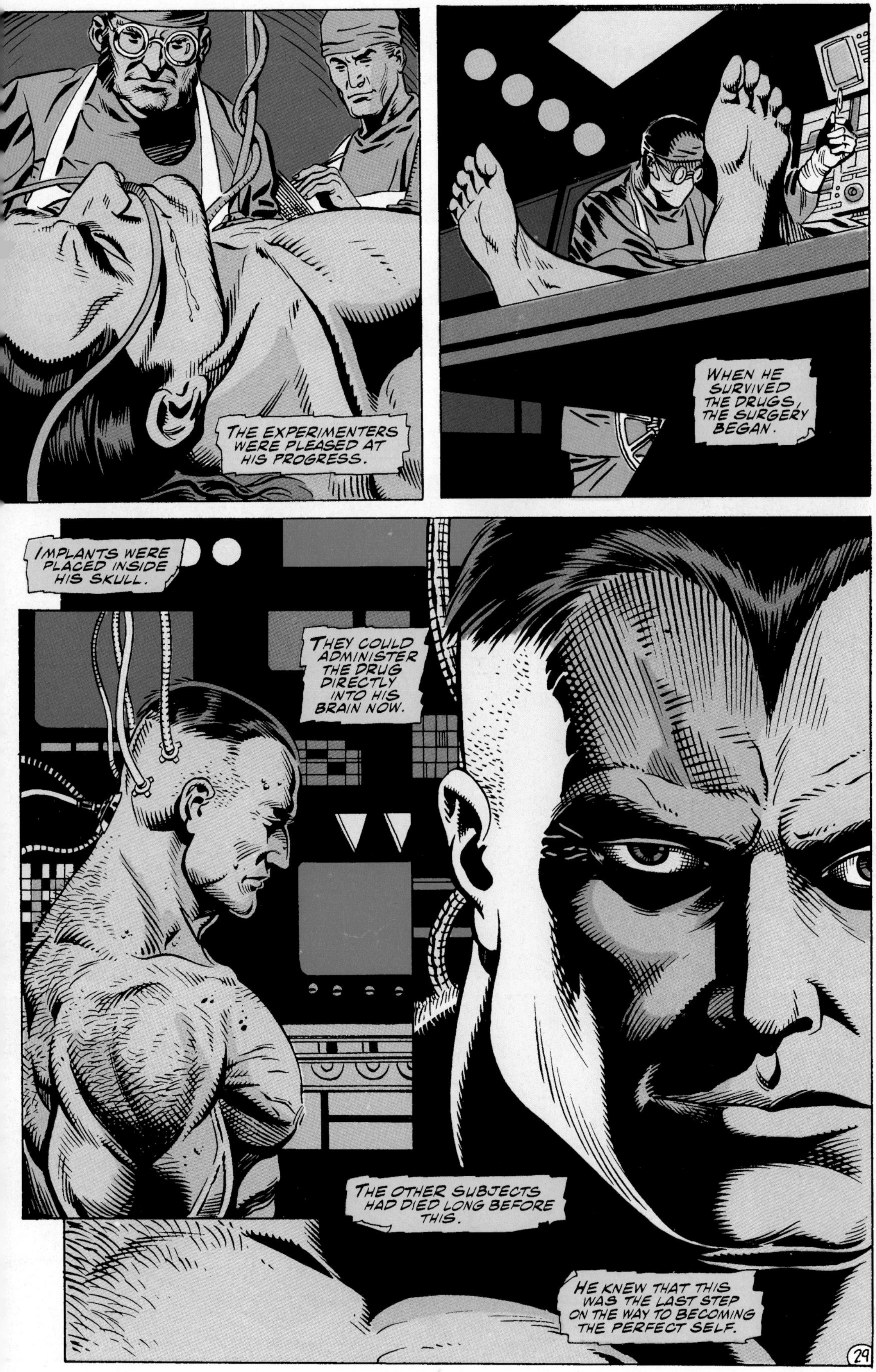
THE EXPERIMENTERS WERE PLEASED AT HIS PROGRESS.
WHEN HE SURVIVED THE DRUGS, THE SURGERY BEGAN.
IMPLANTS WERE PLACED INSIDE HIS SKULL.
THEY COULD ADMINISTER THE DRUG DIRECTLY INTO HIS BRAIN NOW.
THE OTHER SUBJECTS HAD DIED LONG BEFORE THIS.
HE KNEW THAT THIS WAS THE LAST STEP ON THE WAY TO BECOMING THE PERFECT SELF.

I WOULD HAVE TO BE ABLE TO REPLICATE THIS VENOM SO THAT BANE COULD TRANSCEND TO HIS ULTIMATE FORM.

I HAD DONE THIS MANY TIMES IN DESIGNING NARCOTICS FOR MY FORMER EMPLOYERS.

BUT NEVER HAD I SEEN ANY COMBINATION SO COMPLEX. COMPLEX, BUT EASILY COPIED.

A SUPER STEROID DERIVED FROM A DRUG CODE-NAMED VENOM.

IT ALSO CONTAINED ELEMENTS THAT WOULD STIMULATE THE ADRENAL GLANDS.

ANOTHER INGREDIENT TARGETED THE CORPUS CALLOSUM SEGMENT OF THE BRAIN.

THIS DRUG WOULD ULTIMATELY FUSE THE RIGHT AND LEFT HEMISPHERES OF THE BRAIN.

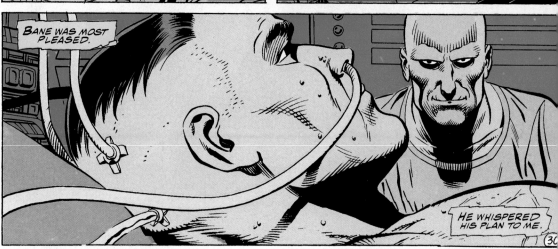

BANE WAS MOST PLEASED.

HE WHISPERED HIS PLAN TO ME.

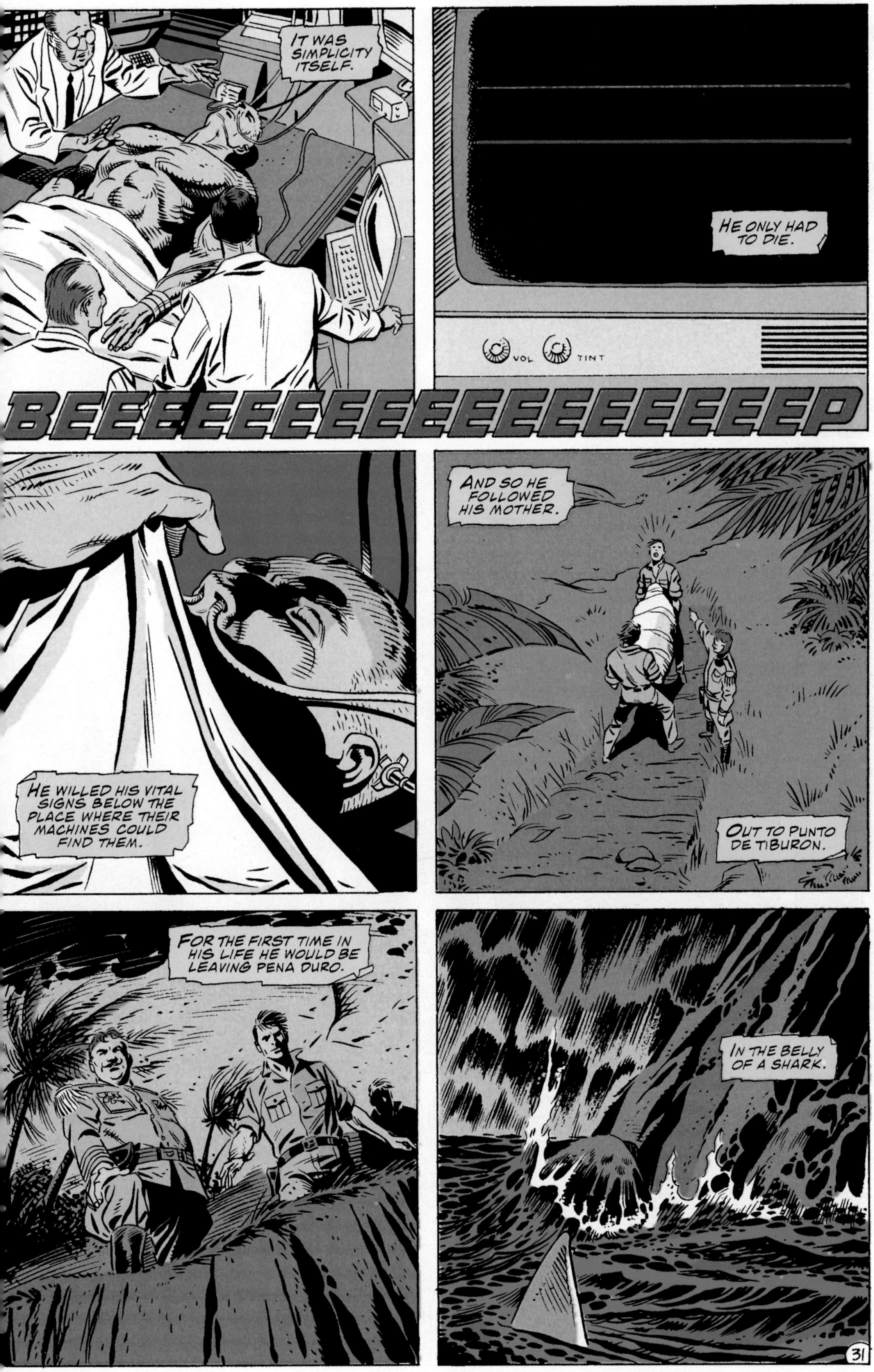
IT WAS SIMPLICITY ITSELF.
HE ONLY HAD TO DIE.
VOL
TINT
BEEEEEEEEEEEEEEEEP
HE WILLED HIS VITAL SIGNS BELOW THE PLACE WHERE THEIR MACHINES COULD FIND THEM.
AND SO HE FOLLOWED HIS MOTHER.
OUT TO PUNTO DE TIBURON.
FOR THE FIRST TIME IN HIS LIFE HE WOULD BE LEAVING PENA DURO.
IN THE BELLY OF A SHARK.

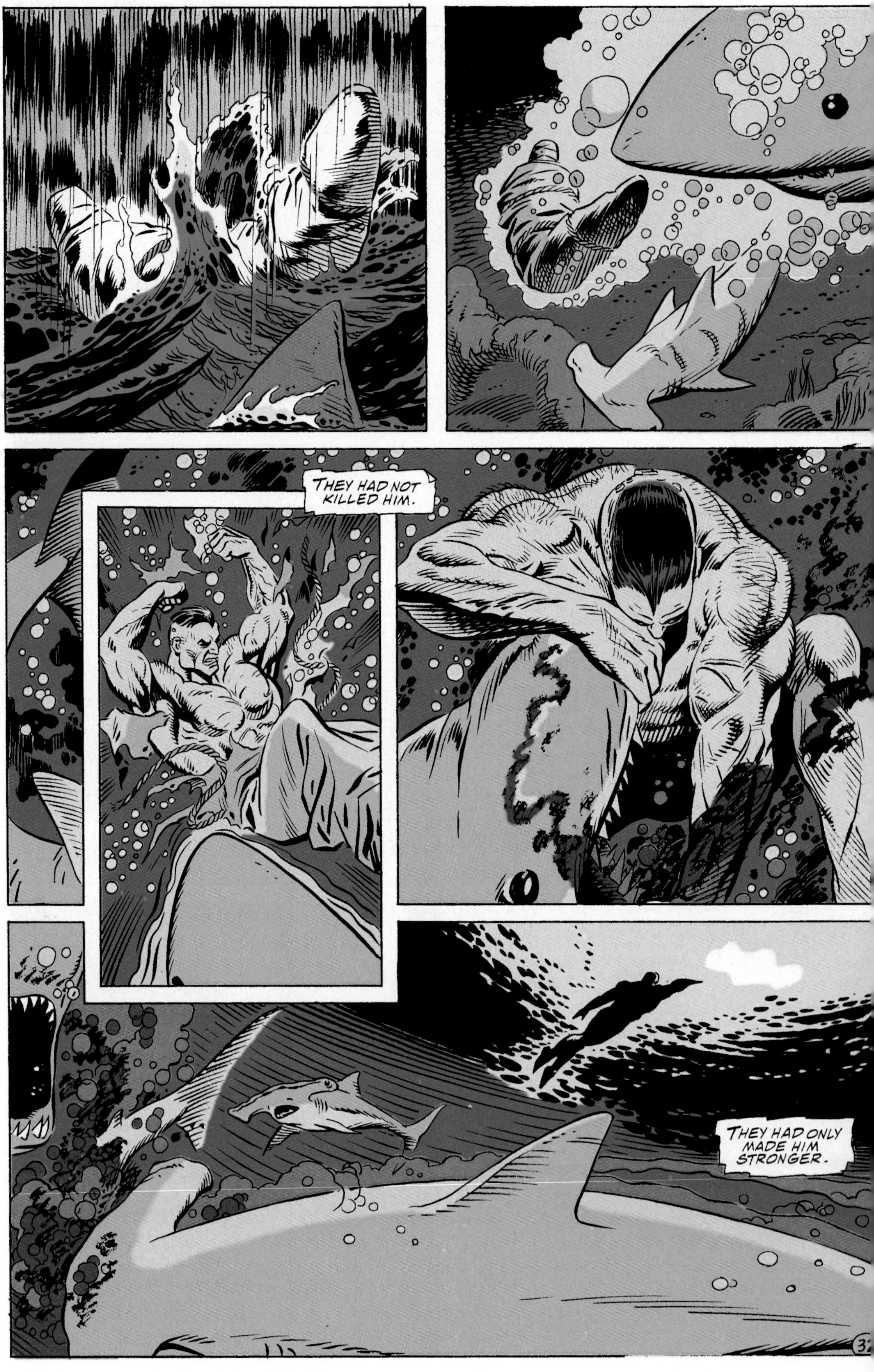
THEY HAD NOT KILLED HIM.
THEY HAD ONLY MADE HIM STRONGER.

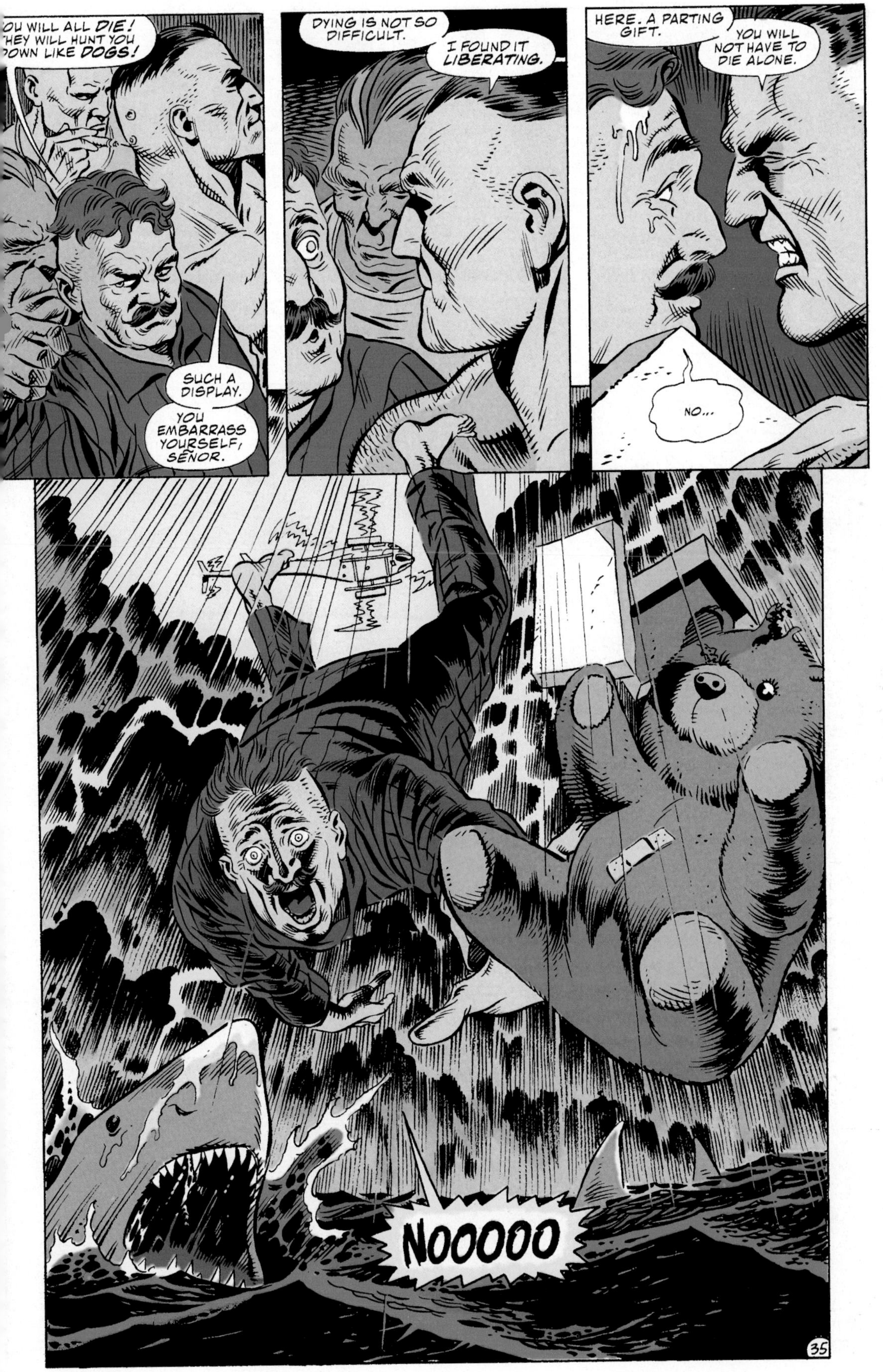
OU WILL ALL DIE! HEY WILL HUNT YOU OWN LIKE DOGS!
SUCH A DISPLAY.
YOU EMBARRASS YOURSELF, SEÑOR.
DYING IS NOT SO DIFFICULT.
I FOUND IT LIBERATING.
HERE. A PARTING GIFT.
YOU WILL NOT HAVE TO DIE ALONE.
NO...
NOOOOO

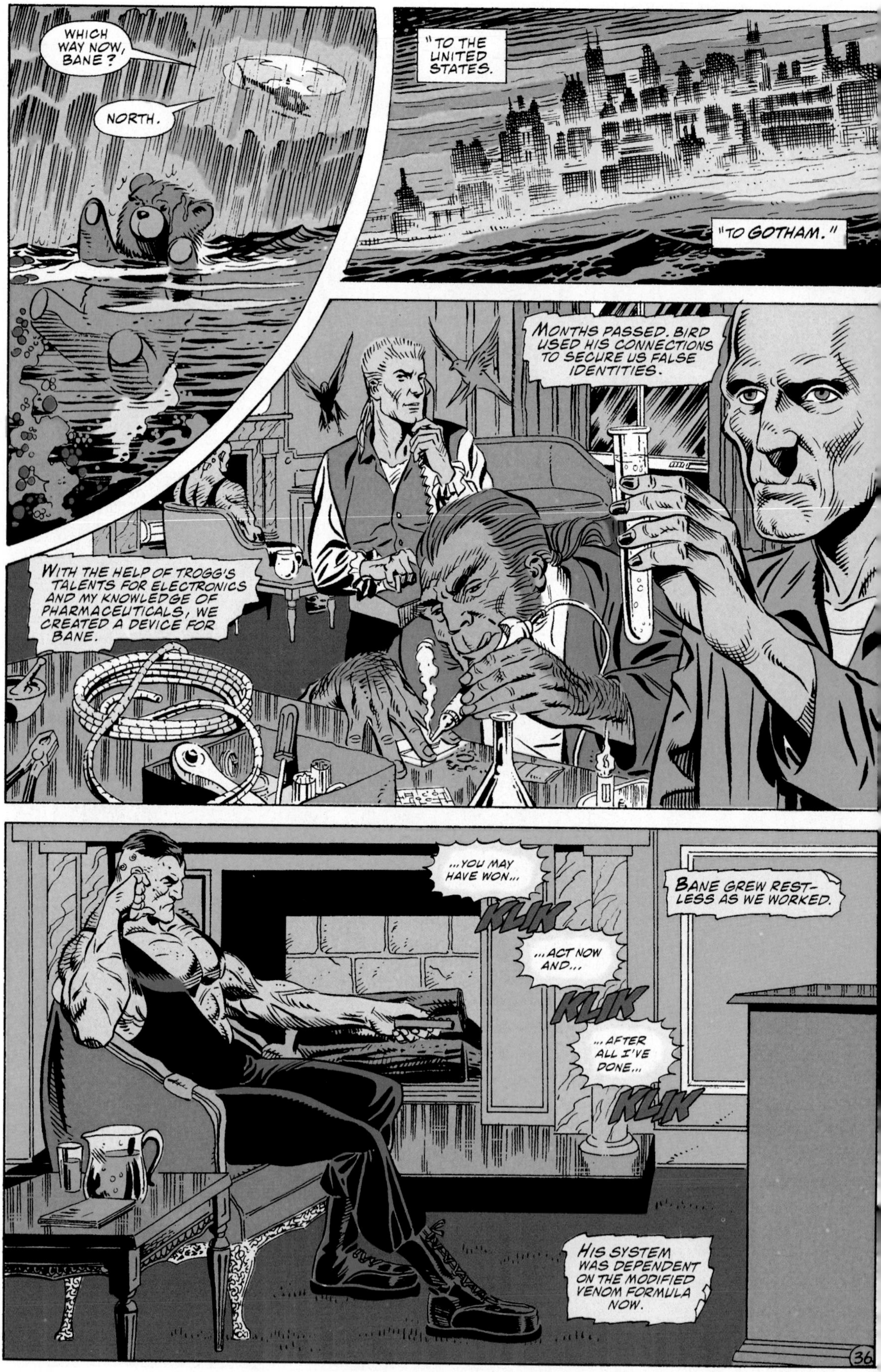

WHICH WAY NOW, BANE?
NORTH.
"TO THE UNITED STATES.
"TO GOTHAM."
MONTHS PASSED. BIRD USED HIS CONNECTIONS TO SECURE US FALSE IDENTITIES.
WITH THE HELP OF TROGG'S TALENTS FOR ELECTRONICS AND MY KNOWLEDGE OF PHARMACEUTICALS, WE CREATED A DEVICE FOR BANE.
BANE GREW RESTLESS AS WE WORKED.
...YOU MAY HAVE WON...
KLIK
...ACT NOW AND...
KLIK
...AFTER ALL I'VE DONE...
KLIK
HIS SYSTEM WAS DEPENDENT ON THE MODIFIED VENOM FORMULA NOW.

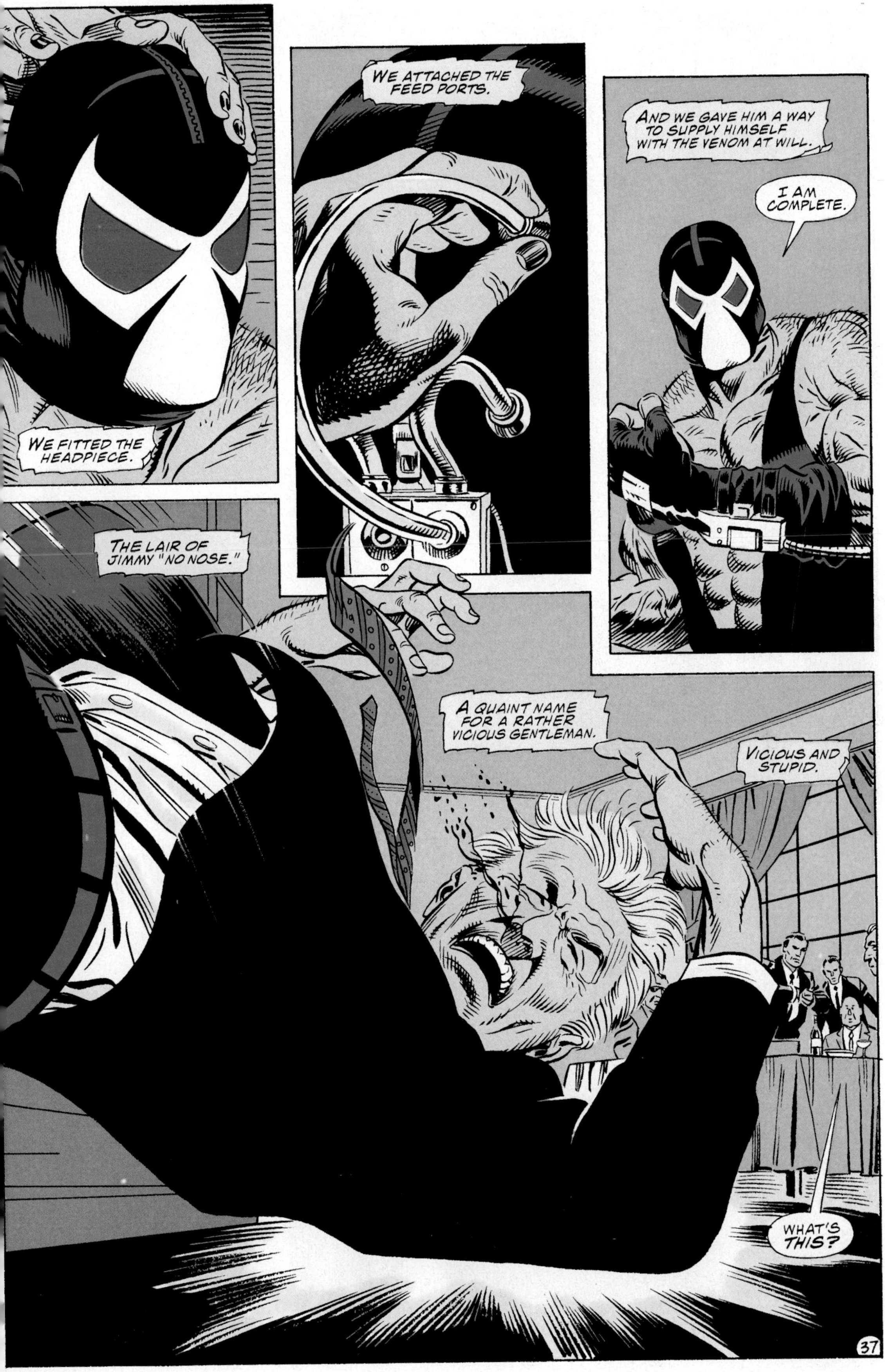

WE FITTED THE HEADPIECE.
WE ATTACHED THE FEED PORTS.
AND WE GAVE HIM A WAY TO SUPPLY HIMSELF WITH THE VENOM AT WILL.
I AM COMPLETE.
THE LAIR OF JIMMY "NO NOSE."
A QUAINT NAME FOR A RATHER VICIOUS GENTLEMAN.
VICIOUS AND STUPID.
WHAT'S THIS?

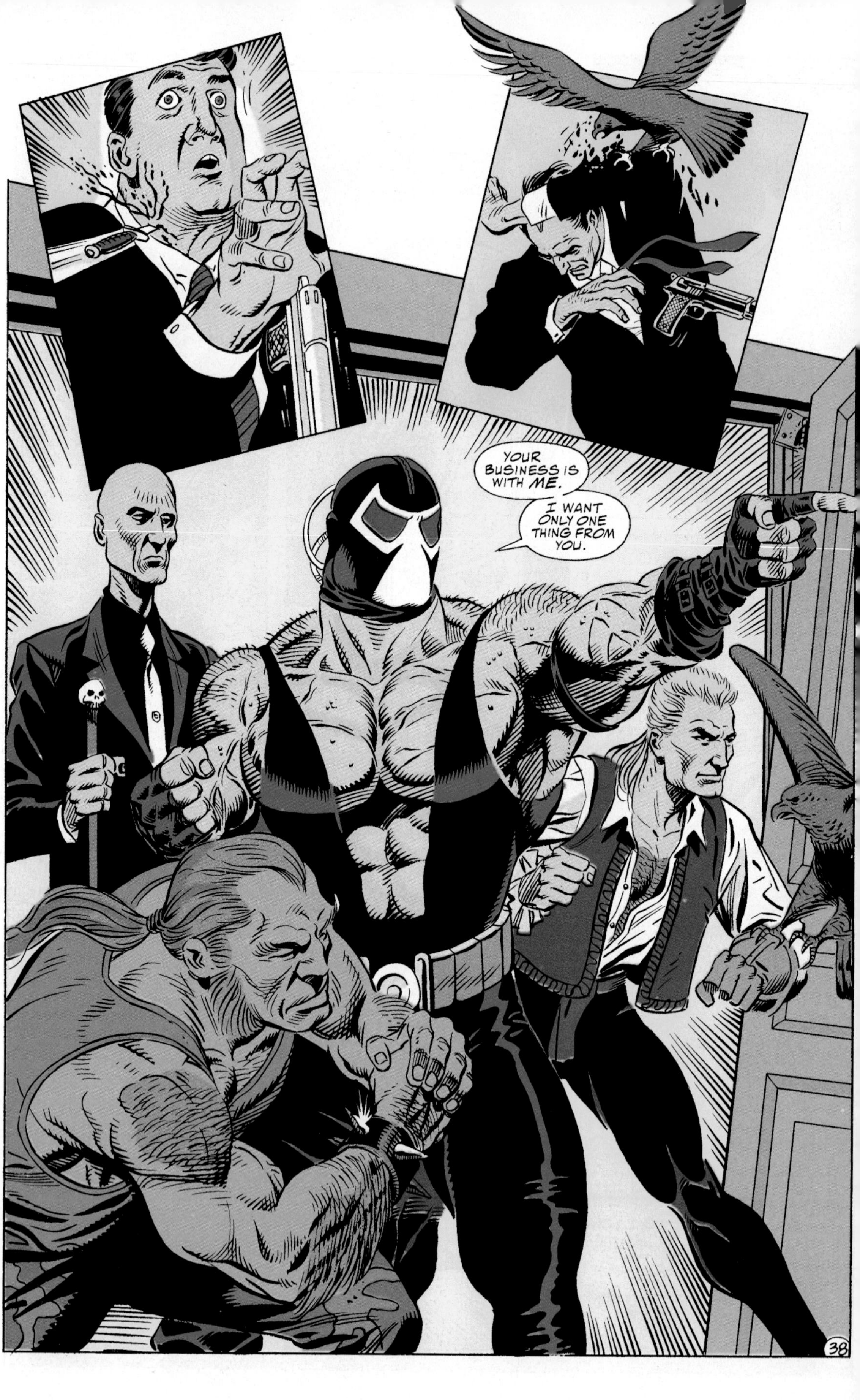
YOUR BUSINESS IS WITH ME.
I WANT ONLY ONE THING FROM YOU.

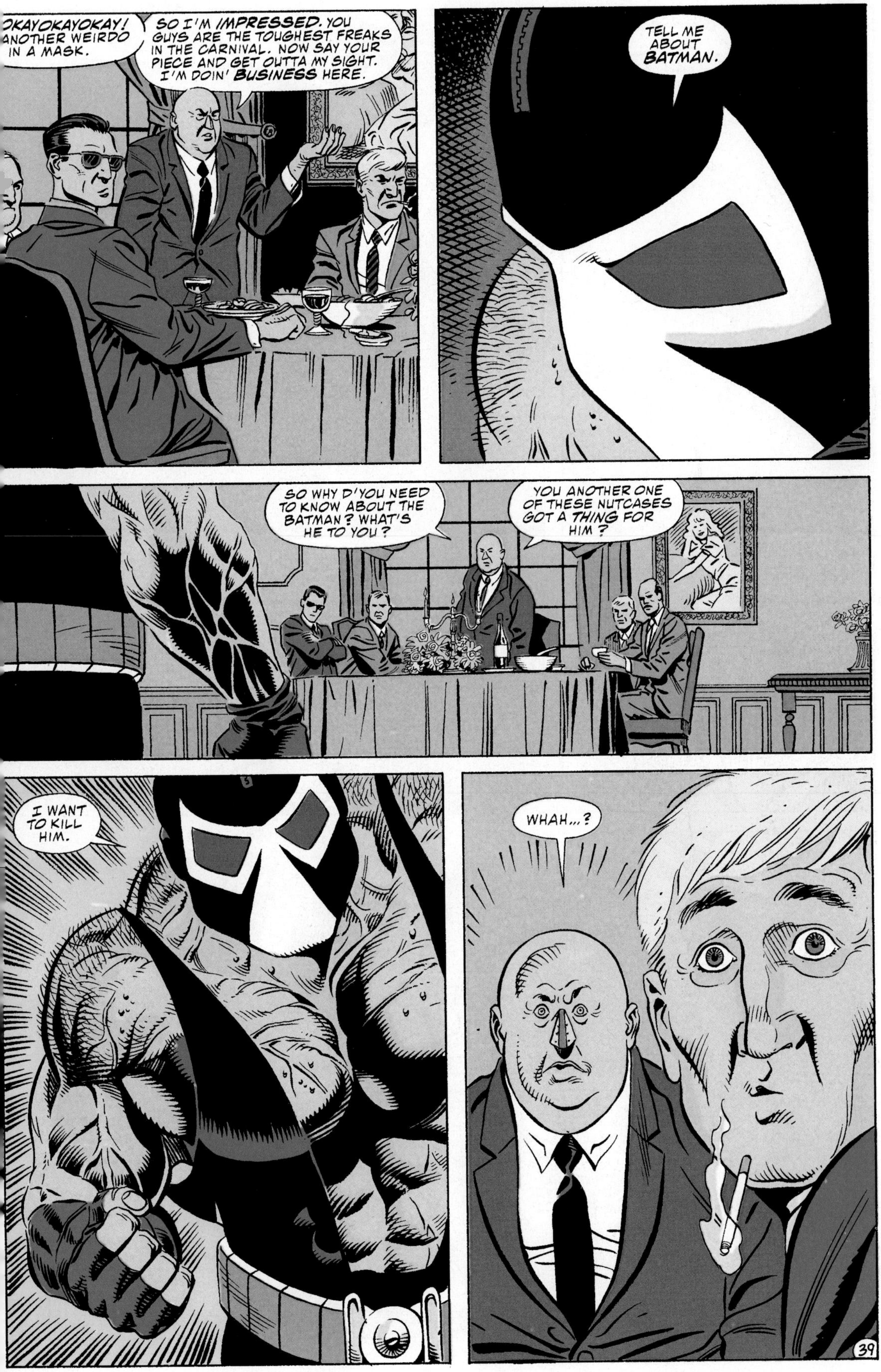
OKAYOKAYOKAY! ANOTHER WEIRDO IN A MASK.
SO I'M IMPRESSED. YOU GUYS ARE THE TOUGHEST FREAKS IN THE CARNIVAL. NOW SAY YOUR PIECE AND GET OUTTA MY SIGHT. I'M DOIN' BUSINESS HERE.
TELL ME ABOUT BATMAN.
SO WHY D'YOU NEED TO KNOW ABOUT THE BATMAN? WHAT'S HE TO YOU?
YOU ANOTHER ONE OF THESE NUTCASES GOT A THING FOR HIM?
I WANT TO KILL HIM.
WHAH...?
39

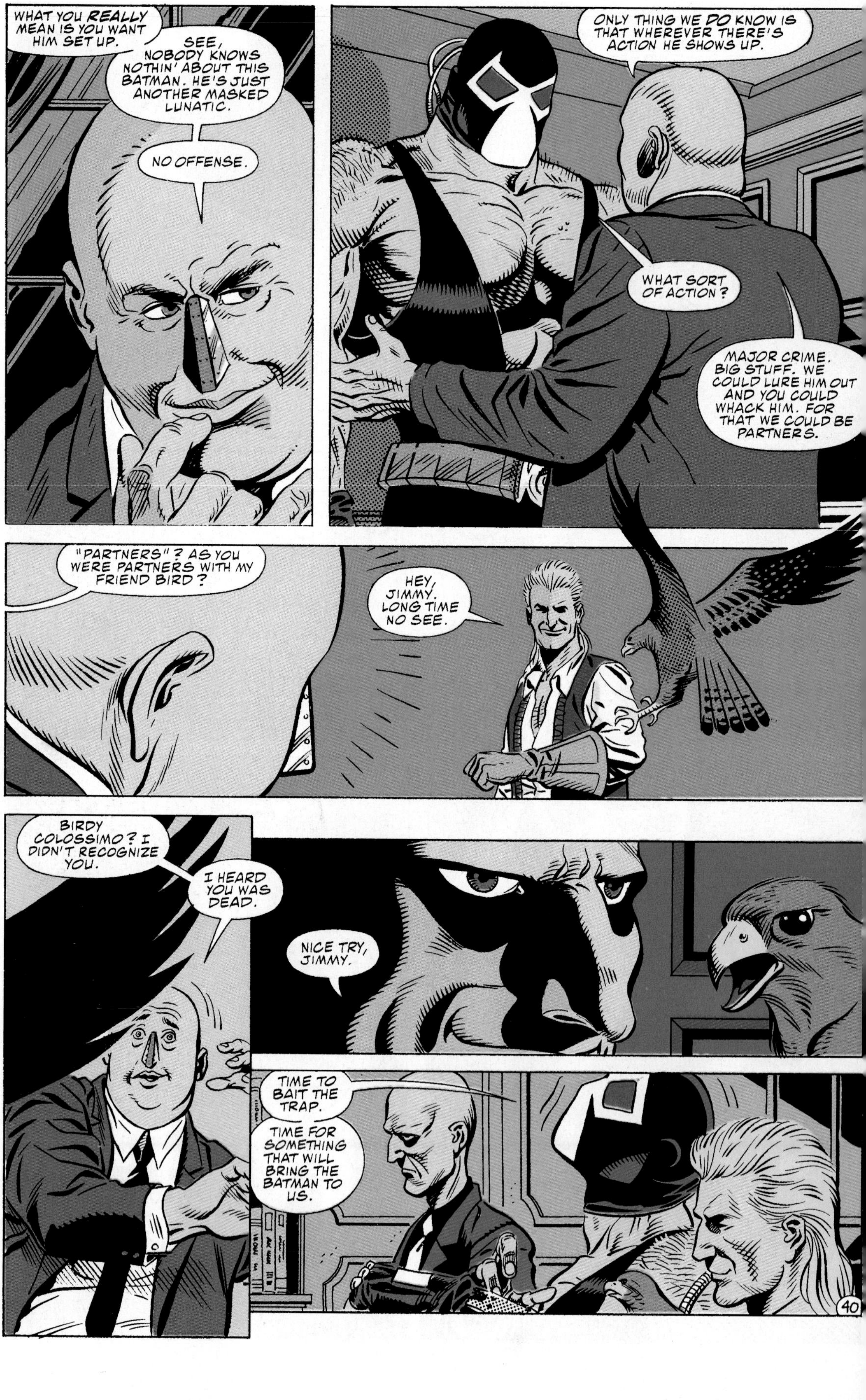
WHAT YOU REALLY MEAN IS YOU WANT HIM SET UP.
SEE, NOBODY KNOWS NOTHIN' ABOUT THIS BATMAN. HE'S JUST ANOTHER MASKED LUNATIC.
NO OFFENSE.
ONLY THING WE DO KNOW IS THAT WHEREVER THERE'S ACTION HE SHOWS UP.
WHAT SORT OF ACTION?
MAJOR CRIME. BIG STUFF. WE COULD LURE HIM OUT AND YOU COULD WHACK HIM. FOR THAT WE COULD BE PARTNERS.
"PARTNERS"? AS YOU WERE PARTNERS WITH MY FRIEND BIRD?
HEY, JIMMY. LONG TIME NO SEE.
BIRDY COLOSSIMO? I DIDN'T RECOGNIZE YOU.
I HEARD YOU WAS DEAD.
NICE TRY, JIMMY.
TIME TO BAIT THE TRAP.
TIME FOR SOMETHING THAT WILL BRING THE BATMAN TO US.

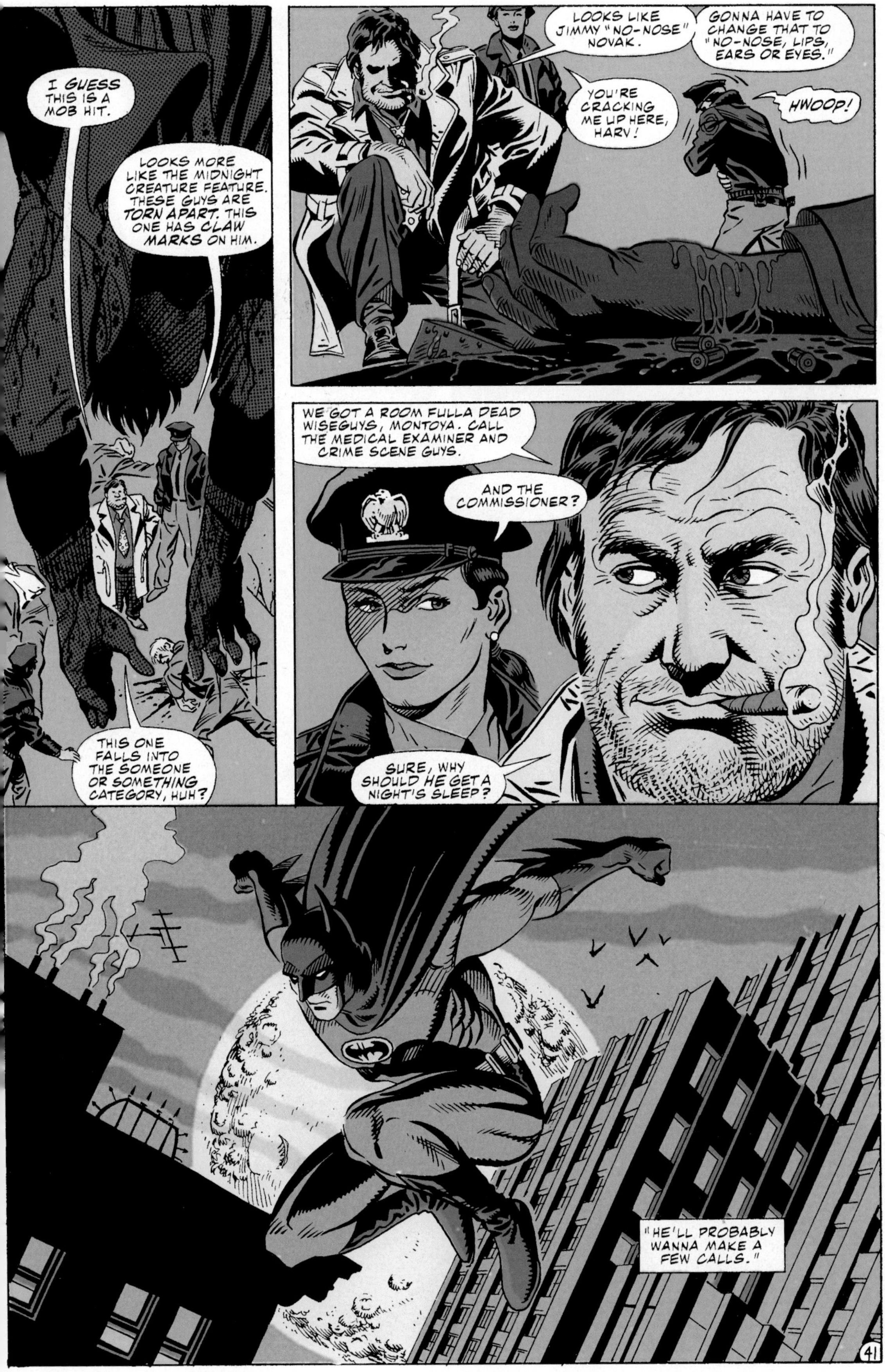
I GUESS THIS IS A MOB HIT.
LOOKS MORE LIKE THE MIDNIGHT CREATURE FEATURE. THESE GUYS ARE TORN APART. THIS ONE HAS CLAW MARKS ON HIM.
THIS ONE FALLS INTO THE SOMEONE OR SOMETHING CATEGORY, HUH?
LOOKS LIKE JIMMY "NO-NOSE" NOVAK.
GONNA HAVE TO CHANGE THAT TO "NO-NOSE, LIPS, EARS OR EYES."
YOU'RE CRACKING ME UP HERE, HARV!
HWOOP!
WE GOT A ROOM FULLA DEAD WISEGUYS, MONTOYA. CALL THE MEDICAL EXAMINER AND CRIME SCENE GUYS.
AND THE COMMISSIONER?
SURE, WHY SHOULD HE GET A NIGHT'S SLEEP?
"HE'LL PROBABLY WANNA MAKE A FEW CALLS."

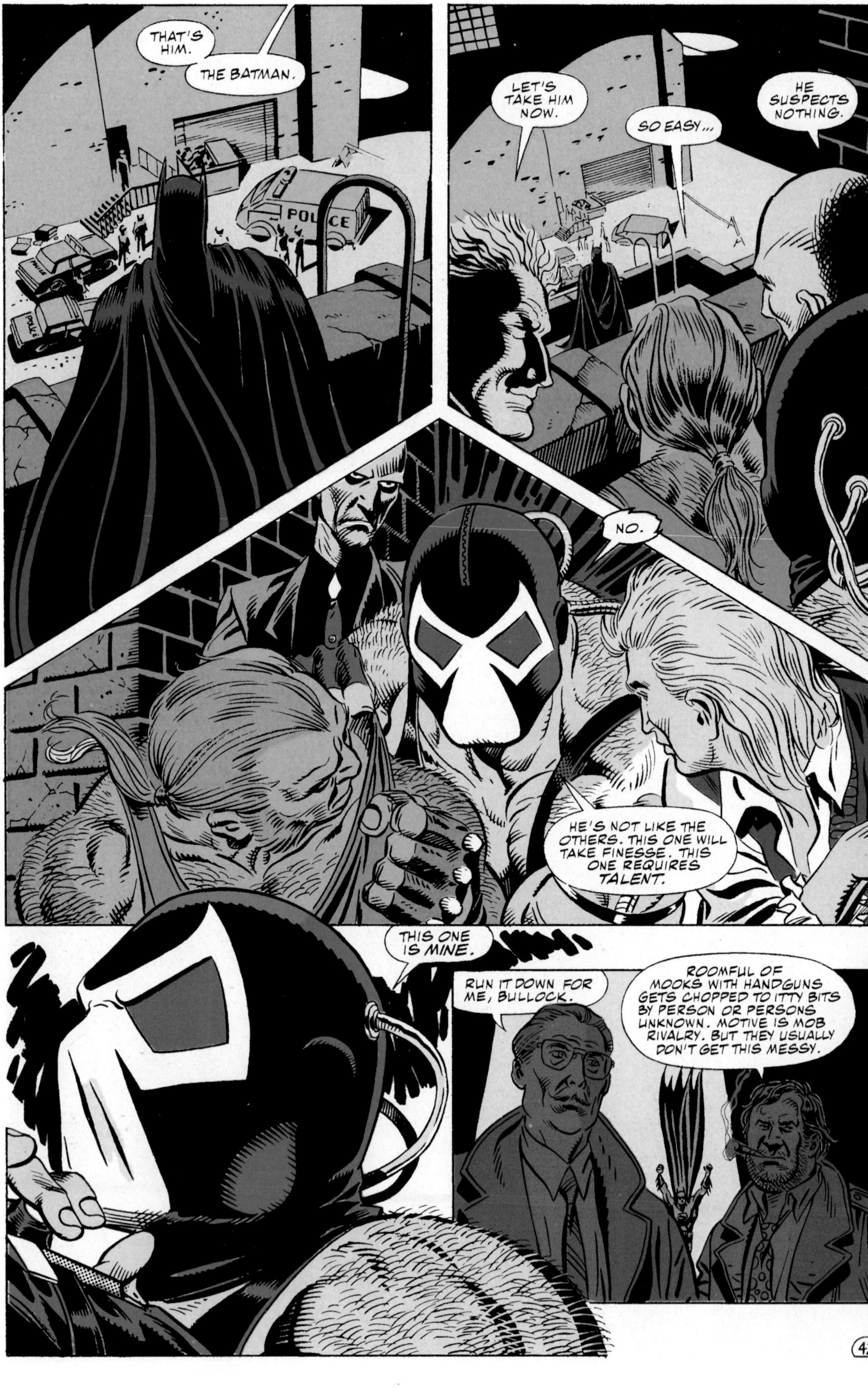
THAT'S HIM.
THE BATMAN.
LET'S TAKE HIM NOW.
SO EASY...
HE SUSPECTS NOTHING.
NO.
HE'S NOT LIKE THE OTHERS. THIS ONE WILL TAKE FINESSE. THIS ONE REQUIRES TALENT.
THIS ONE IS MINE.
RUN IT DOWN FOR ME, BULLOCK.
ROOMFUL OF MOOKS WITH HANDGUNS GETS CHOPPED TO ITTY BITS BY PERSON OR PERSONS UNKNOWN. MOTIVE IS MOB RIVALRY. BUT THEY USUALLY DON'T GET THIS MESSY.
POLICE

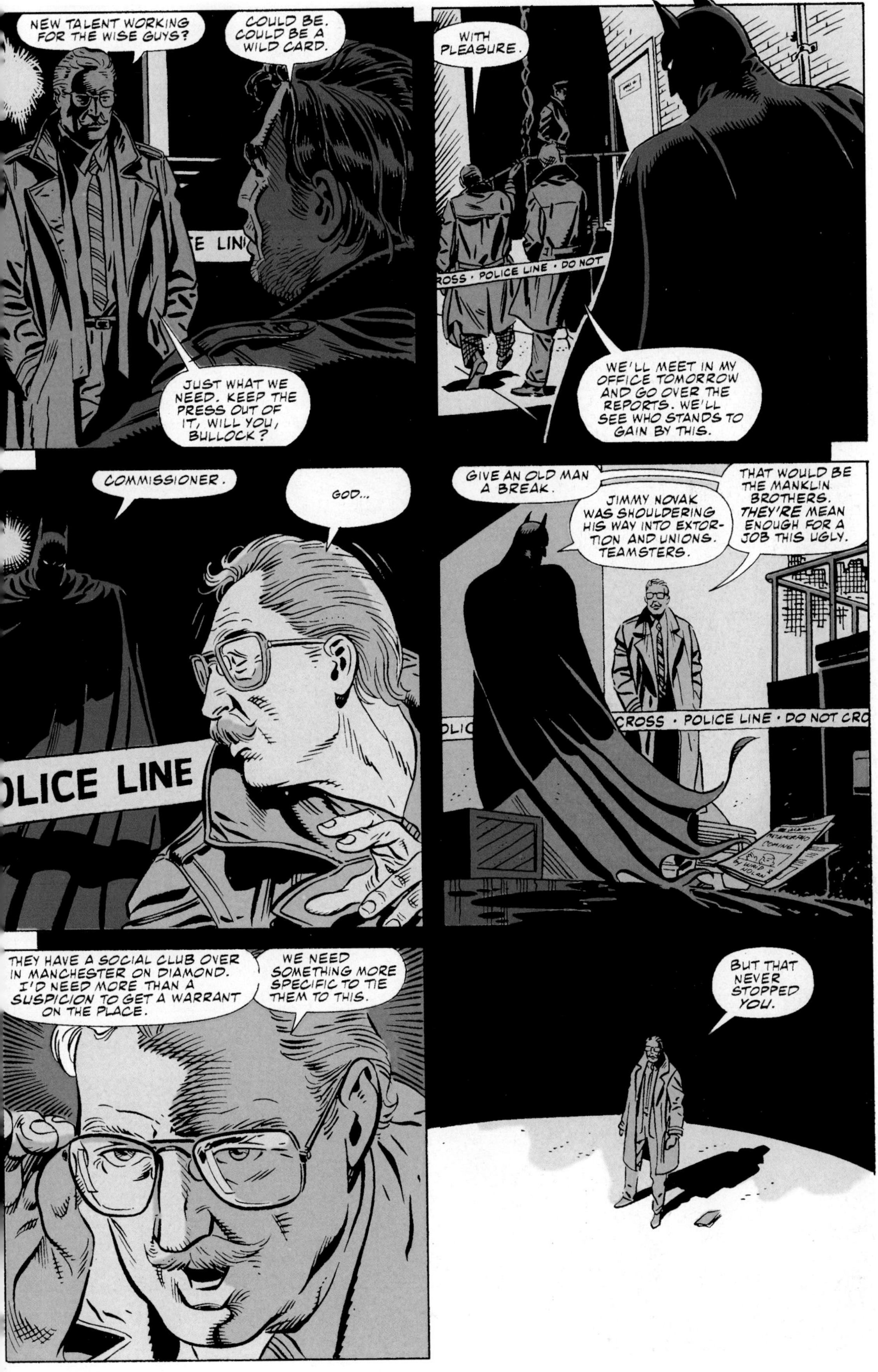
NEW TALENT WORKING FOR THE WISE GUYS?
COULD BE. COULD BE A WILD CARD.
JUST WHAT WE NEED. KEEP THE PRESS OUT OF IT, WILL YOU, BULLOCK?
WITH PLEASURE.
CROSS · POLICE LINE · DO NOT
WE'LL MEET IN MY OFFICE TOMORROW AND GO OVER THE REPORTS. WE'LL SEE WHO STANDS TO GAIN BY THIS.
COMMISSIONER.
GOD...
POLICE LINE
GIVE AN OLD MAN A BREAK.
JIMMY NOVAK WAS SHOULDERING HIS WAY INTO EXTORTION AND UNIONS. TEAMSTERS.
THAT WOULD BE THE MANKLIN BROTHERS. THEY'RE MEAN ENOUGH FOR A JOB THIS UGLY.
CROSS · POLICE LINE · DO NOT CRO
THEY HAVE A SOCIAL CLUB OVER IN MANCHESTER ON DIAMOND. I'D NEED MORE THAN A SUSPICION TO GET A WARRANT ON THE PLACE.
WE NEED SOMETHING MORE SPECIFIC TO TIE THEM TO THIS.
BUT THAT NEVER STOPPED YOU.

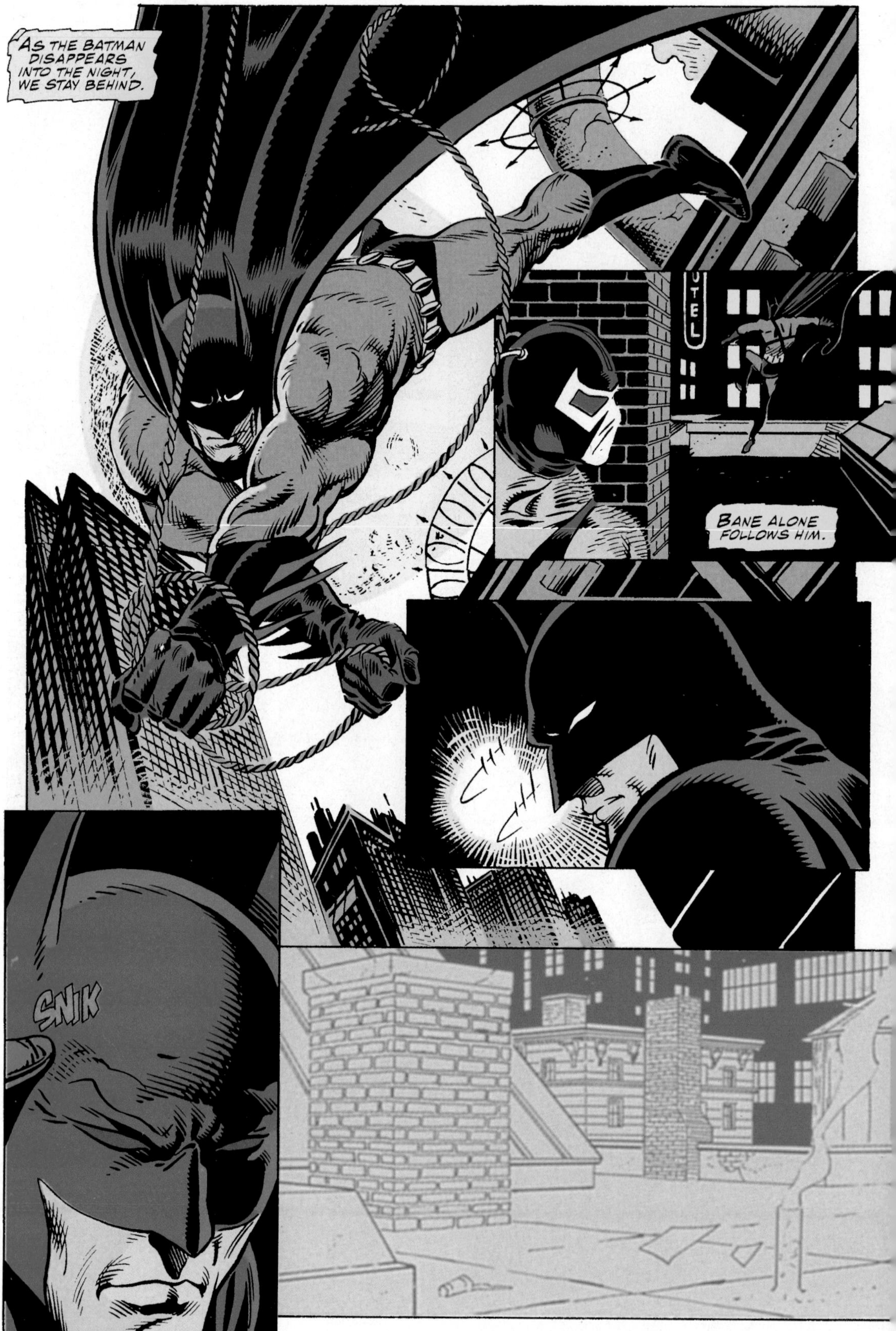
AS THE BATMAN DISAPPEARS INTO THE NIGHT, WE STAY BEHIND.
UTEL
BANE ALONE FOLLOWS HIM.
SNIK

HE WILL CONFRONT THIS CREATURE ON HIS OWN.

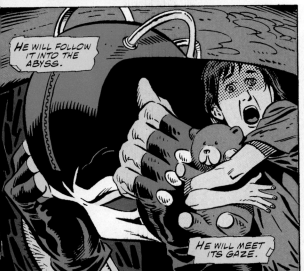

HE WILL FOLLOW IT INTO THE ABYSS.

HE WILL MEET ITS GAZE.

AND HE WILL DESTROY IT.

OR BE DESTROYED.

45

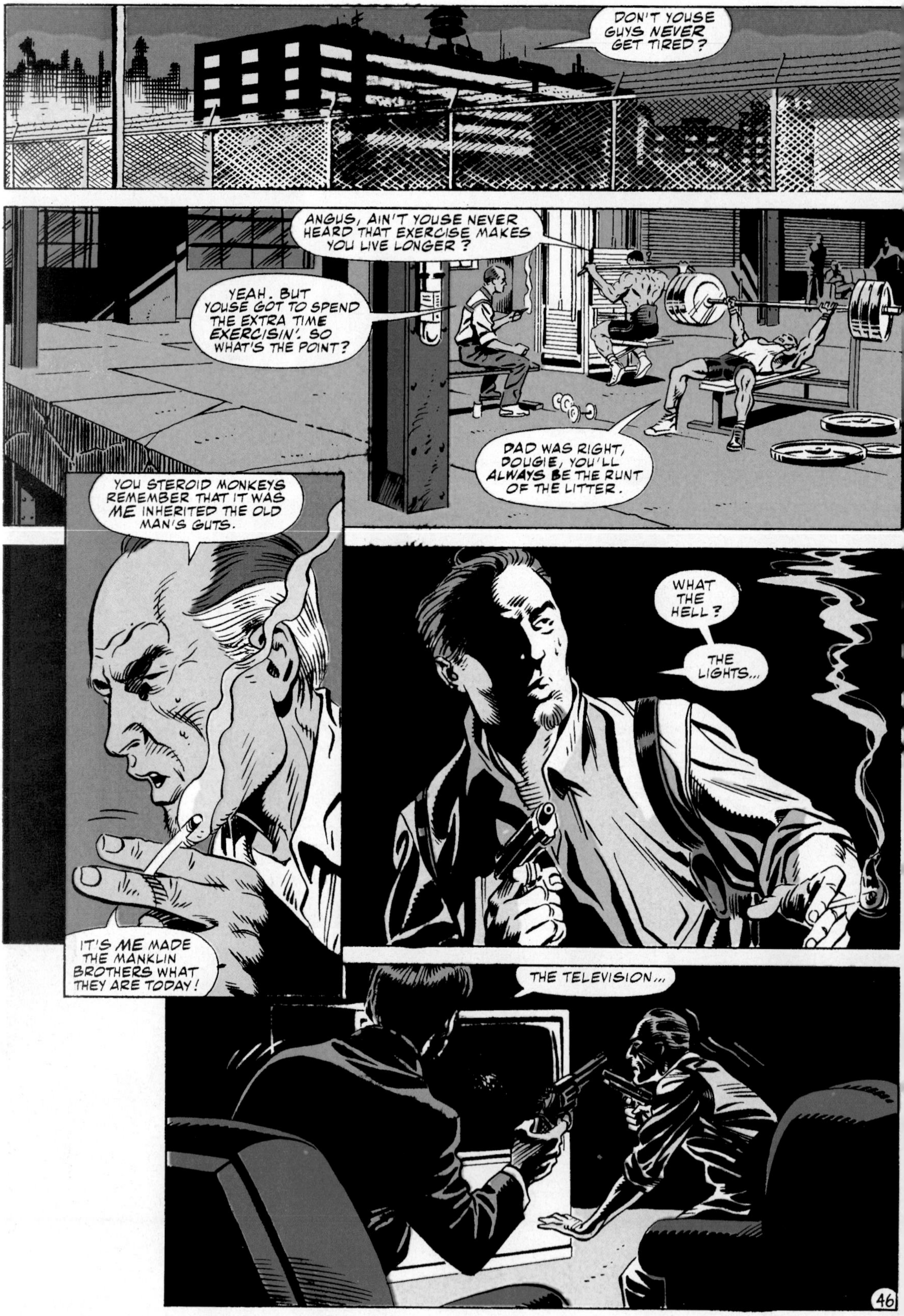
DON'T YOUSE GUYS NEVER GET TIRED?
ANGUS, AIN'T YOUSE NEVER HEARD THAT EXERCISE MAKES YOU LIVE LONGER?
YEAH. BUT YOUSE GOT TO SPEND THE EXTRA TIME EXERCISIN'. SO WHAT'S THE POINT?
DAD WAS RIGHT, DOUGIE, YOU'LL ALWAYS BE THE RUNT OF THE LITTER.
YOU STEROID MONKEYS REMEMBER THAT IT WAS ME INHERITED THE OLD MAN'S GUTS.
IT'S ME MADE THE MANKLIN BROTHERS WHAT THEY ARE TODAY!
WHAT THE HELL?
THE LIGHTS...
THE TELEVISION...
46

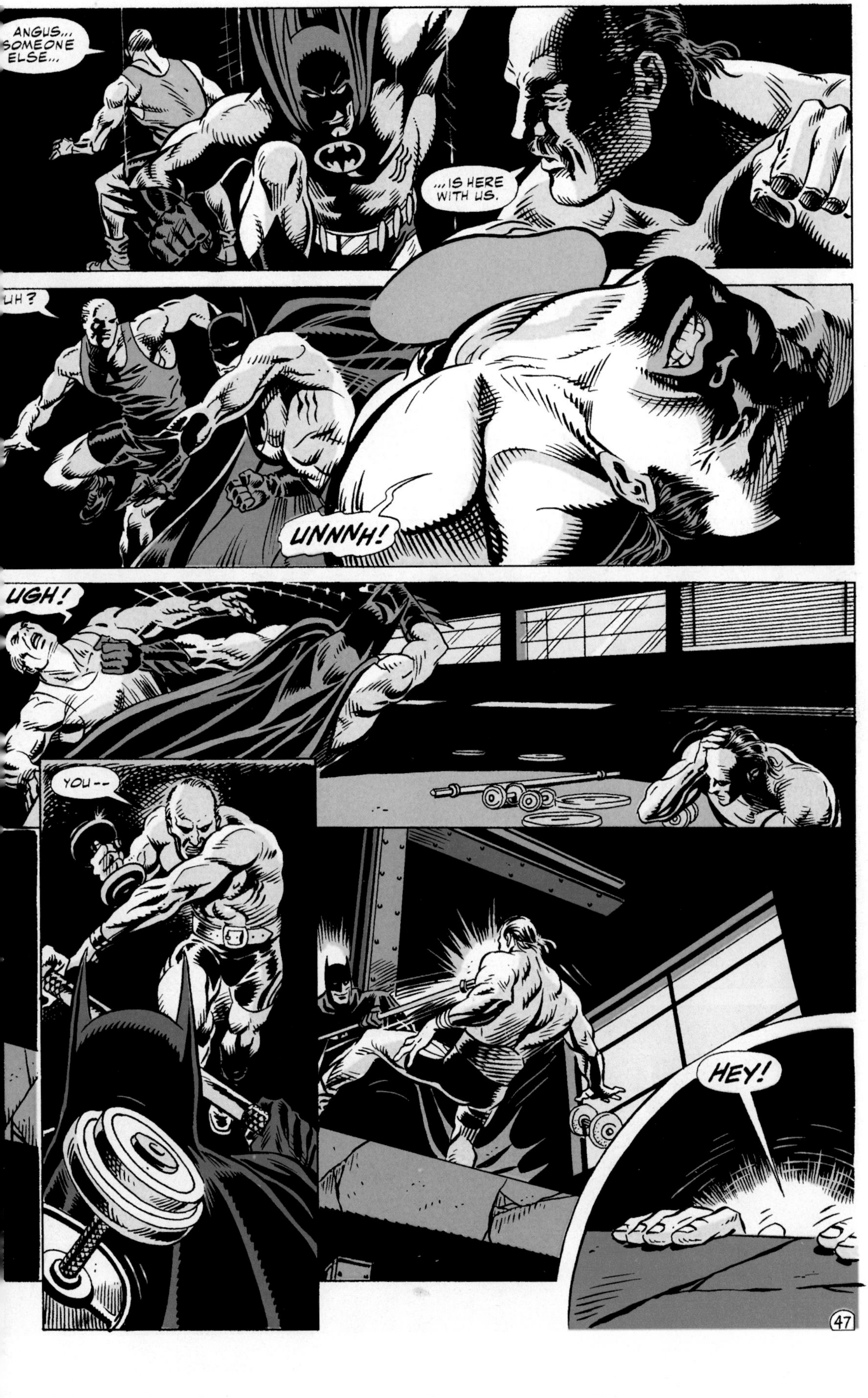

ANGUS... SOMEONE ELSE...
...IS HERE WITH US.
UH?
UNNNH!
UGH!
YOU--
HEY!

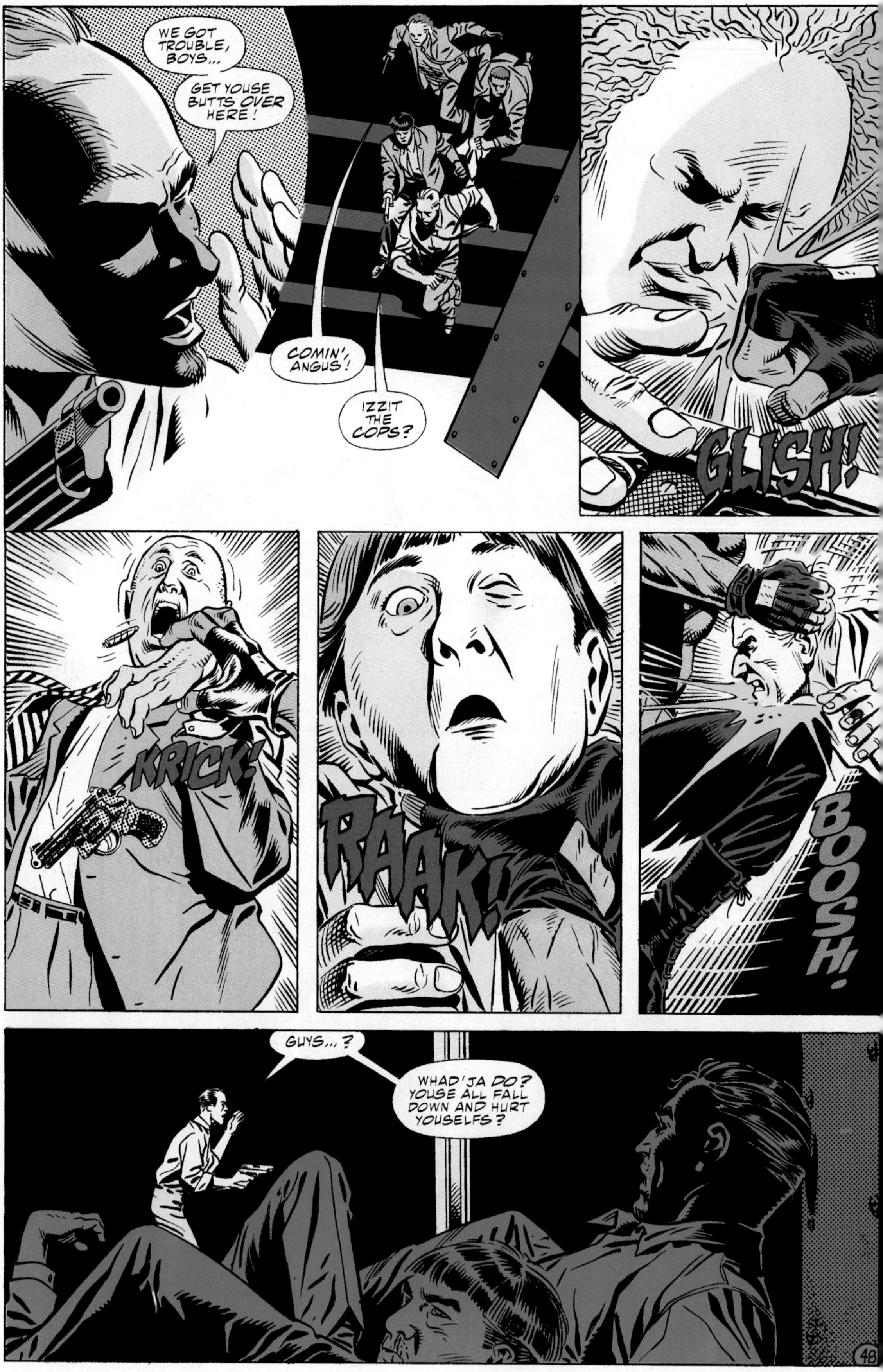

WE GOT TROUBLE, BOYS...
GET YOUSE BUTTS OVER HERE!
COMIN', ANGUS!
IZZIT THE COPS?
GLISH!
KRICK!
RAAK!
BOOSH!
GUYS... ?
WHAD'JA DO? YOUSE ALL FALL DOWN AND HURT YOUSELFS?

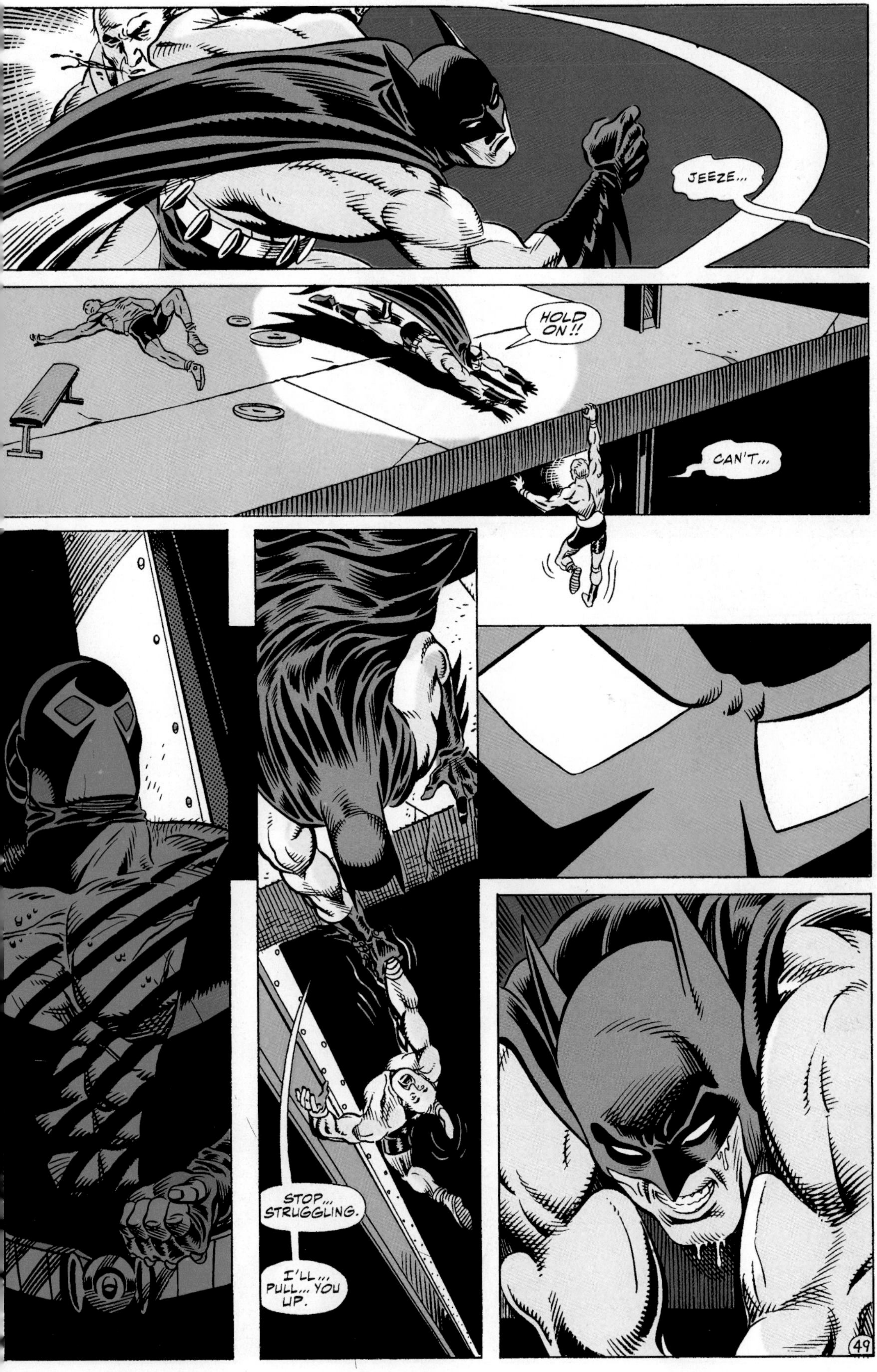
JEEZE...
HOLD ON!!
CAN'T...
STOP... STRUGGLING.
I'LL... PULL... YOU UP.

IT'S DARK. AND YOUSE IS QUICK.

BUT I GOT FOURTEEN MORE SHOTS.

NOBODY'S THAT QUICK.

NOT EVEN YOUSE.

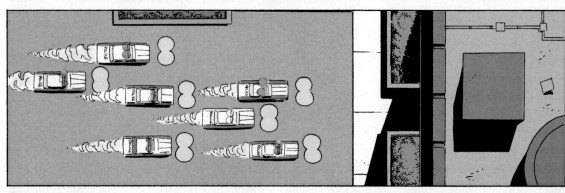

HE IS MINE. NOBODY CAN KILL HIM BUT ME.

NO...

ALMOST... THERE...

50

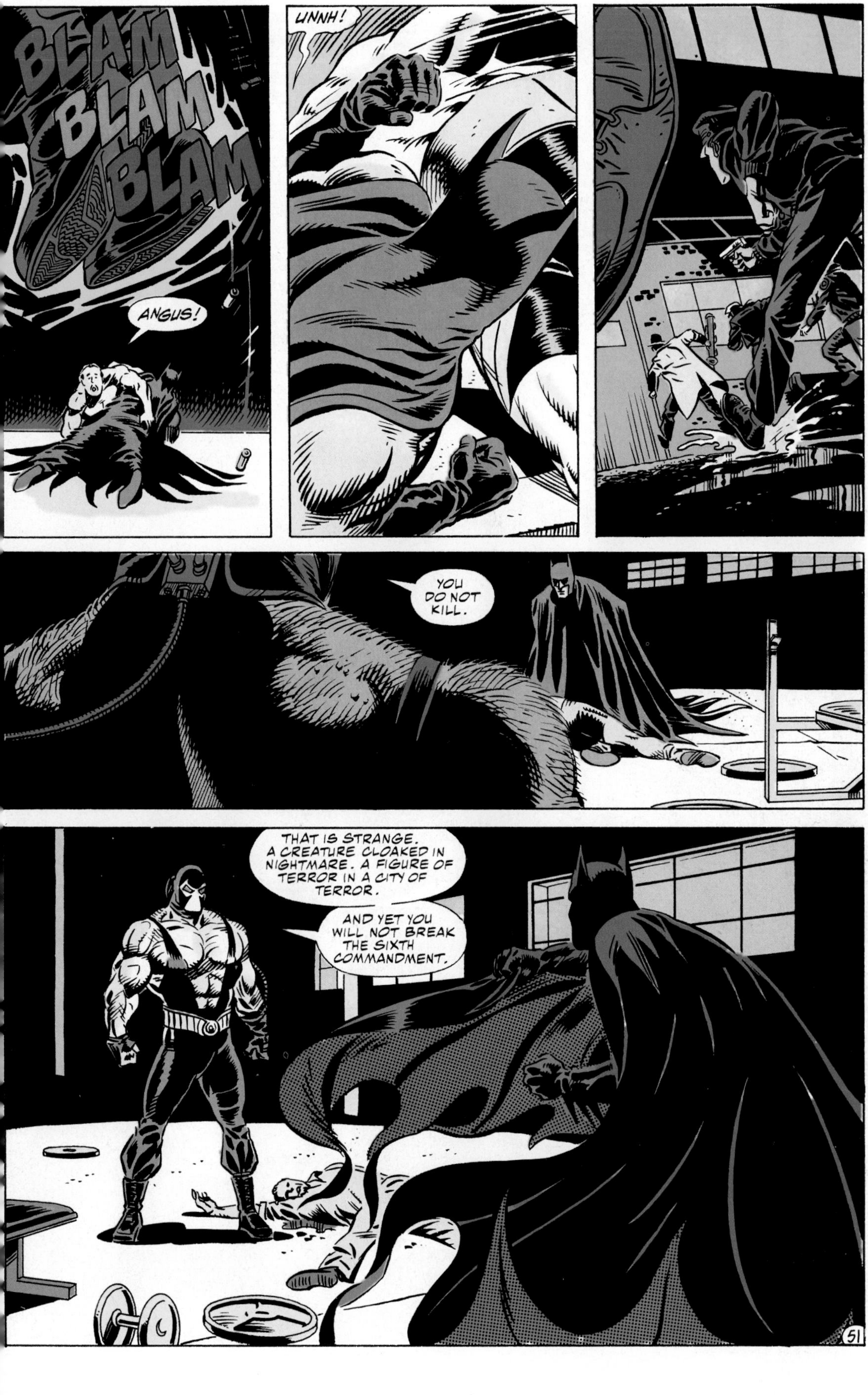
BLAM
BLAM
BLAM
ANGUS!
UNNH!
YOU DO NOT KILL.
THAT IS STRANGE. A CREATURE CLOAKED IN NIGHTMARE. A FIGURE OF TERROR IN A CITY OF TERROR.
AND YET YOU WILL NOT BREAK THE SIXTH COMMANDMENT.
51

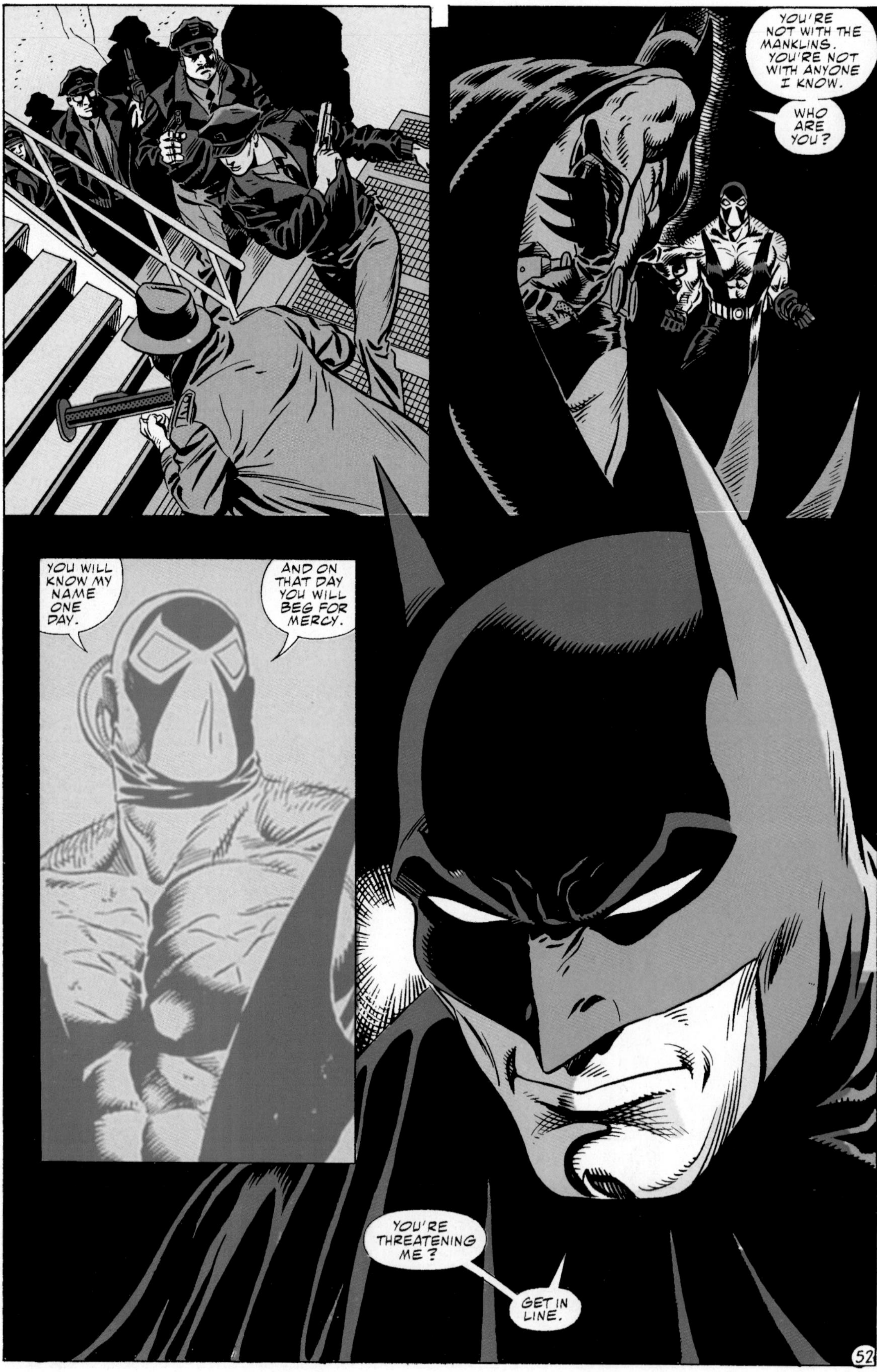
YOU'RE NOT WITH THE MANKLINS. YOU'RE NOT WITH ANYONE I KNOW.
WHO ARE YOU?
YOU WILL KNOW MY NAME ONE DAY.
AND ON THAT DAY YOU WILL BEG FOR MERCY.
YOU'RE THREATENING ME?
GET IN LINE.

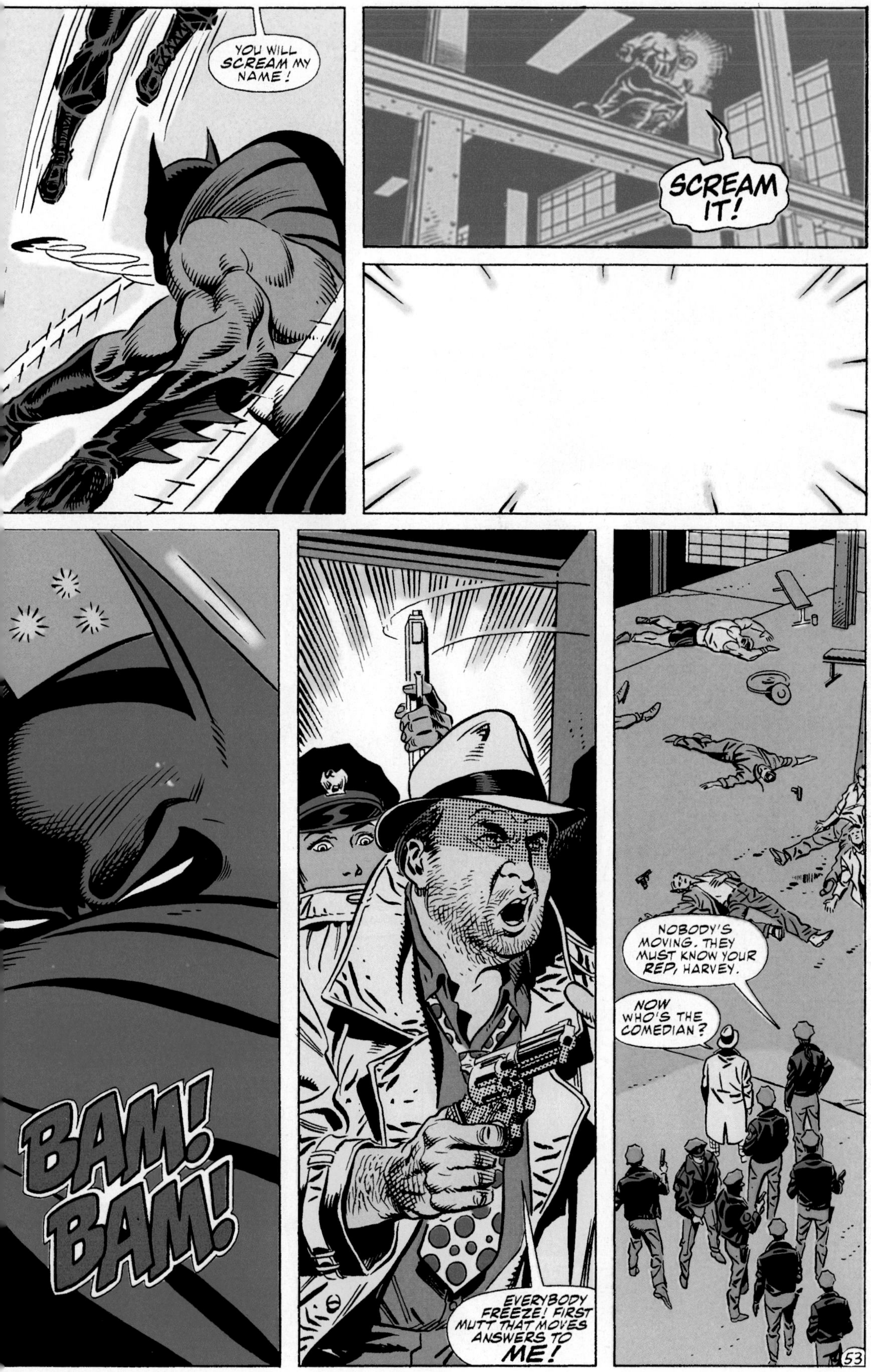

YOU WILL SCREAM MY NAME!
SCREAM IT!
BAM! BAM!
EVERYBODY FREEZE! FIRST MUTT THAT MOVES ANSWERS TO ME!
NOBODY'S MOVING. THEY MUST KNOW YOUR REP, HARVEY.
NOW WHO'S THE COMEDIAN?

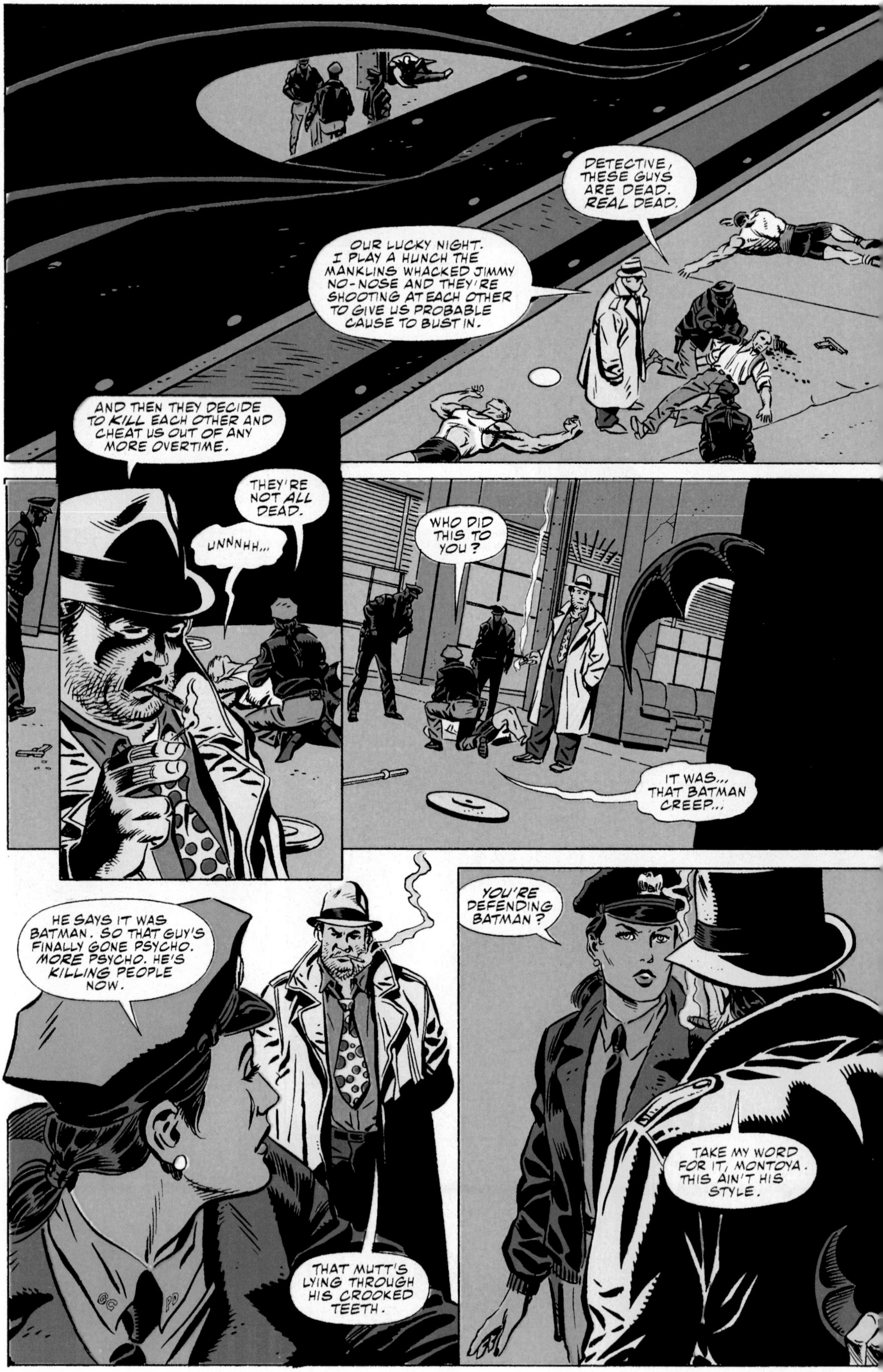
DETECTIVE, THESE GUYS ARE DEAD. REAL DEAD.
OUR LUCKY NIGHT. I PLAY A HUNCH THE MANKLINS WHACKED JIMMY NO-NOSE AND THEY'RE SHOOTING AT EACH OTHER TO GIVE US PROBABLE CAUSE TO BUST IN.
AND THEN THEY DECIDE TO KILL EACH OTHER AND CHEAT US OUT OF ANY MORE OVERTIME.
THEY'RE NOT ALL DEAD.
UNNNHH...
WHO DID THIS TO YOU?
IT WAS... THAT BATMAN CREEP...
HE SAYS IT WAS BATMAN. SO THAT GUY'S FINALLY GONE PSYCHO. MORE PSYCHO. HE'S KILLING PEOPLE NOW.
THAT MUTT'S LYING THROUGH HIS CROOKED TEETH.
YOU'RE DEFENDING BATMAN?
TAKE MY WORD FOR IT, MONTOYA. THIS AIN'T HIS STYLE.

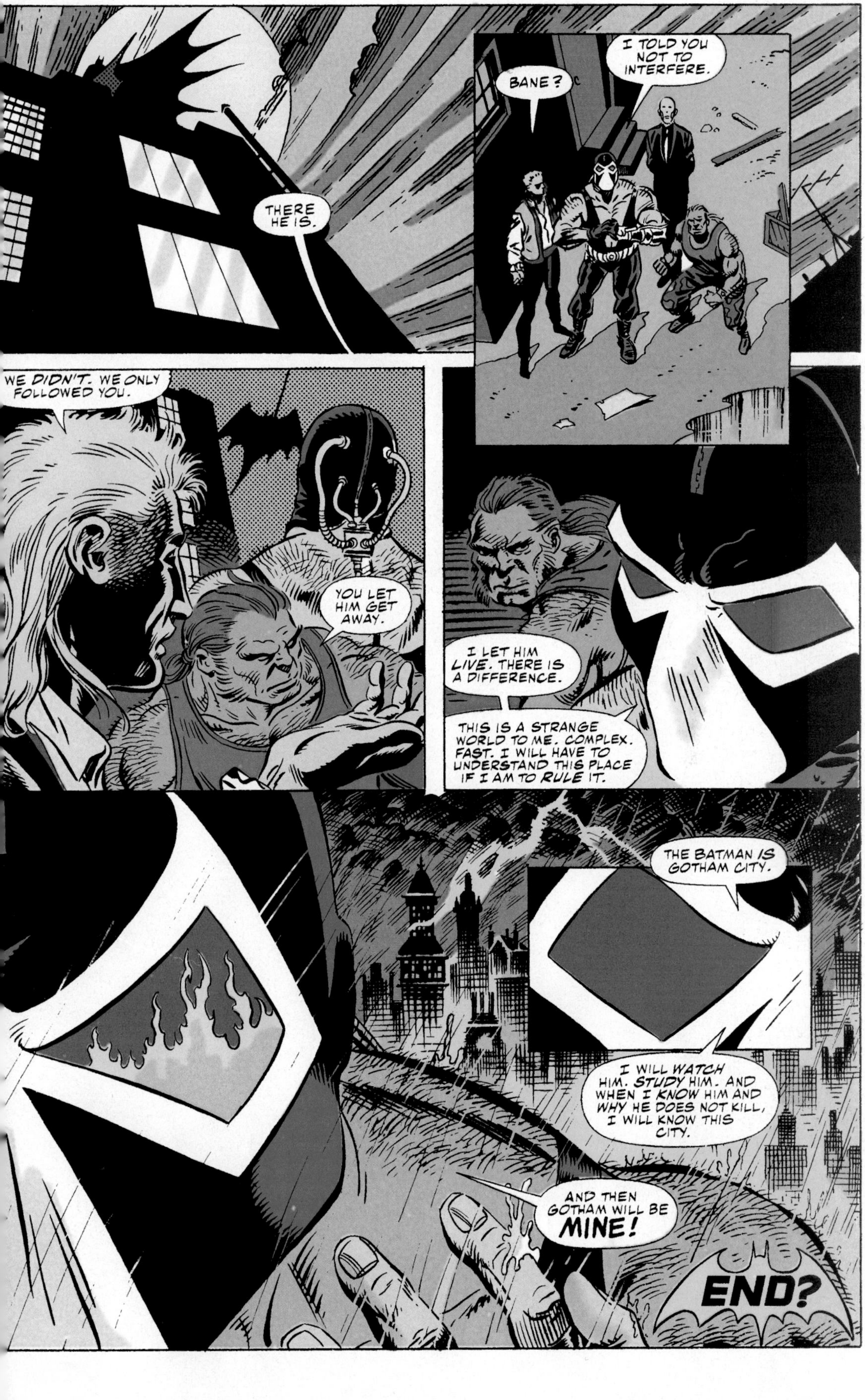
THERE HE IS.
BANE?
I TOLD YOU NOT TO INTERFERE.
WE DIDN'T. WE ONLY FOLLOWED YOU.
YOU LET HIM GET AWAY.
I LET HIM LIVE. THERE IS A DIFFERENCE.
THIS IS A STRANGE WORLD TO ME. COMPLEX. FAST. I WILL HAVE TO UNDERSTAND THIS PLACE IF I AM TO RULE IT.
THE BATMAN IS GOTHAM CITY.
I WILL WATCH HIM. STUDY HIM. AND WHEN I KNOW HIM AND WHY HE DOES NOT KILL, I WILL KNOW THIS CITY.
AND THEN GOTHAM WILL BE MINE!
END?

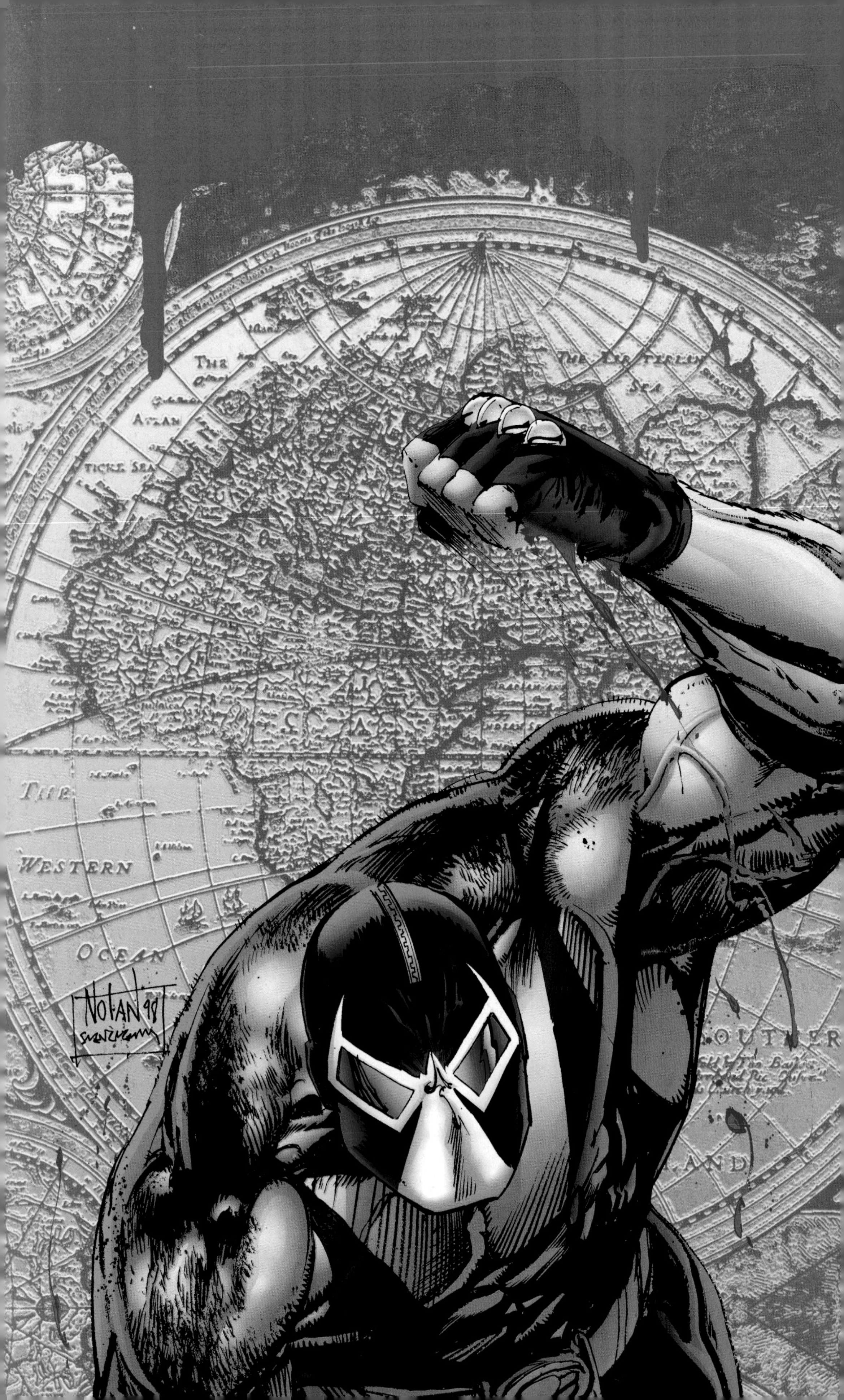
THE
WESTERN
OCEAN

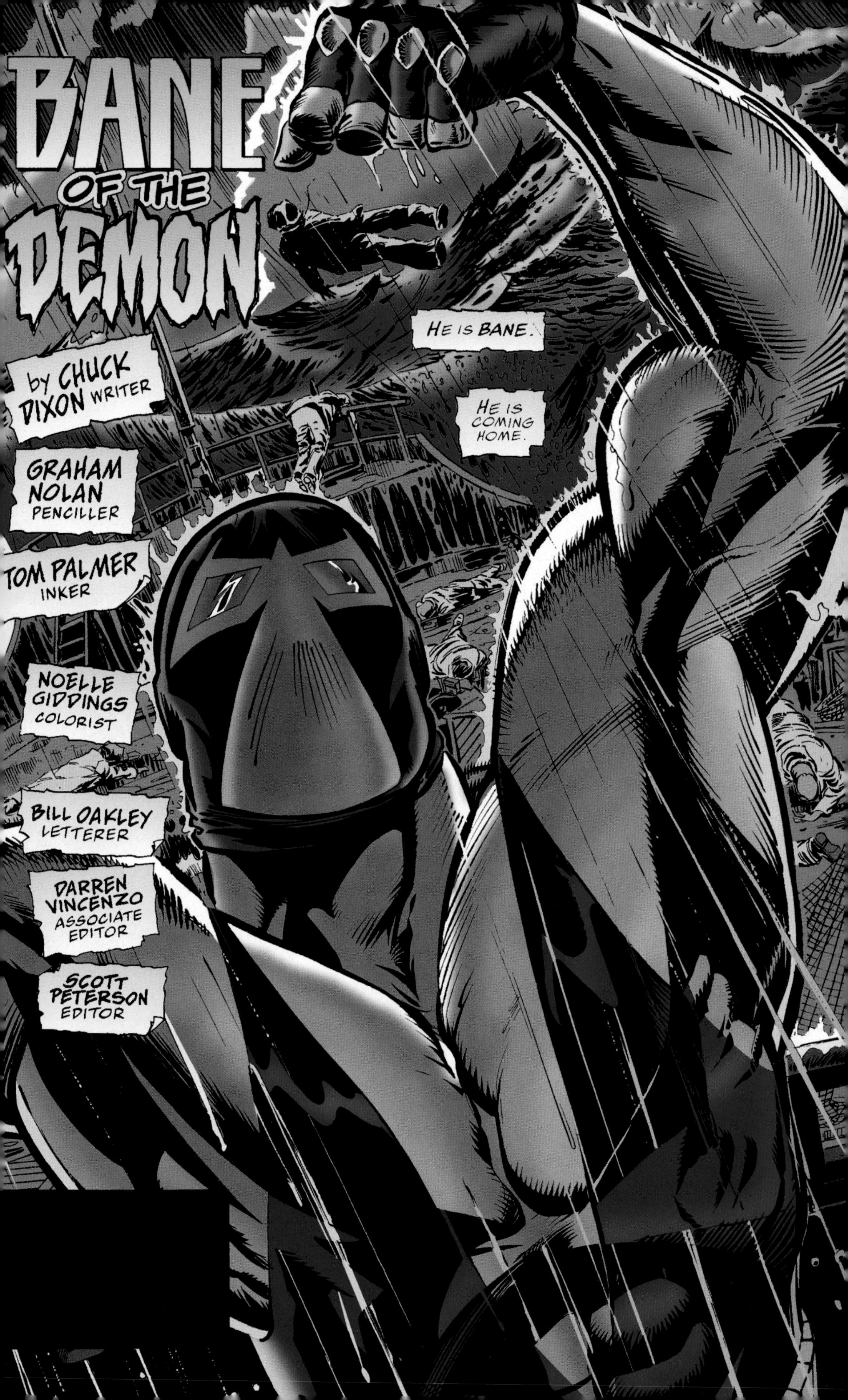
BANE OF THE DEMON
HE IS BANE.
HE IS COMING HOME.
by CHUCK DIXON WRITER
GRAHAM NOLAN PENCILLER
TOM PALMER INKER
NOELLE GIDDINGS COLORIST
BILL OAKLEY LETTERER
DARREN VINCENZO ASSOCIATE EDITOR
SCOTT PETERSON EDITOR

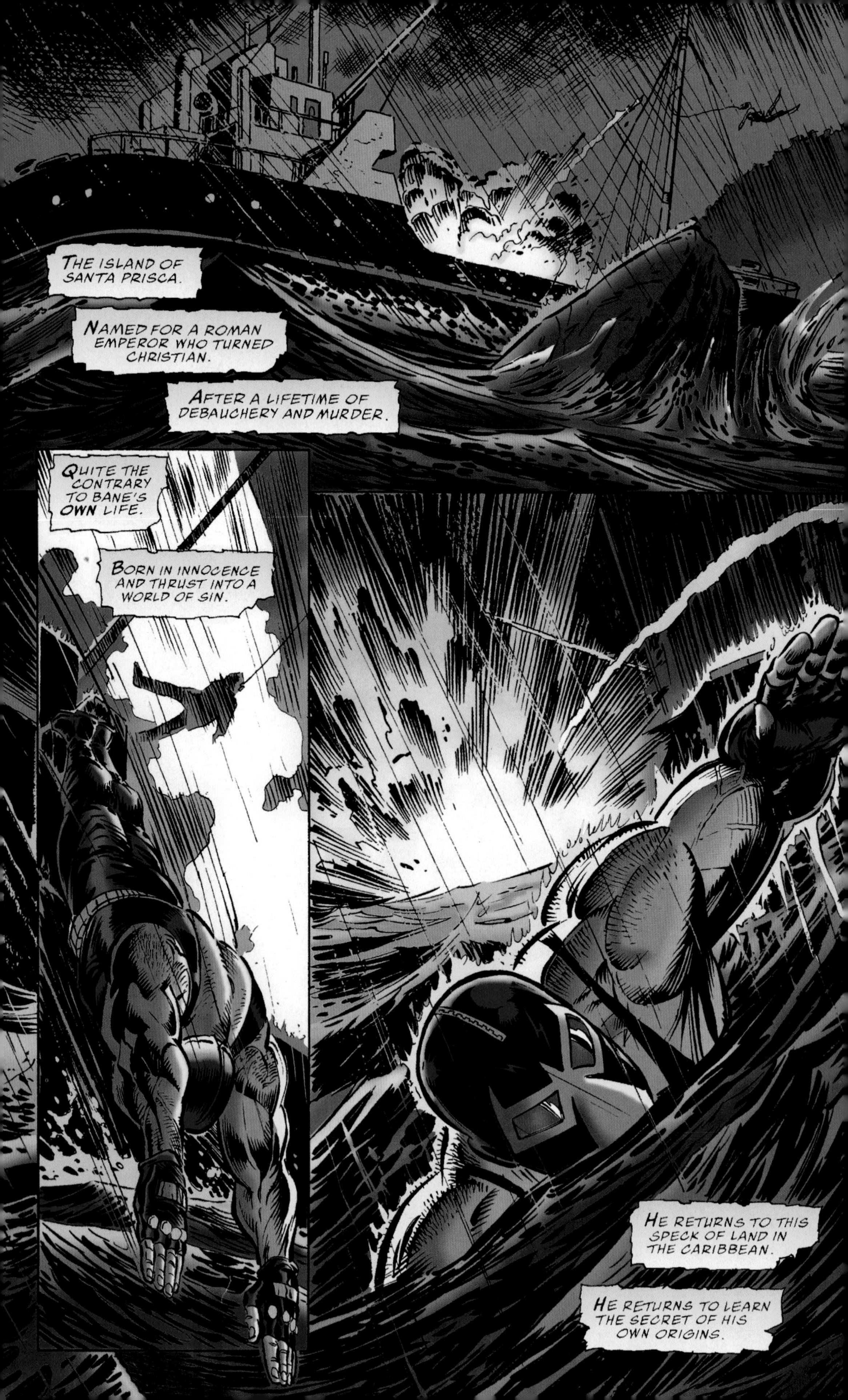
THE ISLAND OF SANTA PRISCA.
NAMED FOR A ROMAN EMPEROR WHO TURNED CHRISTIAN.
AFTER A LIFETIME OF DEBAUCHERY AND MURDER.
QUITE THE CONTRARY TO BANE'S OWN LIFE.
BORN IN INNOCENCE AND THRUST INTO A WORLD OF SIN.
HE RETURNS TO THIS SPECK OF LAND IN THE CARIBBEAN.
HE RETURNS TO LEARN THE SECRET OF HIS OWN ORIGINS.

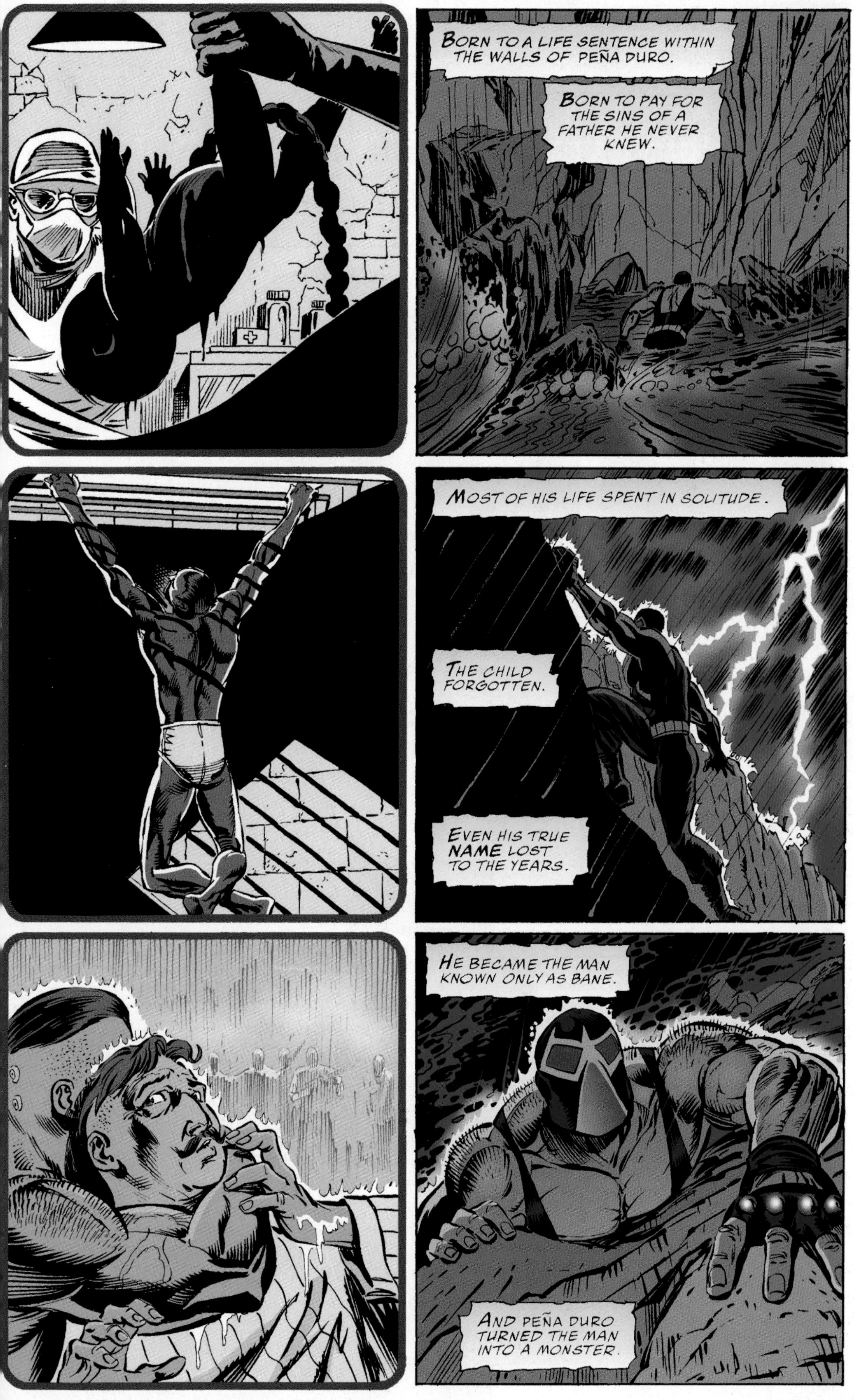
BORN TO A LIFE SENTENCE WITHIN THE WALLS OF PEÑA DURO.
BORN TO PAY FOR THE SINS OF A FATHER HE NEVER KNEW.
MOST OF HIS LIFE SPENT IN SOLITUDE.
THE CHILD FORGOTTEN.
EVEN HIS TRUE NAME LOST TO THE YEARS.
HE BECAME THE MAN KNOWN ONLY AS BANE.
AND PEÑA DURO TURNED THE MAN INTO A MONSTER.

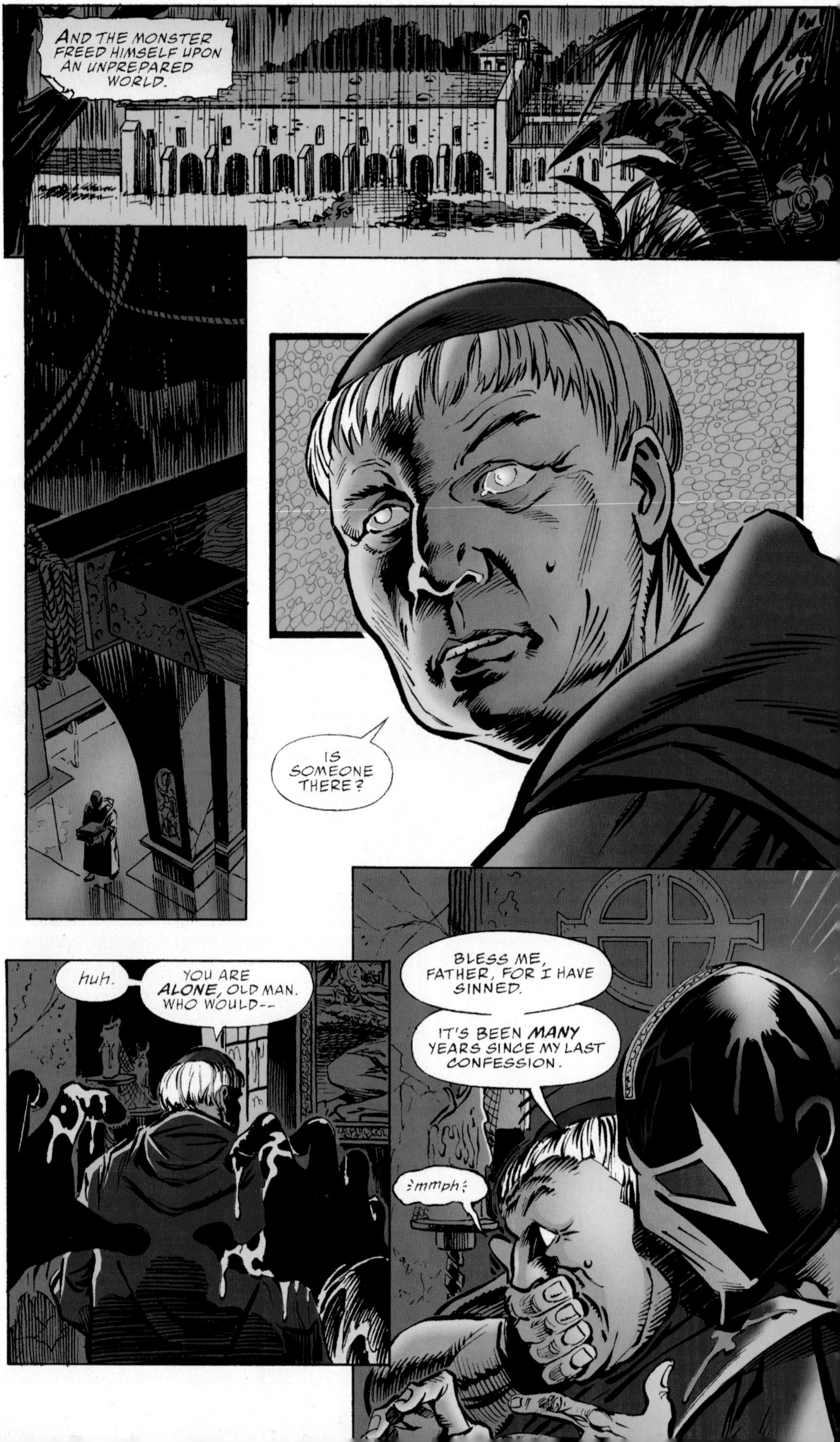

AND THE MONSTER FREED HIMSELF UPON AN UNPREPARED WORLD.
IS SOMEONE THERE?
huh.
YOU ARE ALONE, OLD MAN. WHO WOULD--
BLESS ME, FATHER, FOR I HAVE SINNED.
IT'S BEEN MANY YEARS SINCE MY LAST CONFESSION.
mmph

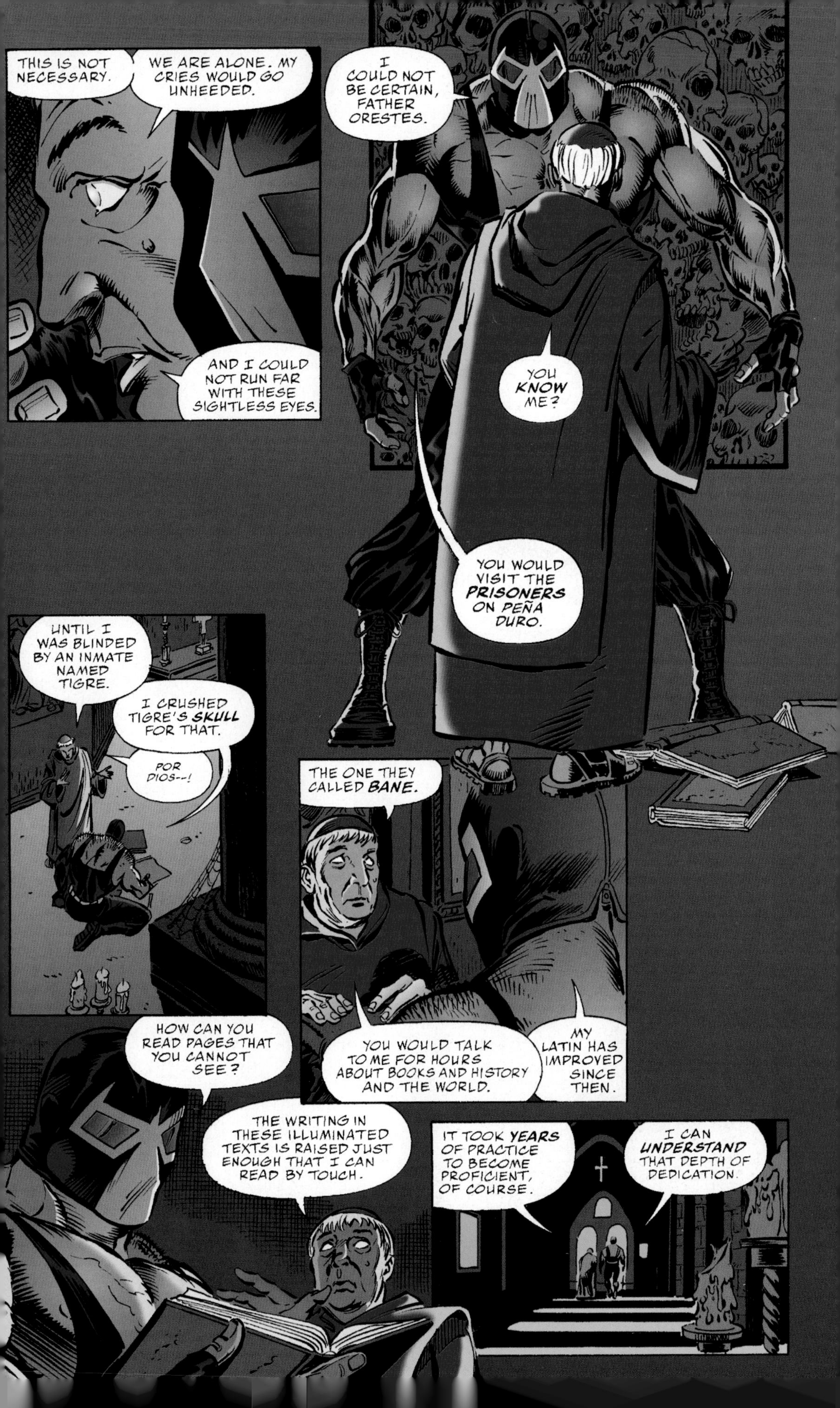

THIS IS NOT NECESSARY.
WE ARE ALONE. MY CRIES WOULD GO UNHEEDED.
AND I COULD NOT RUN FAR WITH THESE SIGHTLESS EYES.
I COULD NOT BE CERTAIN, FATHER ORESTES.
YOU KNOW ME?
YOU WOULD VISIT THE PRISONERS ON PEÑA DURO.
UNTIL I WAS BLINDED BY AN INMATE NAMED TIGRE.
I CRUSHED TIGRE'S SKULL FOR THAT.
POR DIOS--!
THE ONE THEY CALLED BANE.
YOU WOULD TALK TO ME FOR HOURS ABOUT BOOKS AND HISTORY AND THE WORLD.
MY LATIN HAS IMPROVED SINCE THEN.
HOW CAN YOU READ PAGES THAT YOU CANNOT SEE?
THE WRITING IN THESE ILLUMINATED TEXTS IS RAISED JUST ENOUGH THAT I CAN READ BY TOUCH.
IT TOOK YEARS OF PRACTICE TO BECOME PROFICIENT, OF COURSE.
I CAN UNDERSTAND THAT DEPTH OF DEDICATION.

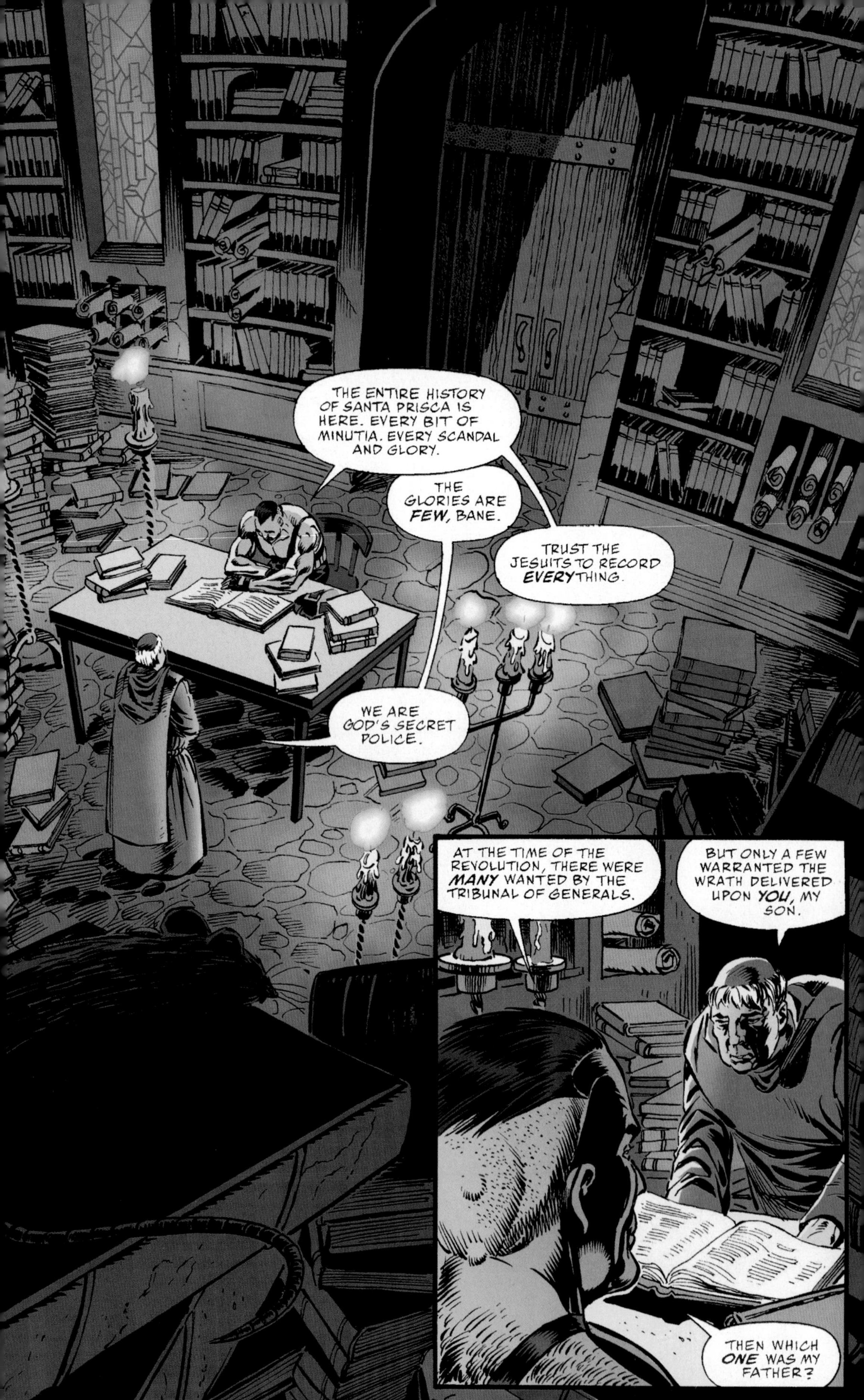
THE ENTIRE HISTORY OF SANTA PRISCA IS HERE. EVERY BIT OF MINUTIA. EVERY SCANDAL AND GLORY.
THE GLORIES ARE *FEW*, BANE.
TRUST THE JESUITS TO RECORD *EVERY*THING.
WE ARE GOD'S SECRET POLICE.
AT THE TIME OF THE REVOLUTION, THERE WERE *MANY* WANTED BY THE TRIBUNAL OF GENERALS.
BUT ONLY A FEW WARRANTED THE WRATH DELIVERED UPON *YOU*, MY SON.
THEN WHICH *ONE* WAS MY FATHER?

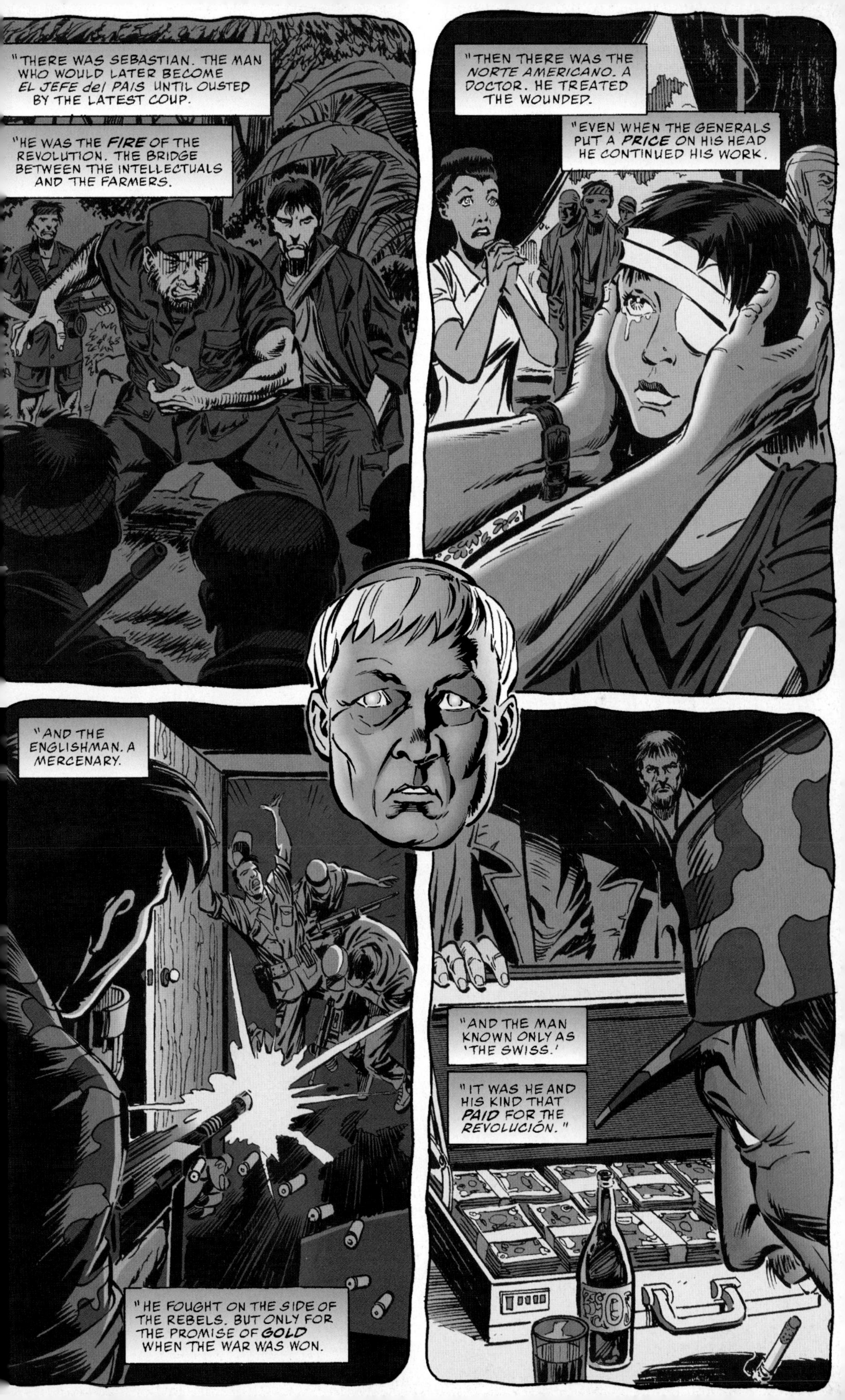
"THERE WAS SEBASTIAN. THE MAN WHO WOULD LATER BECOME *EL JEFE del PAIS* UNTIL OUSTED BY THE LATEST COUP.
"HE WAS THE ***FIRE*** OF THE REVOLUTION. THE BRIDGE BETWEEN THE INTELLECTUALS AND THE FARMERS.
"THEN THERE WAS THE *NORTE AMERICANO*. A DOCTOR. HE TREATED THE WOUNDED.
"EVEN WHEN THE GENERALS PUT A ***PRICE*** ON HIS HEAD HE CONTINUED HIS WORK.
"AND THE ENGLISHMAN. A MERCENARY.
"HE FOUGHT ON THE SIDE OF THE REBELS. BUT ONLY FOR THE PROMISE OF ***GOLD*** WHEN THE WAR WAS WON.
"AND THE MAN KNOWN ONLY AS 'THE SWISS.'
"IT WAS HE AND HIS KIND THAT ***PAID*** FOR THE *REVOLUCIÓN*."

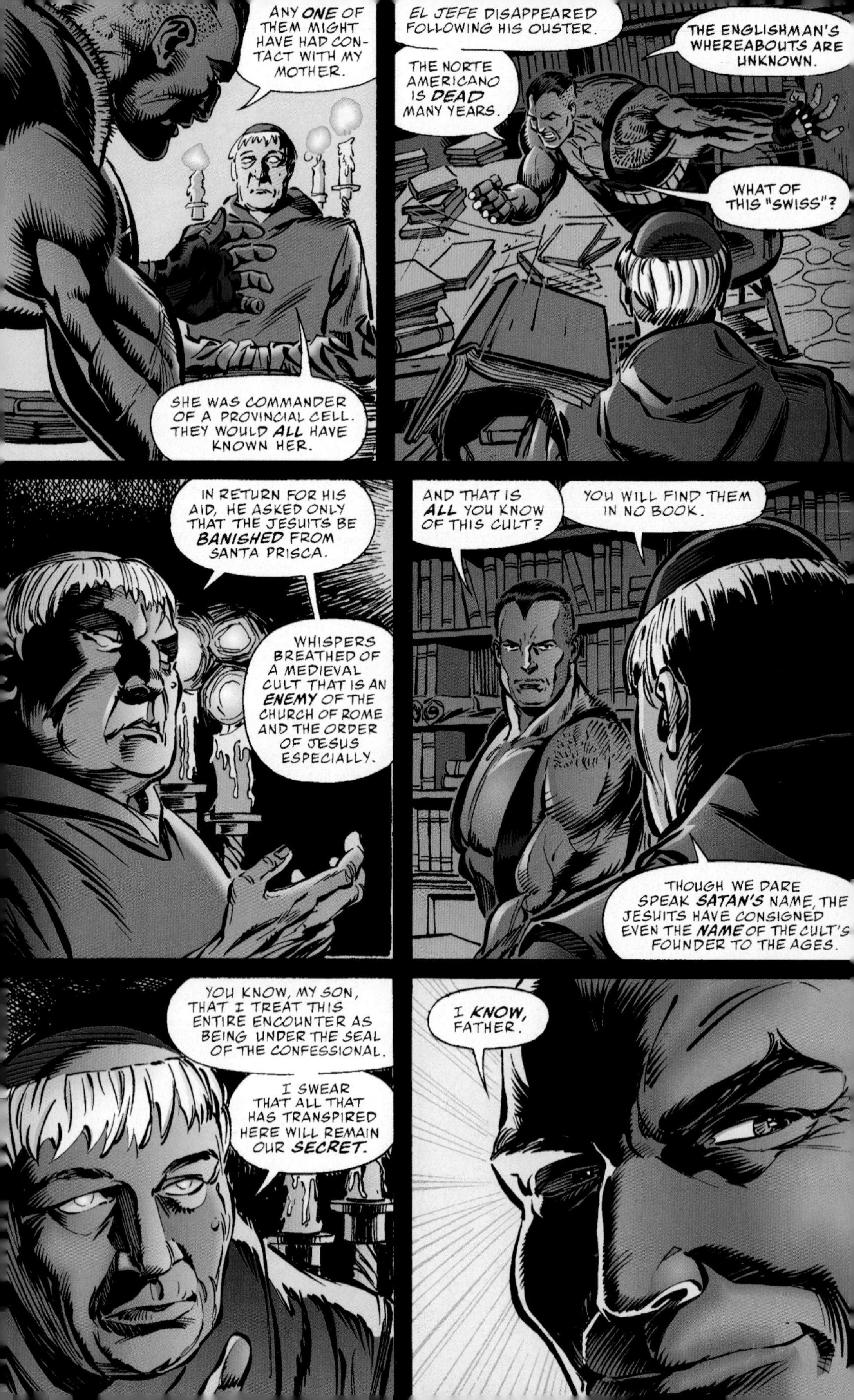
ANY ONE OF THEM MIGHT HAVE HAD CONTACT WITH MY MOTHER.
SHE WAS COMMANDER OF A PROVINCIAL CELL. THEY WOULD ALL HAVE KNOWN HER.
EL JEFE DISAPPEARED FOLLOWING HIS OUSTER.
THE NORTE AMERICANO IS DEAD MANY YEARS.
THE ENGLISHMAN'S WHEREABOUTS ARE UNKNOWN.
WHAT OF THIS "SWISS"?
IN RETURN FOR HIS AID, HE ASKED ONLY THAT THE JESUITS BE BANISHED FROM SANTA PRISCA.
WHISPERS BREATHED OF A MEDIEVAL CULT THAT IS AN ENEMY OF THE CHURCH OF ROME AND THE ORDER OF JESUS ESPECIALLY.
AND THAT IS ALL YOU KNOW OF THIS CULT?
YOU WILL FIND THEM IN NO BOOK.
THOUGH WE DARE SPEAK SATAN'S NAME, THE JESUITS HAVE CONSIGNED EVEN THE NAME OF THE CULT'S FOUNDER TO THE AGES.
YOU KNOW, MY SON, THAT I TREAT THIS ENTIRE ENCOUNTER AS BEING UNDER THE SEAL OF THE CONFESSIONAL.
I SWEAR THAT ALL THAT HAS TRANSPIRED HERE WILL REMAIN OUR SECRET.
I KNOW, FATHER.

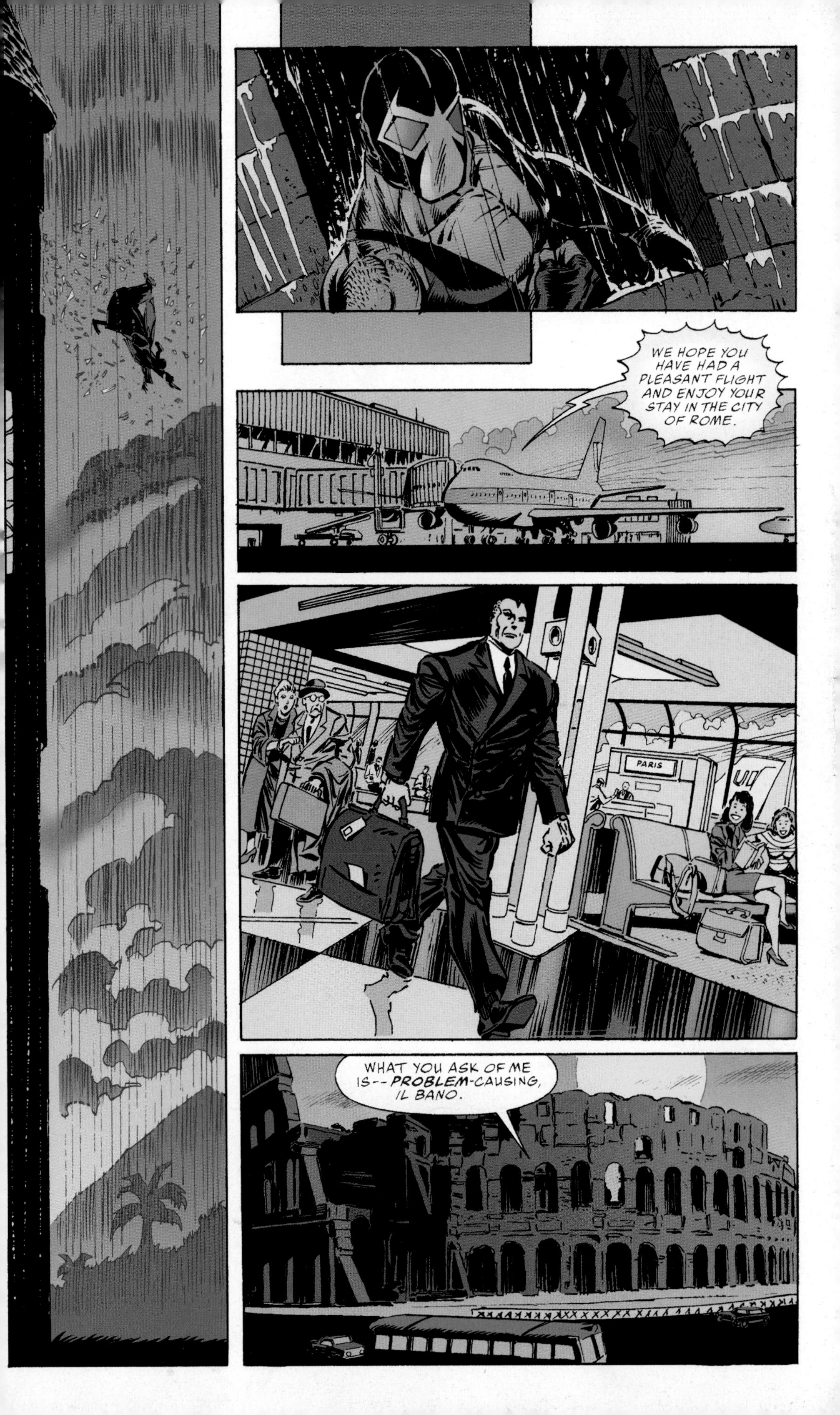
WE HOPE YOU HAVE HAD A PLEASANT FLIGHT AND ENJOY YOUR STAY IN THE CITY OF ROME.
PARIS
WHAT YOU ASK OF ME IS-- PROBLEM-CAUSING, IL BANO.

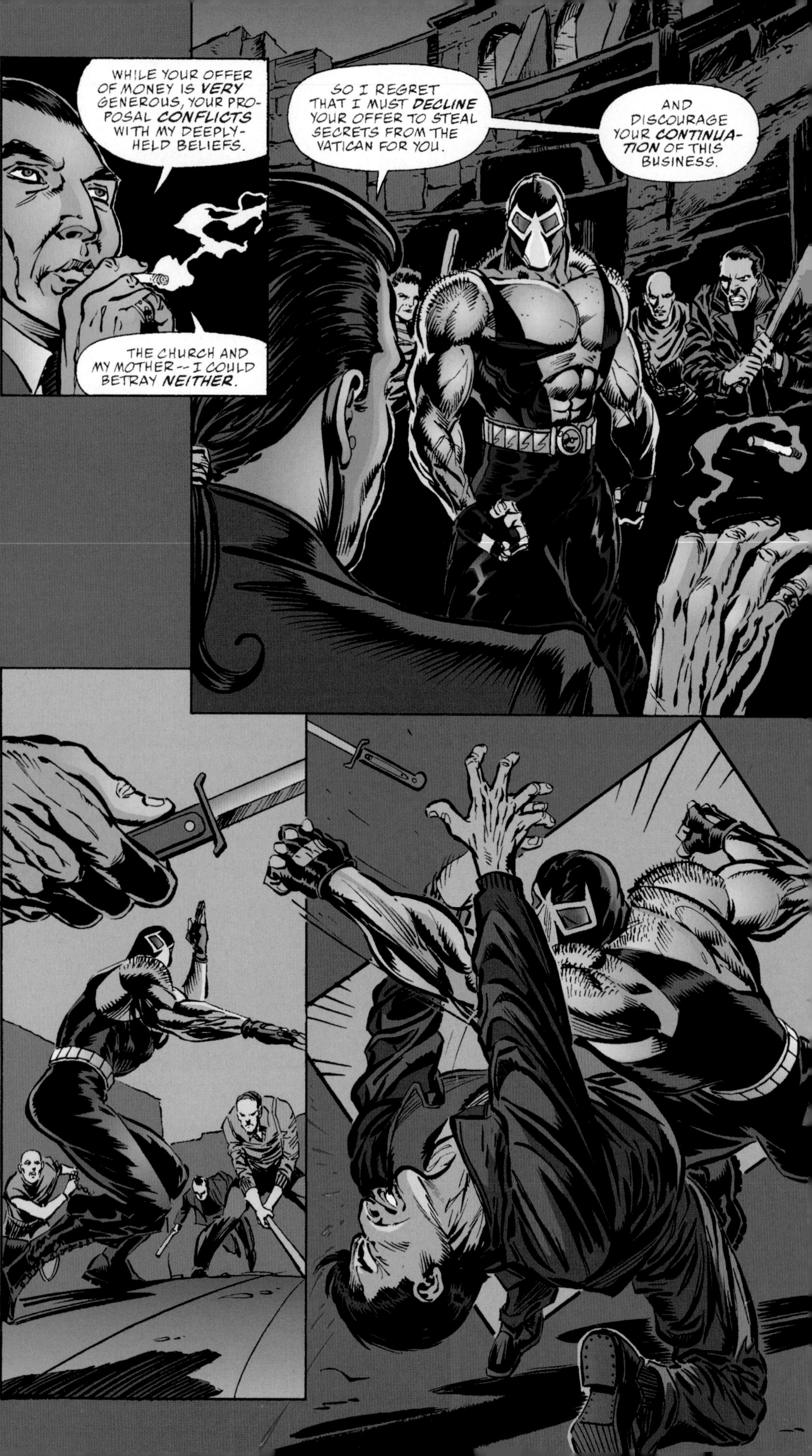
WHILE YOUR OFFER OF MONEY IS VERY GENEROUS, YOUR PROPOSAL CONFLICTS WITH MY DEEPLY-HELD BELIEFS.
THE CHURCH AND MY MOTHER -- I COULD BETRAY NEITHER.
SO I REGRET THAT I MUST DECLINE YOUR OFFER TO STEAL SECRETS FROM THE VATICAN FOR YOU.
AND DISCOURAGE YOUR CONTINUATION OF THIS BUSINESS.

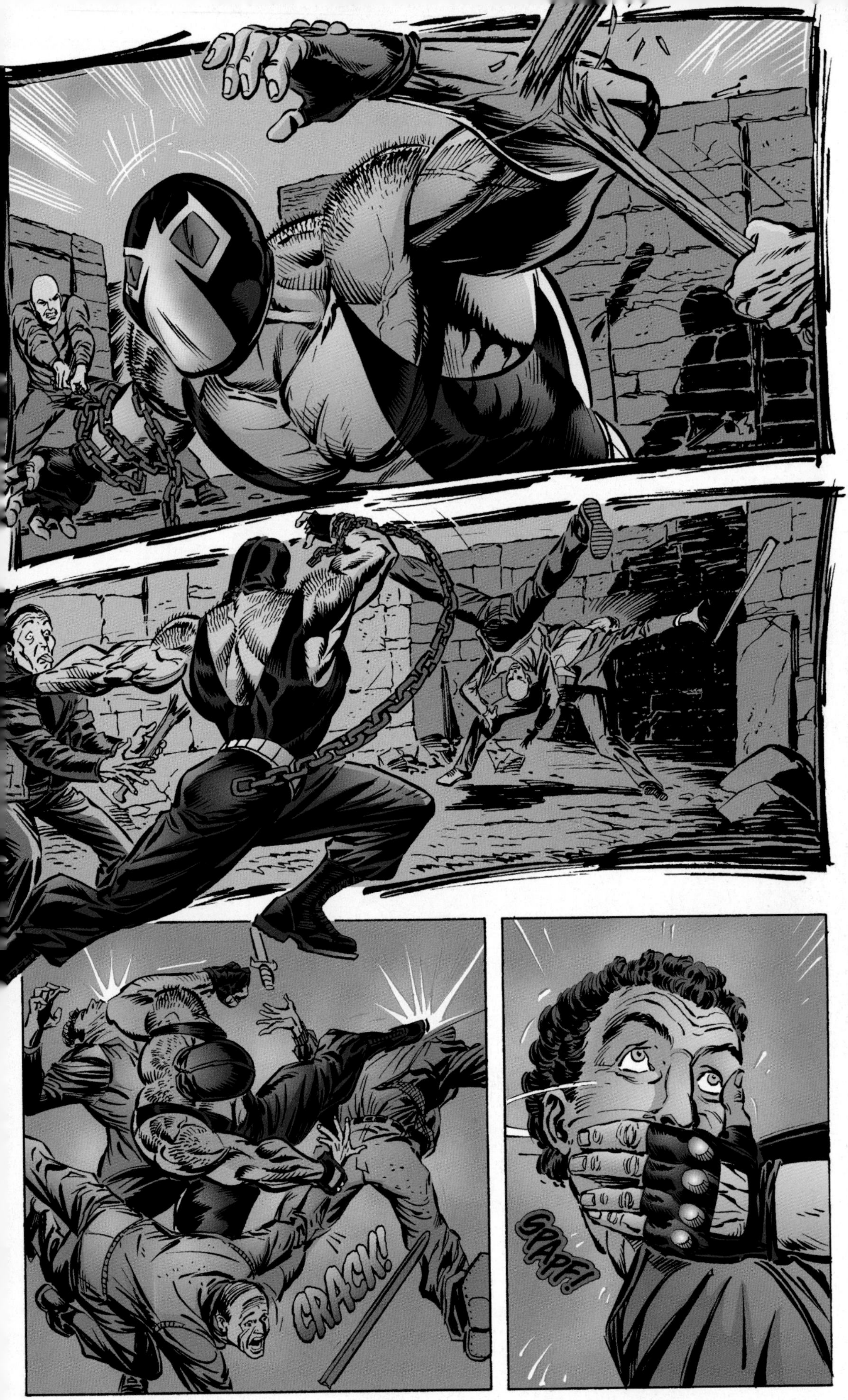

CRACK!
GRAPF!

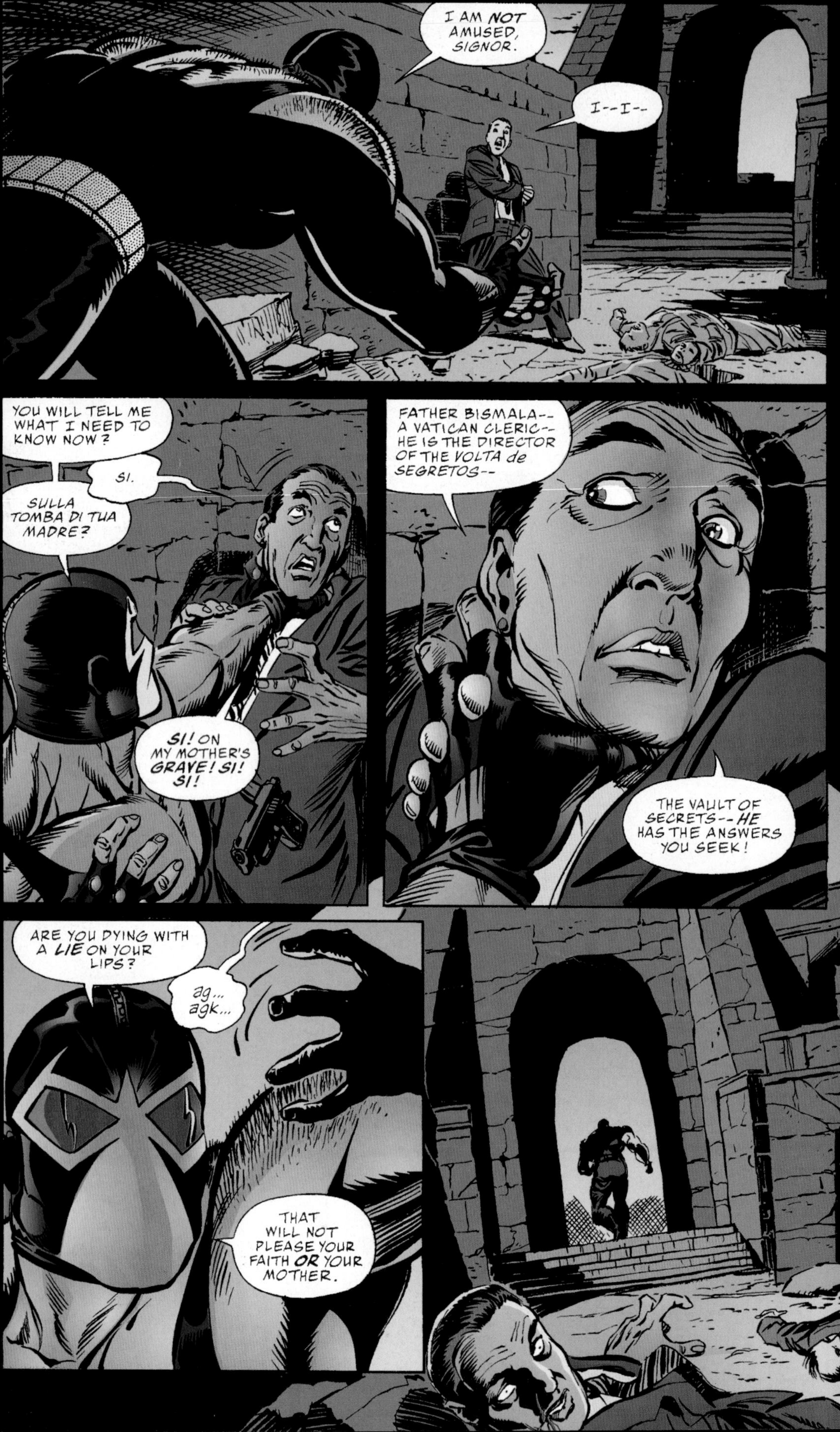
I AM NOT AMUSED, SIGNOR.
I--I--
YOU WILL TELL ME WHAT I NEED TO KNOW NOW?
SI.
SULLA TOMBA DI TUA MADRE?
SI! ON MY MOTHER'S GRAVE! SI! SI!
FATHER BISMALA-- A VATICAN CLERIC-- HE IS THE DIRECTOR OF THE VOLTA de SEGRETOS--
THE VAULT OF SECRETS--HE HAS THE ANSWERS YOU SEEK!
ARE YOU DYING WITH A LIE ON YOUR LIPS?
ag... agk...
THAT WILL NOT PLEASE YOUR FAITH OR YOUR MOTHER.

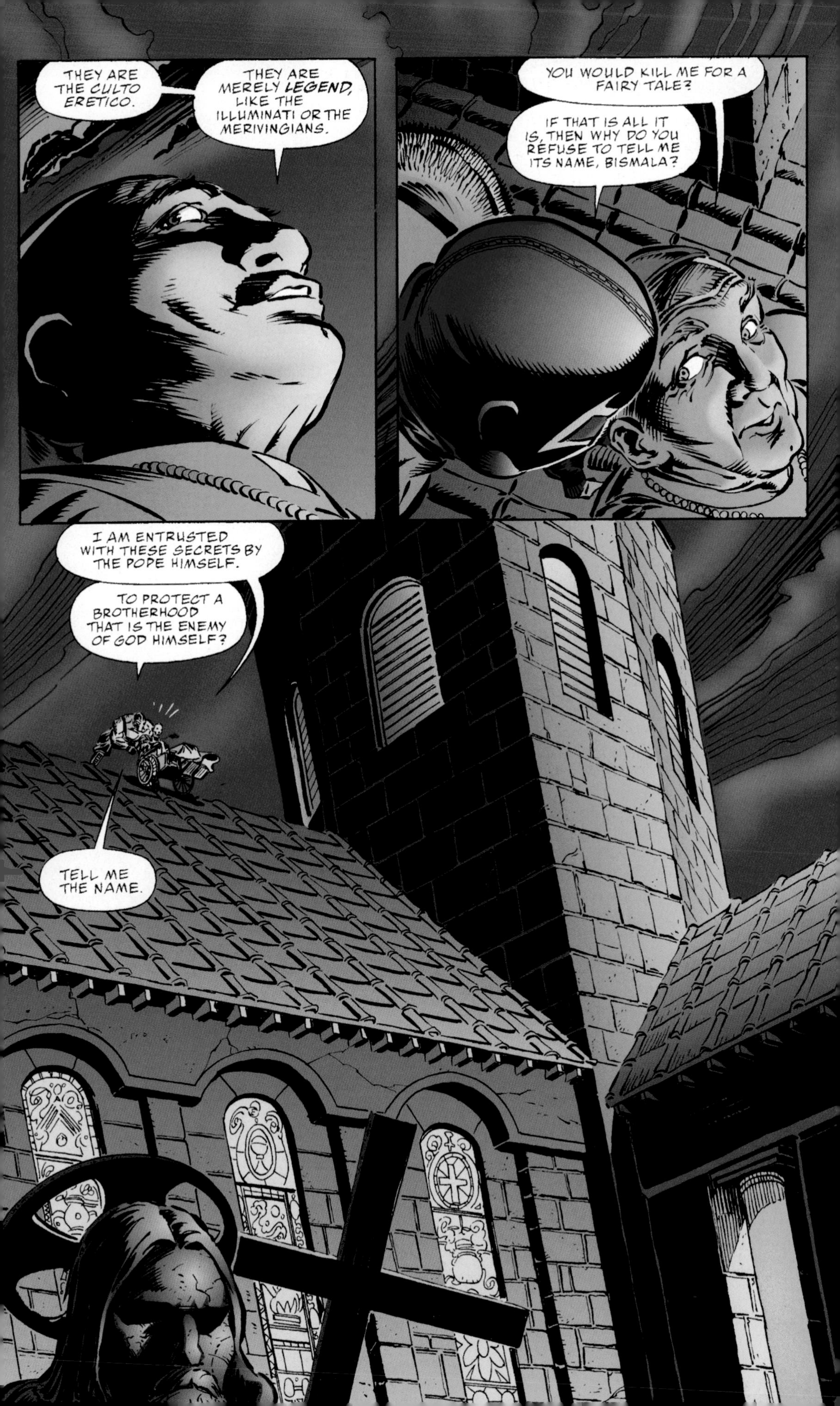
THEY ARE THE CULTO ERETICO.
THEY ARE MERELY LEGEND, LIKE THE ILLUMINATI OR THE MERIVINGIANS.
YOU WOULD KILL ME FOR A FAIRY TALE?
IF THAT IS ALL IT IS, THEN WHY DO YOU REFUSE TO TELL ME ITS NAME, BISMALA?
I AM ENTRUSTED WITH THESE SECRETS BY THE POPE HIMSELF.
TO PROTECT A BROTHERHOOD THAT IS THE ENEMY OF GOD HIMSELF?
TELL ME THE NAME.

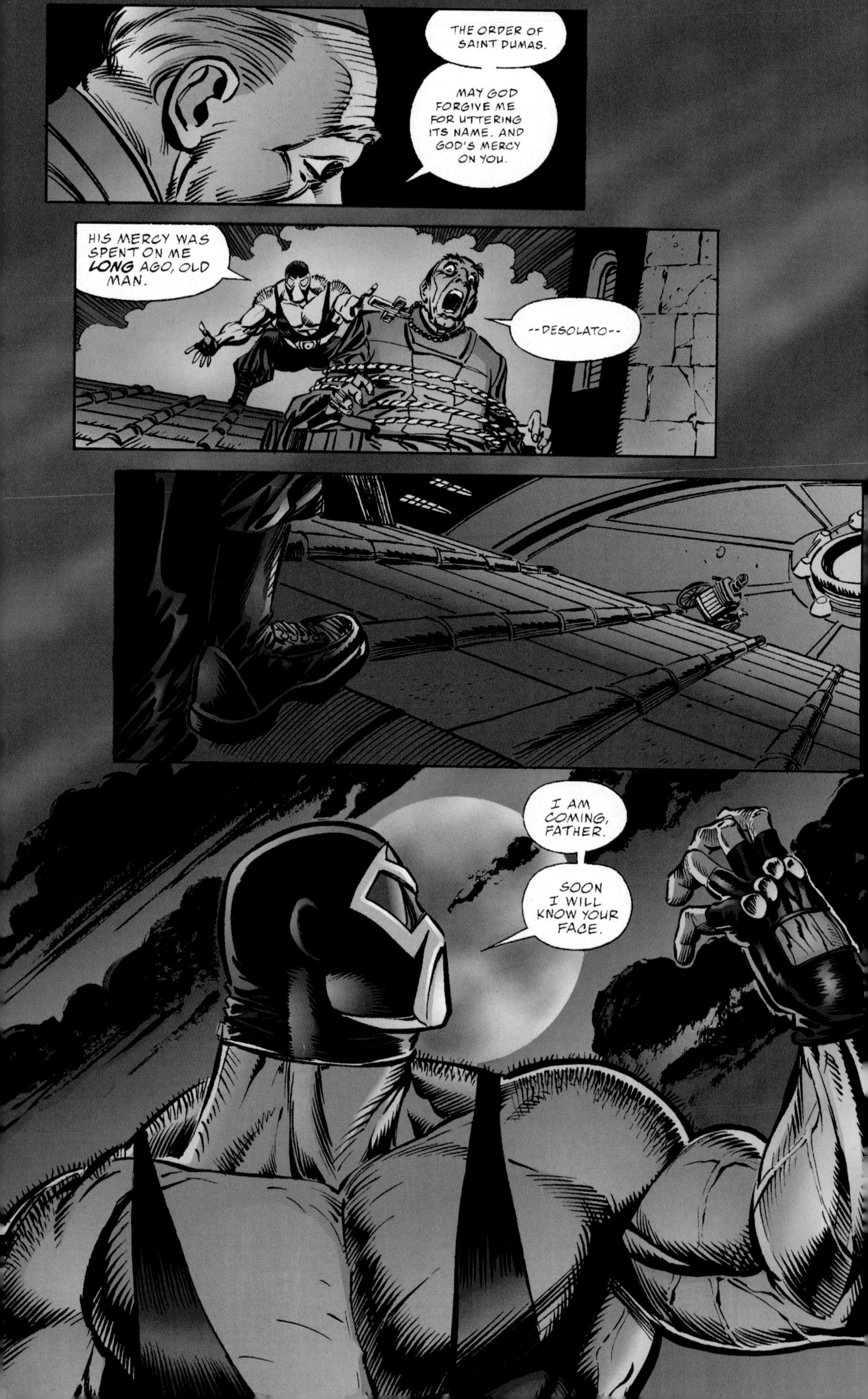
THE ORDER OF SAINT DUMAS.
MAY GOD FORGIVE ME FOR UTTERING ITS NAME. AND GOD'S MERCY ON YOU.
HIS MERCY WAS SPENT ON ME **LONG** AGO, OLD MAN.
--DESOLATO--
I AM COMING, FATHER.
SOON I WILL KNOW YOUR FACE.

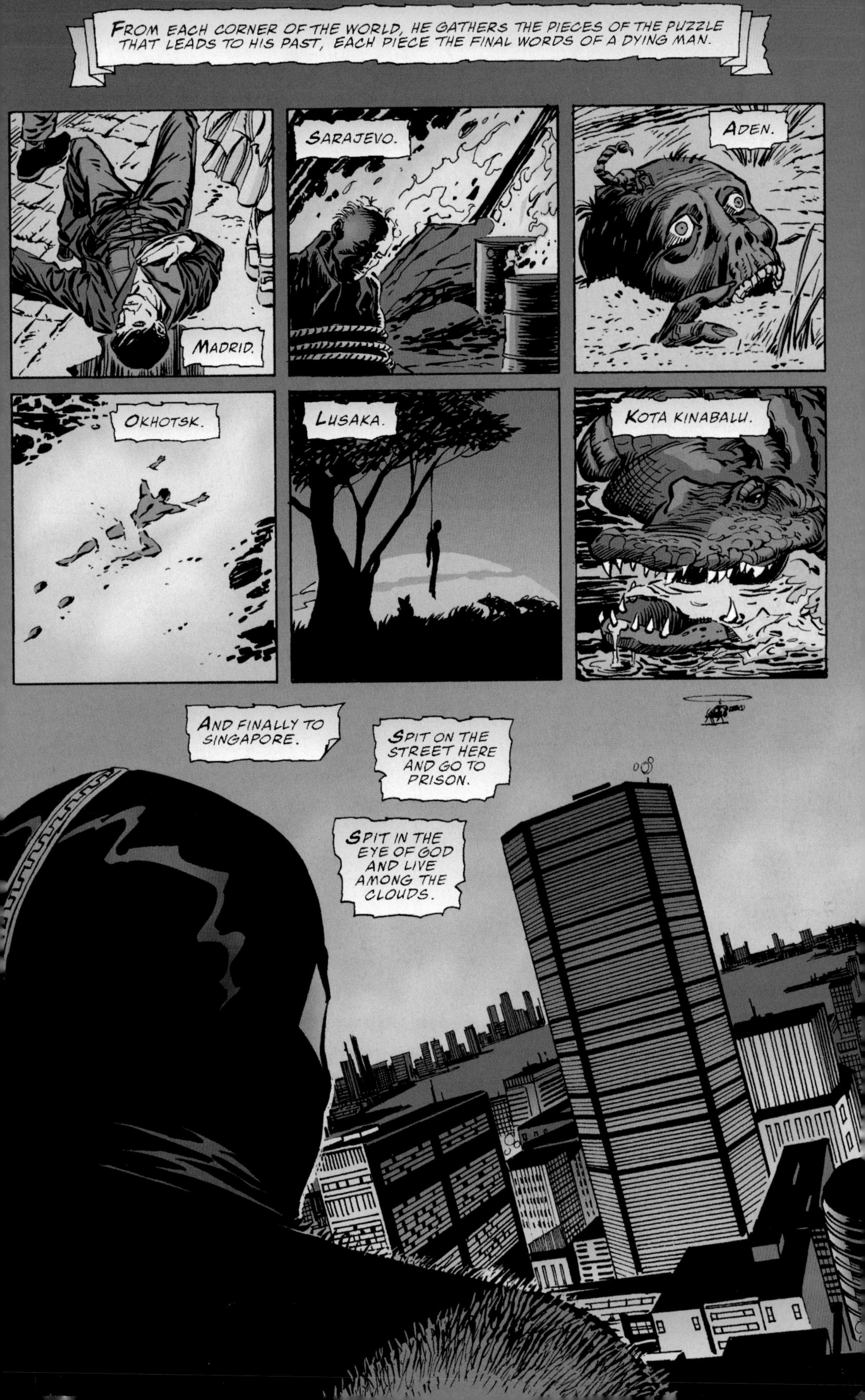
FROM EACH CORNER OF THE WORLD, HE GATHERS THE PIECES OF THE PUZZLE THAT LEADS TO HIS PAST, EACH PIECE THE FINAL WORDS OF A DYING MAN.
MADRID.
SARAJEVO.
ADEN.
OKHOTSK.
LUSAKA.
KOTA KINABALU.
AND FINALLY TO SINGAPORE.
SPIT ON THE STREET HERE AND GO TO PRISON.
SPIT IN THE EYE OF GOD AND LIVE AMONG THE CLOUDS.

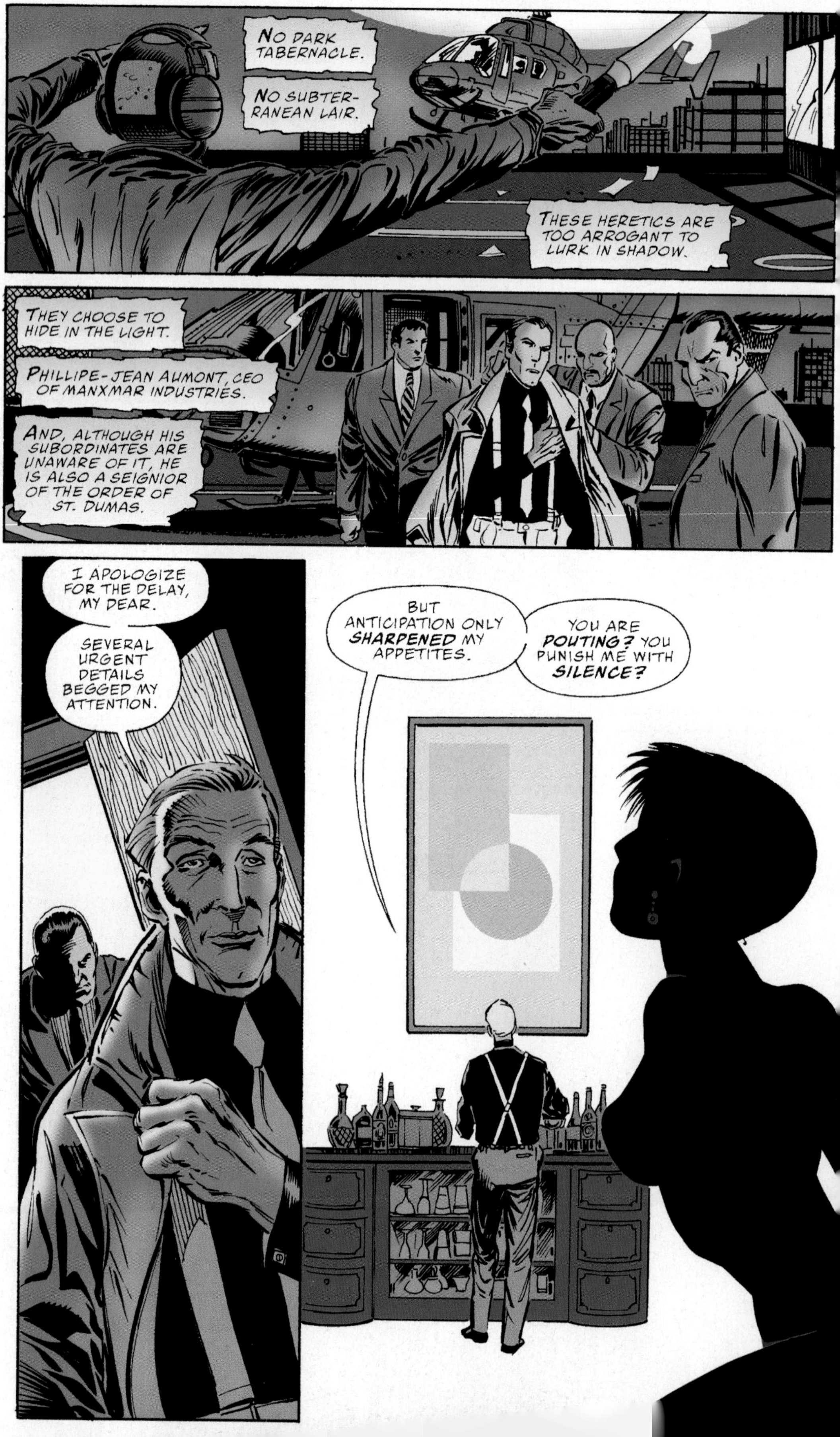
NO DARK TABERNACLE.
NO SUBTERRANEAN LAIR.
THESE HERETICS ARE TOO ARROGANT TO LURK IN SHADOW.
THEY CHOOSE TO HIDE IN THE LIGHT.
PHILLIPE-JEAN AUMONT, CEO OF MANXMAR INDUSTRIES.
AND, ALTHOUGH HIS SUBORDINATES ARE UNAWARE OF IT, HE IS ALSO A SEIGNIOR OF THE ORDER OF ST. DUMAS.
I APOLOGIZE FOR THE DELAY, MY DEAR.
SEVERAL URGENT DETAILS BEGGED MY ATTENTION.
BUT ANTICIPATION ONLY **SHARPENED** MY APPETITES.
YOU ARE **POUTING?** YOU PUNISH ME WITH **SILENCE?**

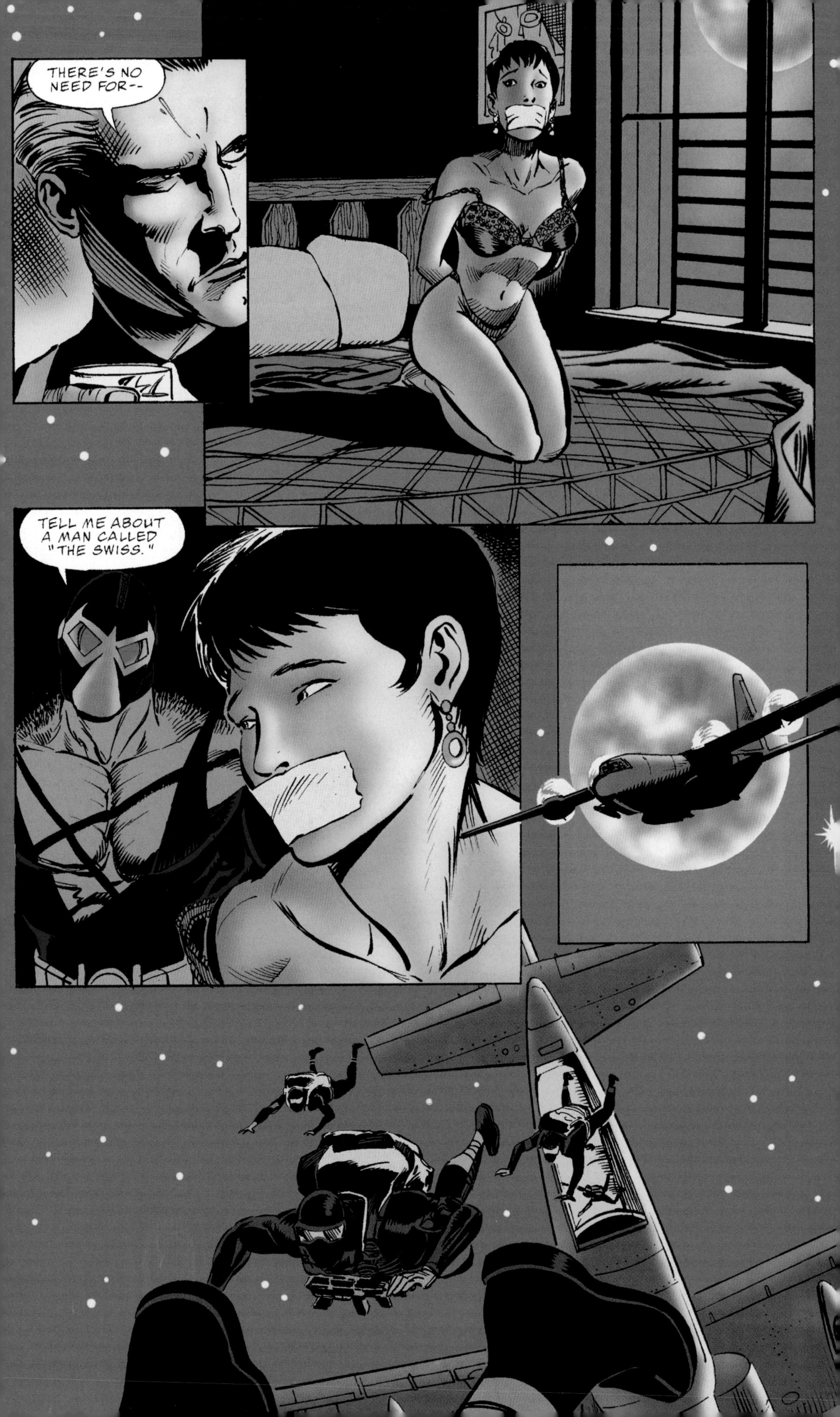
THERE'S NO NEED FOR--
TELL ME ABOUT A MAN CALLED "THE SWISS."

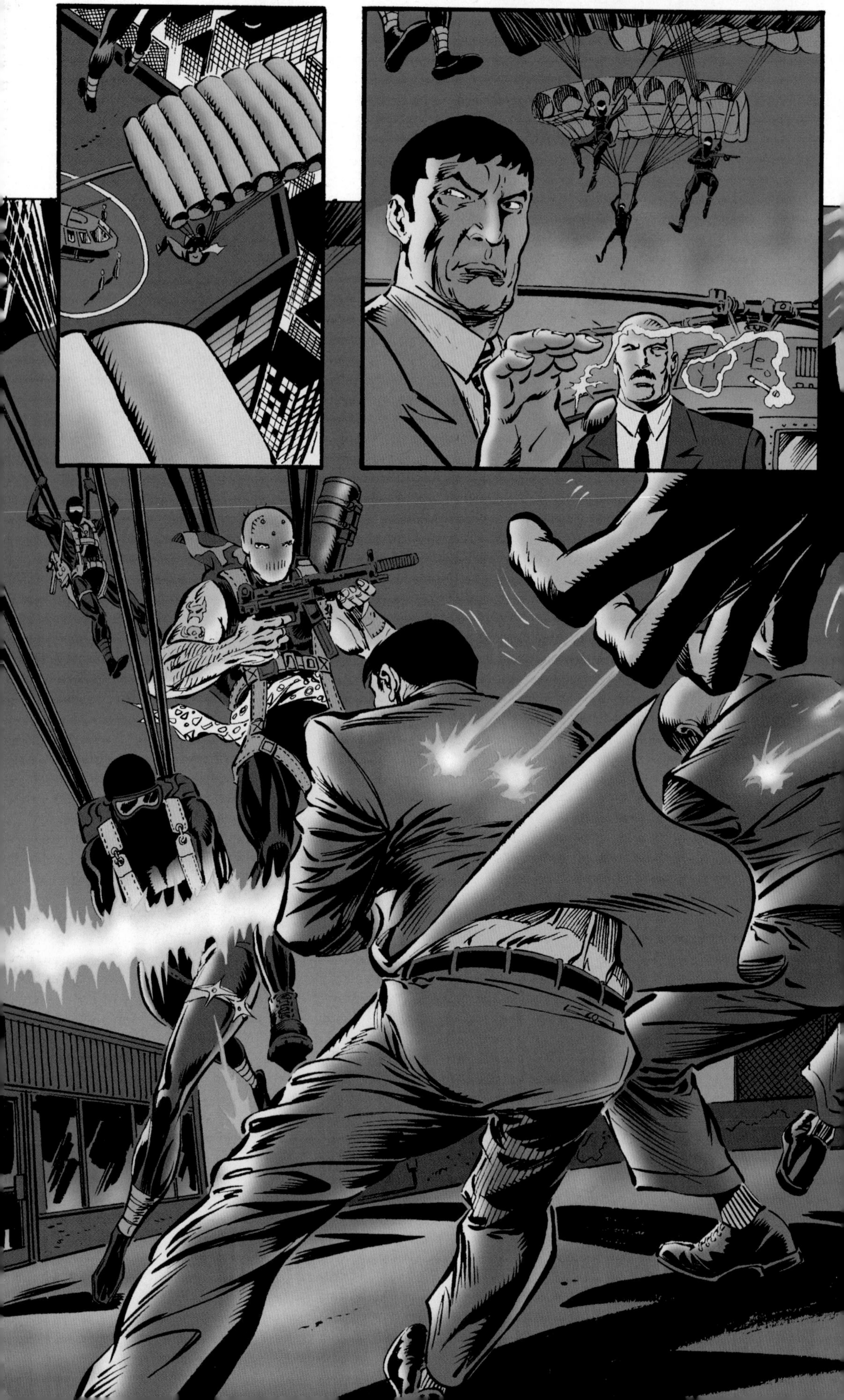

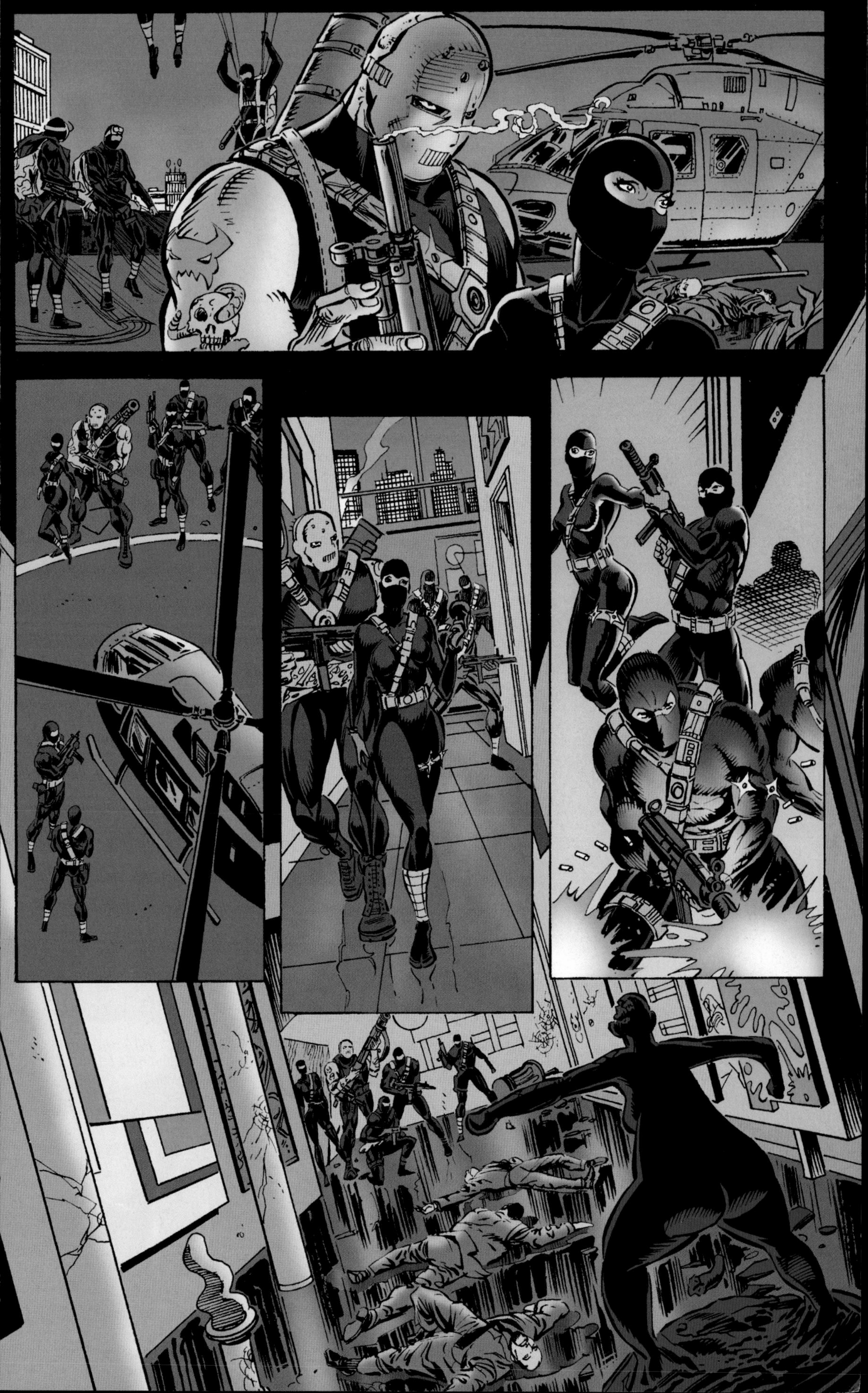

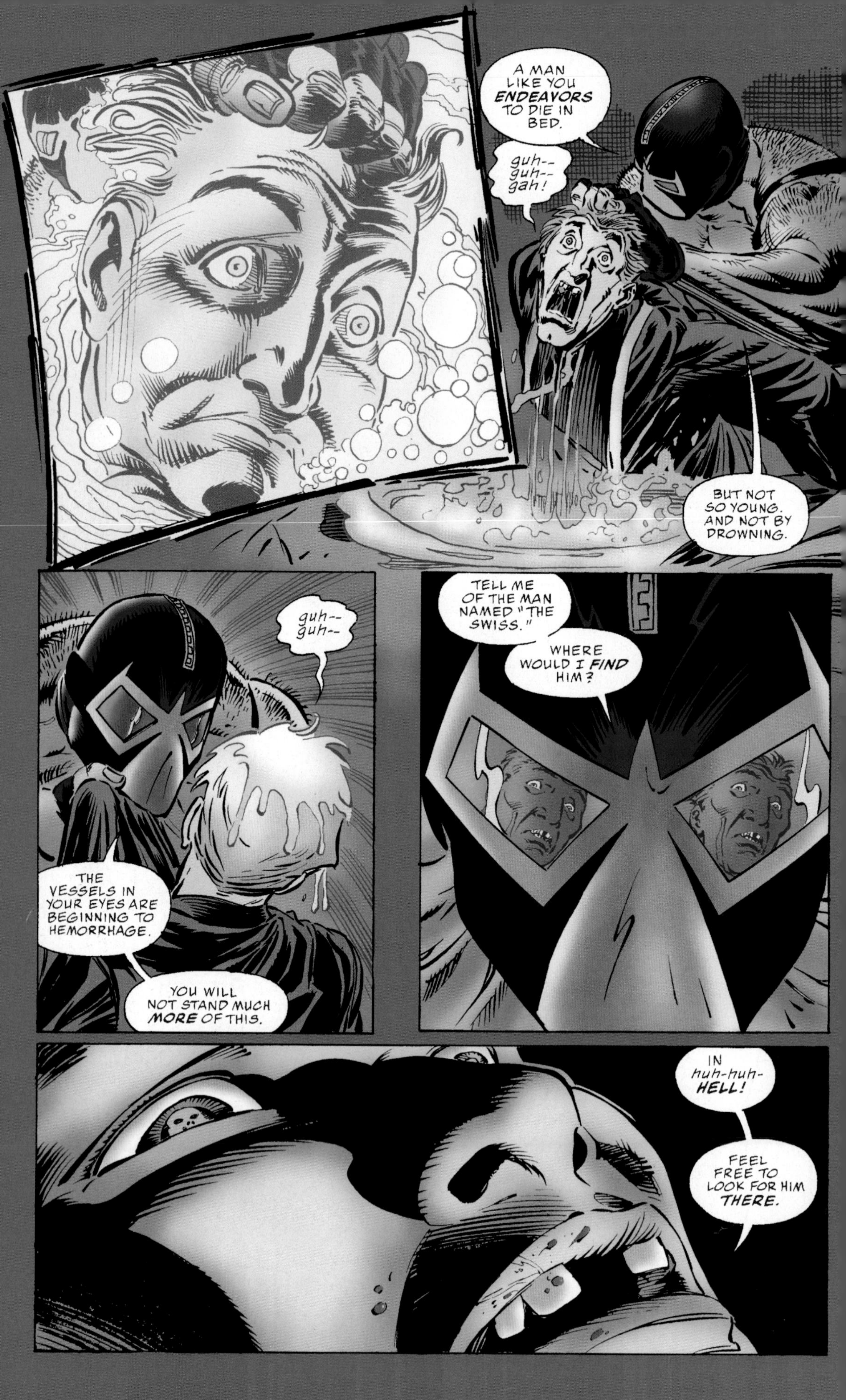
A MAN LIKE YOU ENDEAVORS TO DIE IN BED.
guh-- guh-- gah!
BUT NOT SO YOUNG. AND NOT BY DROWNING.
guh-- guh--
THE VESSELS IN YOUR EYES ARE BEGINNING TO HEMORRHAGE.
YOU WILL NOT STAND MUCH MORE OF THIS.
TELL ME OF THE MAN NAMED "THE SWISS."
WHERE WOULD I FIND HIM?
IN huh-huh- HELL!
FEEL FREE TO LOOK FOR HIM THERE.

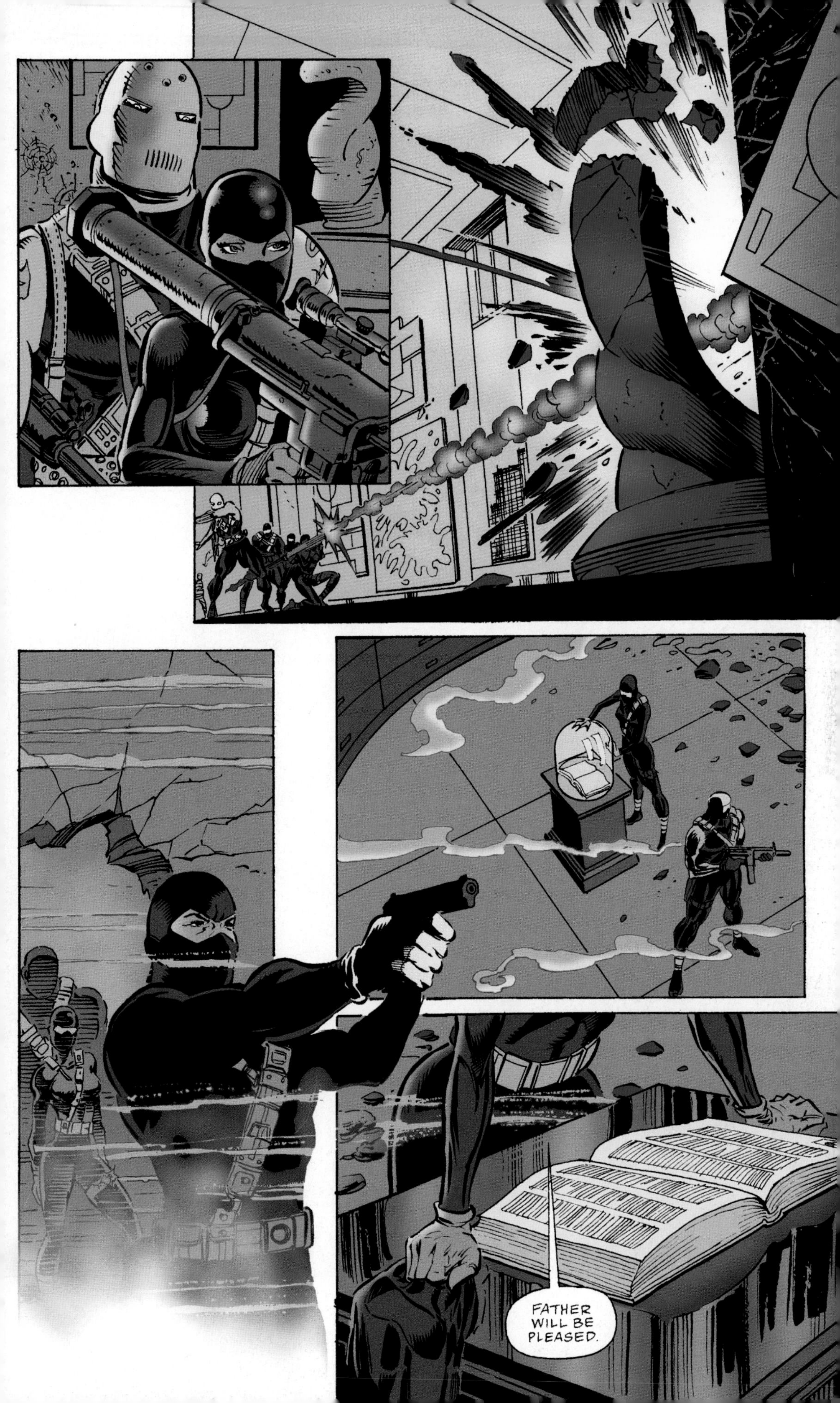
FATHER WILL BE PLEASED.

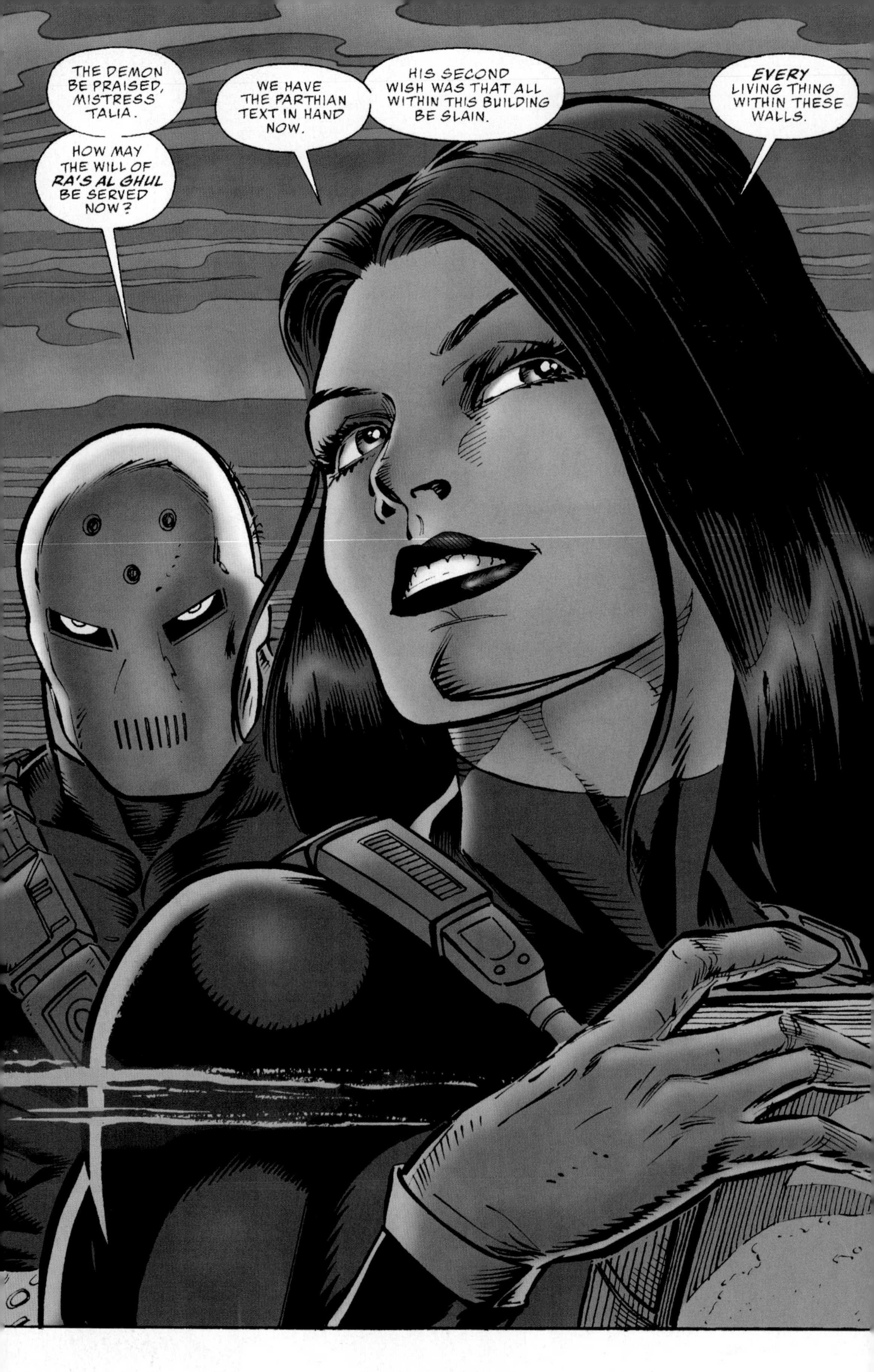
THE DEMON BE PRAISED, MISTRESS TALIA.
HOW MAY THE WILL OF RA'S AL GHUL BE SERVED NOW?
WE HAVE THE PARTHIAN TEXT IN HAND NOW.
HIS SECOND WISH WAS THAT ALL WITHIN THIS BUILDING BE SLAIN.
EVERY LIVING THING WITHIN THESE WALLS.

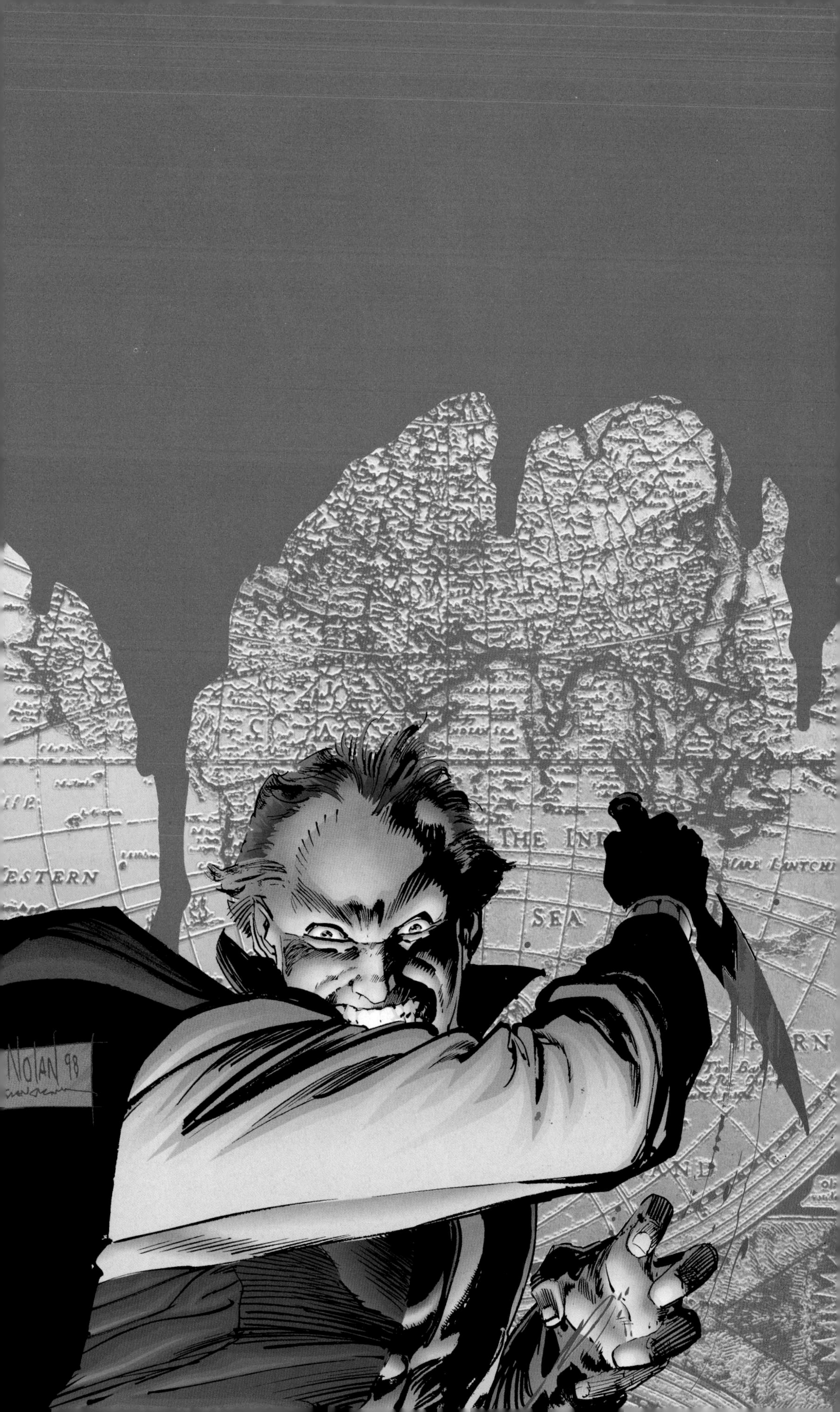
ESTERN
THE IND
SEA
NOLAN 98

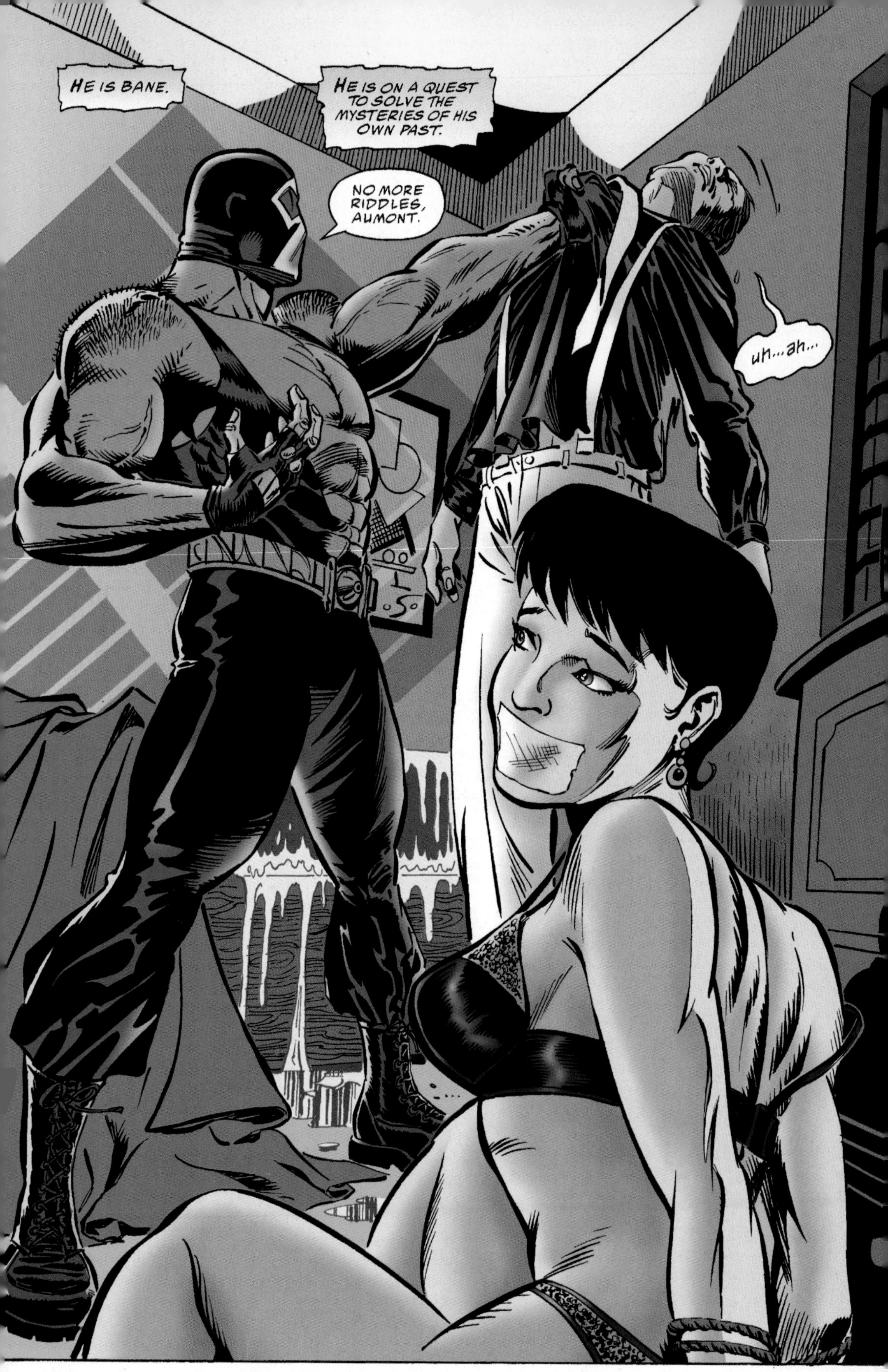
HE IS BANE.
HE IS ON A QUEST TO SOLVE THE MYSTERIES OF HIS OWN PAST.
NO MORE RIDDLES, AUMONT.
uh...ah...

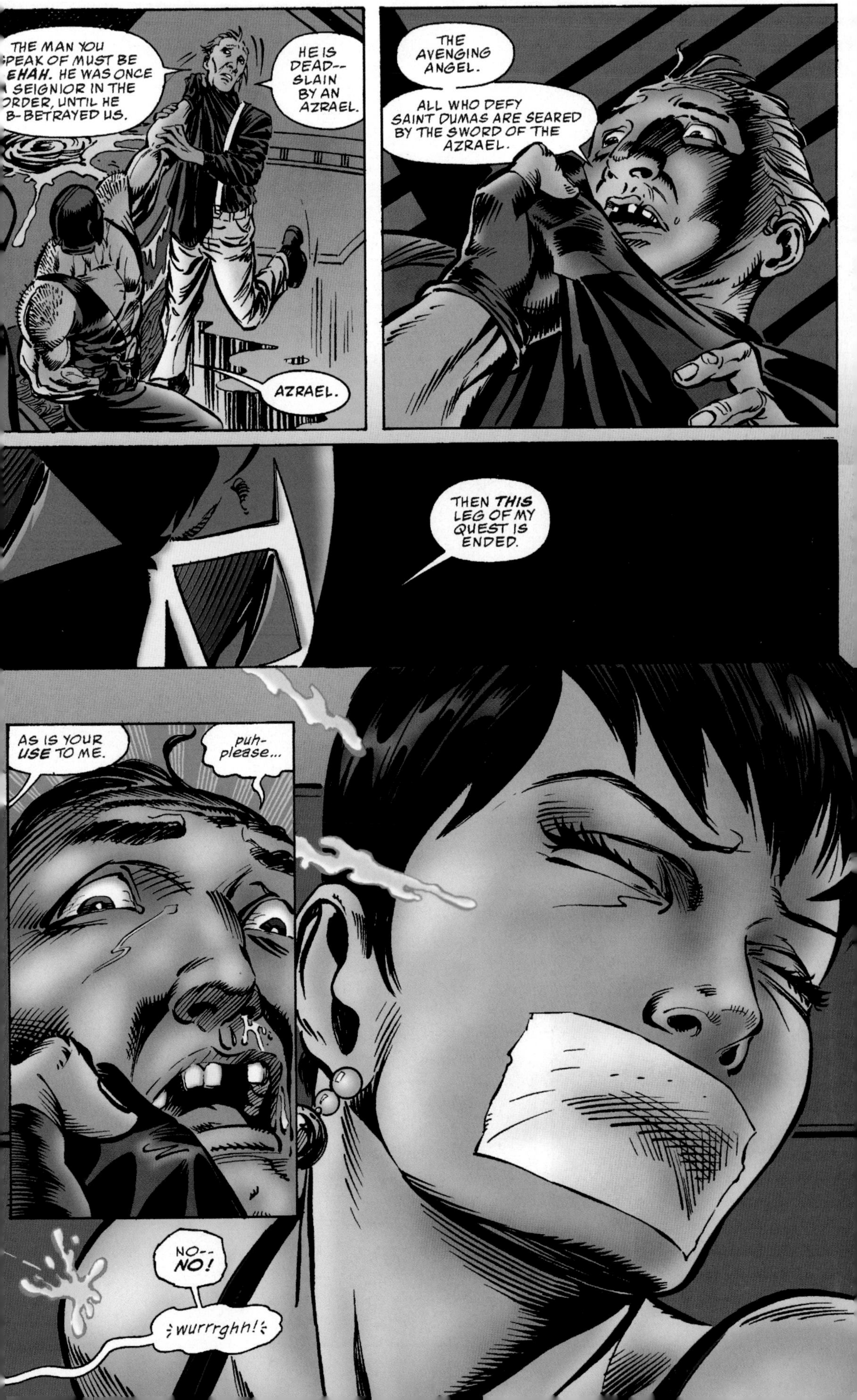
THE MAN YOU
SPEAK OF MUST BE EHAH. HE WAS ONCE A SEIGNIOR IN THE ORDER, UNTIL HE B-BETRAYED US.
HE IS DEAD-- SLAIN BY AN AZRAEL.
AZRAEL.
THE AVENGING ANGEL.
ALL WHO DEFY SAINT DUMAS ARE SEARED BY THE SWORD OF THE AZRAEL.
THEN THIS LEG OF MY QUEST IS ENDED.
AS IS YOUR USE TO ME.
puh-please...
NO-- NO!
wurrrghh!

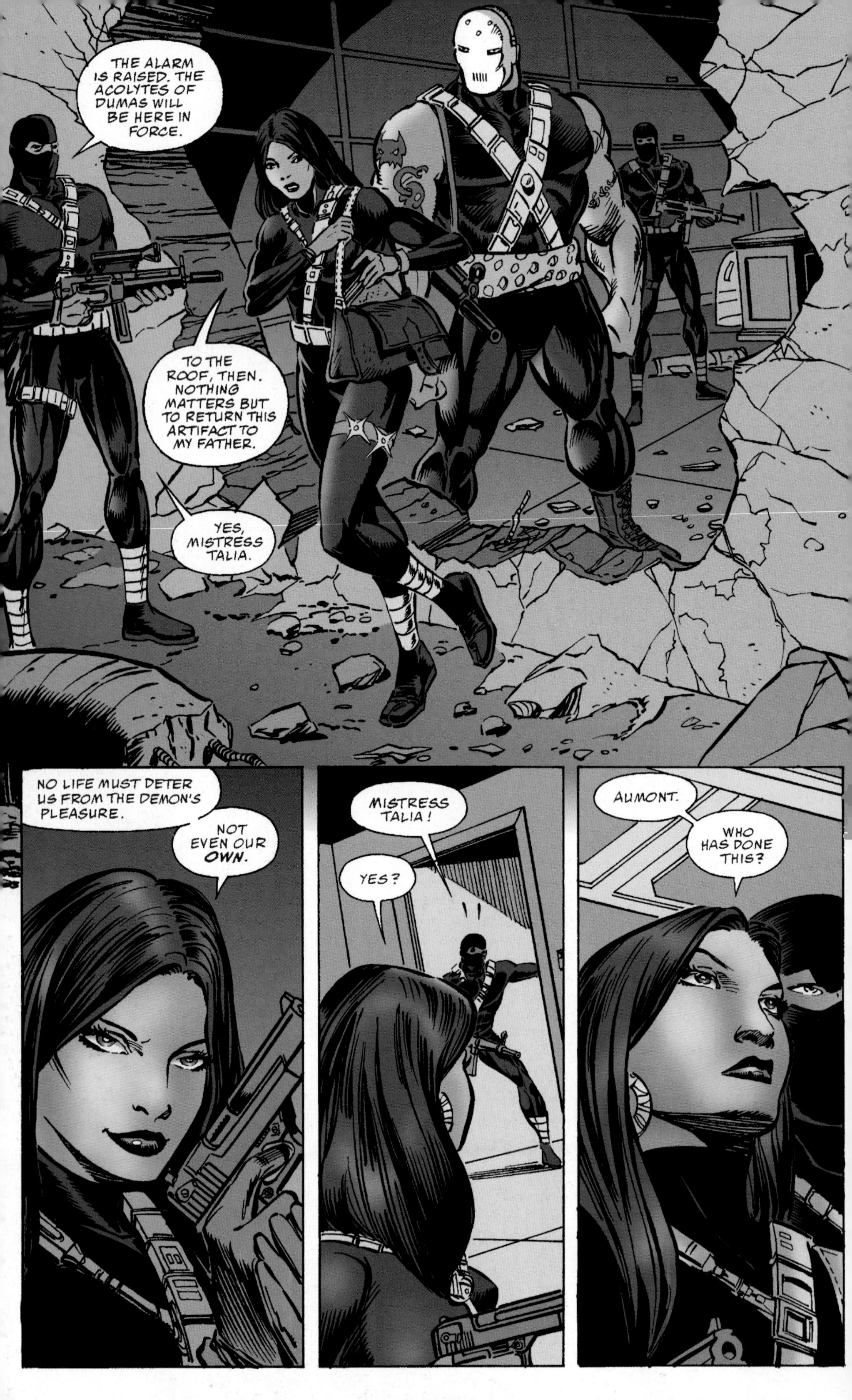
THE ALARM IS RAISED. THE ACOLYTES OF DUMAS WILL BE HERE IN FORCE.
TO THE ROOF, THEN. NOTHING MATTERS BUT TO RETURN THIS ARTIFACT TO MY FATHER.
YES, MISTRESS TALIA.
NO LIFE MUST DETER US FROM THE DEMON'S PLEASURE.
NOT EVEN OUR **OWN**.
MISTRESS TALIA!
YES?
AUMONT.
WHO HAS DONE THIS?

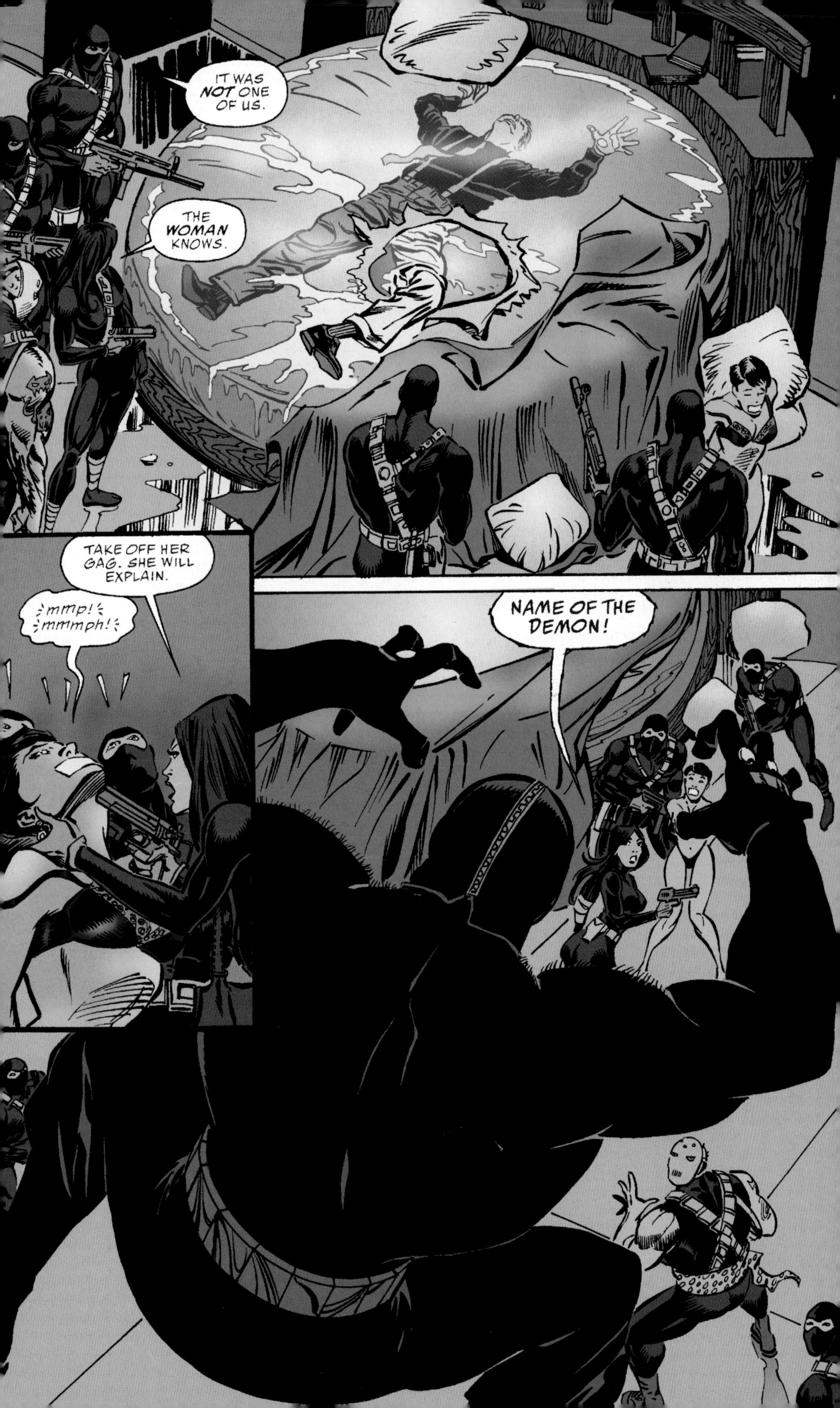
IT WAS NOT ONE OF US.
THE WOMAN KNOWS.
TAKE OFF HER GAG. SHE WILL EXPLAIN.
mmp! mmmph!
NAME OF THE DEMON!

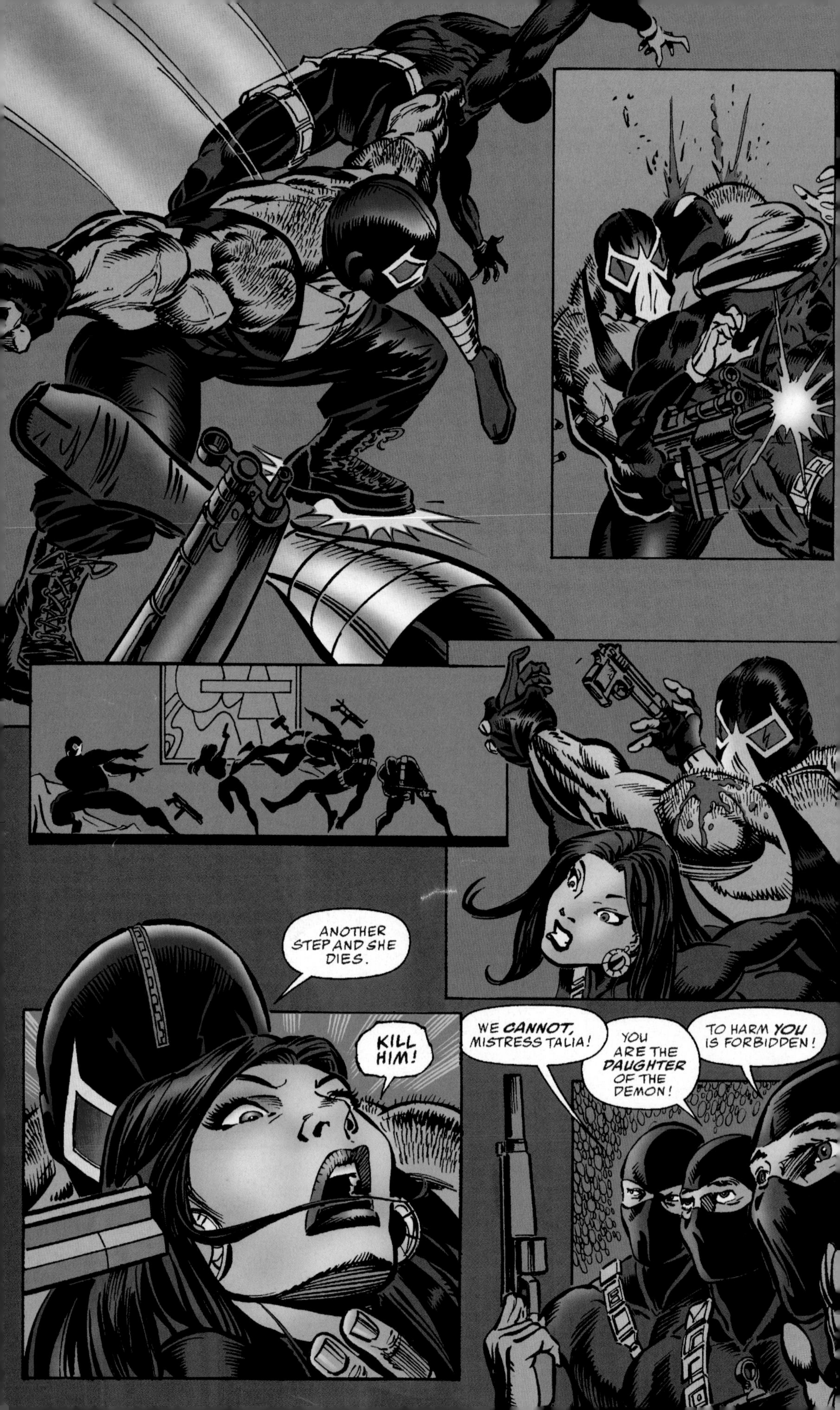
ANOTHER STEP AND SHE DIES.
KILL HIM!
WE CANNOT, MISTRESS TALIA!
YOU ARE THE DAUGHTER OF THE DEMON!
TO HARM YOU IS FORBIDDEN!

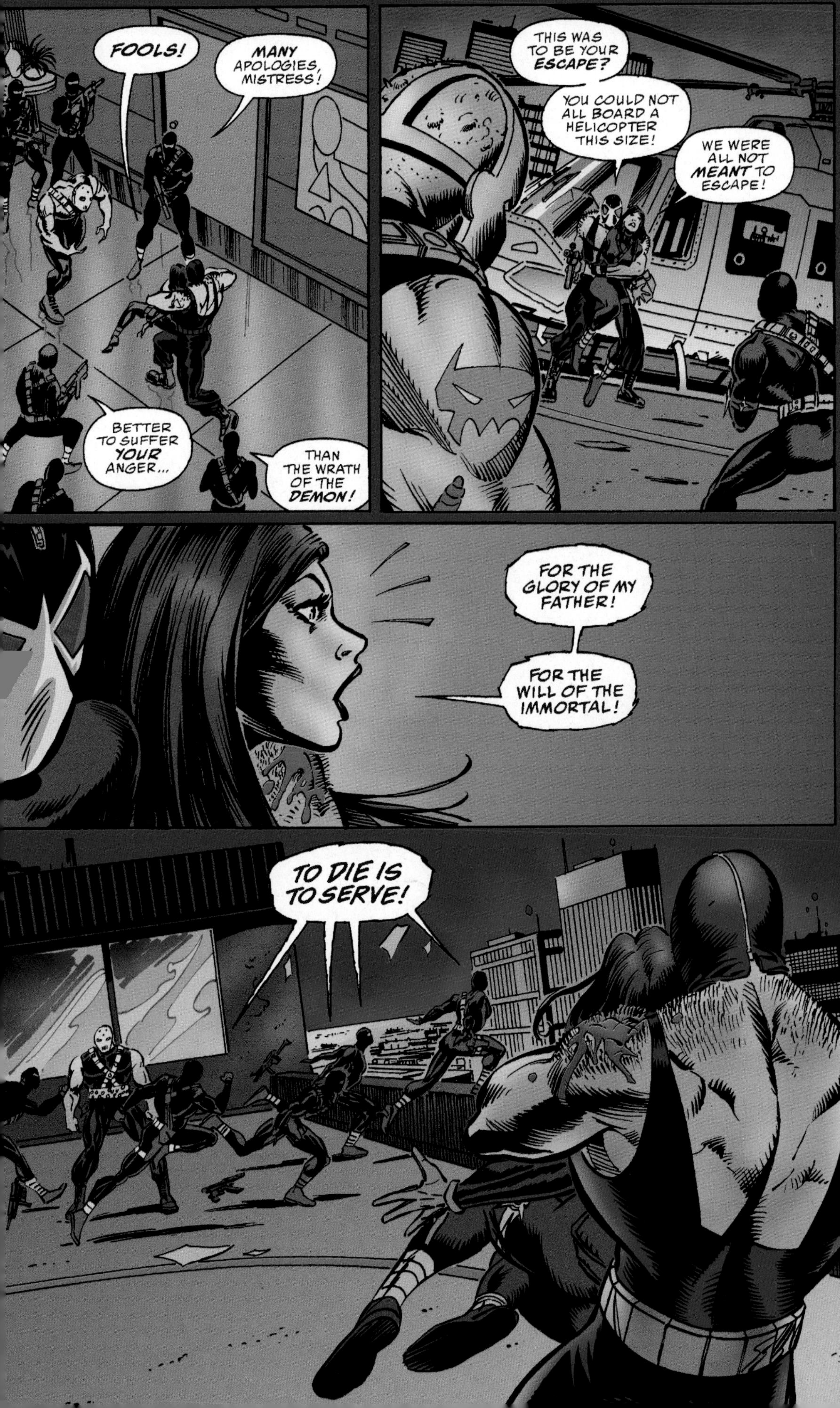

FOOLS!
MANY APOLOGIES, MISTRESS!
BETTER TO SUFFER YOUR ANGER...
THAN THE WRATH OF THE DEMON!
THIS WAS TO BE YOUR ESCAPE?
YOU COULD NOT ALL BOARD A HELICOPTER THIS SIZE!
WE WERE ALL NOT MEANT TO ESCAPE!
FOR THE GLORY OF MY FATHER!
FOR THE WILL OF THE IMMORTAL!
TO DIE IS TO SERVE!

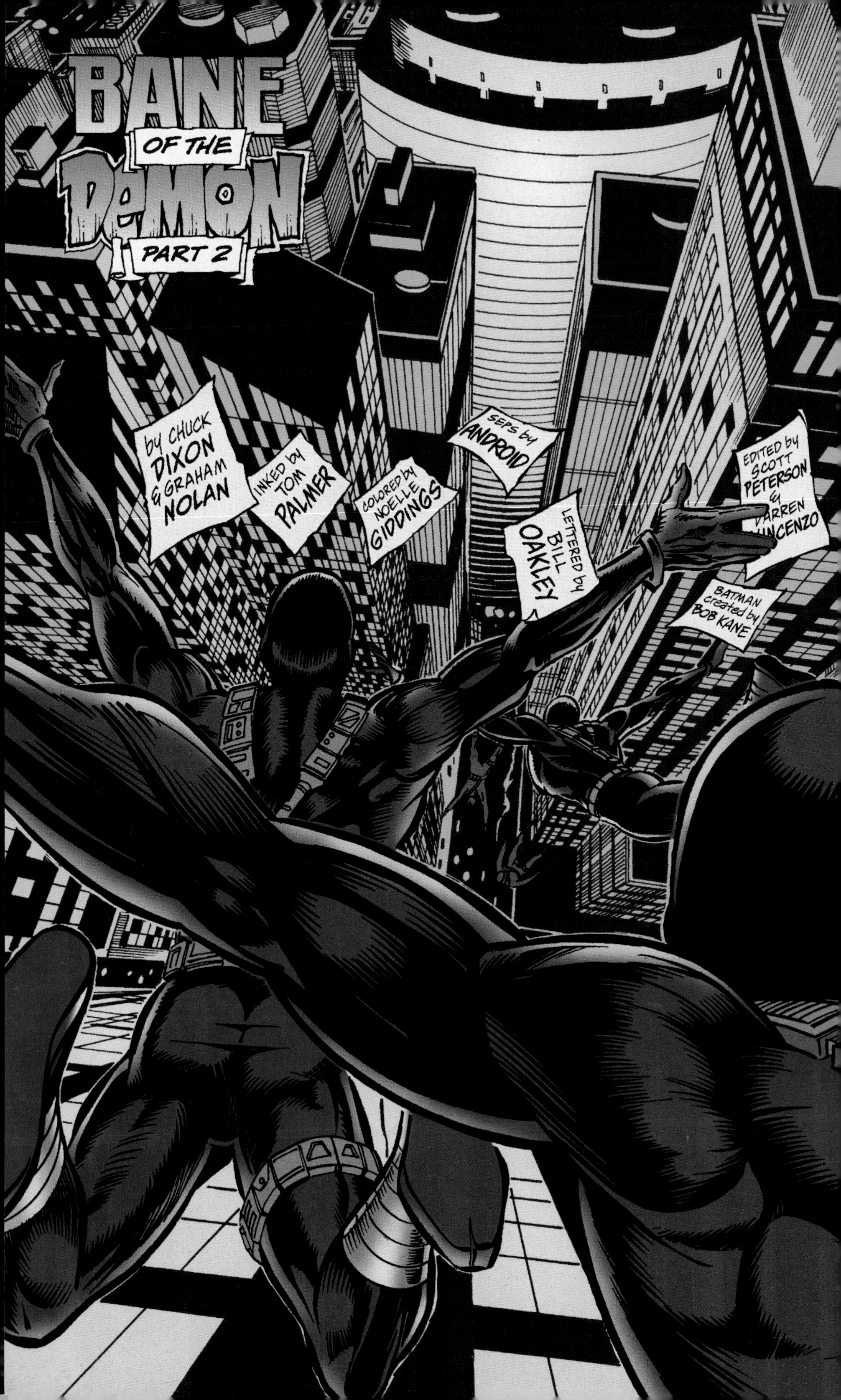
BANE OF THE DEMON
PART 2
by CHUCK DIXON & GRAHAM NOLAN
INKED by TOM PALMER
COLORED by NOELLE GIDDINGS
SEPS by ANDROID
LETTERED by BILL OAKLEY
EDITED by SCOTT PETERSON & DARREN VINCENZO
BATMAN created by BOB KANE

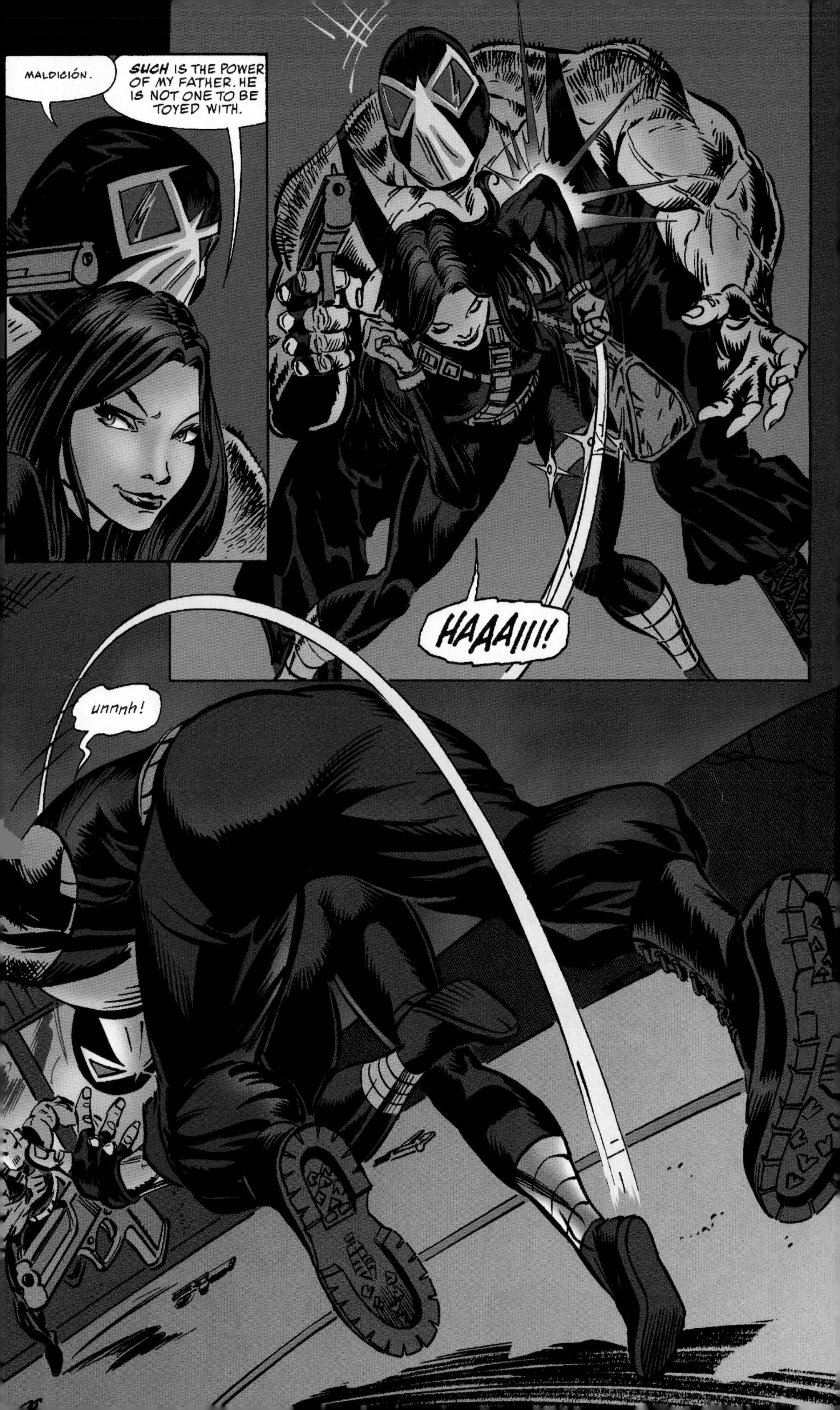

MALDICIÓN.
SUCH IS THE POWER OF MY FATHER. HE IS NOT ONE TO BE TOYED WITH.
HAAAIII!
unnnh!

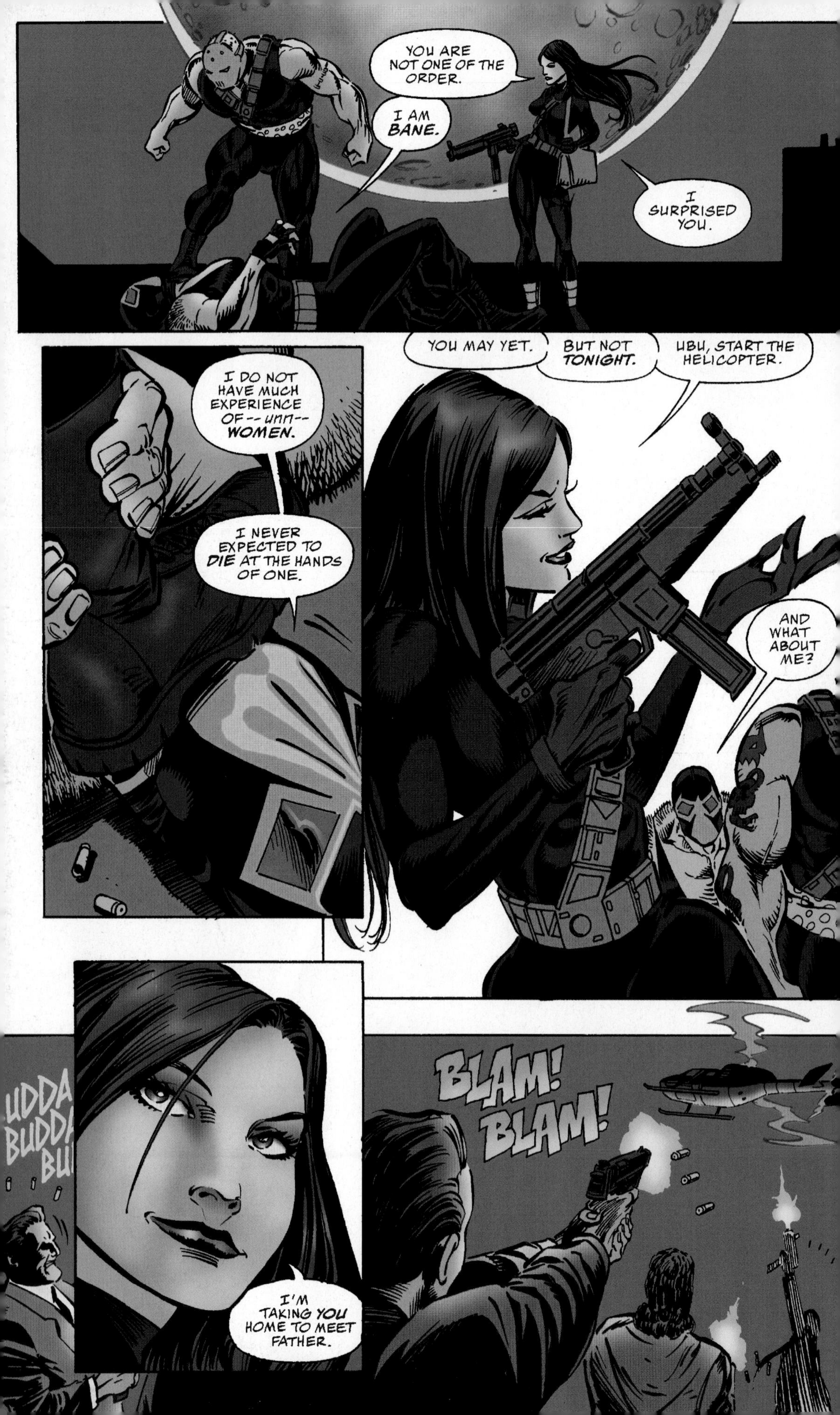
YOU ARE NOT ONE OF THE ORDER.
I AM BANE.
I SURPRISED YOU.
YOU MAY YET.
BUT NOT TONIGHT.
UBU, START THE HELICOPTER.
I DO NOT HAVE MUCH EXPERIENCE OF -- umm-- WOMEN.
I NEVER EXPECTED TO DIE AT THE HANDS OF ONE.
AND WHAT ABOUT ME?
I'M TAKING YOU HOME TO MEET FATHER.
BLAM! BLAM!

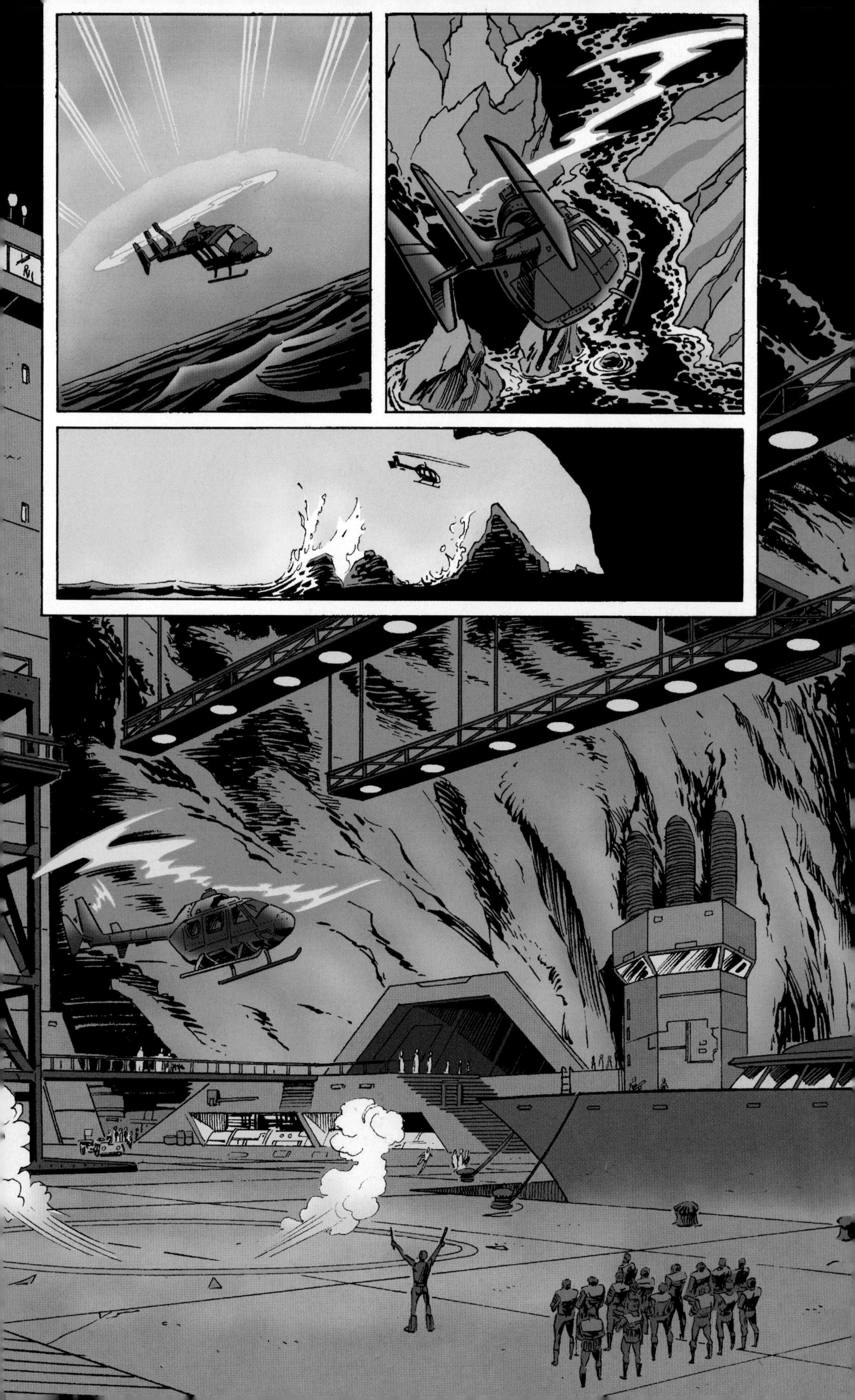

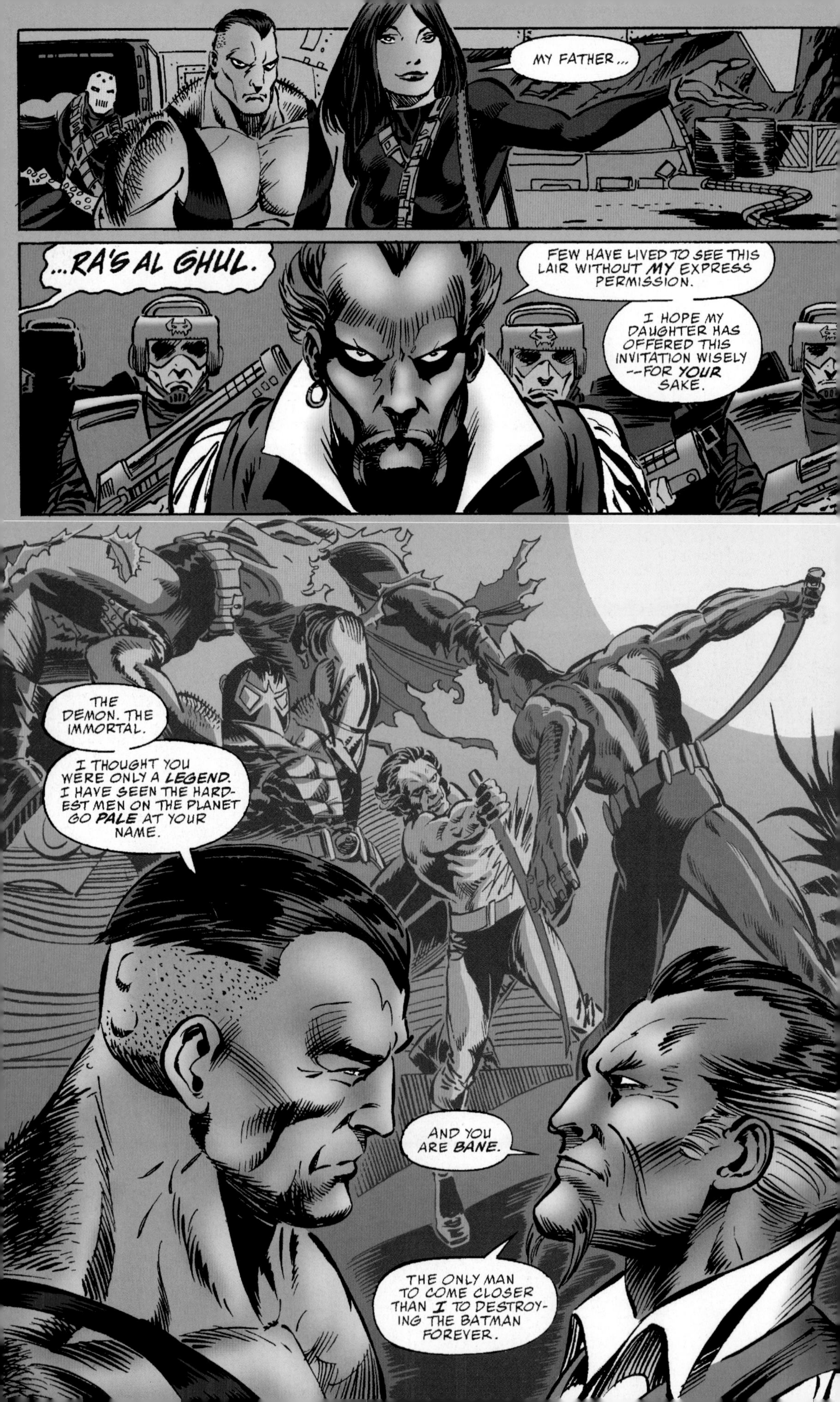
MY FATHER...
...RA'S AL GHUL.
FEW HAVE LIVED TO SEE THIS LAIR WITHOUT MY EXPRESS PERMISSION.
I HOPE MY DAUGHTER HAS OFFERED THIS INVITATION WISELY --FOR YOUR SAKE.
THE DEMON. THE IMMORTAL.
I THOUGHT YOU WERE ONLY A LEGEND. I HAVE SEEN THE HARDEST MEN ON THE PLANET GO PALE AT YOUR NAME.
AND YOU ARE BANE.
THE ONLY MAN TO COME CLOSER THAN I TO DESTROYING THE BATMAN FOREVER.

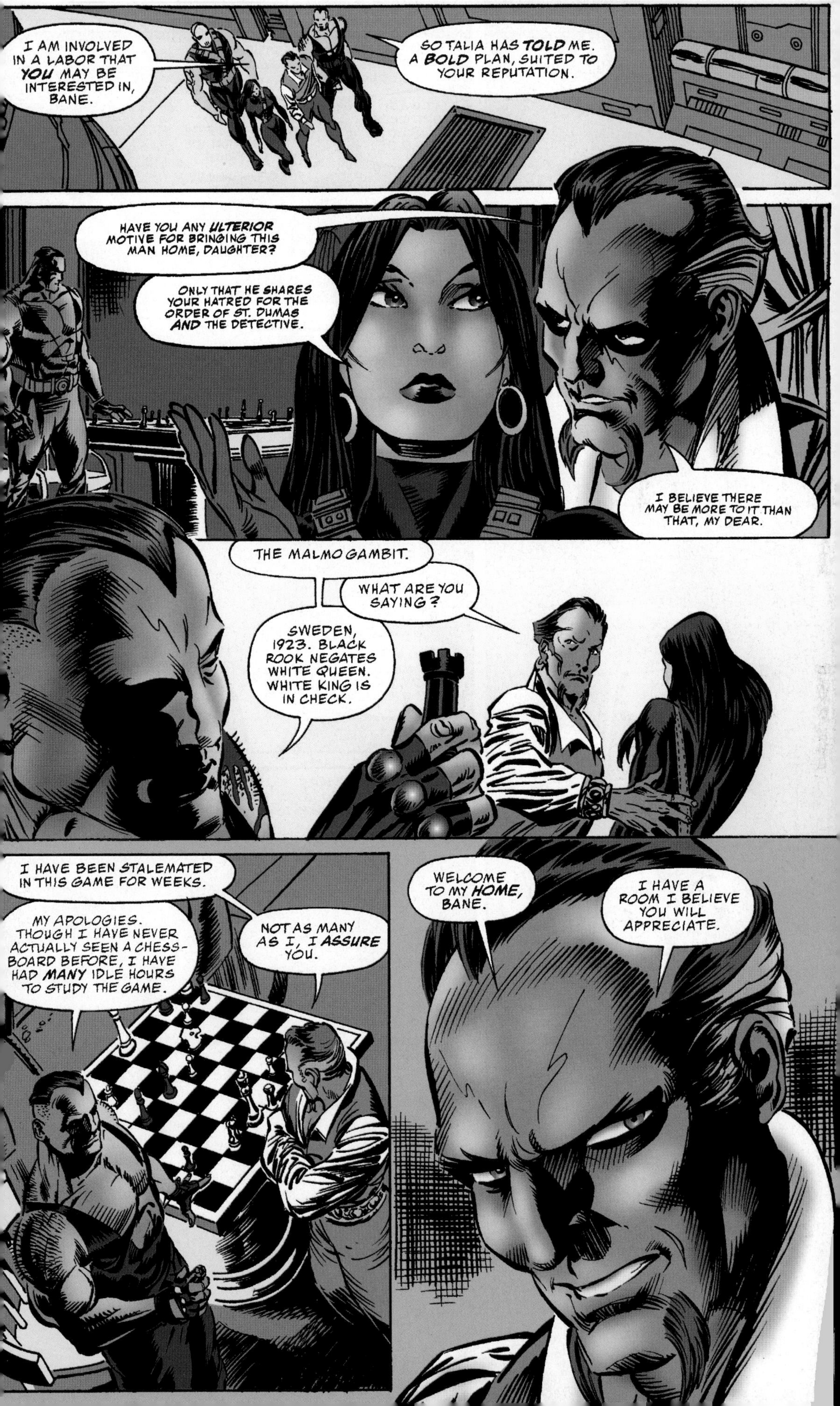

I AM INVOLVED IN A LABOR THAT YOU MAY BE INTERESTED IN, BANE.
SO TALIA HAS TOLD ME. A BOLD PLAN, SUITED TO YOUR REPUTATION.
HAVE YOU ANY ULTERIOR MOTIVE FOR BRINGING THIS MAN HOME, DAUGHTER?
ONLY THAT HE SHARES YOUR HATRED FOR THE ORDER OF ST. DUMAS AND THE DETECTIVE.
I BELIEVE THERE MAY BE MORE TO IT THAN THAT, MY DEAR.
THE MALMO GAMBIT.
WHAT ARE YOU SAYING?
SWEDEN, 1923. BLACK ROOK NEGATES WHITE QUEEN. WHITE KING IS IN CHECK.
I HAVE BEEN STALEMATED IN THIS GAME FOR WEEKS.
MY APOLOGIES. THOUGH I HAVE NEVER ACTUALLY SEEN A CHESS-BOARD BEFORE, I HAVE HAD MANY IDLE HOURS TO STUDY THE GAME.
NOT AS MANY AS I, I ASSURE YOU.
WELCOME TO MY HOME, BANE.
I HAVE A ROOM I BELIEVE YOU WILL APPRECIATE.

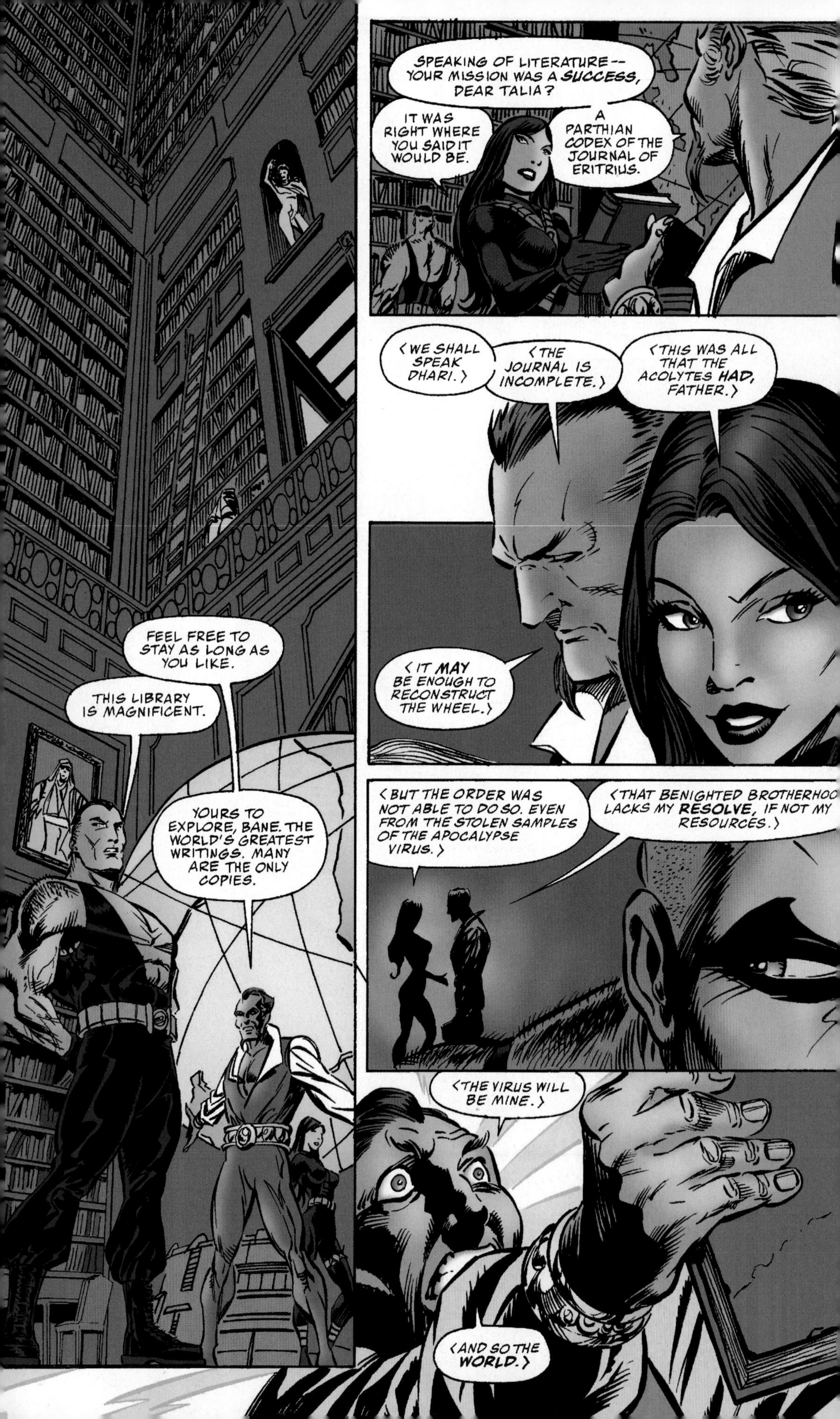
THIS LIBRARY IS MAGNIFICENT.
FEEL FREE TO STAY AS LONG AS YOU LIKE.
YOURS TO EXPLORE, BANE. THE WORLD'S GREATEST WRITINGS. MANY ARE THE ONLY COPIES.
SPEAKING OF LITERATURE-- YOUR MISSION WAS A SUCCESS, DEAR TALIA?
IT WAS RIGHT WHERE YOU SAID IT WOULD BE.
A PARTHIAN CODEX OF THE JOURNAL OF ERITRIUS.
〈WE SHALL SPEAK DHARI.〉
〈THE JOURNAL IS INCOMPLETE.〉
〈THIS WAS ALL THAT THE ACOLYTES HAD, FATHER.〉
〈IT MAY BE ENOUGH TO RECONSTRUCT THE WHEEL.〉
〈BUT THE ORDER WAS NOT ABLE TO DO SO. EVEN FROM THE STOLEN SAMPLES OF THE APOCALYPSE VIRUS.〉
〈THAT BENIGHTED BROTHERHOO LACKS MY RESOLVE, IF NOT MY RESOURCES.〉
〈THE VIRUS WILL BE MINE.〉
〈AND SO THE WORLD.〉

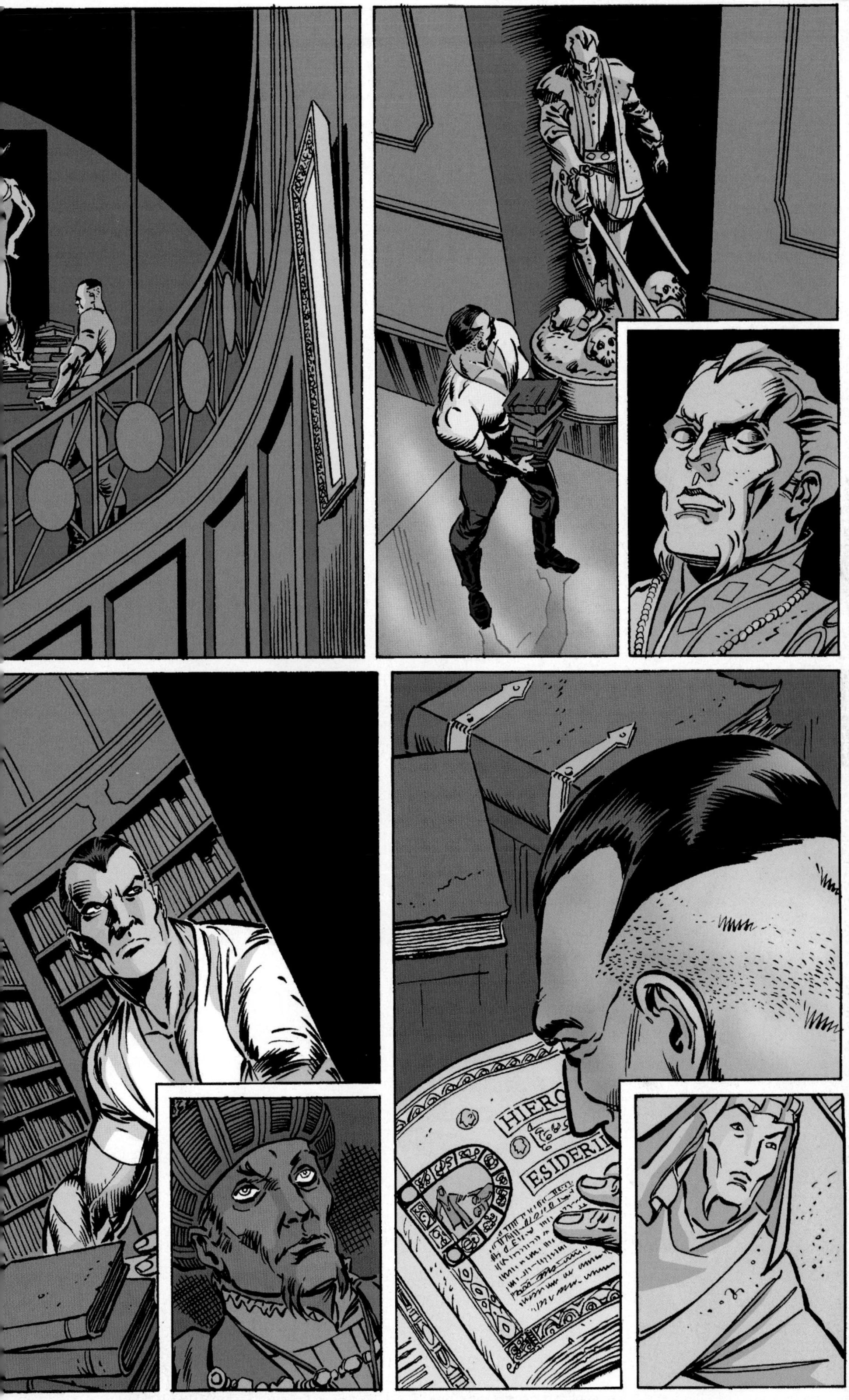

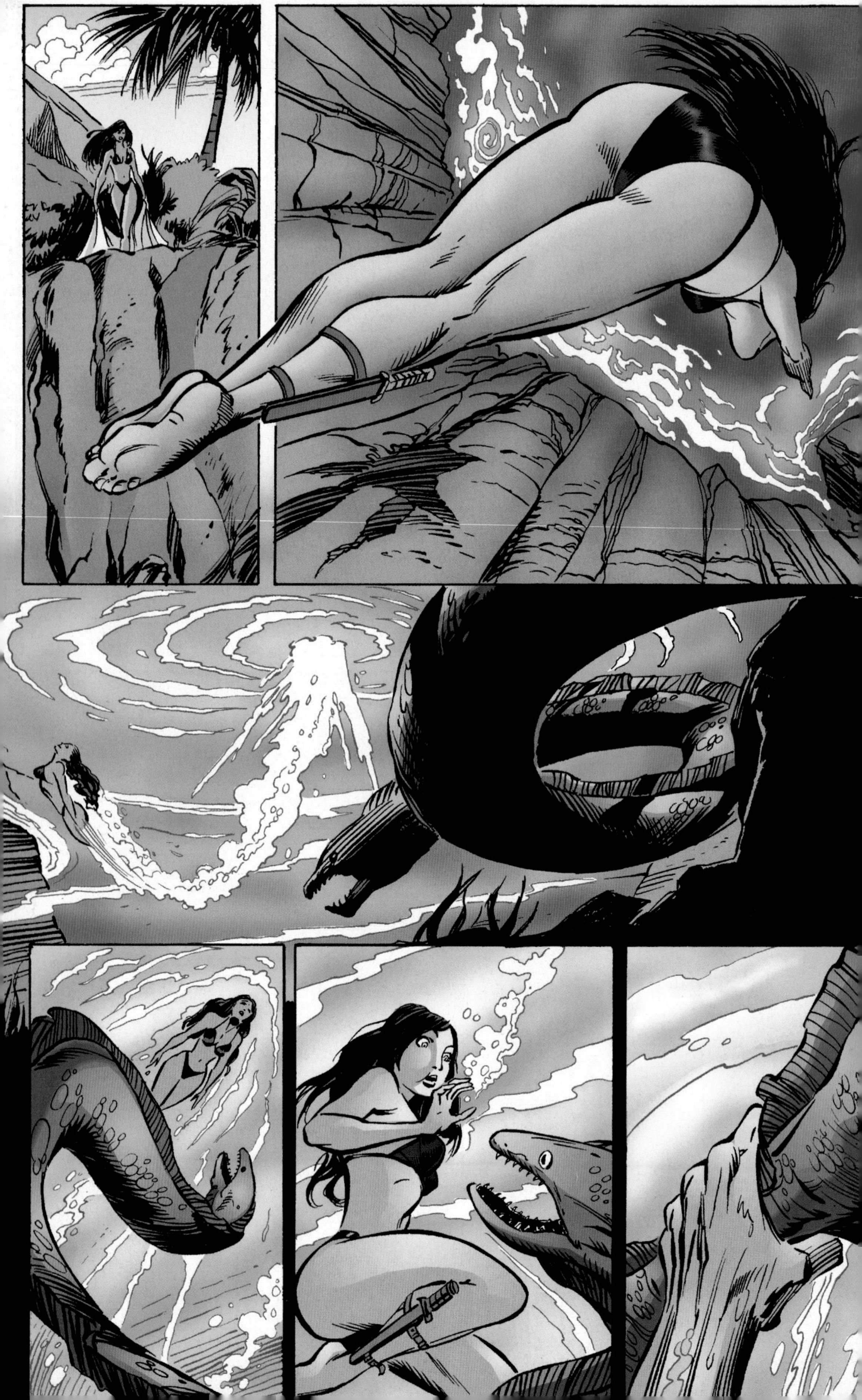

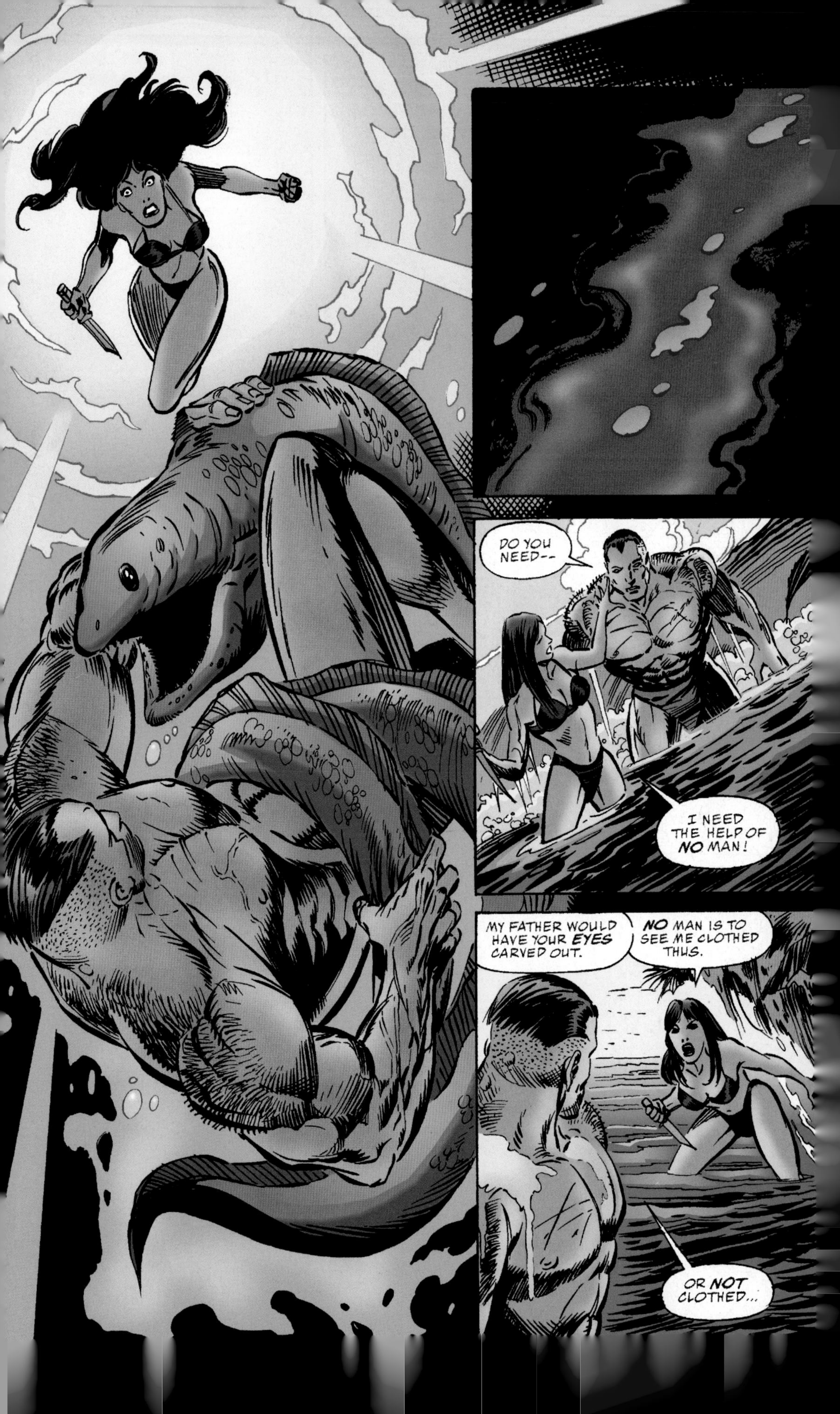
DO YOU NEED--
I NEED THE HELP OF NO MAN!
MY FATHER WOULD HAVE YOUR EYES CARVED OUT.
NO MAN IS TO SEE ME CLOTHED THUS.
OR NOT CLOTHED...

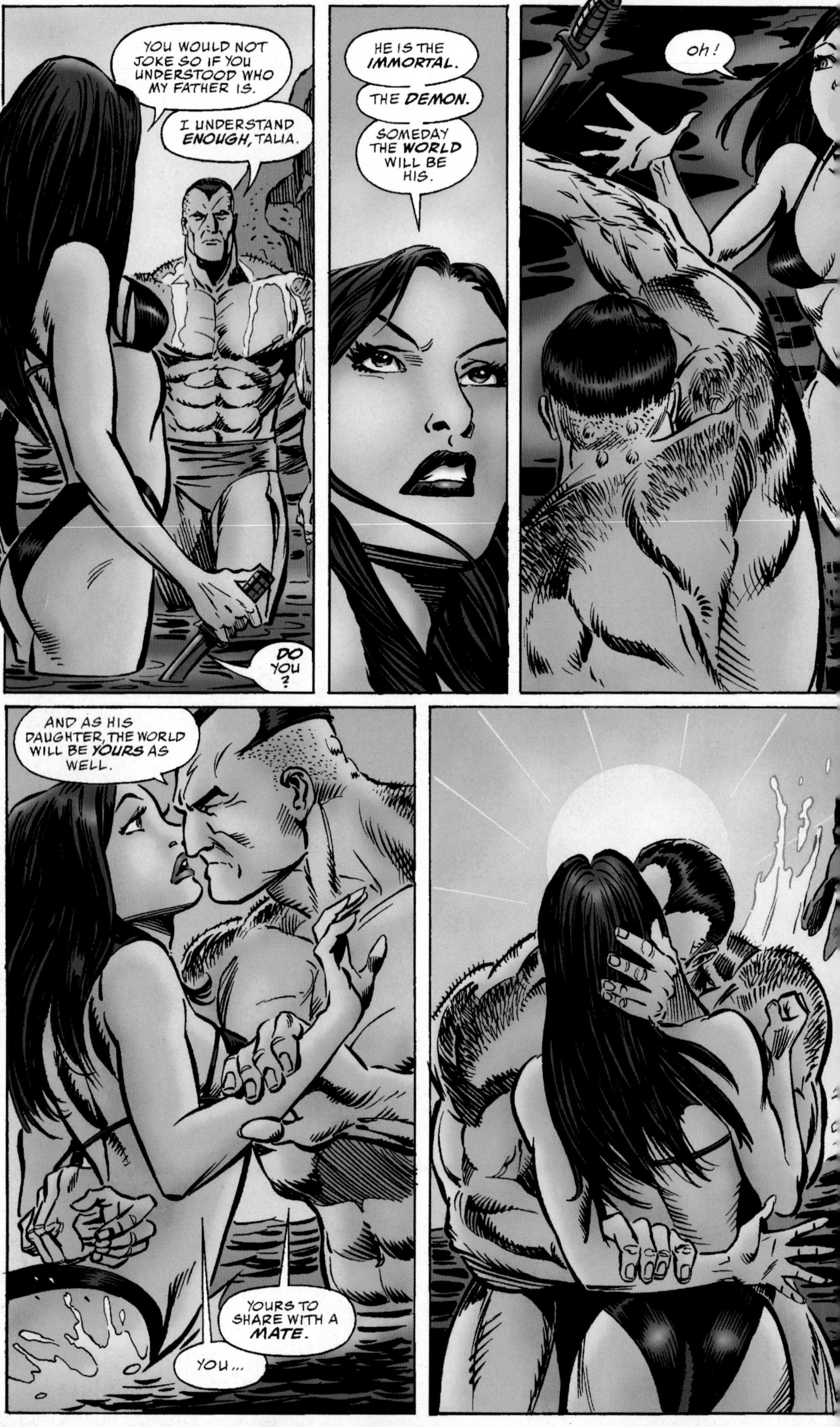
YOU WOULD NOT JOKE SO IF YOU UNDERSTOOD WHO MY FATHER IS.
I UNDERSTAND ENOUGH, TALIA.
DO YOU?
HE IS THE IMMORTAL.
THE DEMON.
SOMEDAY THE WORLD WILL BE HIS.
oh!
AND AS HIS DAUGHTER, THE WORLD WILL BE YOURS AS WELL.
YOURS TO SHARE WITH A MATE.
YOU...

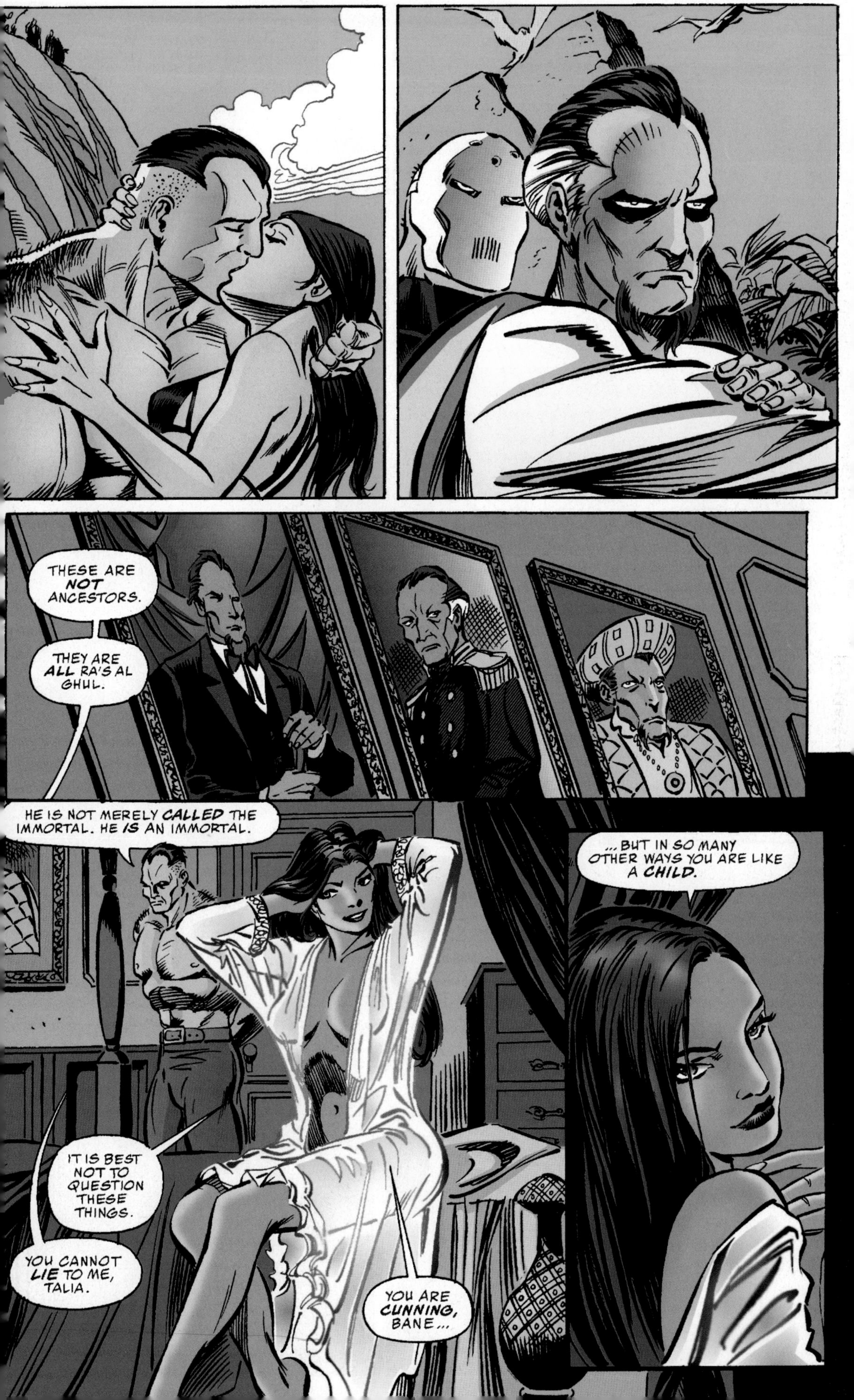
THESE ARE NOT ANCESTORS.
THEY ARE ALL RA'S AL GHUL.
HE IS NOT MERELY CALLED THE IMMORTAL. HE IS AN IMMORTAL.
IT IS BEST NOT TO QUESTION THESE THINGS.
YOU CANNOT LIE TO ME, TALIA.
YOU ARE CUNNING, BANE...
...BUT IN SO MANY OTHER WAYS YOU ARE LIKE A CHILD.

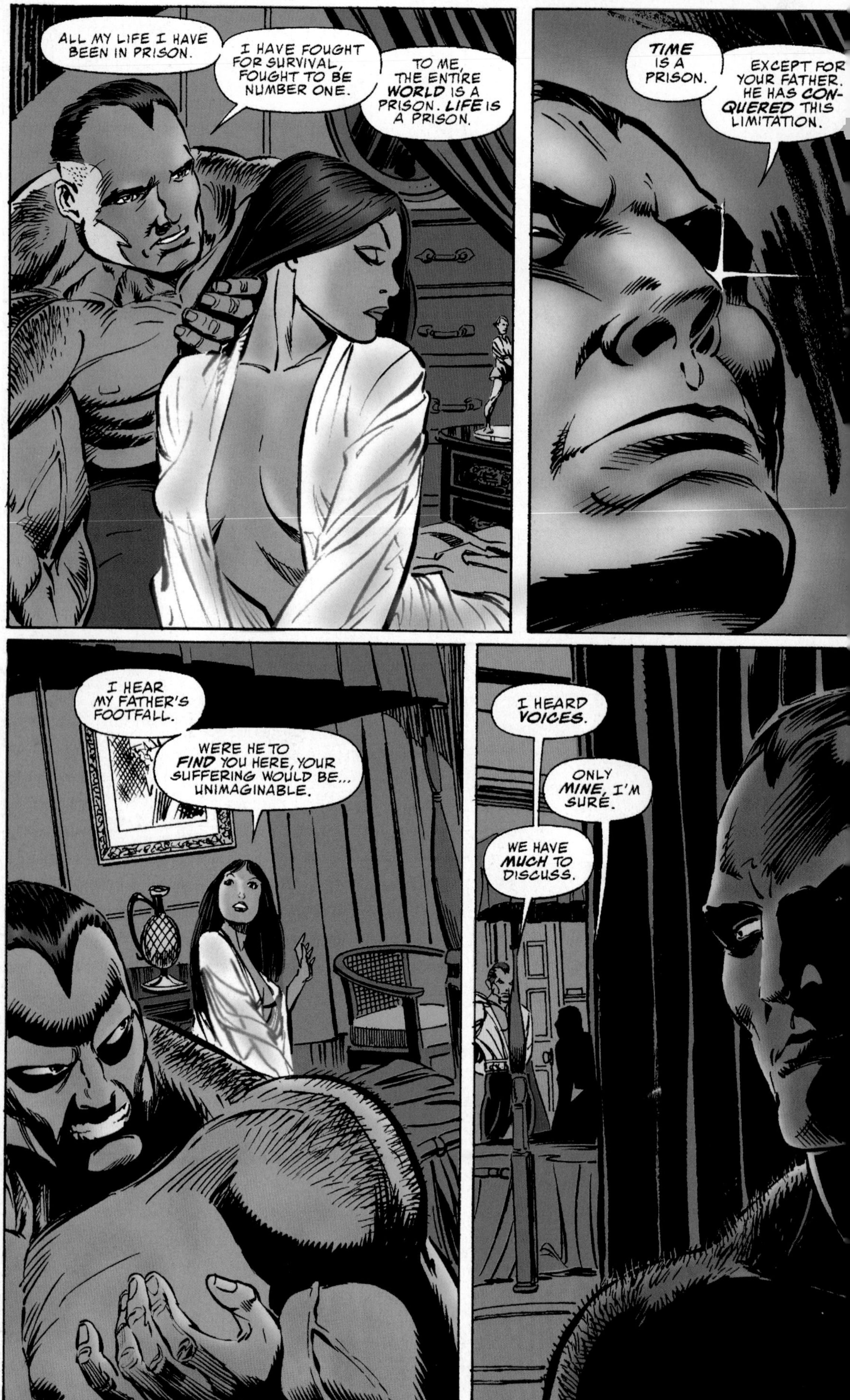
ALL MY LIFE I HAVE BEEN IN PRISON.
I HAVE FOUGHT FOR SURVIVAL, FOUGHT TO BE NUMBER ONE.
TO ME, THE ENTIRE WORLD IS A PRISON. LIFE IS A PRISON.
TIME IS A PRISON.
EXCEPT FOR YOUR FATHER. HE HAS CONQUERED THIS LIMITATION.
I HEAR MY FATHER'S FOOTFALL.
WERE HE TO FIND YOU HERE, YOUR SUFFERING WOULD BE... UNIMAGINABLE.
I HEARD VOICES.
ONLY MINE, I'M SURE.
WE HAVE MUCH TO DISCUSS.

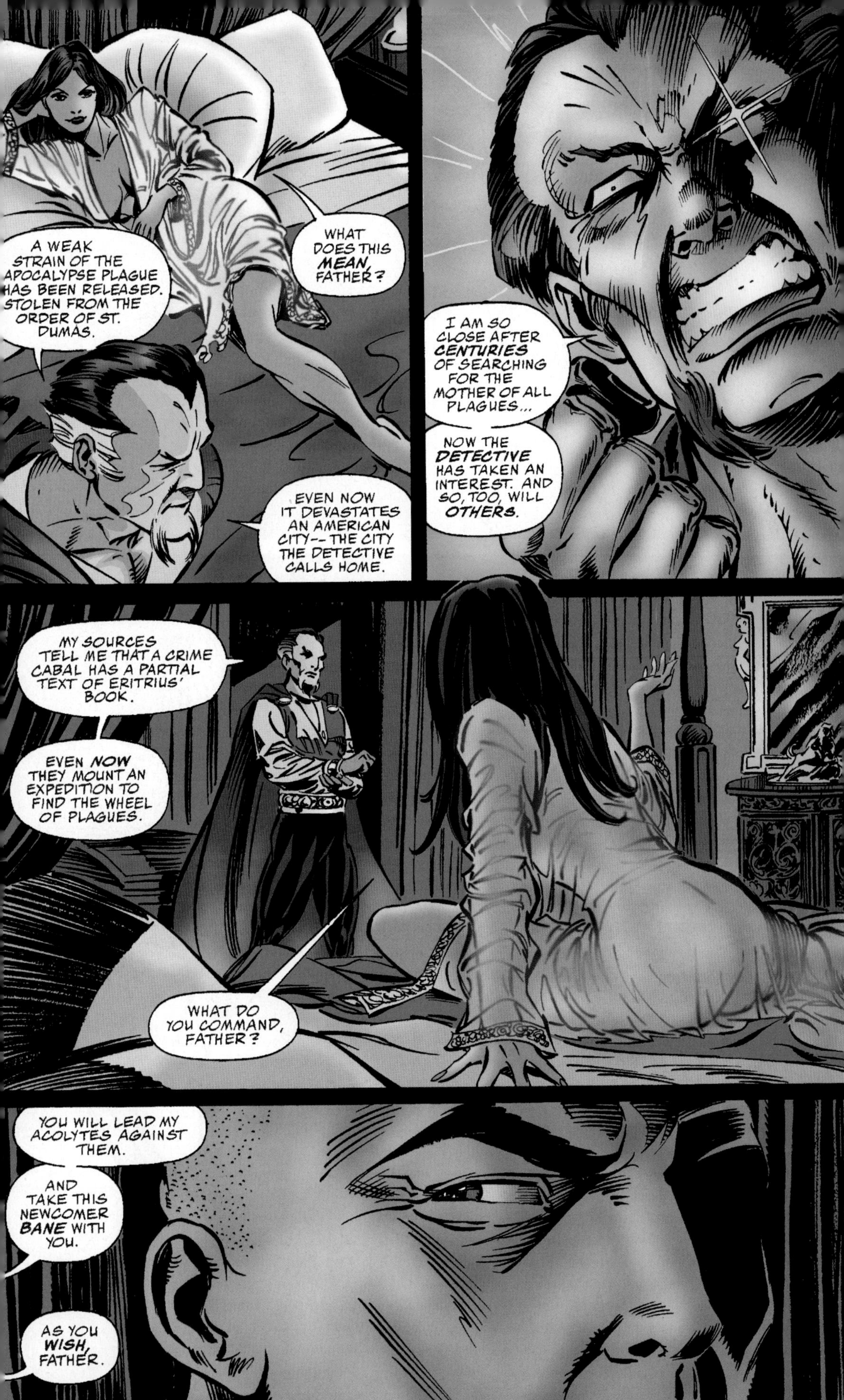

A WEAK STRAIN OF THE APOCALYPSE PLAGUE HAS BEEN RELEASED. STOLEN FROM THE ORDER OF ST. DUMAS.
WHAT DOES THIS MEAN, FATHER?
EVEN NOW IT DEVASTATES AN AMERICAN CITY-- THE CITY THE DETECTIVE CALLS HOME.
I AM SO CLOSE AFTER CENTURIES OF SEARCHING FOR THE MOTHER OF ALL PLAGUES...
NOW THE DETECTIVE HAS TAKEN AN INTEREST. AND SO, TOO, WILL OTHERS.
MY SOURCES TELL ME THAT A CRIME CABAL HAS A PARTIAL TEXT OF ERITRIUS' BOOK.
EVEN NOW THEY MOUNT AN EXPEDITION TO FIND THE WHEEL OF PLAGUES.
WHAT DO YOU COMMAND, FATHER?
YOU WILL LEAD MY ACOLYTES AGAINST THEM.
AND TAKE THIS NEWCOMER BANE WITH YOU.
AS YOU WISH, FATHER.

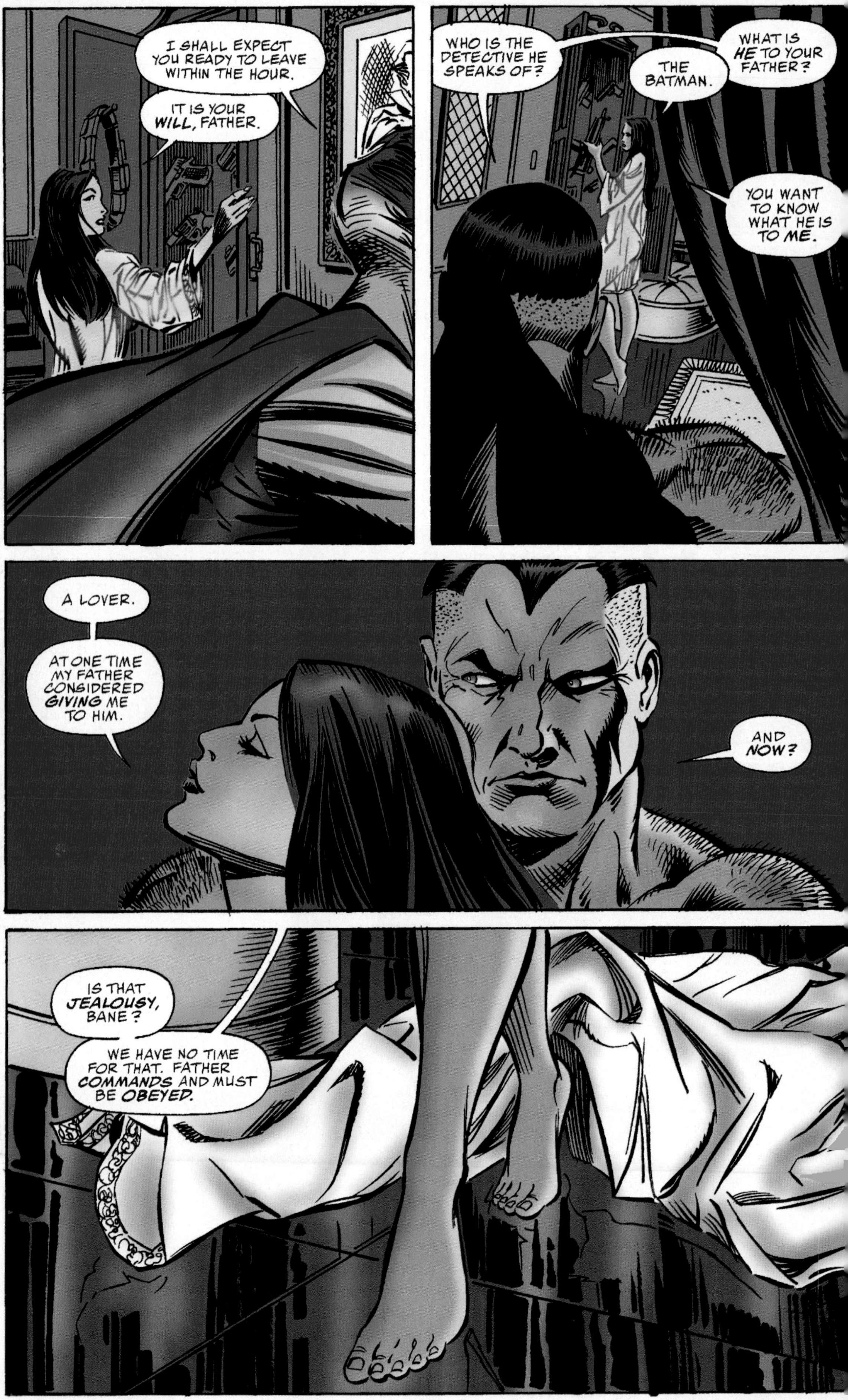
I SHALL EXPECT YOU READY TO LEAVE WITHIN THE HOUR.
IT IS YOUR WILL, FATHER.
WHO IS THE DETECTIVE HE SPEAKS OF?
THE BATMAN.
WHAT IS HE TO YOUR FATHER?
YOU WANT TO KNOW WHAT HE IS TO ME.
A LOVER.
AT ONE TIME MY FATHER CONSIDERED GIVING ME TO HIM.
AND NOW?
IS THAT JEALOUSY, BANE?
WE HAVE NO TIME FOR THAT. FATHER COMMANDS AND MUST BE OBEYED.

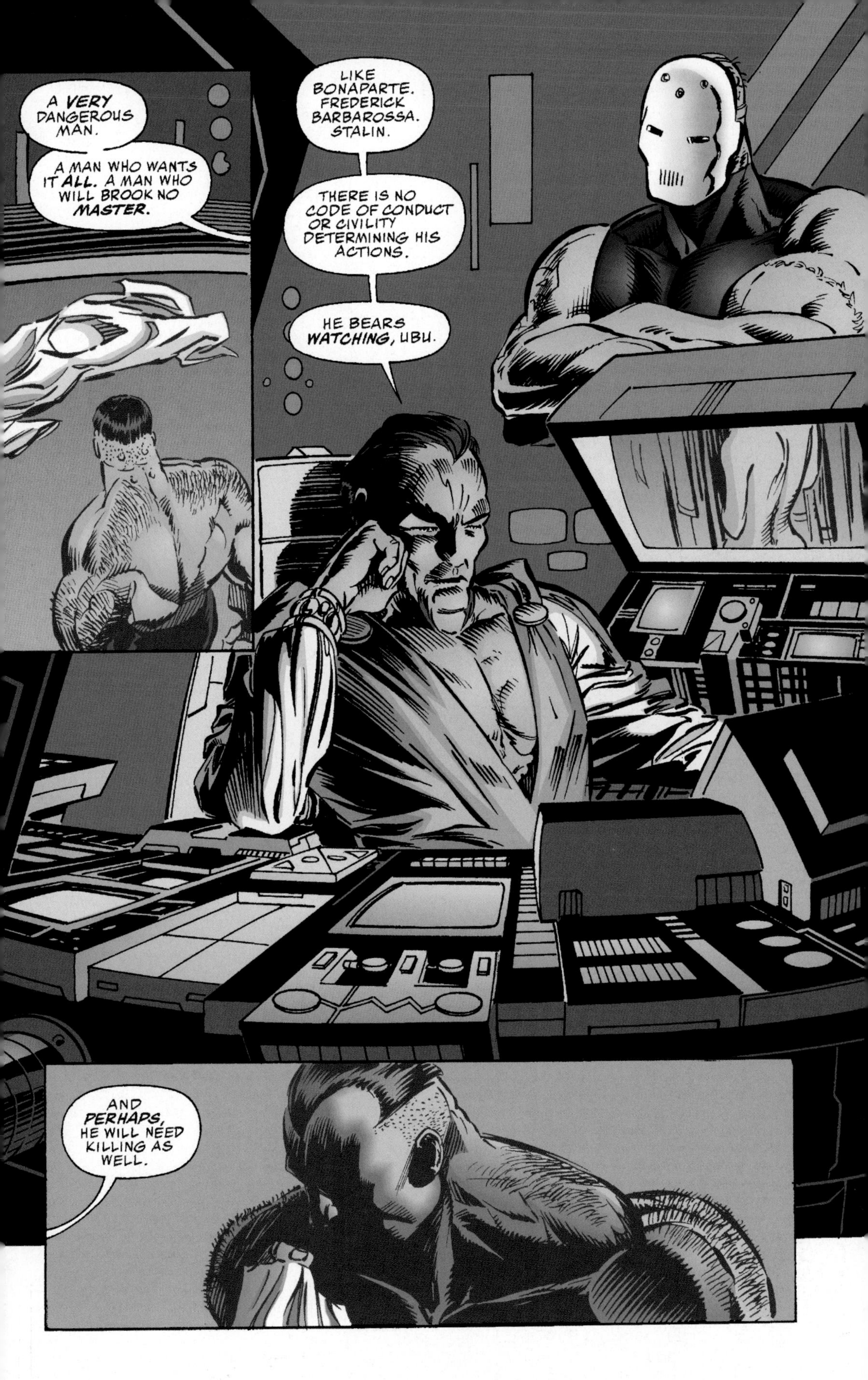
A VERY DANGEROUS MAN.
A MAN WHO WANTS IT ALL. A MAN WHO WILL BROOK NO MASTER.
LIKE BONAPARTE. FREDERICK BARBAROSSA. STALIN.
THERE IS NO CODE OF CONDUCT OR CIVILITY DETERMINING HIS ACTIONS.
HE BEARS WATCHING, UBU.
AND PERHAPS, HE WILL NEED KILLING AS WELL.

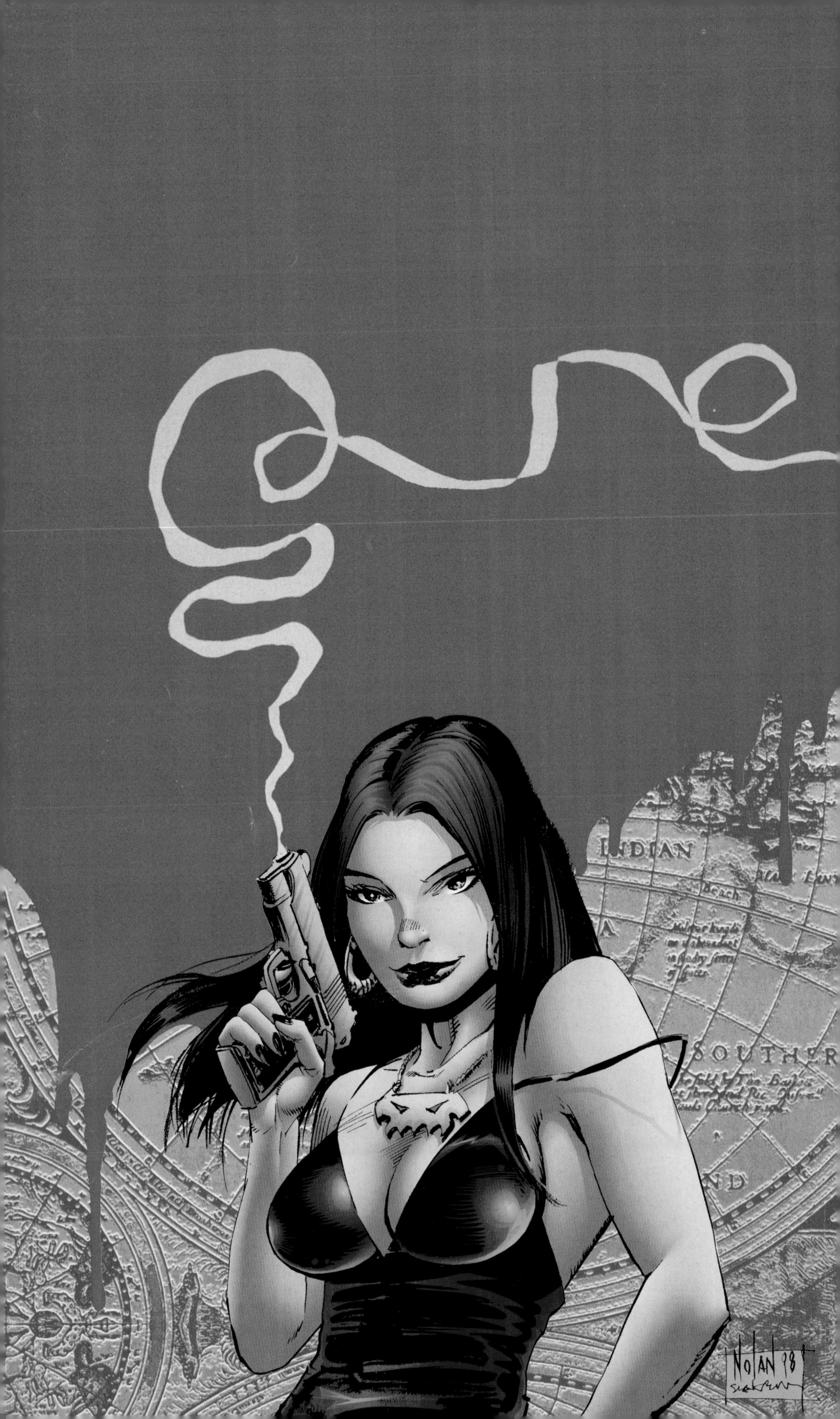
Gone
INDIAN
SOUTHER
NOLAN 98

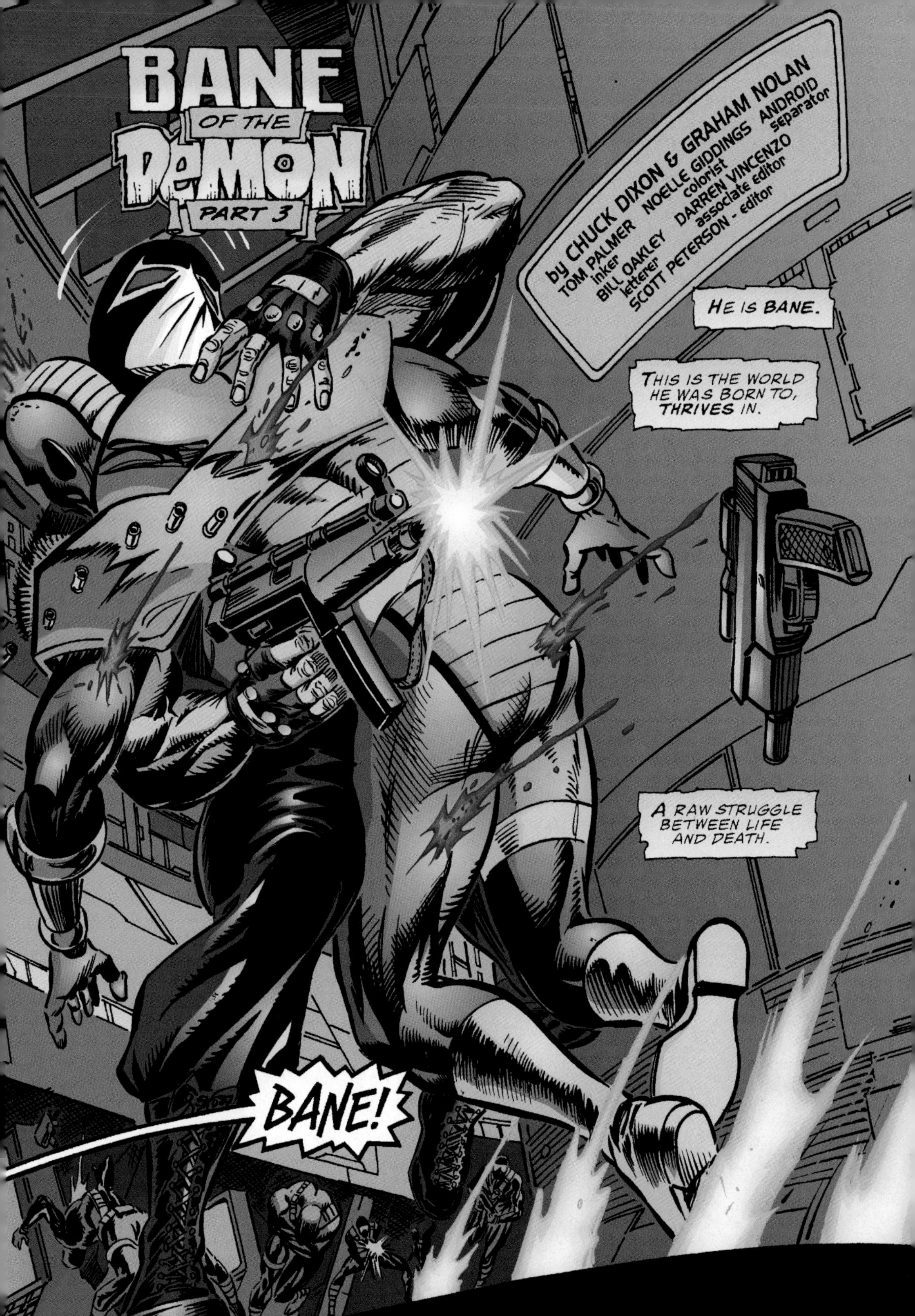
BANE OF THE DEMON
PART 3
by CHUCK DIXON & GRAHAM NOLAN
TOM PALMER inker NOELLE GIDDINGS colorist ANDROID separator
BILL OAKLEY letterer DARREN VINCENZO associate editor
SCOTT PETERSON - editor
HE IS BANE.
THIS IS THE WORLD HE WAS BORN TO, THRIVES IN.
A RAW STRUGGLE BETWEEN LIFE AND DEATH.
BANE!

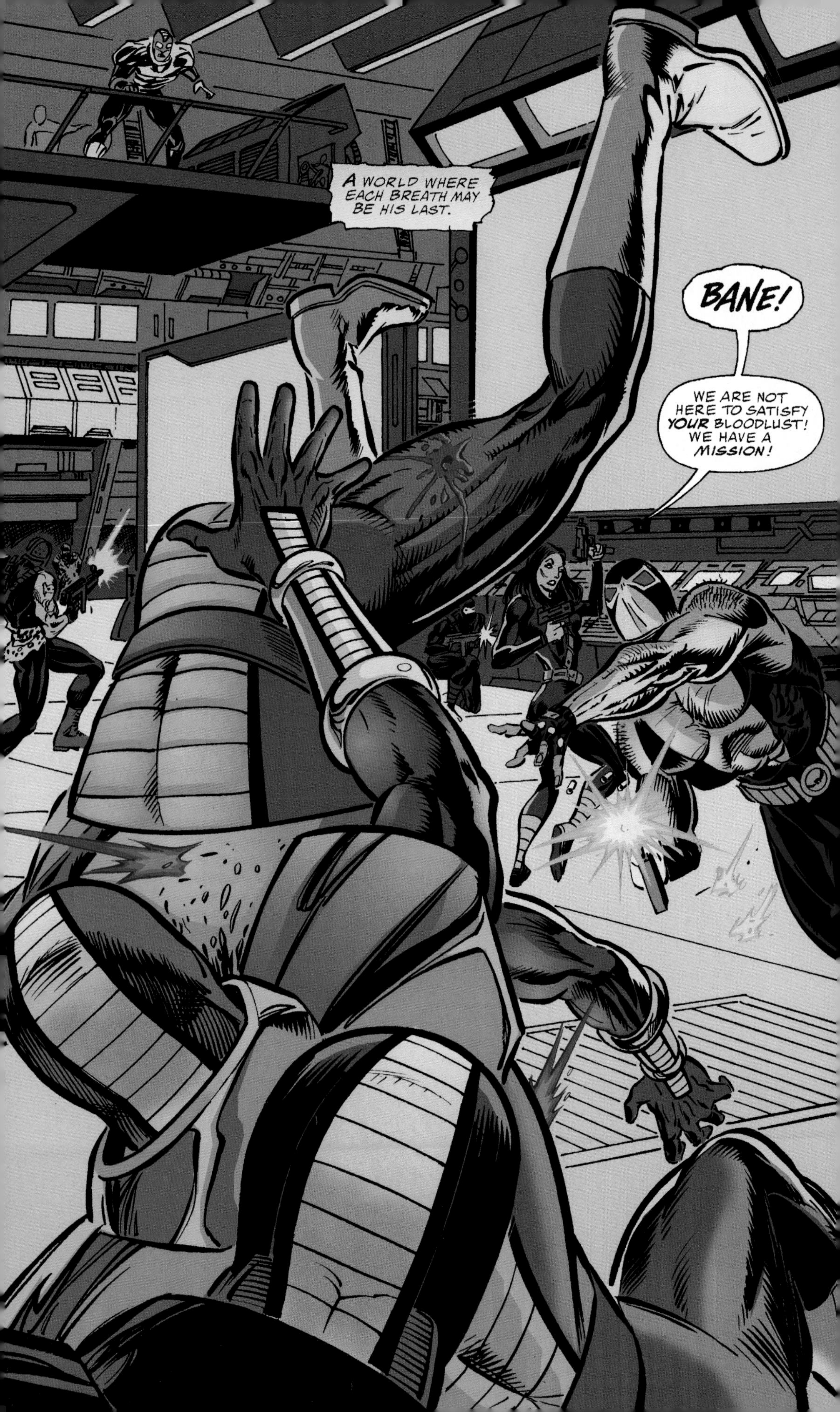

A WORLD WHERE EACH BREATH MAY BE HIS LAST.
BANE!
WE ARE NOT HERE TO SATISFY YOUR BLOODLUST! WE HAVE A MISSION!

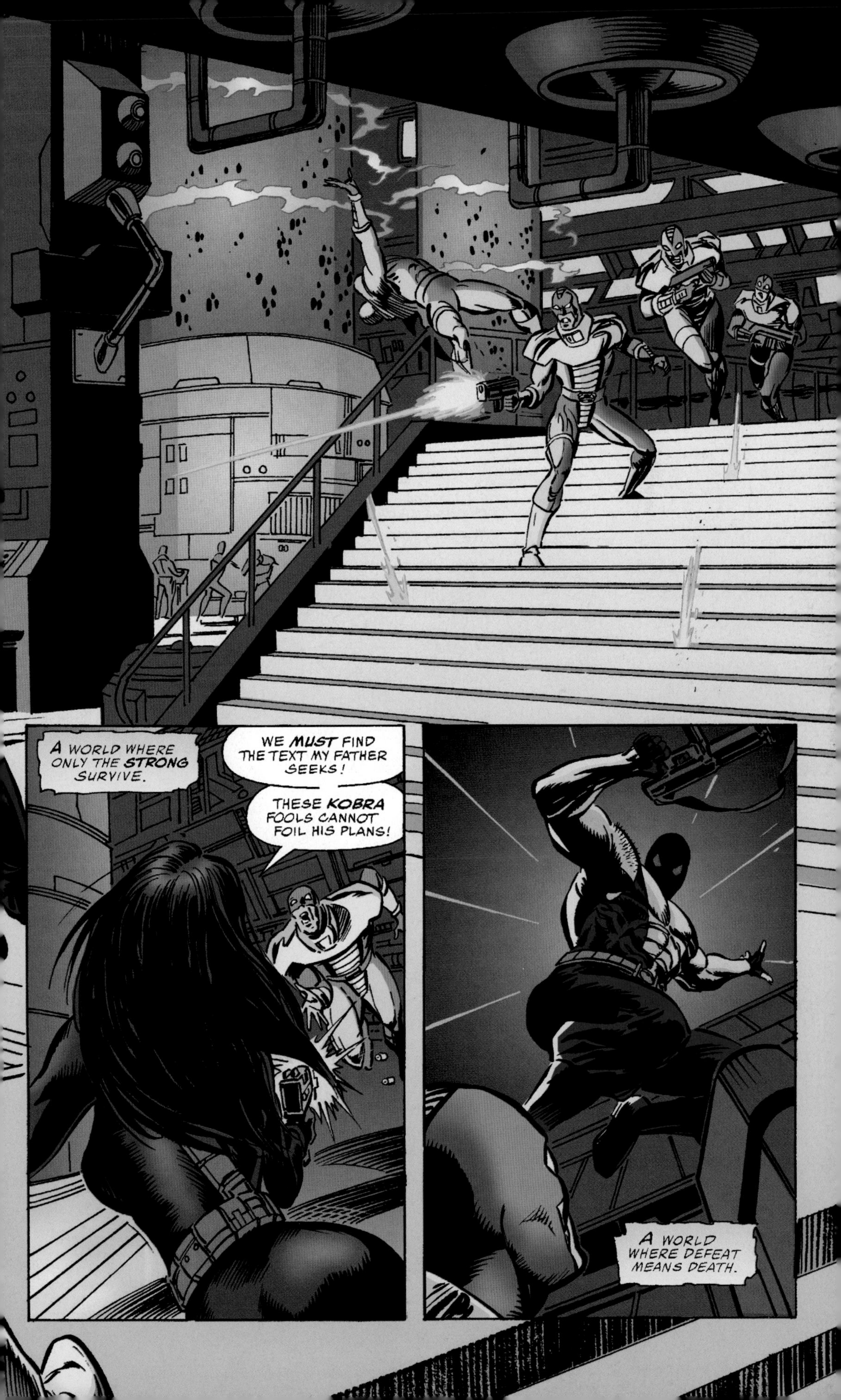
A WORLD WHERE ONLY THE STRONG SURVIVE.
WE MUST FIND THE TEXT MY FATHER SEEKS!
THESE KOBRA FOOLS CANNOT FOIL HIS PLANS!
A WORLD WHERE DEFEAT MEANS DEATH.

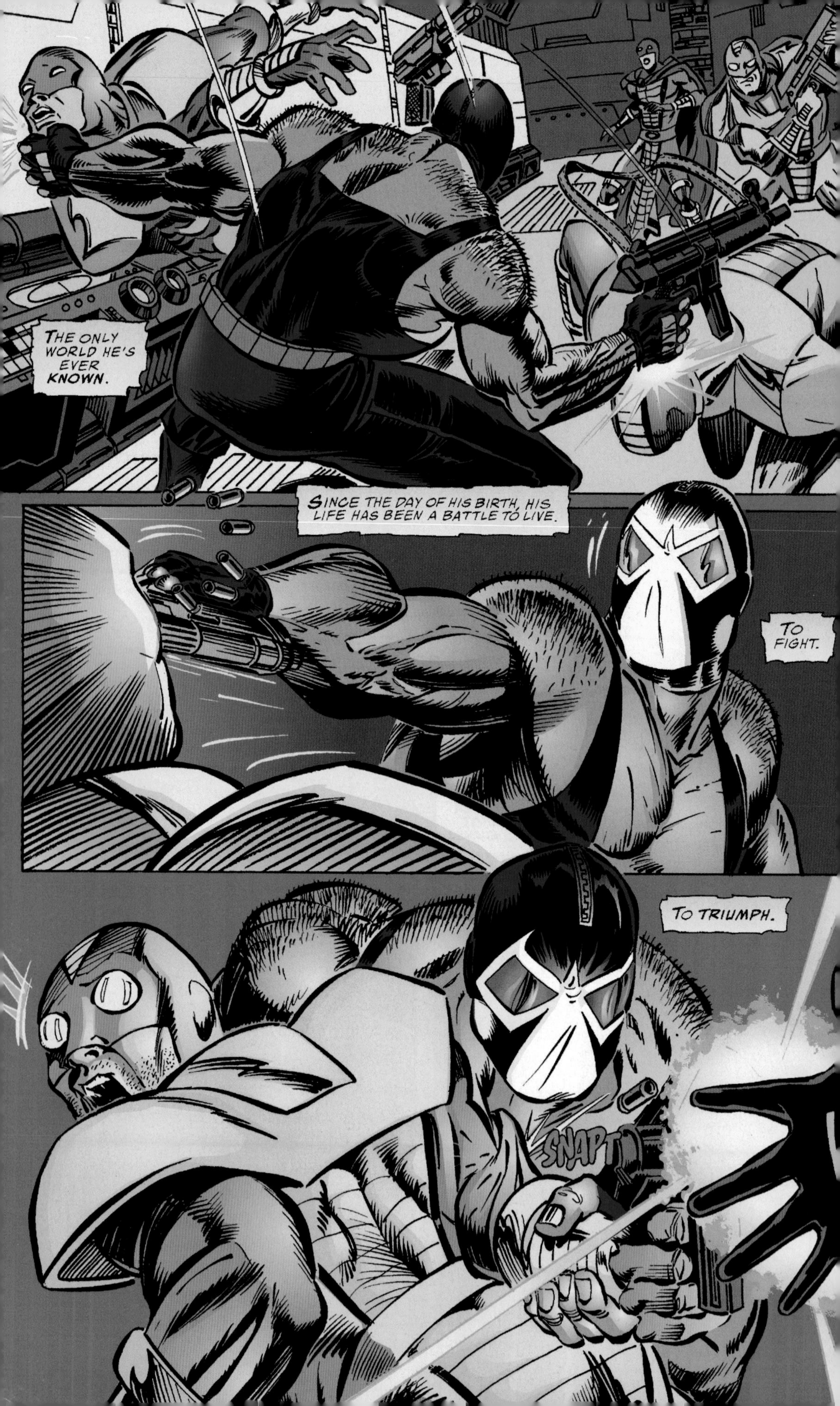
THE ONLY WORLD HE'S EVER KNOWN.
SINCE THE DAY OF HIS BIRTH, HIS LIFE HAS BEEN A BATTLE TO LIVE.
TO FIGHT.
TO TRIUMPH.
SNAP!

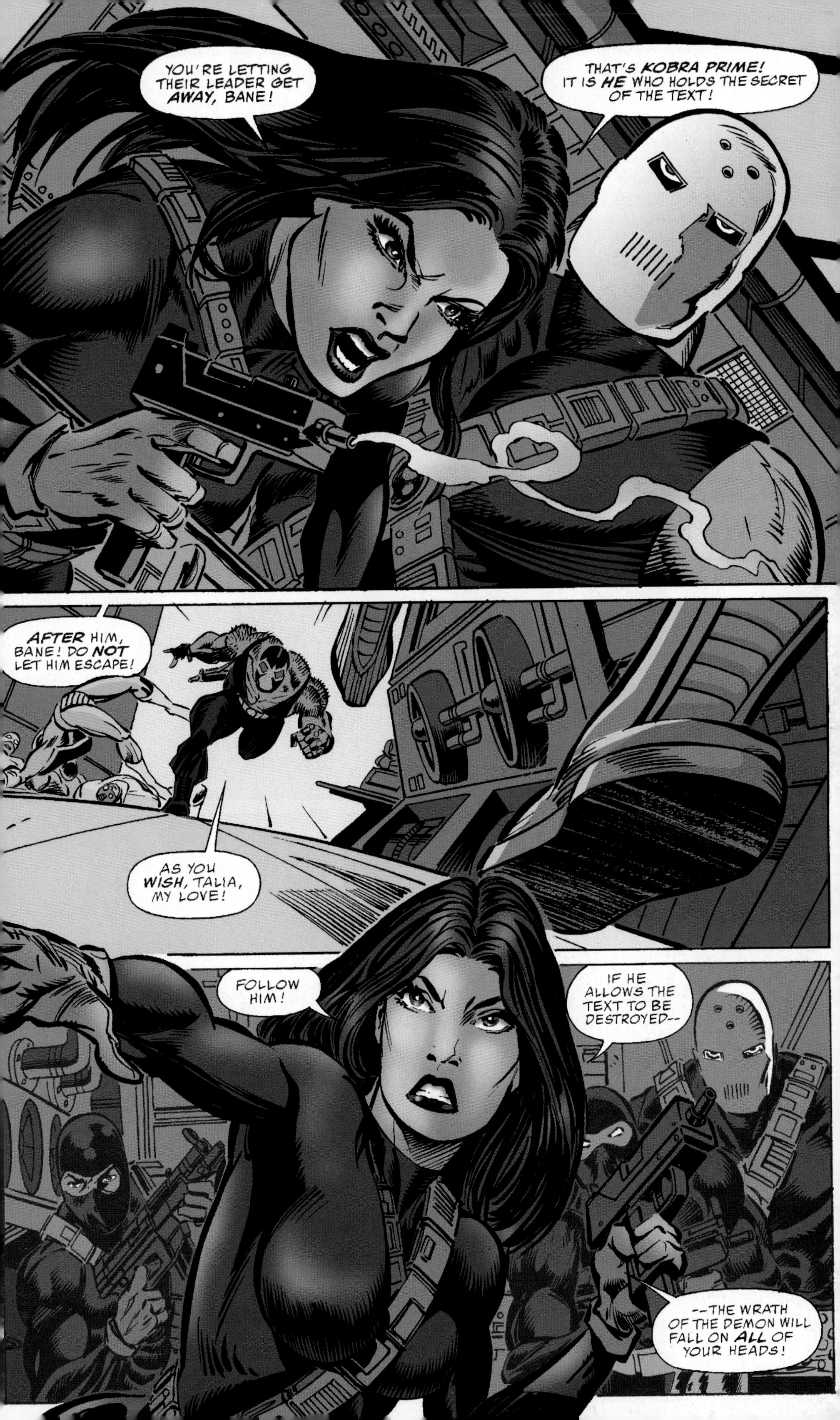

YOU'RE LETTING THEIR LEADER GET AWAY, BANE!
THAT'S KOBRA PRIME! IT IS HE WHO HOLDS THE SECRET OF THE TEXT!
AFTER HIM, BANE! DO NOT LET HIM ESCAPE!
AS YOU WISH, TALIA, MY LOVE!
FOLLOW HIM!
IF HE ALLOWS THE TEXT TO BE DESTROYED--
--THE WRATH OF THE DEMON WILL FALL ON ALL OF YOUR HEADS!

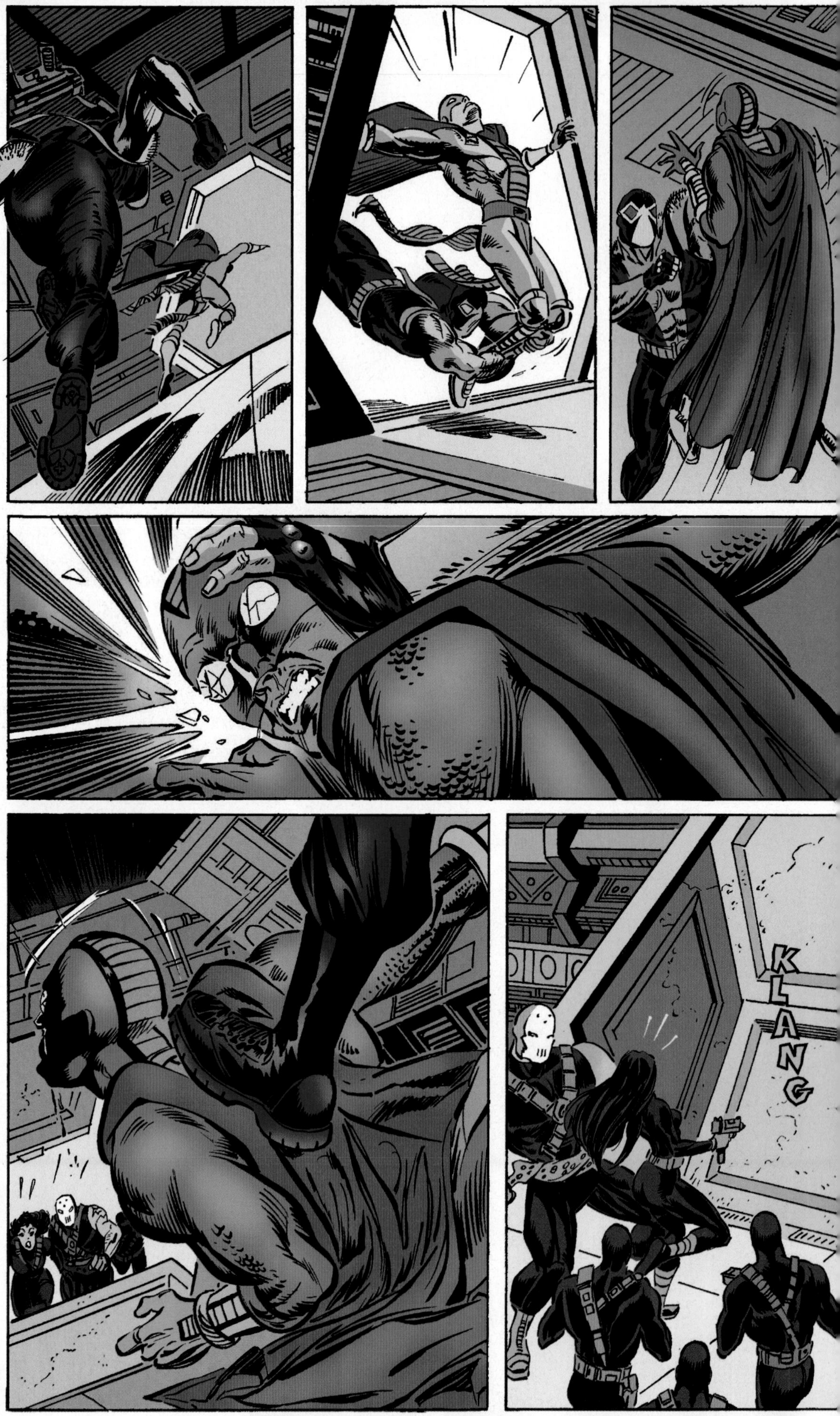
KLANG

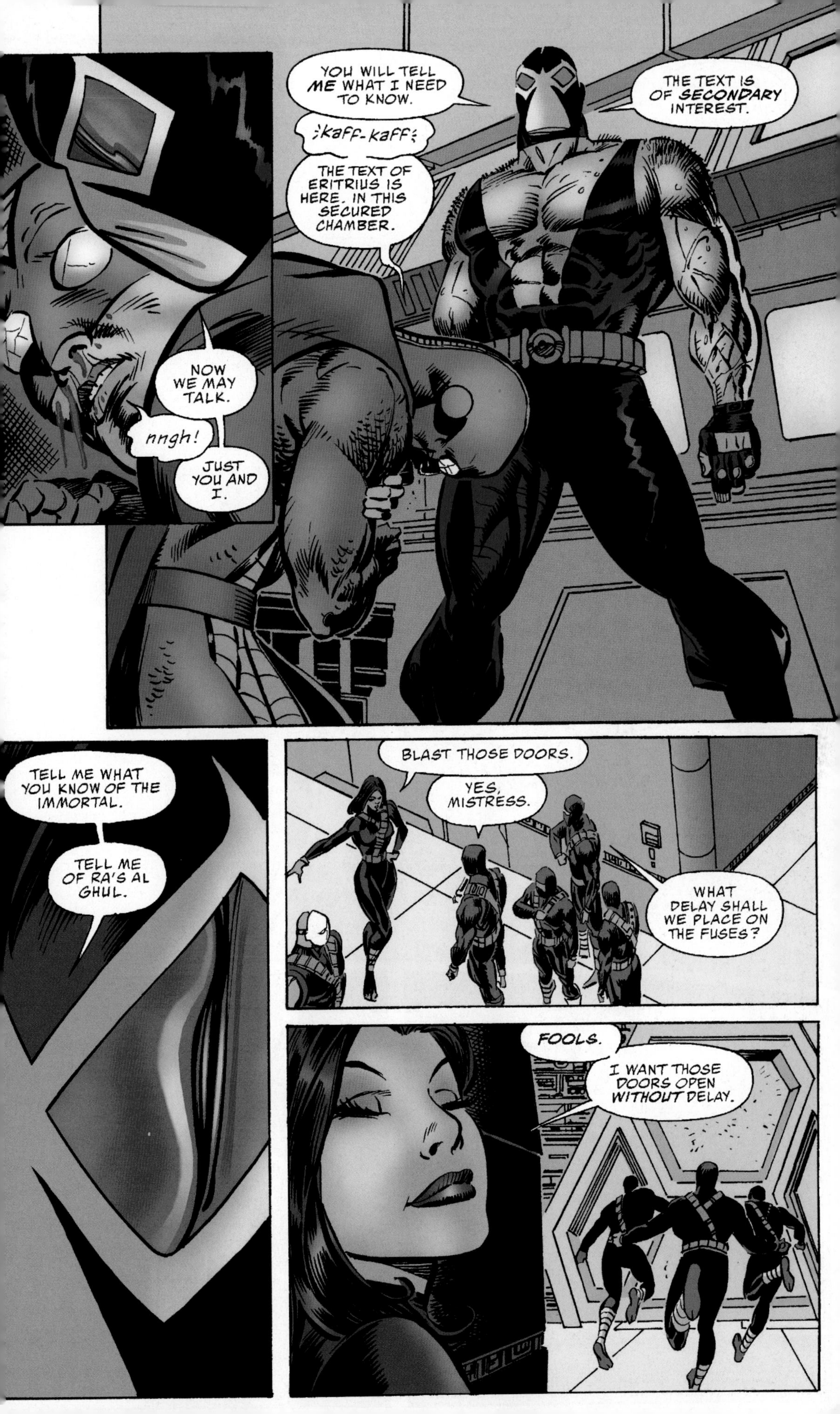
YOU WILL TELL ME WHAT I NEED TO KNOW.
:kaff-kaff:
THE TEXT OF ERITRIUS IS HERE. IN THIS SECURED CHAMBER.
THE TEXT IS OF SECONDARY INTEREST.
NOW WE MAY TALK.
nngh!
JUST YOU AND I.
TELL ME WHAT YOU KNOW OF THE IMMORTAL.
TELL ME OF RA'S AL GHUL.
BLAST THOSE DOORS.
YES, MISTRESS.
WHAT DELAY SHALL WE PLACE ON THE FUSES?
FOOLS.
I WANT THOSE DOORS OPEN WITHOUT DELAY.

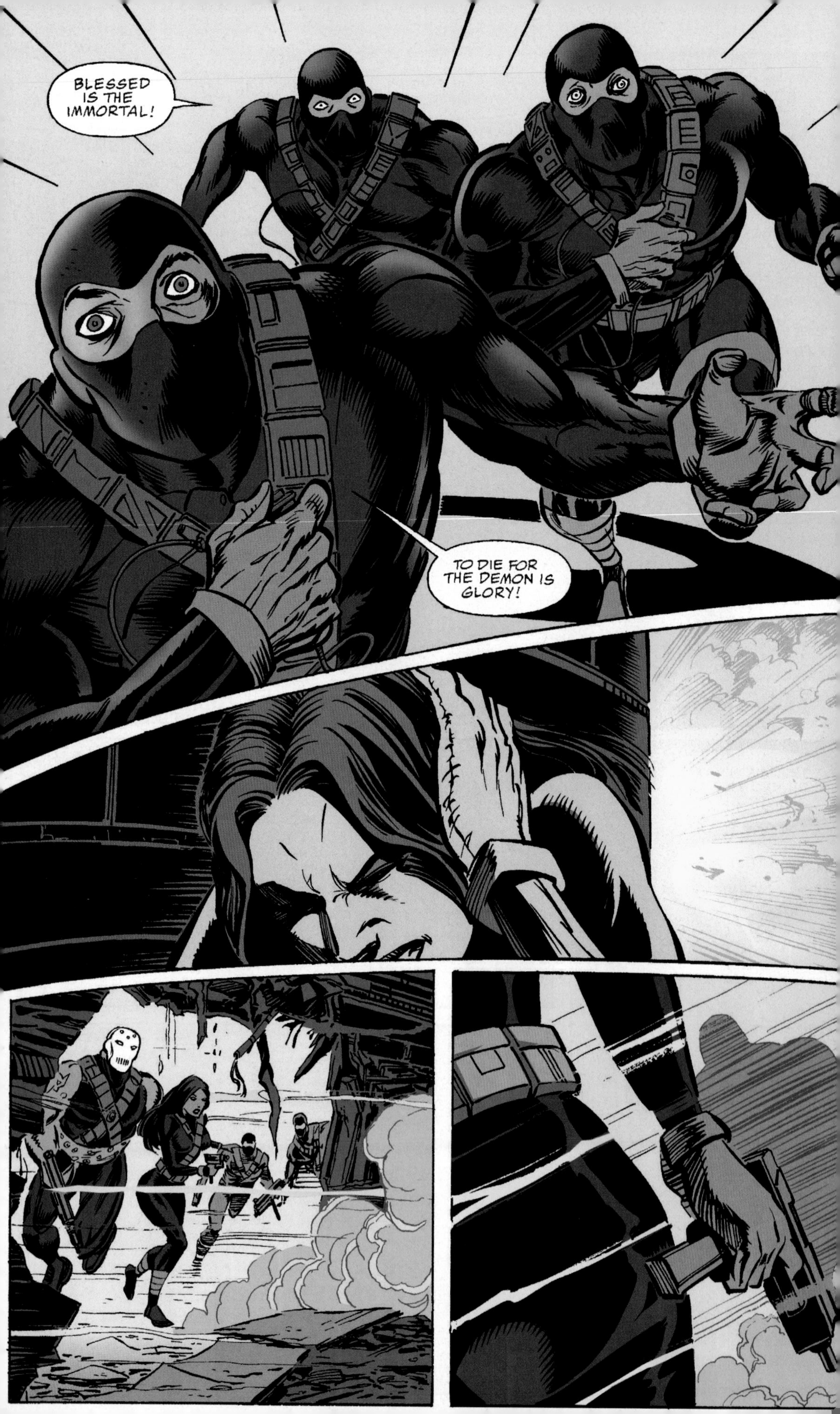
BLESSED IS THE IMMORTAL!
TO DIE FOR THE DEMON IS GLORY!

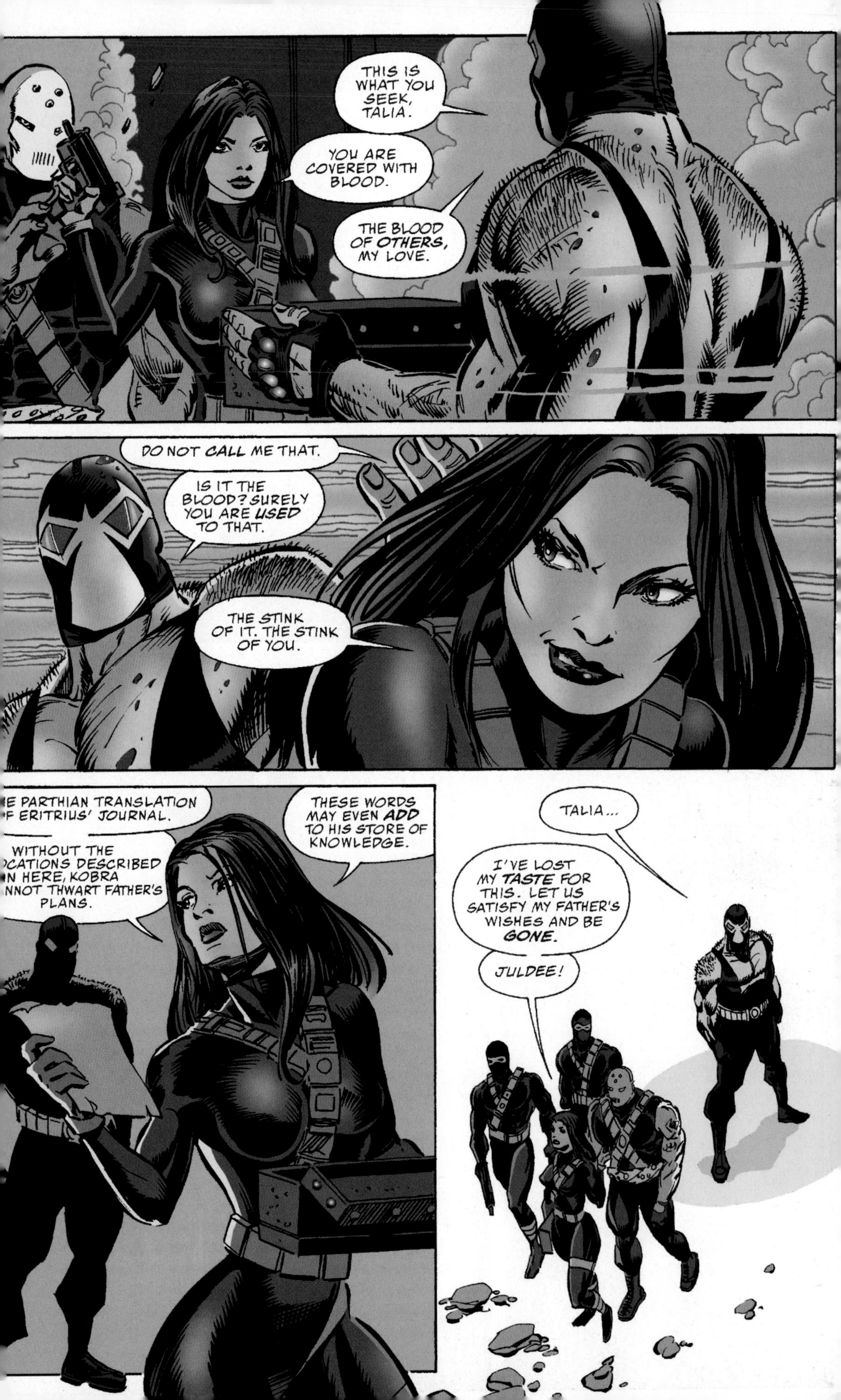

THIS IS WHAT YOU SEEK, TALIA.
YOU ARE COVERED WITH BLOOD.
THE BLOOD OF OTHERS, MY LOVE.
DO NOT CALL ME THAT.
IS IT THE BLOOD? SURELY YOU ARE USED TO THAT.
THE STINK OF IT. THE STINK OF YOU.
E PARTHIAN TRANSLATION F ERITRIUS' JOURNAL.
WITHOUT THE OCATIONS DESCRIBED N HERE, KOBRA NNOT THWART FATHER'S PLANS.
THESE WORDS MAY EVEN ADD TO HIS STORE OF KNOWLEDGE.
TALIA...
I'VE LOST MY TASTE FOR THIS. LET US SATISFY MY FATHER'S WISHES AND BE GONE.
JULDEE!

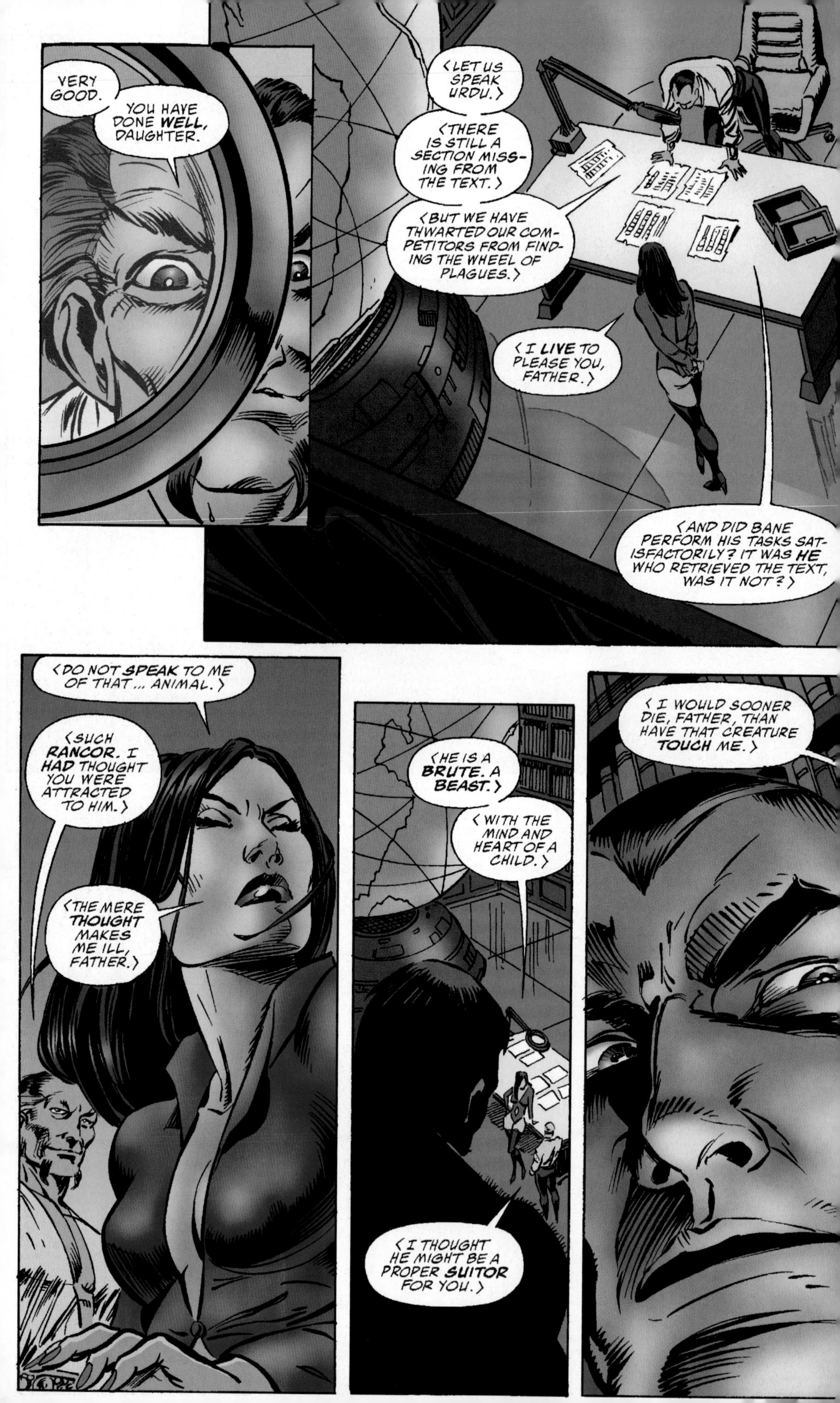

VERY GOOD.
YOU HAVE DONE WELL, DAUGHTER.
<LET US SPEAK URDU.>
<THERE IS STILL A SECTION MISSING FROM THE TEXT.>
<BUT WE HAVE THWARTED OUR COMPETITORS FROM FINDING THE WHEEL OF PLAGUES.>
<I LIVE TO PLEASE YOU, FATHER.>
<AND DID BANE PERFORM HIS TASKS SATISFACTORILY? IT WAS HE WHO RETRIEVED THE TEXT, WAS IT NOT?>
<DO NOT SPEAK TO ME OF THAT... ANIMAL.>
<SUCH RANCOR. I HAD THOUGHT YOU WERE ATTRACTED TO HIM.>
<THE MERE THOUGHT MAKES ME ILL, FATHER.>
<HE IS A BRUTE. A BEAST.>
<WITH THE MIND AND HEART OF A CHILD.>
<I THOUGHT HE MIGHT BE A PROPER SUITOR FOR YOU.>
<I WOULD SOONER DIE, FATHER, THAN HAVE THAT CREATURE TOUCH ME.>

⟨BUT HE INSPIRES SUCH *PASSION* IN YOU. EVEN *HATRED* MAY TURN TO--⟩

⟨YOU SEE *PASSION* WHERE THERE IS ONLY *REVULSION*.⟩

⟨IF HE DISPLEASES YOU SO, I WILL HAVE HIM SLAIN.⟩

⟨NO. HE IS USEFUL. AS A MINION. A *TOOL*.⟩

⟨VERY WELL THEN, DEAR DAUGHTER.⟩

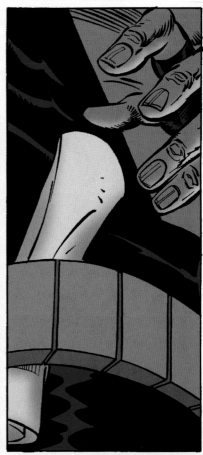

SHUF

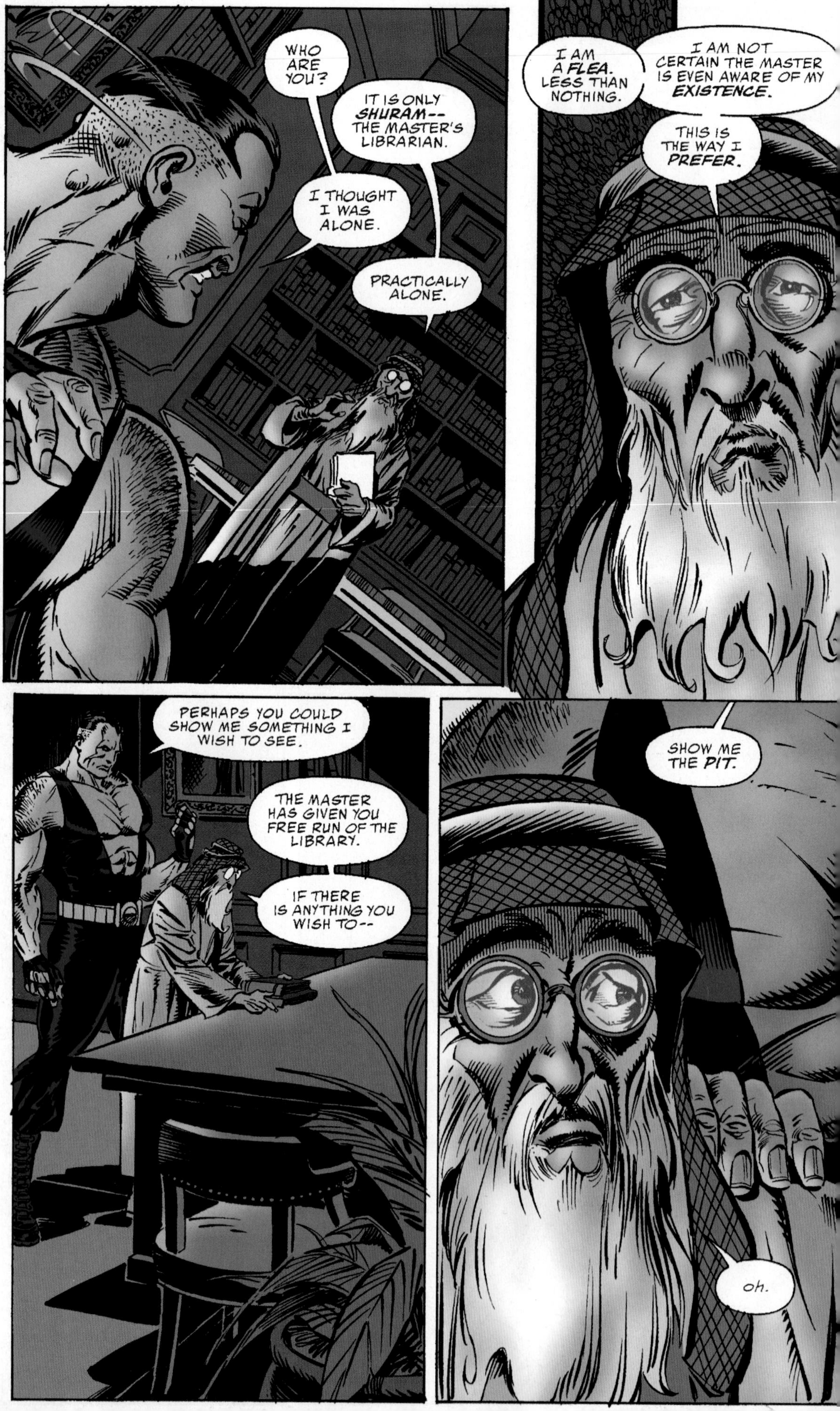
WHO ARE YOU?
IT IS ONLY *SHURAM*-- THE MASTER'S LIBRARIAN.
I THOUGHT I WAS ALONE.
PRACTICALLY ALONE.
I AM A *FLEA*. LESS THAN NOTHING.
I AM NOT CERTAIN THE MASTER IS EVEN AWARE OF MY *EXISTENCE*.
THIS IS THE WAY I *PREFER*.
PERHAPS YOU COULD SHOW ME SOMETHING I WISH TO SEE.
THE MASTER HAS GIVEN YOU FREE RUN OF THE LIBRARY.
IF THERE IS ANYTHING YOU WISH TO--
SHOW ME THE *PIT*.
oh.

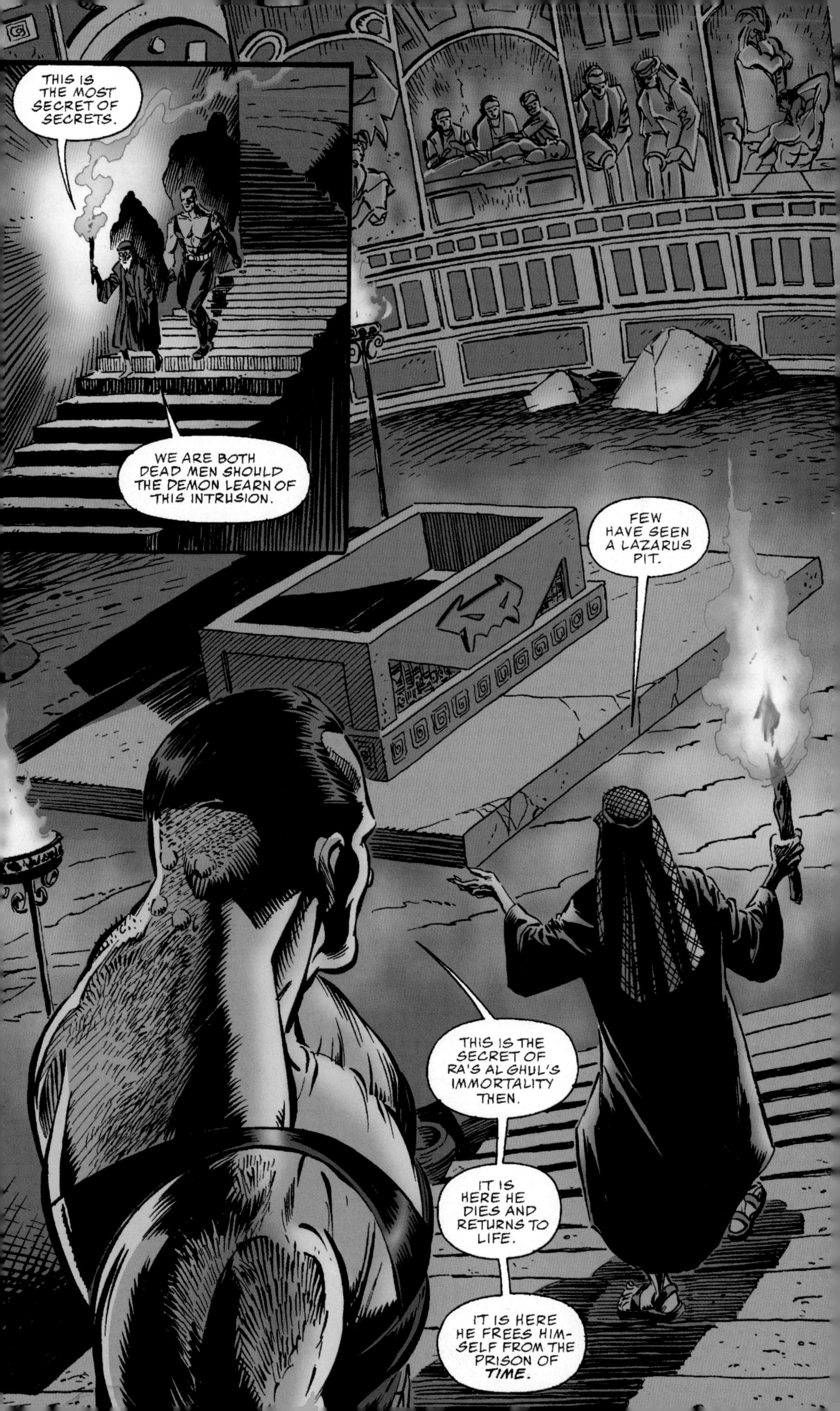
THIS IS THE MOST SECRET OF SECRETS.
WE ARE BOTH DEAD MEN SHOULD THE DEMON LEARN OF THIS INTRUSION.
FEW HAVE SEEN A LAZARUS PIT.
THIS IS THE SECRET OF RA'S AL GHUL'S IMMORTALITY THEN.
IT IS HERE HE DIES AND RETURNS TO LIFE.
IT IS HERE HE FREES HIM-SELF FROM THE PRISON OF TIME.

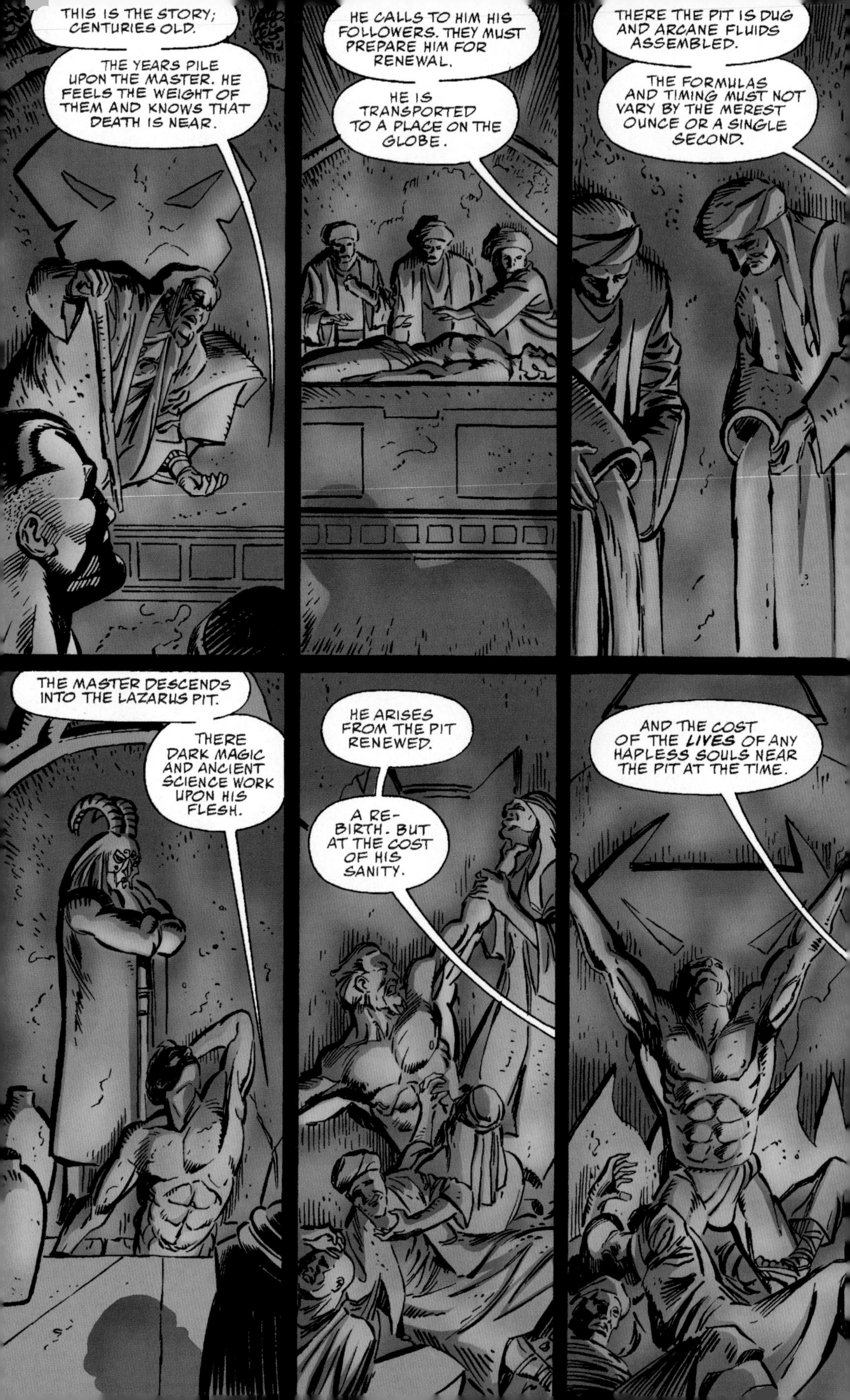
THIS IS THE STORY; CENTURIES OLD.
THE YEARS PILE UPON THE MASTER. HE FEELS THE WEIGHT OF THEM AND KNOWS THAT DEATH IS NEAR.
HE CALLS TO HIM HIS FOLLOWERS. THEY MUST PREPARE HIM FOR RENEWAL.
HE IS TRANSPORTED TO A PLACE ON THE GLOBE.
THERE THE PIT IS DUG AND ARCANE FLUIDS ASSEMBLED.
THE FORMULAS AND TIMING MUST NOT VARY BY THE MEREST OUNCE OR A SINGLE SECOND.
THE MASTER DESCENDS INTO THE LAZARUS PIT.
THERE DARK MAGIC AND ANCIENT SCIENCE WORK UPON HIS FLESH.
HE ARISES FROM THE PIT RENEWED.
A RE-BIRTH. BUT AT THE COST OF HIS SANITY.
AND THE COST OF THE *LIVES* OF ANY HAPLESS SOULS NEAR THE PIT AT THE TIME.

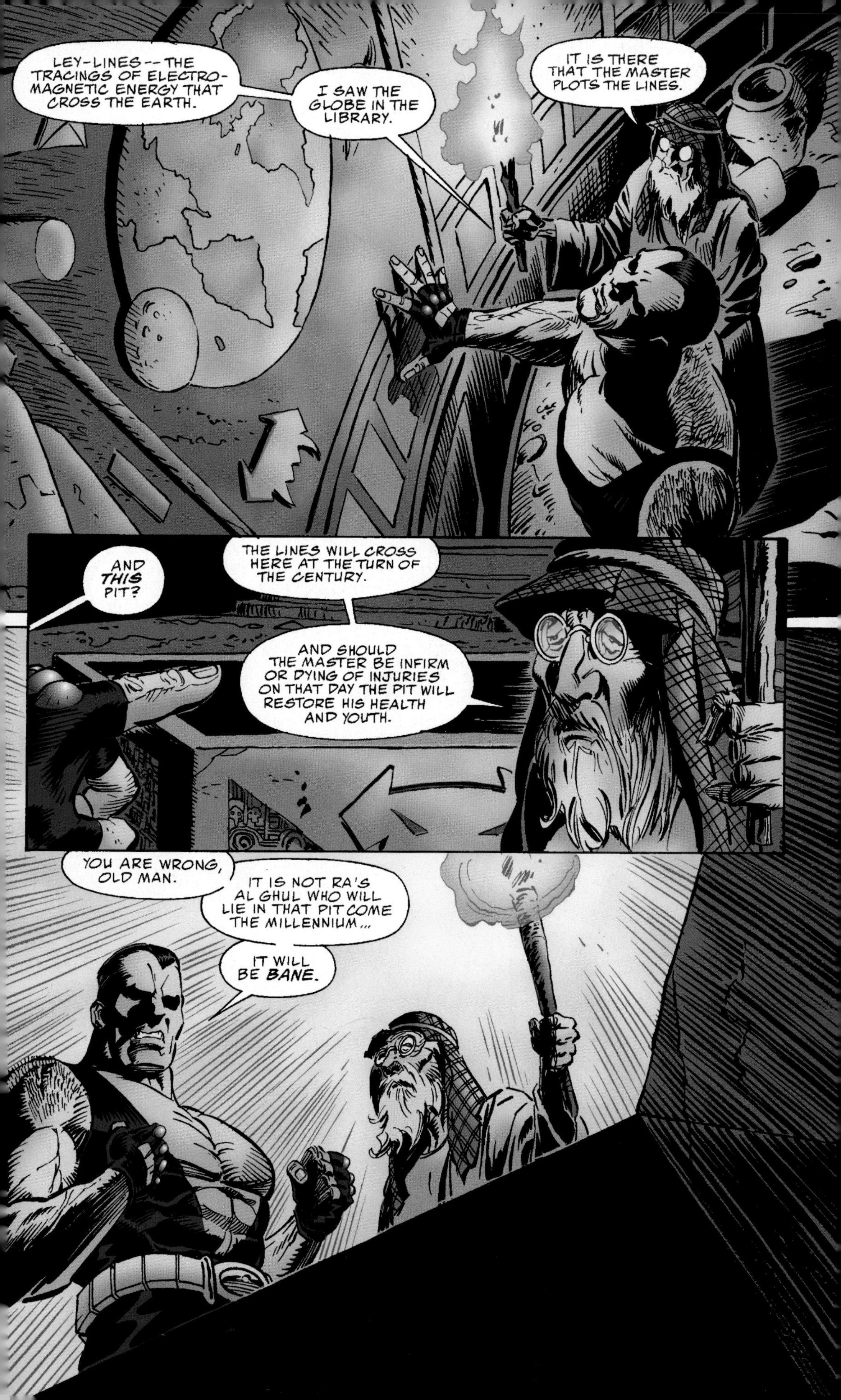

LEY-LINES--THE TRACINGS OF ELECTRO-MAGNETIC ENERGY THAT CROSS THE EARTH.
I SAW THE GLOBE IN THE LIBRARY.
IT IS THERE THAT THE MASTER PLOTS THE LINES.
AND THIS PIT?
THE LINES WILL CROSS HERE AT THE TURN OF THE CENTURY.
AND SHOULD THE MASTER BE INFIRM OR DYING OF INJURIES ON THAT DAY THE PIT WILL RESTORE HIS HEALTH AND YOUTH.
YOU ARE WRONG, OLD MAN.
IT IS NOT RA'S AL GHUL WHO WILL LIE IN THAT PIT COME THE MILLENNIUM...
IT WILL BE BANE.

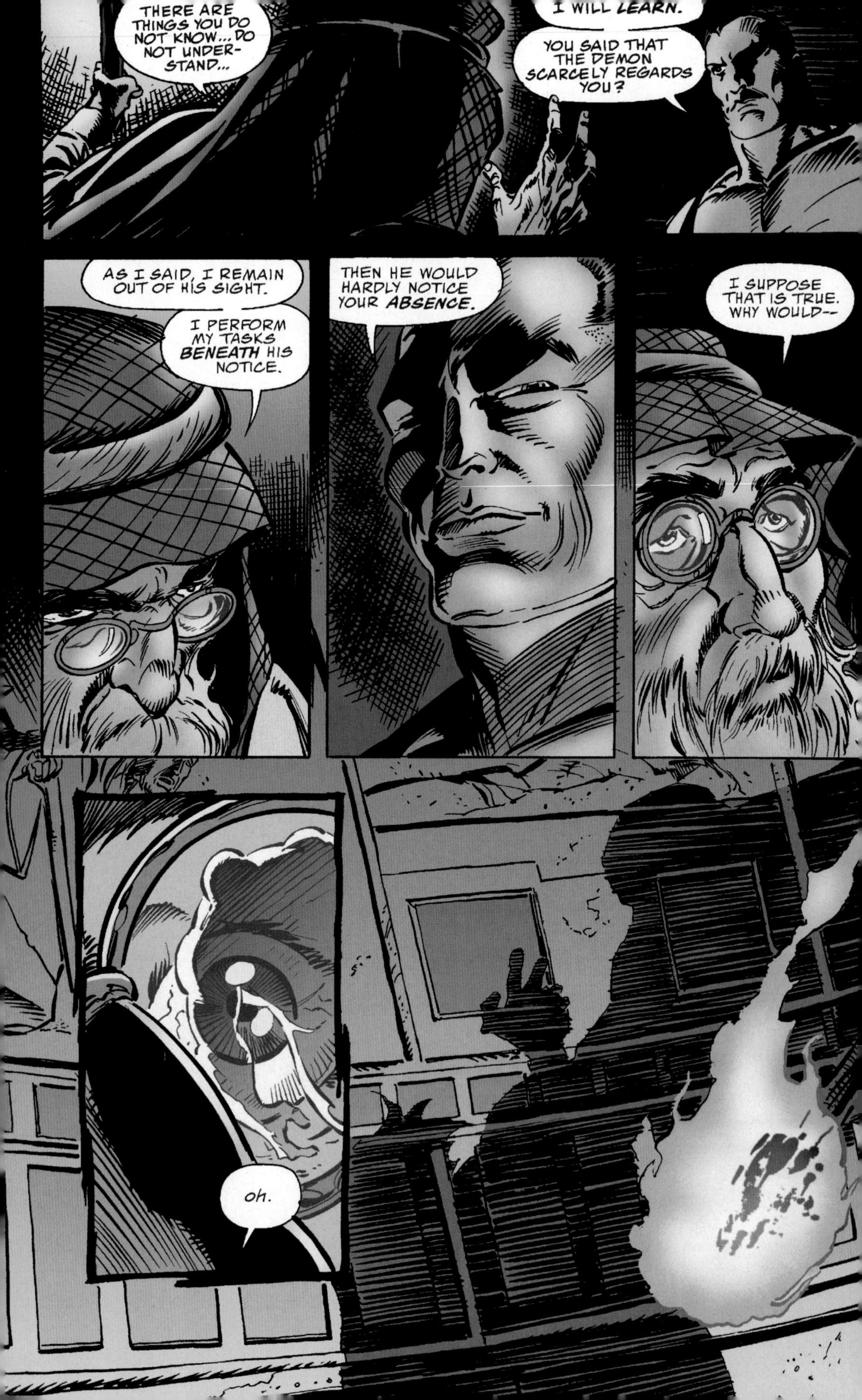
THERE ARE THINGS YOU DO NOT KNOW... DO NOT UNDER-STAND...
I WILL LEARN.
YOU SAID THAT THE DEMON SCARCELY REGARDS YOU?
AS I SAID, I REMAIN OUT OF HIS SIGHT.
I PERFORM MY TASKS BENEATH HIS NOTICE.
THEN HE WOULD HARDLY NOTICE YOUR ABSENCE.
I SUPPOSE THAT IS TRUE. WHY WOULD--
oh.

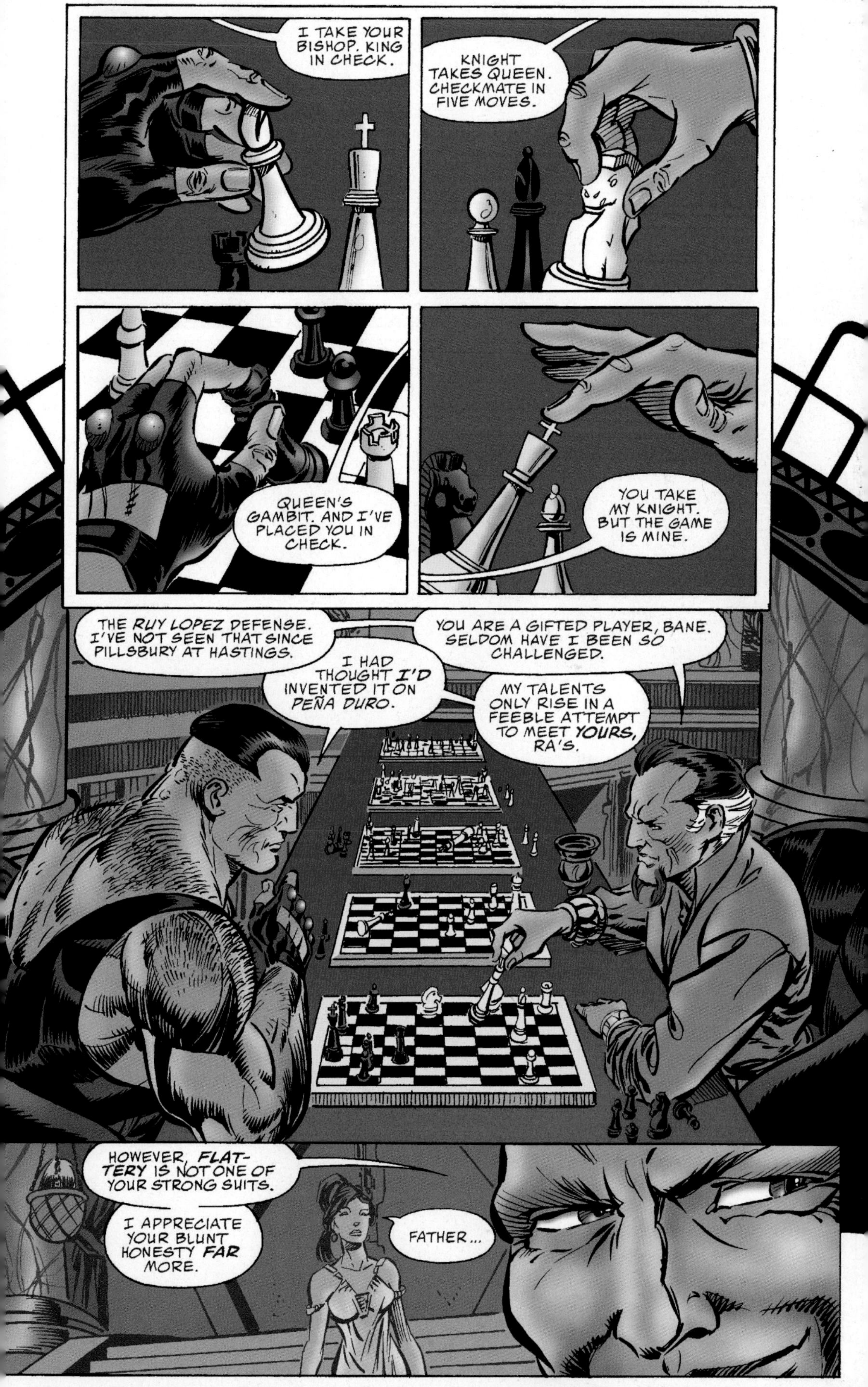
I TAKE YOUR BISHOP. KING IN CHECK.
KNIGHT TAKES QUEEN. CHECKMATE IN FIVE MOVES.
QUEEN'S GAMBIT. AND I'VE PLACED YOU IN CHECK.
YOU TAKE MY KNIGHT. BUT THE GAME IS MINE.
THE RUY LOPEZ DEFENSE. I'VE NOT SEEN THAT SINCE PILLSBURY AT HASTINGS.
I HAD THOUGHT I'D INVENTED IT ON PEÑA DURO.
YOU ARE A GIFTED PLAYER, BANE. SELDOM HAVE I BEEN SO CHALLENGED.
MY TALENTS ONLY RISE IN A FEEBLE ATTEMPT TO MEET YOURS, RA'S.
HOWEVER, FLATTERY IS NOT ONE OF YOUR STRONG SUITS.
I APPRECIATE YOUR BLUNT HONESTY FAR MORE.
FATHER...

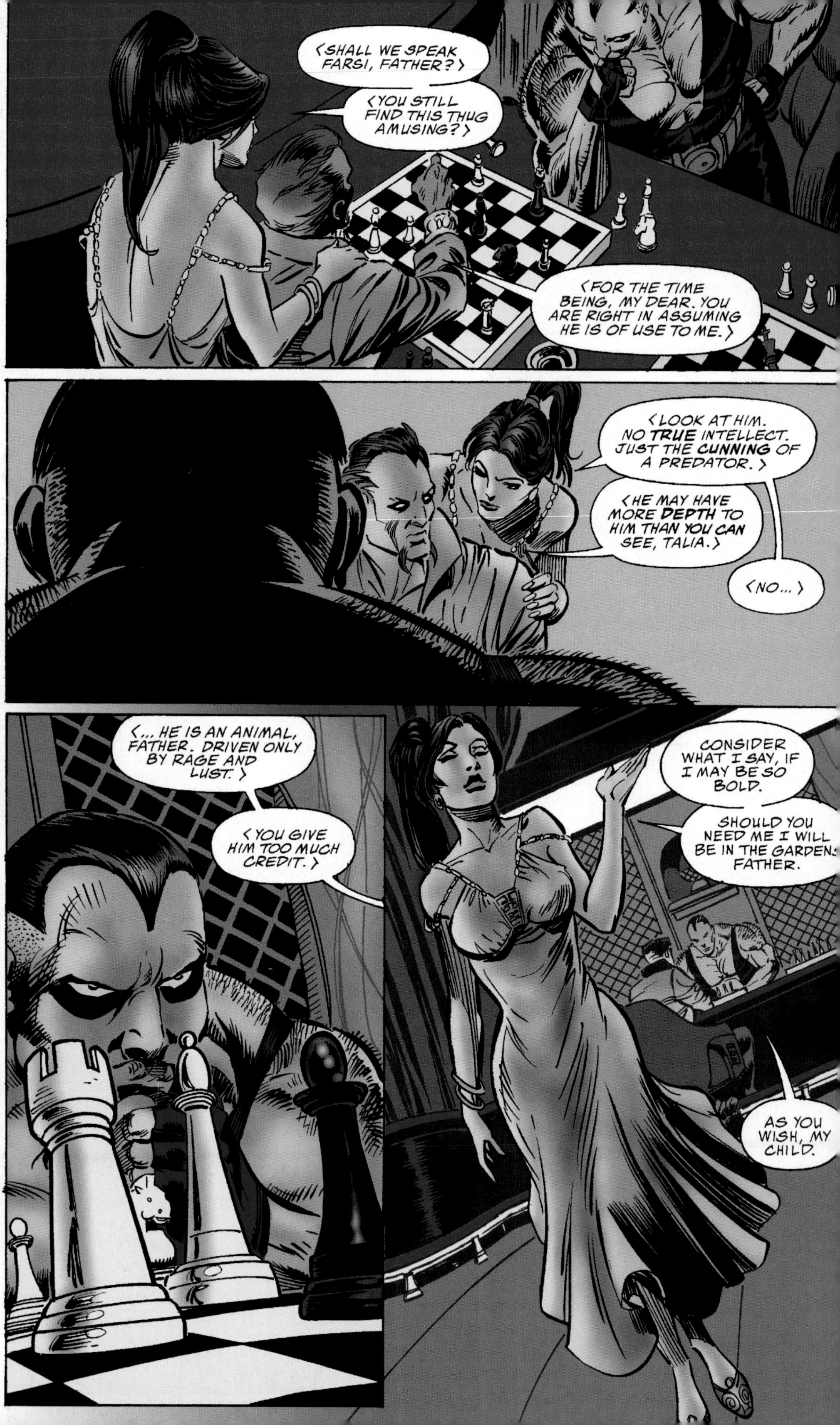

‹SHALL WE SPEAK FARSI, FATHER?›
‹YOU STILL FIND THIS THUG AMUSING?›
‹FOR THE TIME BEING, MY DEAR. YOU ARE RIGHT IN ASSUMING HE IS OF USE TO ME.›
‹LOOK AT HIM. NO TRUE INTELLECT. JUST THE CUNNING OF A PREDATOR.›
‹HE MAY HAVE MORE DEPTH TO HIM THAN YOU CAN SEE, TALIA.›
‹NO...›
‹... HE IS AN ANIMAL, FATHER. DRIVEN ONLY BY RAGE AND LUST.›
‹YOU GIVE HIM TOO MUCH CREDIT.›
CONSIDER WHAT I SAY, IF I MAY BE SO BOLD.
SHOULD YOU NEED ME I WILL BE IN THE GARDEN, FATHER.
AS YOU WISH, MY CHILD.

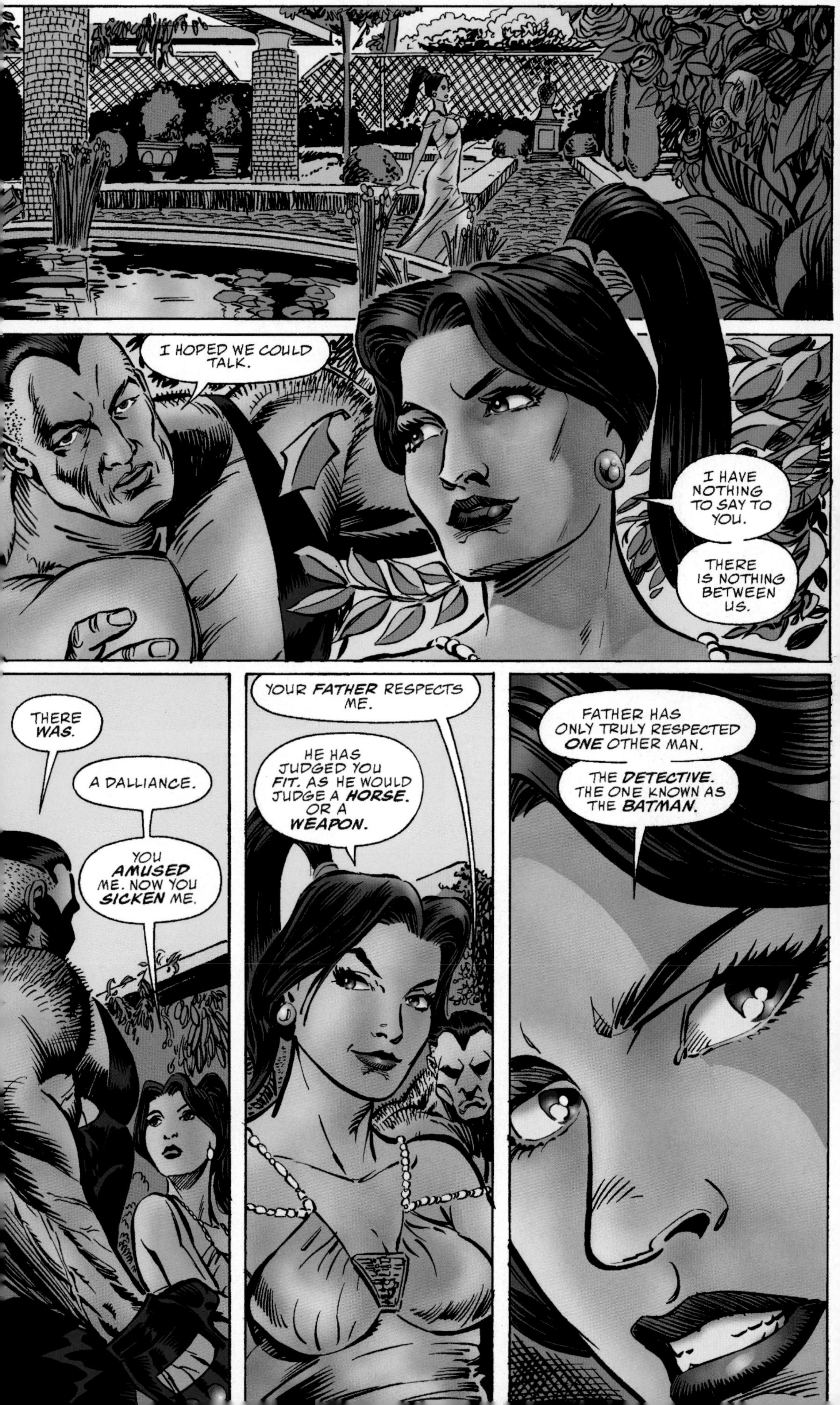
I HOPED WE COULD TALK.
I HAVE NOTHING TO SAY TO YOU.
THERE IS NOTHING BETWEEN US.
THERE WAS.
A DALLIANCE.
YOU AMUSED ME. NOW YOU SICKEN ME.
YOUR FATHER RESPECTS ME.
HE HAS JUDGED YOU FIT. AS HE WOULD JUDGE A HORSE. OR A WEAPON.
FATHER HAS ONLY TRULY RESPECTED ONE OTHER MAN.
THE DETECTIVE. THE ONE KNOWN AS THE BATMAN.

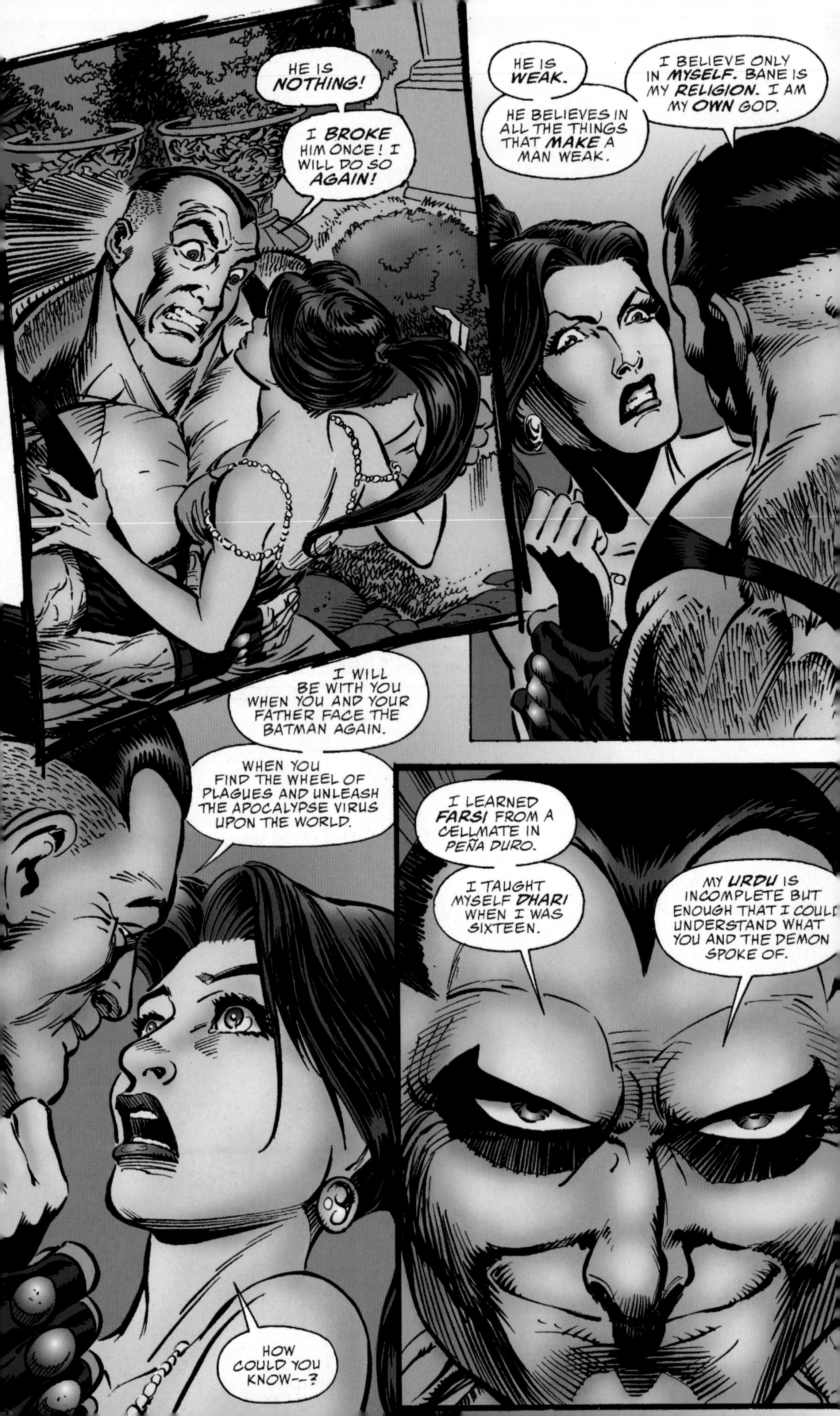
HE IS NOTHING!
I BROKE HIM ONCE! I WILL DO SO AGAIN!
HE IS WEAK.
HE BELIEVES IN ALL THE THINGS THAT MAKE A MAN WEAK.
I BELIEVE ONLY IN MYSELF. BANE IS MY RELIGION. I AM MY OWN GOD.
I WILL BE WITH YOU WHEN YOU AND YOUR FATHER FACE THE BATMAN AGAIN.
WHEN YOU FIND THE WHEEL OF PLAGUES AND UNLEASH THE APOCALYPSE VIRUS UPON THE WORLD.
HOW COULD YOU KNOW--?
I LEARNED FARSI FROM A CELLMATE IN PEÑA DURO.
I TAUGHT MYSELF DHARI WHEN I WAS SIXTEEN.
MY URDU IS INCOMPLETE BUT ENOUGH THAT I COUL UNDERSTAND WHAT YOU AND THE DEMON SPOKE OF.

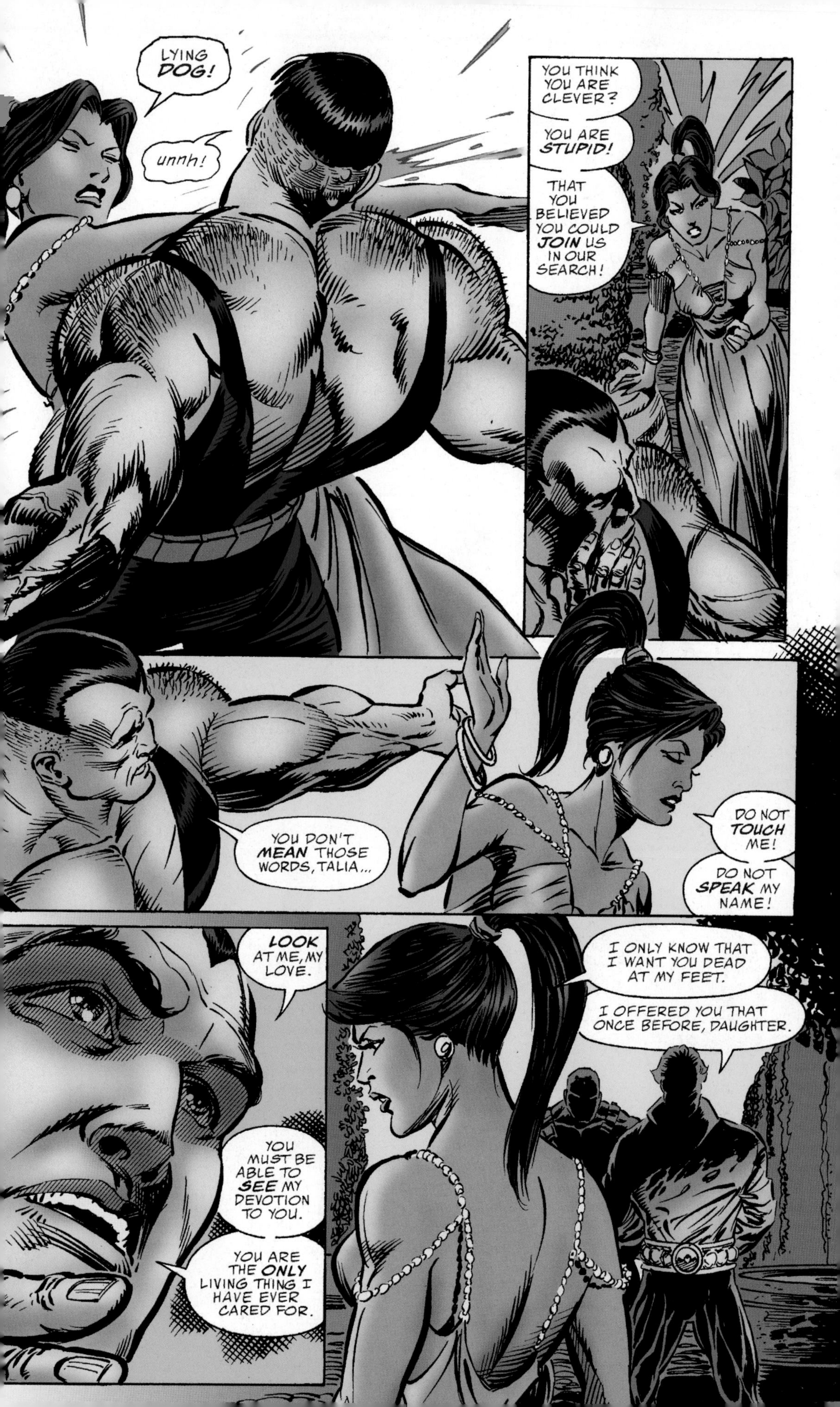

LYING DOG!
unnh!
YOU THINK YOU ARE CLEVER?
YOU ARE STUPID!
THAT YOU BELIEVED YOU COULD JOIN US IN OUR SEARCH!
YOU DON'T MEAN THOSE WORDS, TALIA...
DO NOT TOUCH ME!
DO NOT SPEAK MY NAME!
LOOK AT ME, MY LOVE.
YOU MUST BE ABLE TO SEE MY DEVOTION TO YOU.
YOU ARE THE ONLY LIVING THING I HAVE EVER CARED FOR.
I ONLY KNOW THAT I WANT YOU DEAD AT MY FEET.
I OFFERED YOU THAT ONCE BEFORE, DAUGHTER.

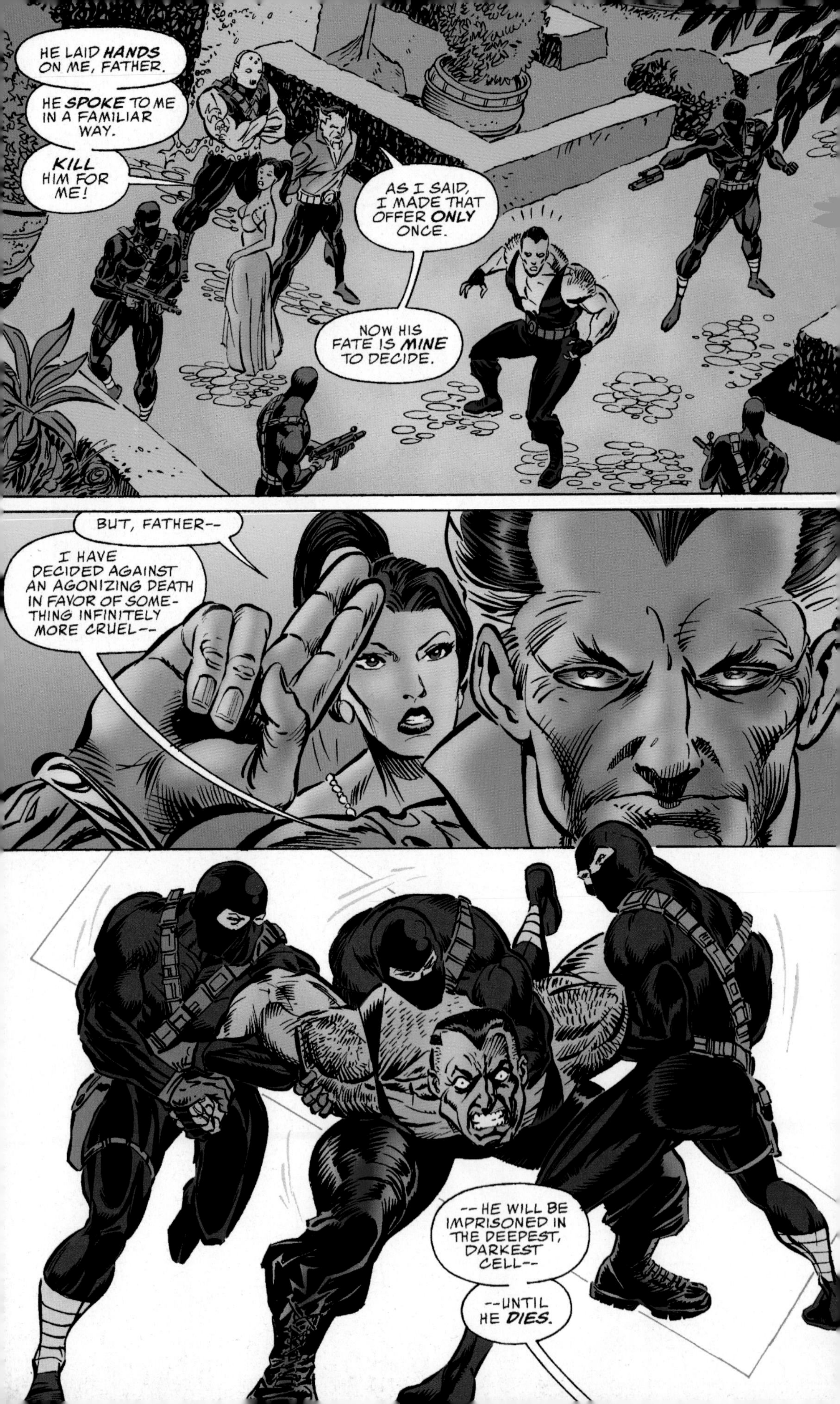
HE LAID HANDS ON ME, FATHER.
HE SPOKE TO ME IN A FAMILIAR WAY.
KILL HIM FOR ME!
AS I SAID, I MADE THAT OFFER ONLY ONCE.
NOW HIS FATE IS MINE TO DECIDE.
BUT, FATHER--
I HAVE DECIDED AGAINST AN AGONIZING DEATH IN FAVOR OF SOMETHING INFINITELY MORE CRUEL--
--HE WILL BE IMPRISONED IN THE DEEPEST, DARKEST CELL--
--UNTIL HE DIES.

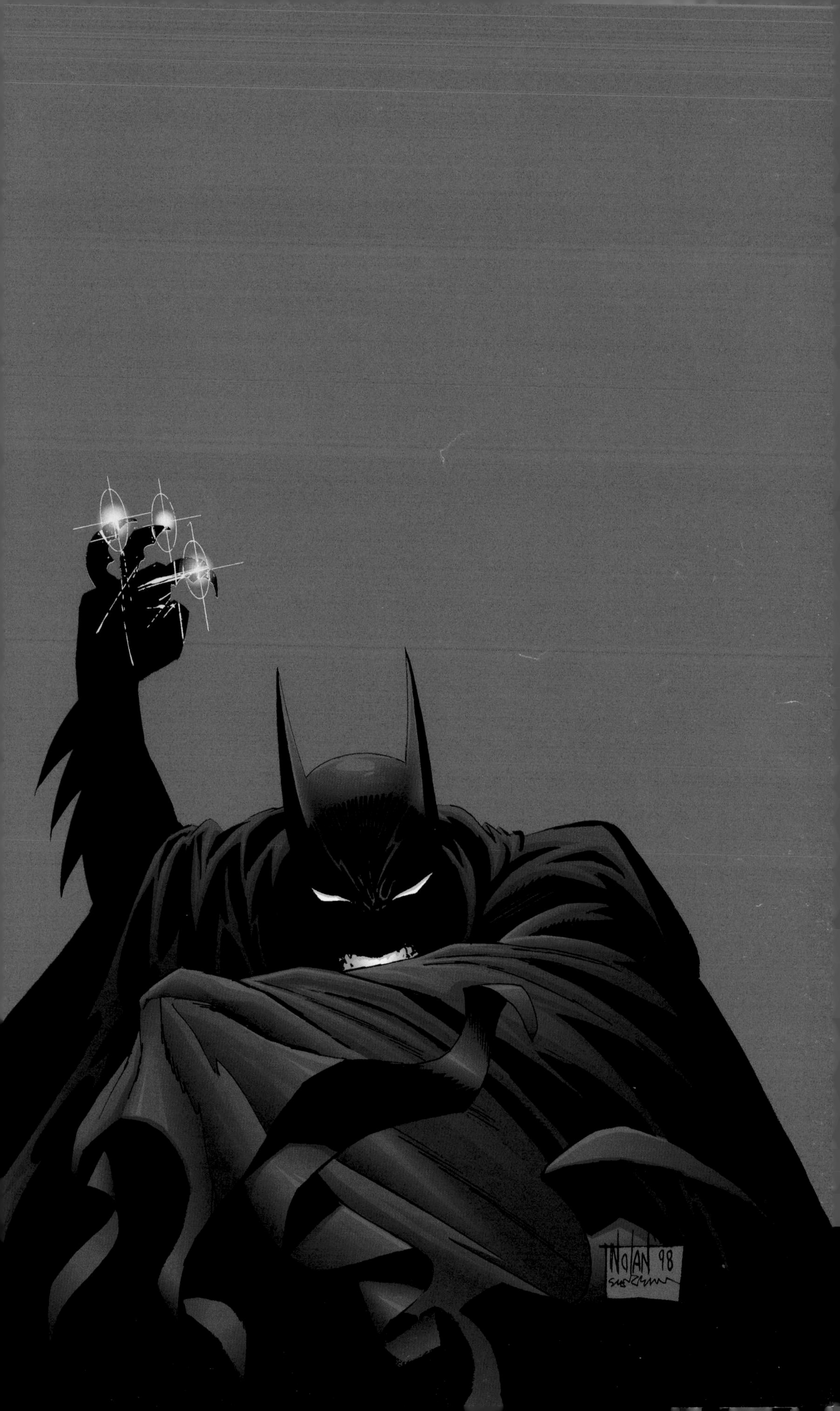
NOLAN 98

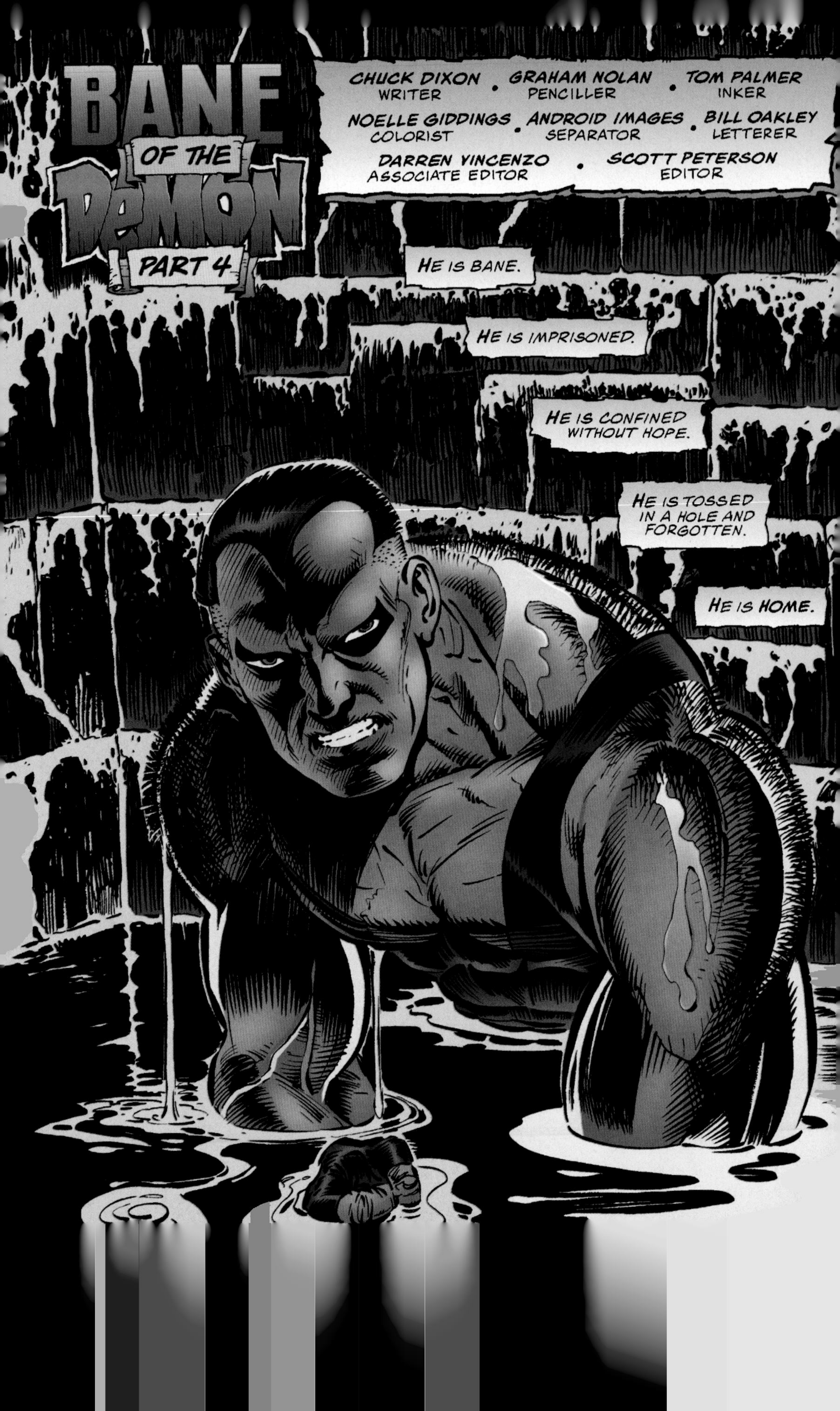
BANE OF THE DEMON
PART 4
CHUCK DIXON WRITER • GRAHAM NOLAN PENCILLER • TOM PALMER INKER
NOELLE GIDDINGS COLORIST • ANDROID IMAGES SEPARATOR • BILL OAKLEY LETTERER
DARREN VINCENZO ASSOCIATE EDITOR • SCOTT PETERSON EDITOR
HE IS BANE.
HE IS IMPRISONED.
HE IS CONFINED WITHOUT HOPE.
HE IS TOSSED IN A HOLE AND FORGOTTEN.
HE IS HOME.

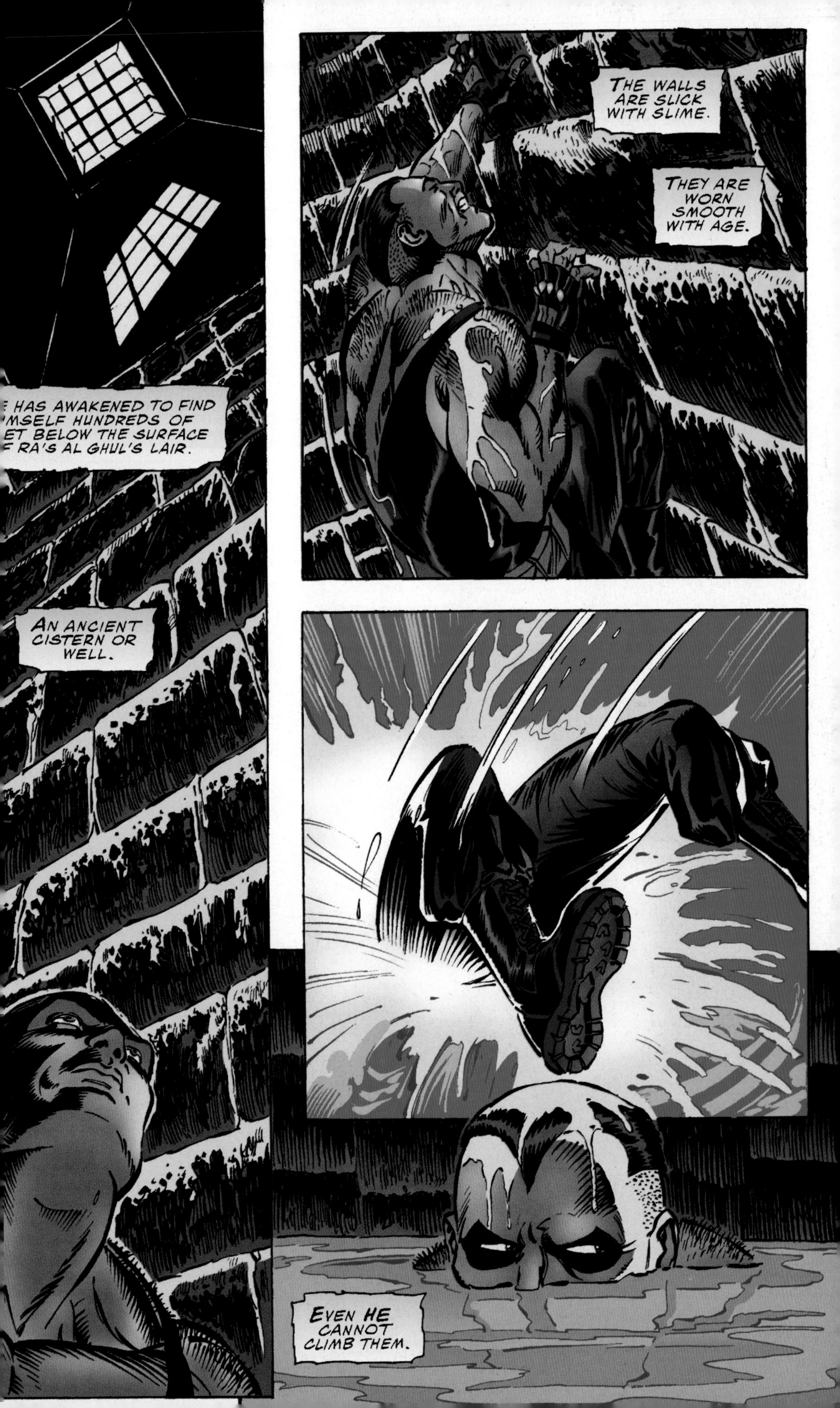
E HAS AWAKENED TO FIND
MSELF HUNDREDS OF
ET BELOW THE SURFACE
F RA'S AL GHUL'S LAIR.
AN ANCIENT CISTERN OR WELL.
THE WALLS ARE SLICK WITH SLIME.
THEY ARE WORN SMOOTH WITH AGE.
EVEN HE CANNOT CLIMB THEM.

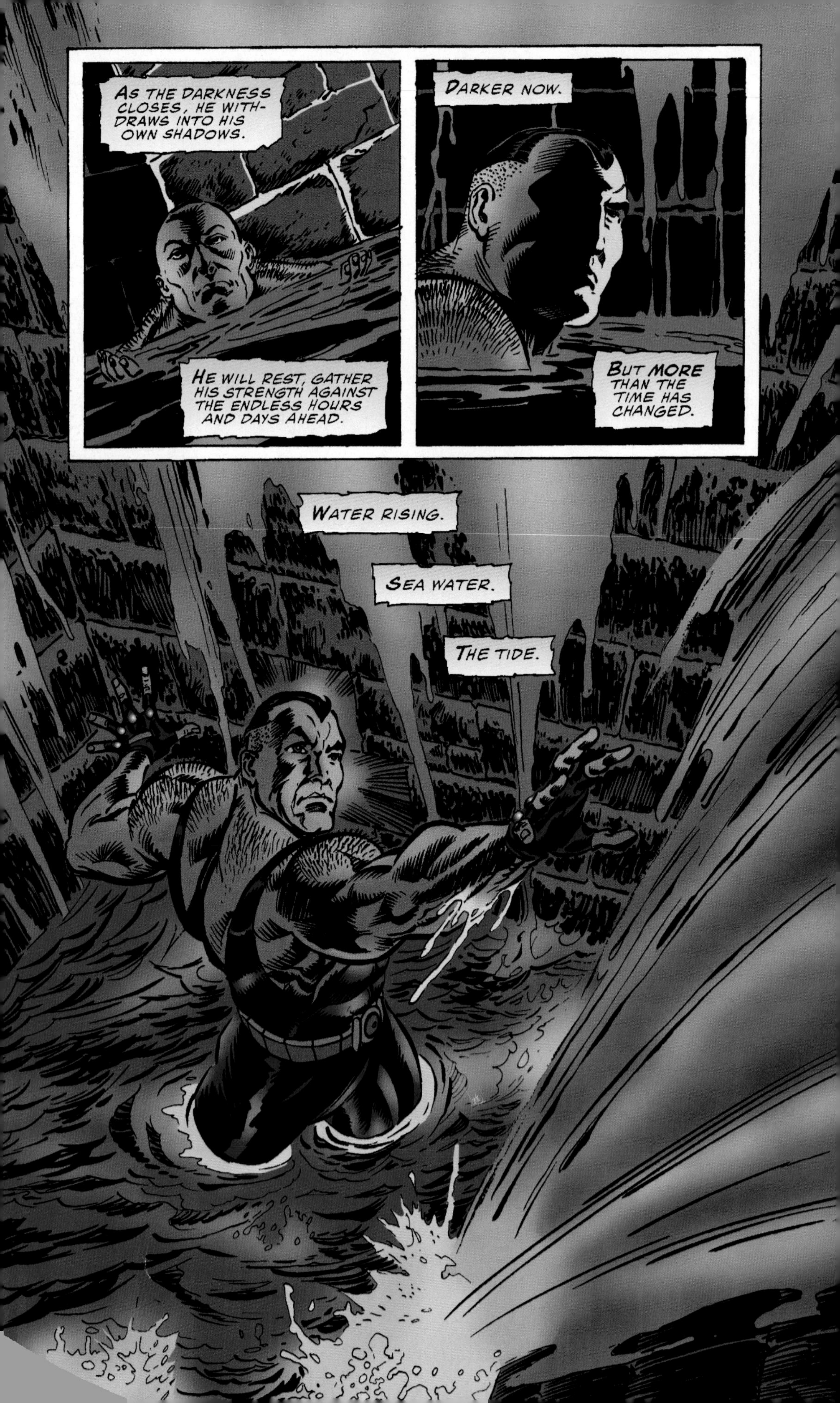
AS THE DARKNESS CLOSES, HE WITH-DRAWS INTO HIS OWN SHADOWS.
HE WILL REST, GATHER HIS STRENGTH AGAINST THE ENDLESS HOURS AND DAYS AHEAD.
DARKER NOW.
BUT MORE THAN THE TIME HAS CHANGED.
WATER RISING.
SEA WATER.
THE TIDE.

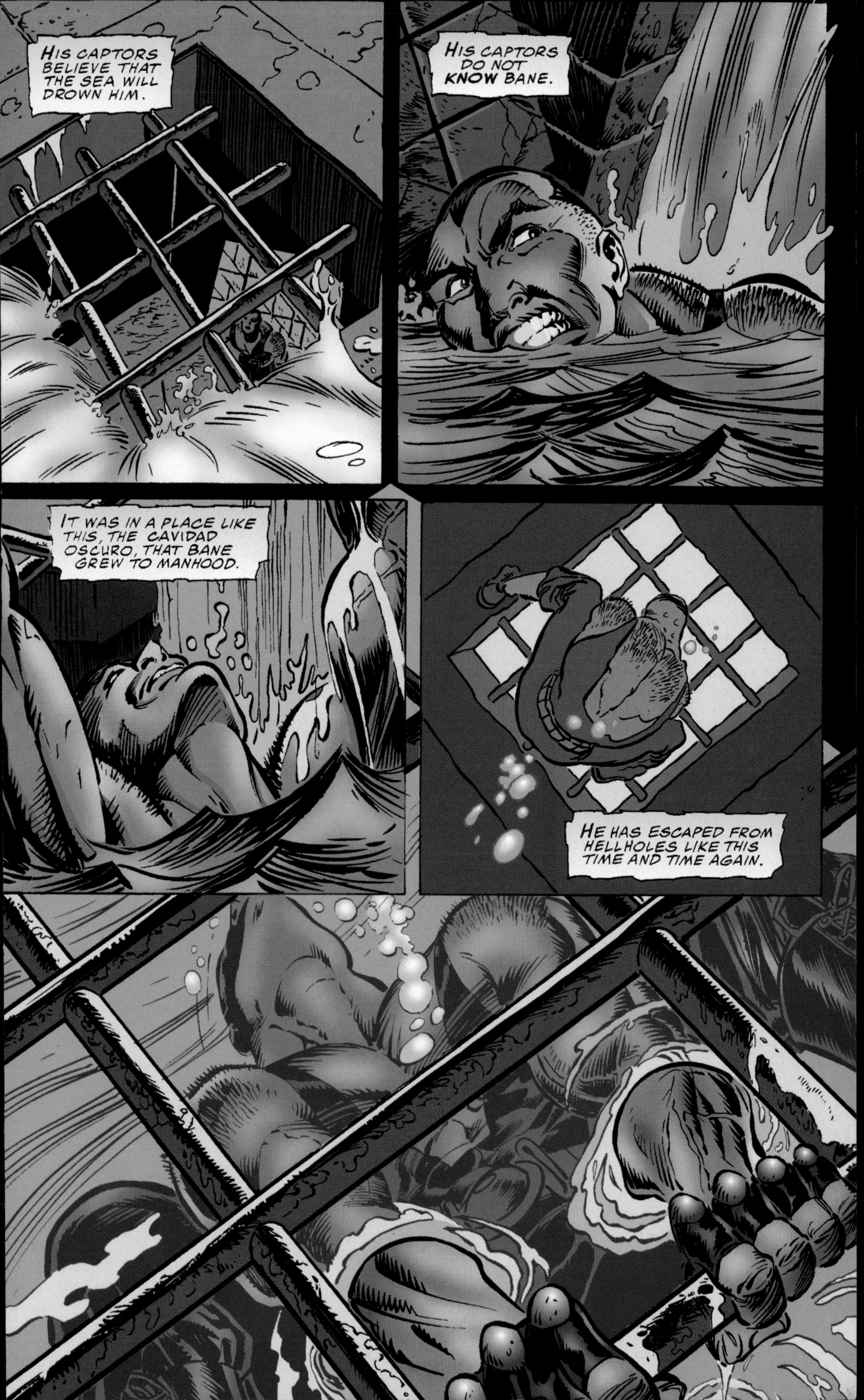
HIS CAPTORS BELIEVE THAT THE SEA WILL DROWN HIM.
HIS CAPTORS DO NOT KNOW BANE.
IT WAS IN A PLACE LIKE THIS, THE CAVIDAD OSCURO, THAT BANE GREW TO MANHOOD.
HE HAS ESCAPED FROM HELLHOLES LIKE THIS TIME AND TIME AGAIN.

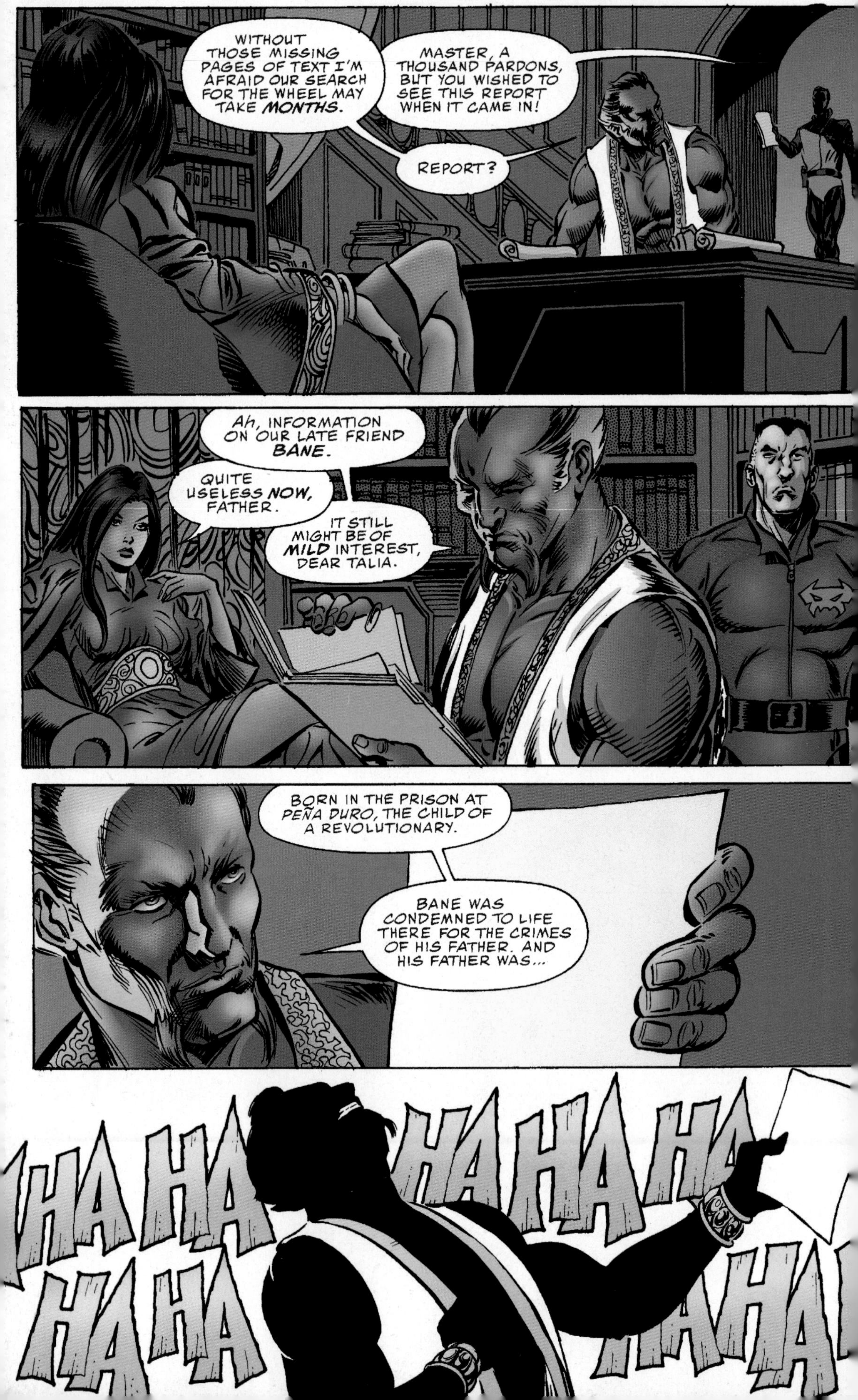
WITHOUT THOSE MISSING PAGES OF TEXT I'M AFRAID OUR SEARCH FOR THE WHEEL MAY TAKE *MONTHS*.
MASTER, A THOUSAND PARDONS, BUT YOU WISHED TO SEE THIS REPORT WHEN IT CAME IN!
REPORT?
Ah, INFORMATION ON OUR LATE FRIEND **BANE**.
QUITE USELESS *NOW*, FATHER.
IT STILL MIGHT BE OF *MILD* INTEREST, DEAR TALIA.
BORN IN THE PRISON AT *PEÑA DURO*, THE CHILD OF A REVOLUTIONARY.
BANE WAS CONDEMNED TO LIFE THERE FOR THE CRIMES OF HIS FATHER. AND HIS FATHER WAS...
HA HA HA HA HA HA HA
HA HA HA HA HA

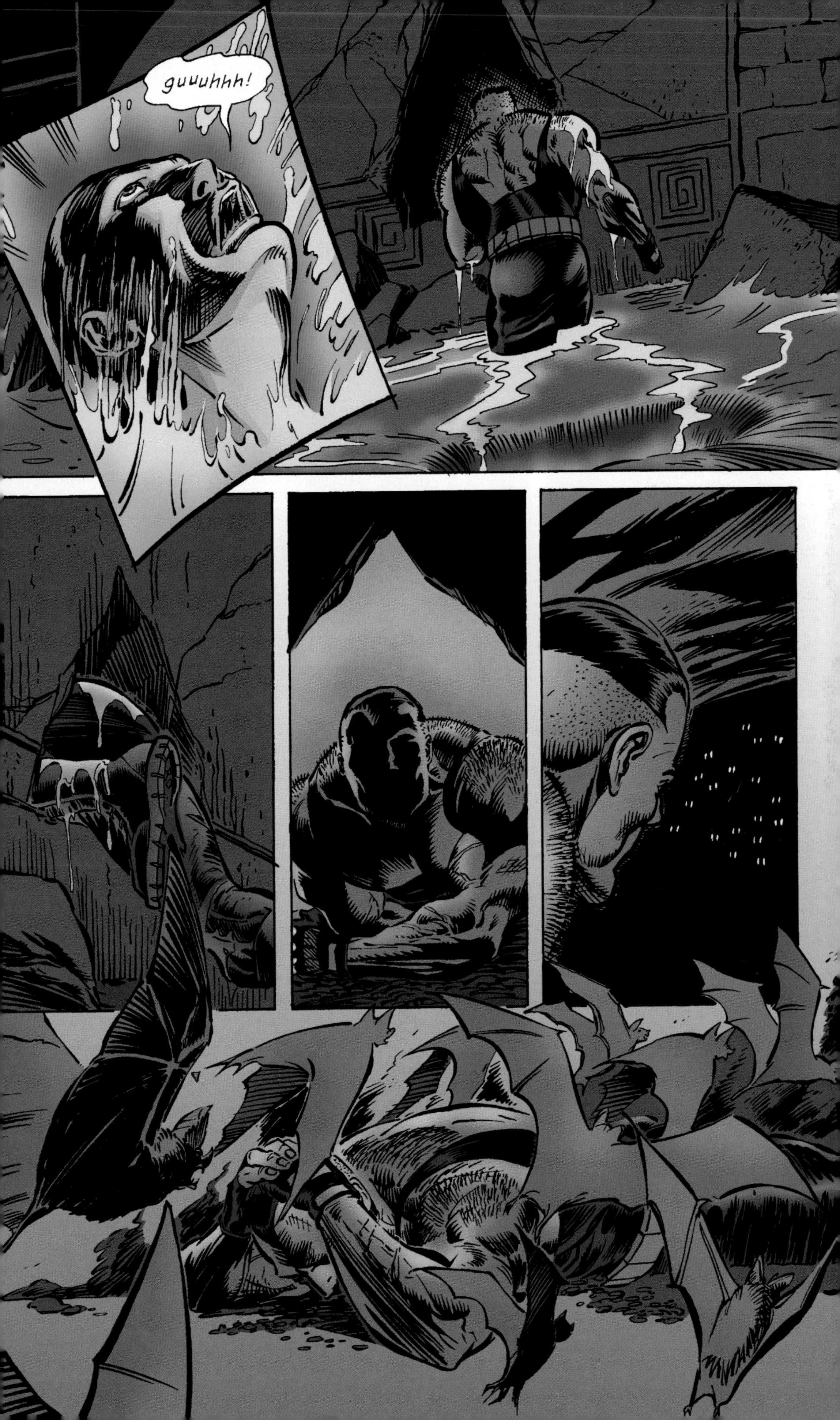
guuuhhh!

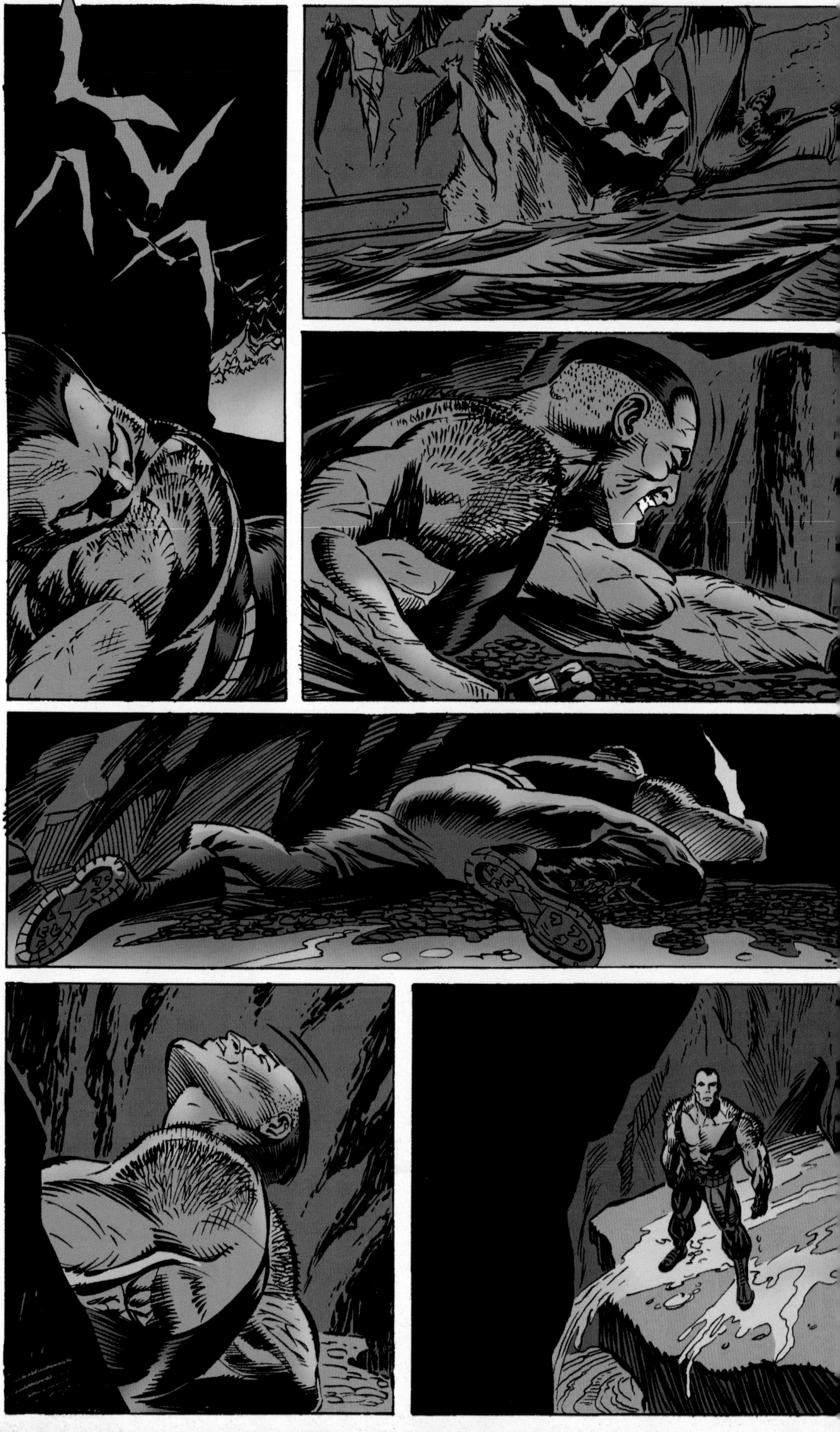

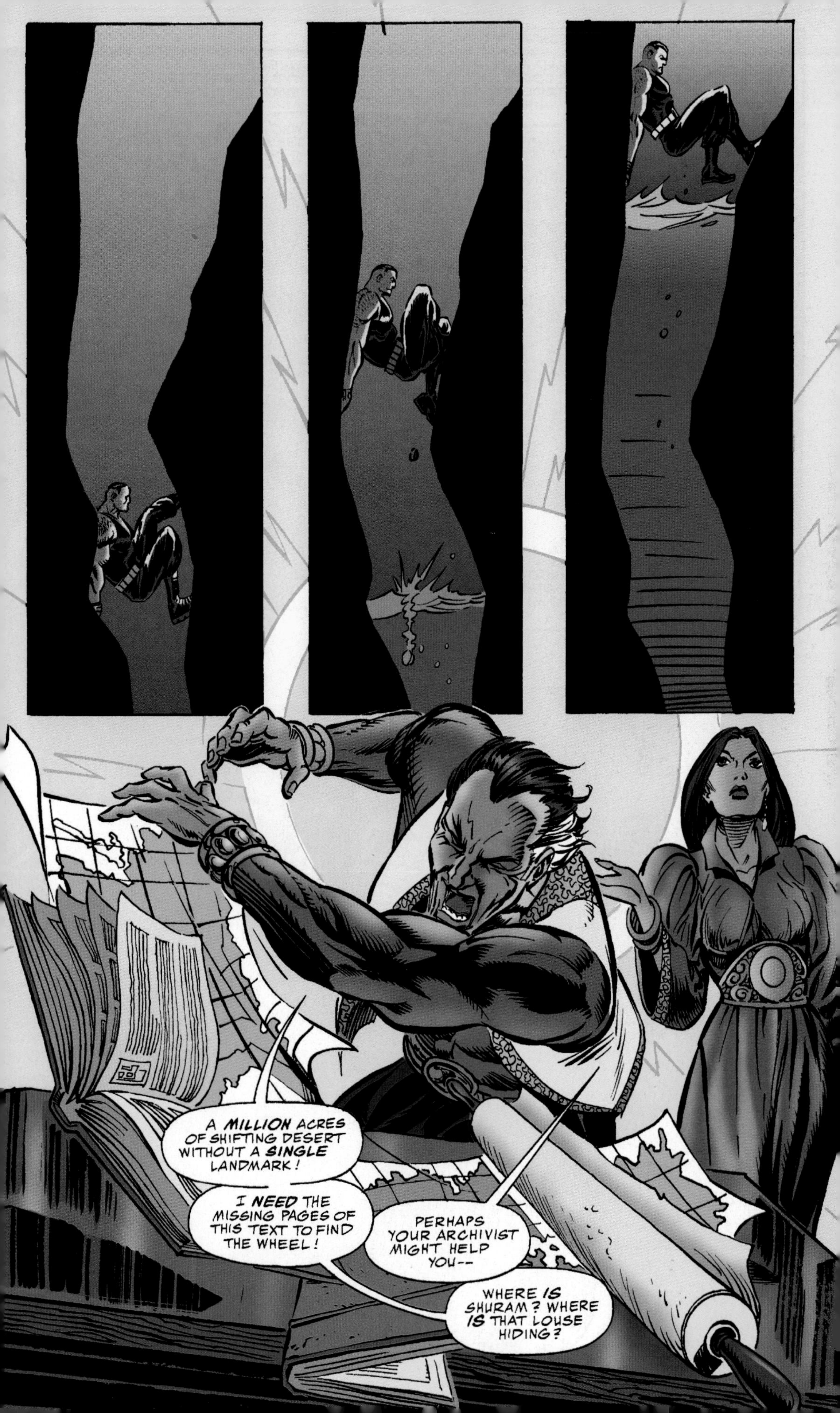
A MILLION ACRES OF SHIFTING DESERT WITHOUT A SINGLE LANDMARK!
I NEED THE MISSING PAGES OF THIS TEXT TO FIND THE WHEEL!
PERHAPS YOUR ARCHIVIST MIGHT HELP YOU--
WHERE IS SHURAM? WHERE IS THAT LOUSE HIDING?

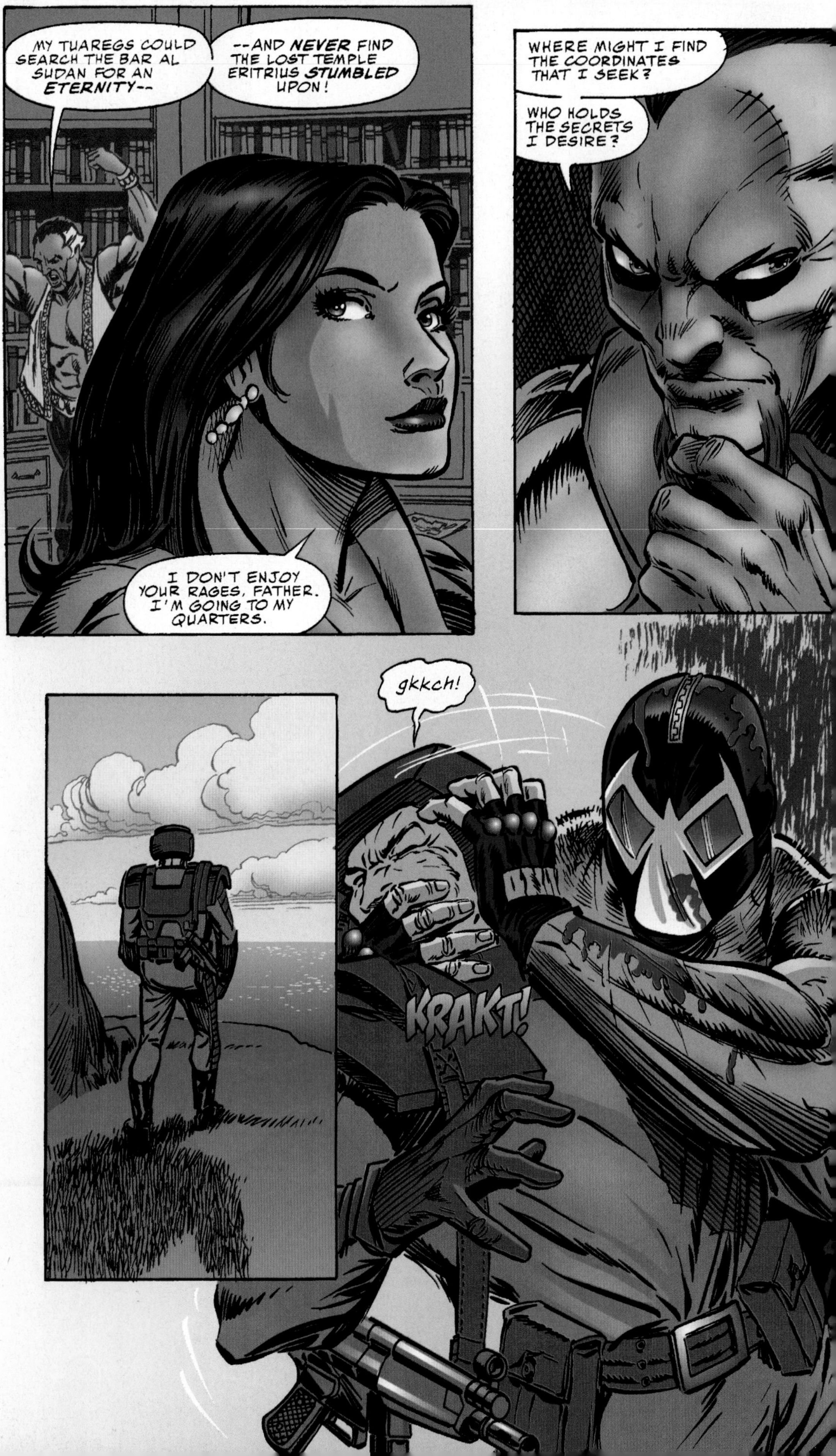
MY TUAREGS COULD SEARCH THE BAR AL SUDAN FOR AN ETERNITY--
--AND NEVER FIND THE LOST TEMPLE ERITRIUS STUMBLED UPON!
I DON'T ENJOY YOUR RAGES, FATHER. I'M GOING TO MY QUARTERS.
WHERE MIGHT I FIND THE COORDINATES THAT I SEEK?
WHO HOLDS THE SECRETS I DESIRE?
gkkch!
KRAKT!

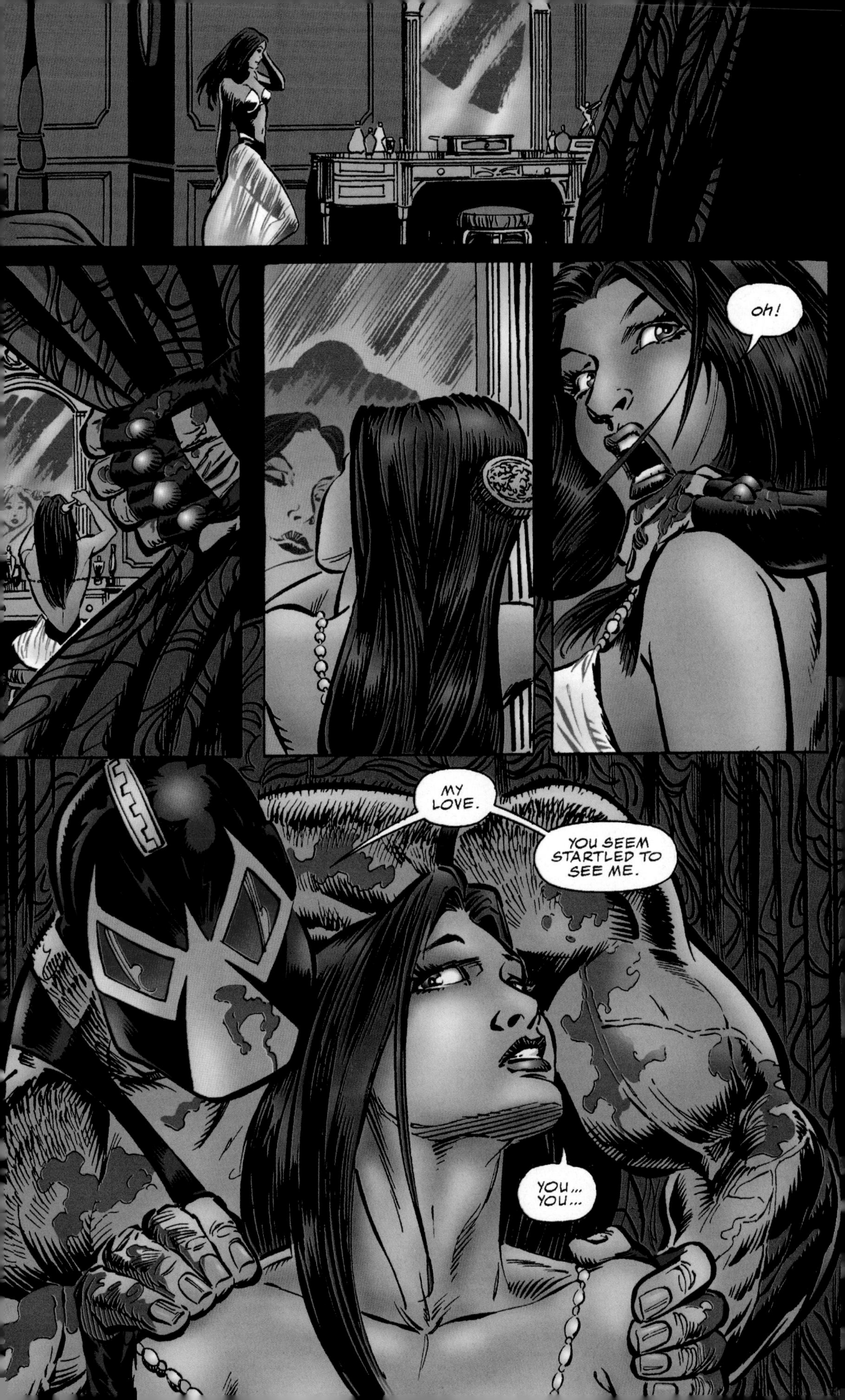
oh!
MY LOVE.
YOU SEEM STARTLED TO SEE ME.
YOU... YOU...

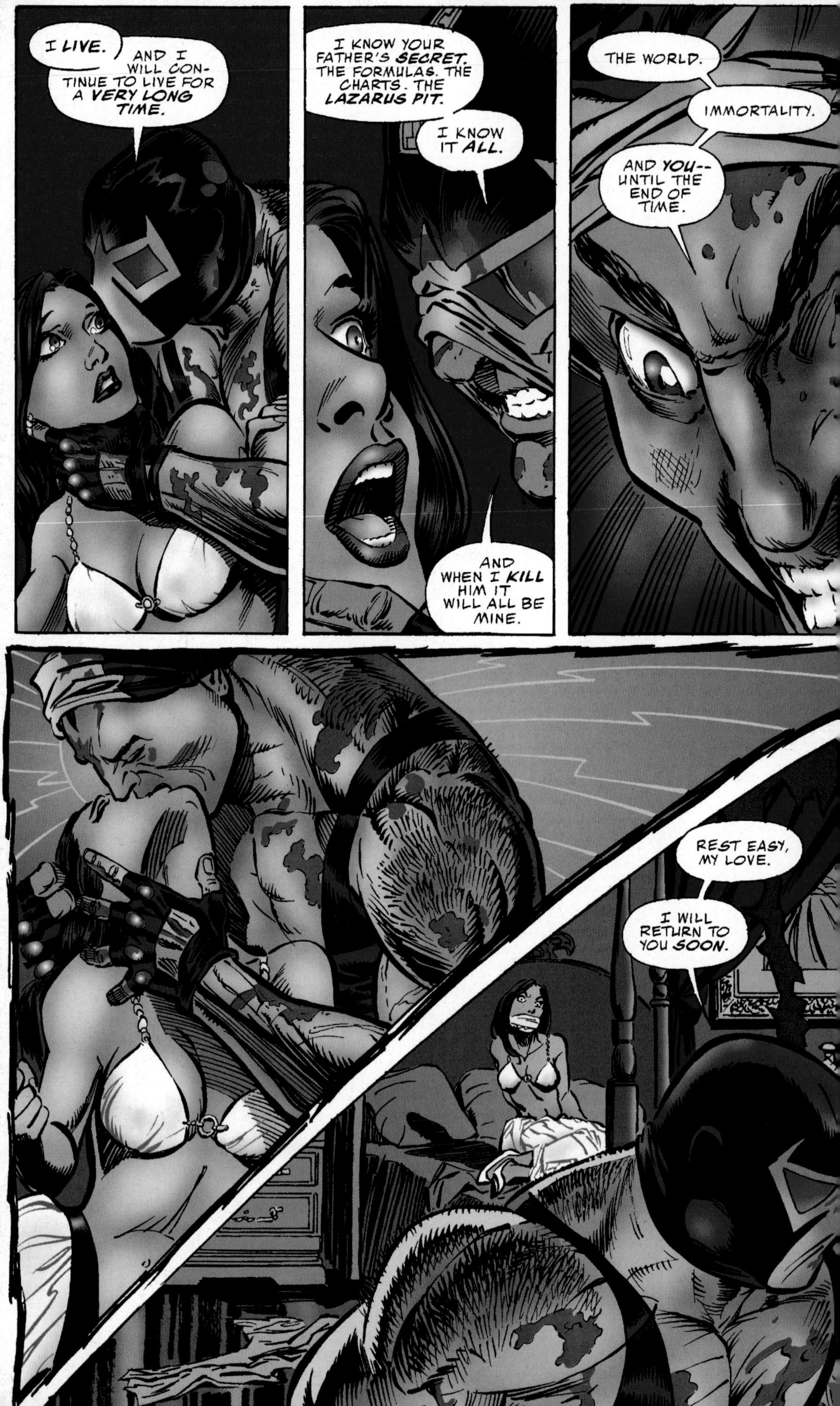
I LIVE.
AND I WILL CONTINUE TO LIVE FOR A VERY LONG TIME.
I KNOW YOUR FATHER'S SECRET. THE FORMULAS. THE CHARTS. THE LAZARUS PIT.
I KNOW IT ALL.
AND WHEN I KILL HIM IT WILL ALL BE MINE.
THE WORLD.
IMMORTALITY.
AND YOU-- UNTIL THE END OF TIME.
REST EASY, MY LOVE.
I WILL RETURN TO YOU SOON.

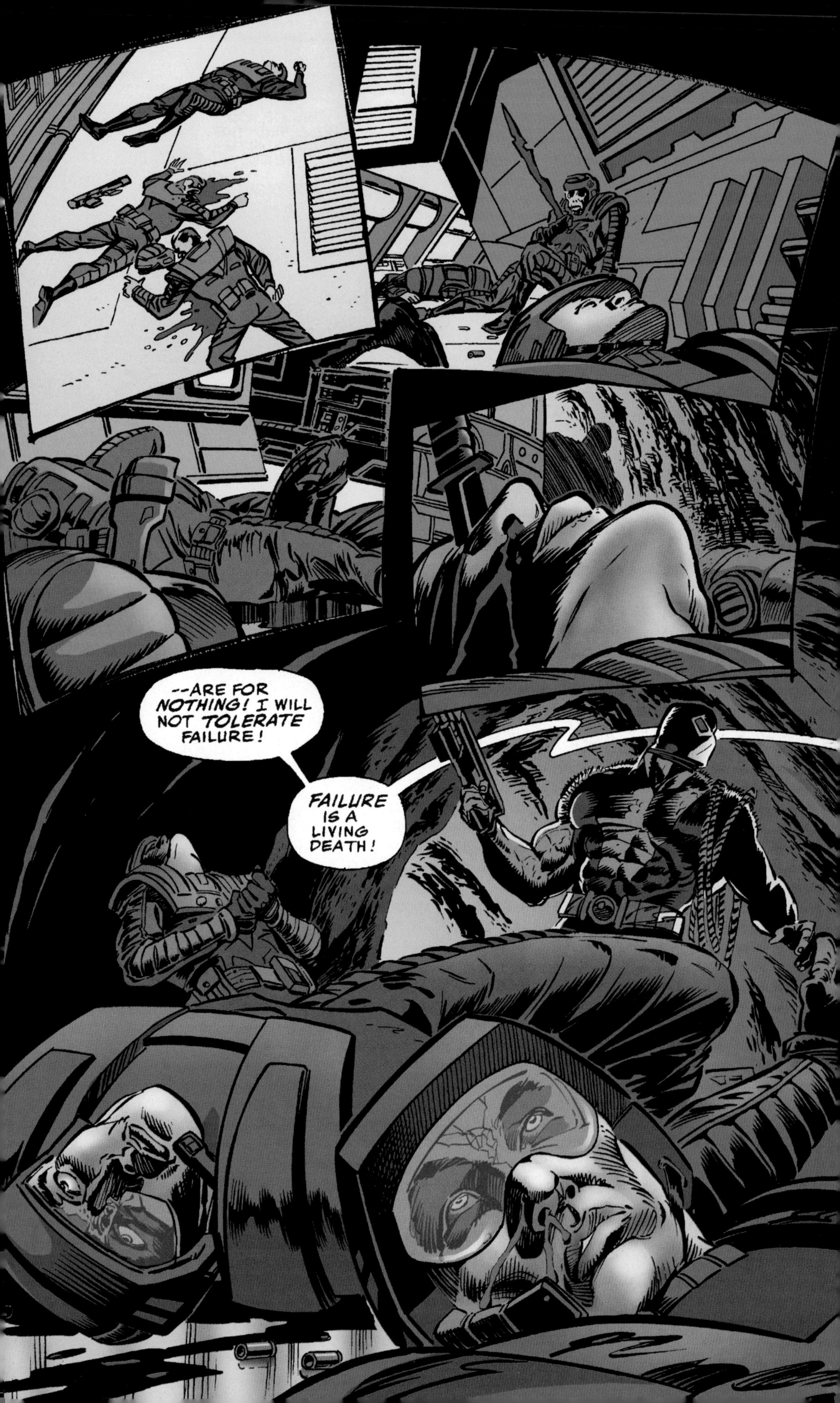
--ARE FOR *NOTHING!* I WILL NOT *TOLERATE* FAILURE!
FAILURE IS A LIVING DEATH!

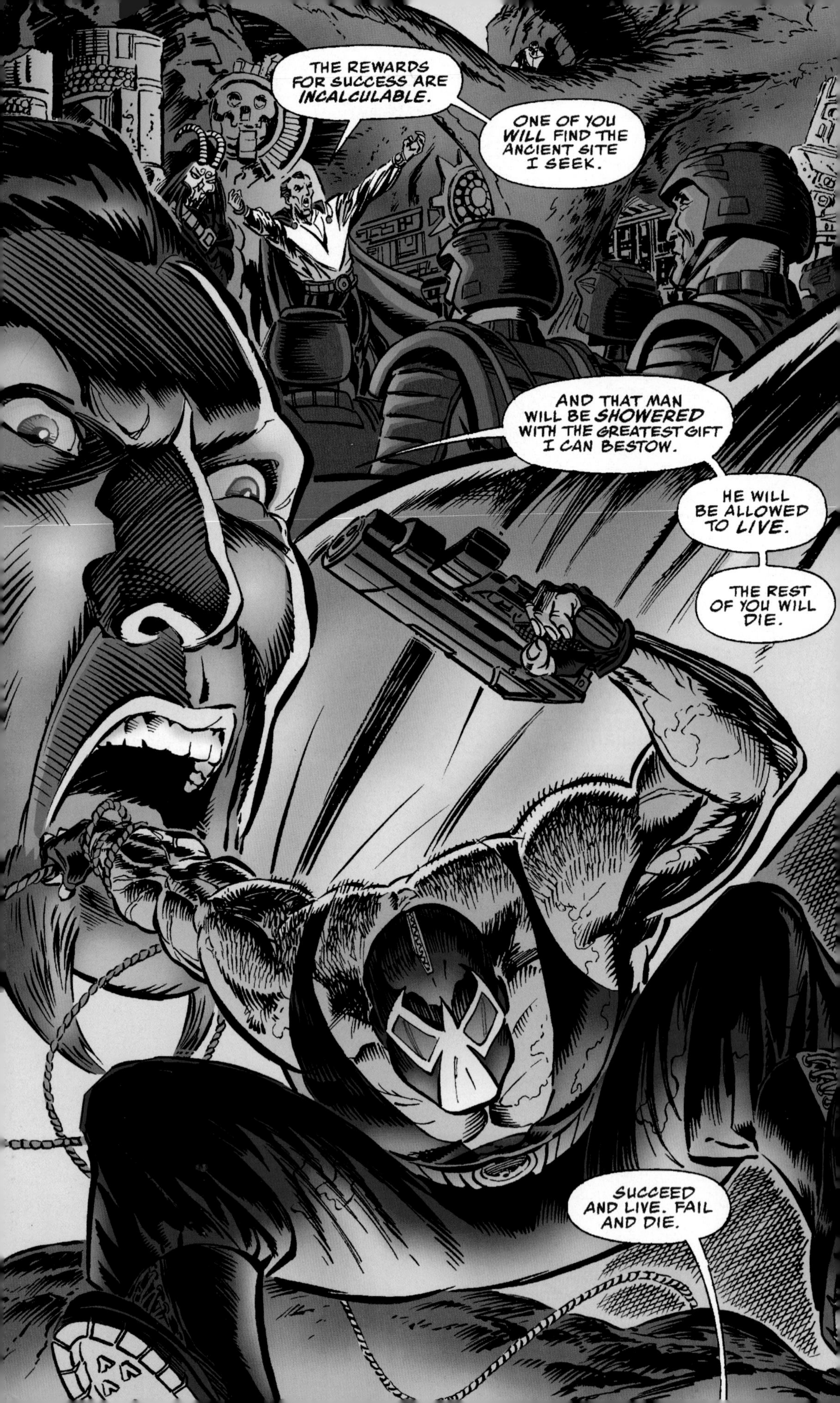
THE REWARDS FOR SUCCESS ARE INCALCULABLE.
ONE OF YOU WILL FIND THE ANCIENT SITE I SEEK.
AND THAT MAN WILL BE SHOWERED WITH THE GREATEST GIFT I CAN BESTOW.
HE WILL BE ALLOWED TO LIVE.
THE REST OF YOU WILL DIE.
SUCCEED AND LIVE. FAIL AND DIE.

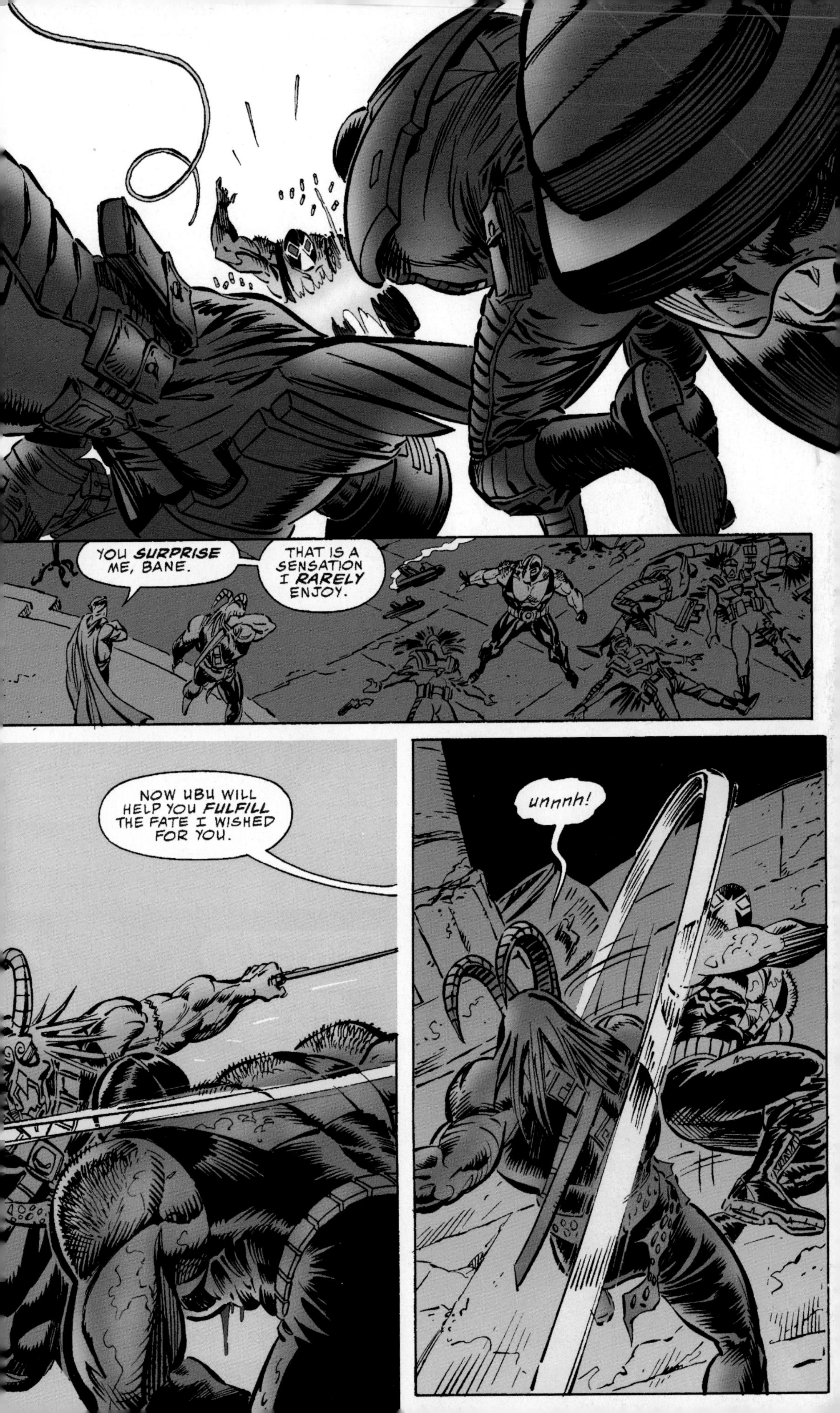
YOU SURPRISE ME, BANE.
THAT IS A SENSATION I RARELY ENJOY.
NOW UBU WILL HELP YOU FULFILL THE FATE I WISHED FOR YOU.
unnnh!

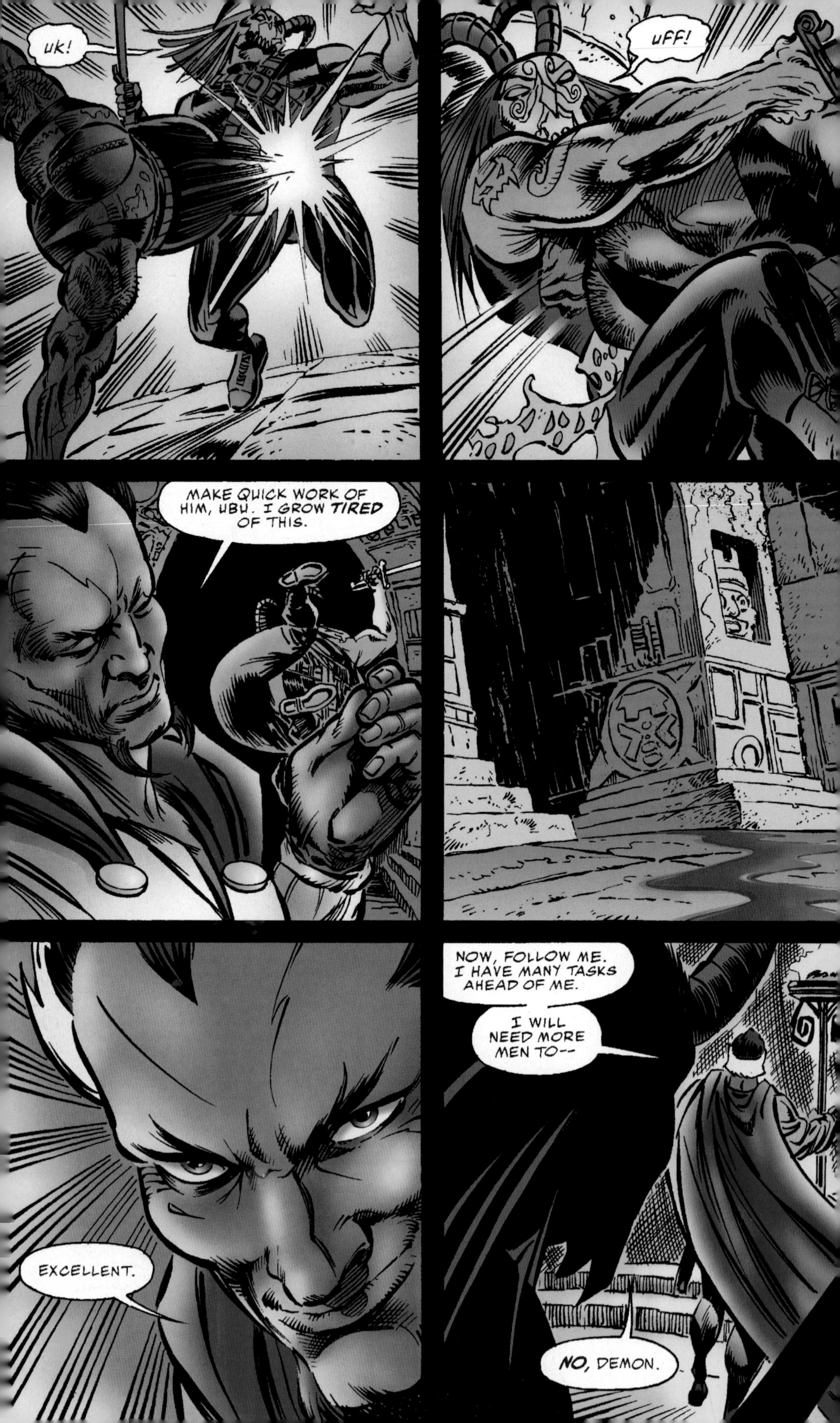
UK!
UFF!
MAKE QUICK WORK OF HIM, UBU. I GROW TIRED OF THIS.
EXCELLENT.
NOW, FOLLOW ME. I HAVE MANY TASKS AHEAD OF ME.
I WILL NEED MORE MEN TO--
NO, DEMON.

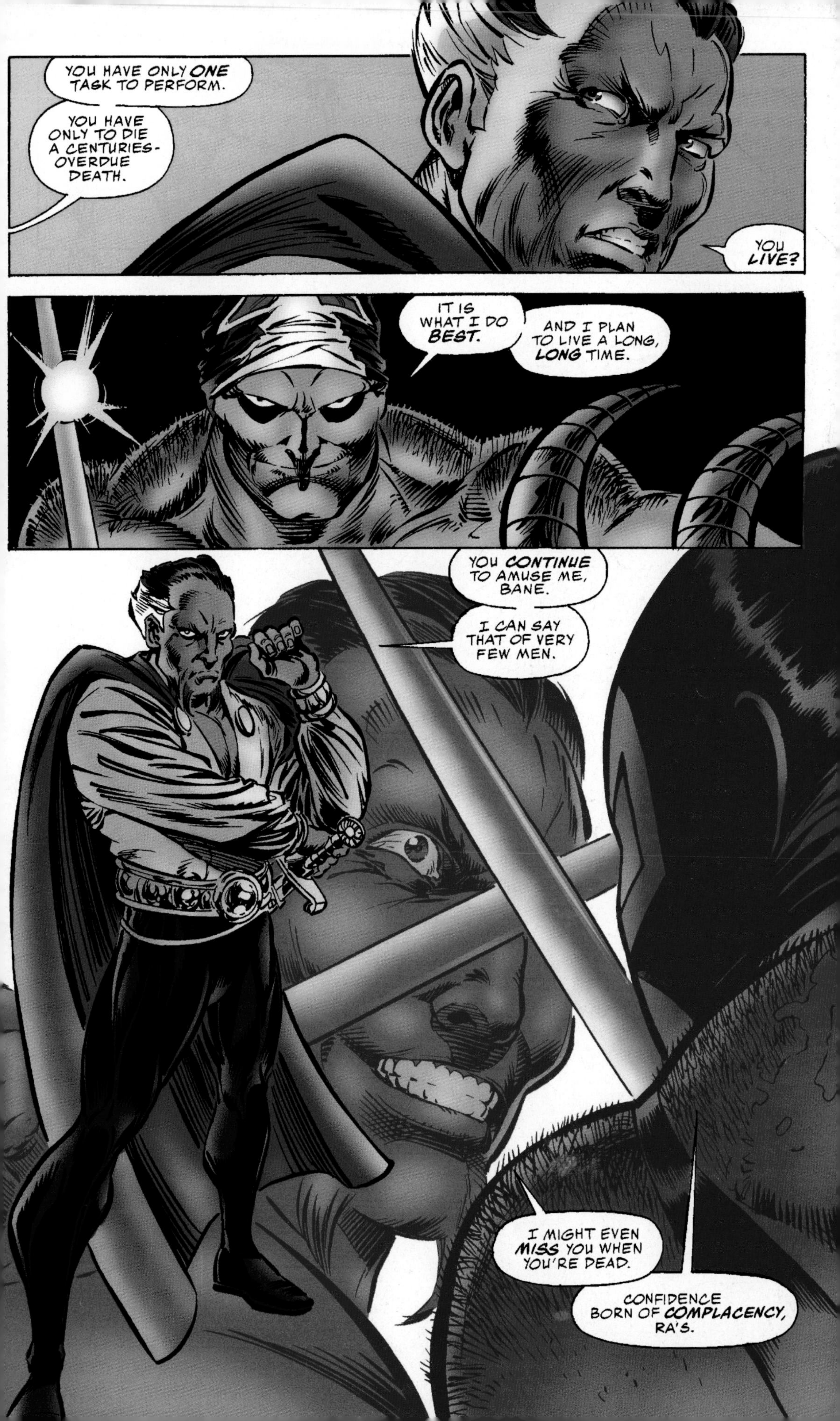
YOU HAVE ONLY ONE TASK TO PERFORM.
YOU HAVE ONLY TO DIE A CENTURIES-OVERDUE DEATH.
YOU LIVE?
IT IS WHAT I DO BEST.
AND I PLAN TO LIVE A LONG, LONG TIME.
YOU CONTINUE TO AMUSE ME, BANE.
I CAN SAY THAT OF VERY FEW MEN.
I MIGHT EVEN MISS YOU WHEN YOU'RE DEAD.
CONFIDENCE BORN OF COMPLACENCY, RA'S.

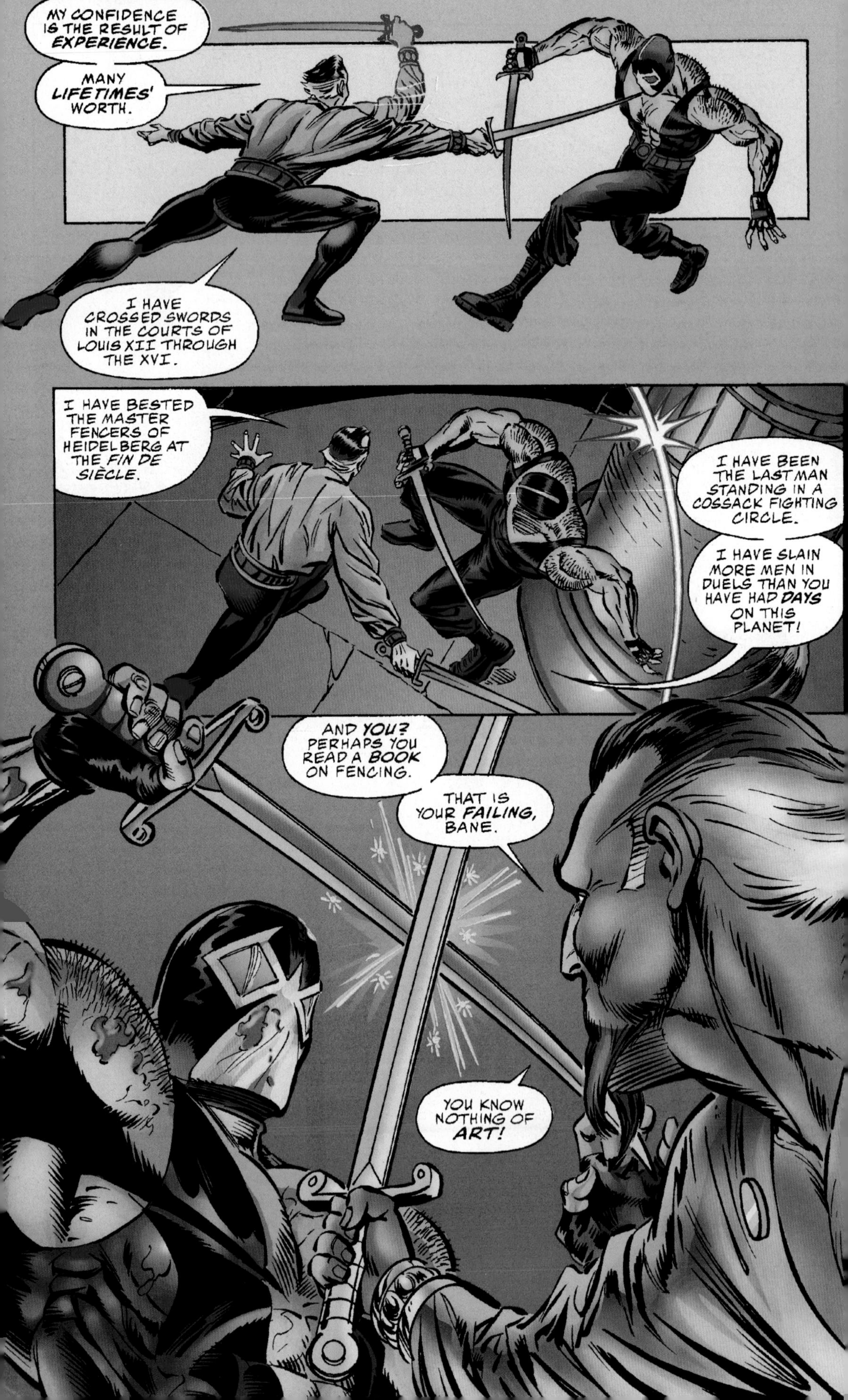
MY CONFIDENCE IS THE RESULT OF EXPERIENCE.
MANY LIFETIMES' WORTH.
I HAVE CROSSED SWORDS IN THE COURTS OF LOUIS XII THROUGH THE XVI.
I HAVE BESTED THE MASTER FENCERS OF HEIDELBERG AT THE FIN DE SIÈCLE.
I HAVE BEEN THE LAST MAN STANDING IN A COSSACK FIGHTING CIRCLE.
I HAVE SLAIN MORE MEN IN DUELS THAN YOU HAVE HAD DAYS ON THIS PLANET!
AND YOU? PERHAPS YOU READ A BOOK ON FENCING.
THAT IS YOUR FAILING, BANE.
YOU KNOW NOTHING OF ART!

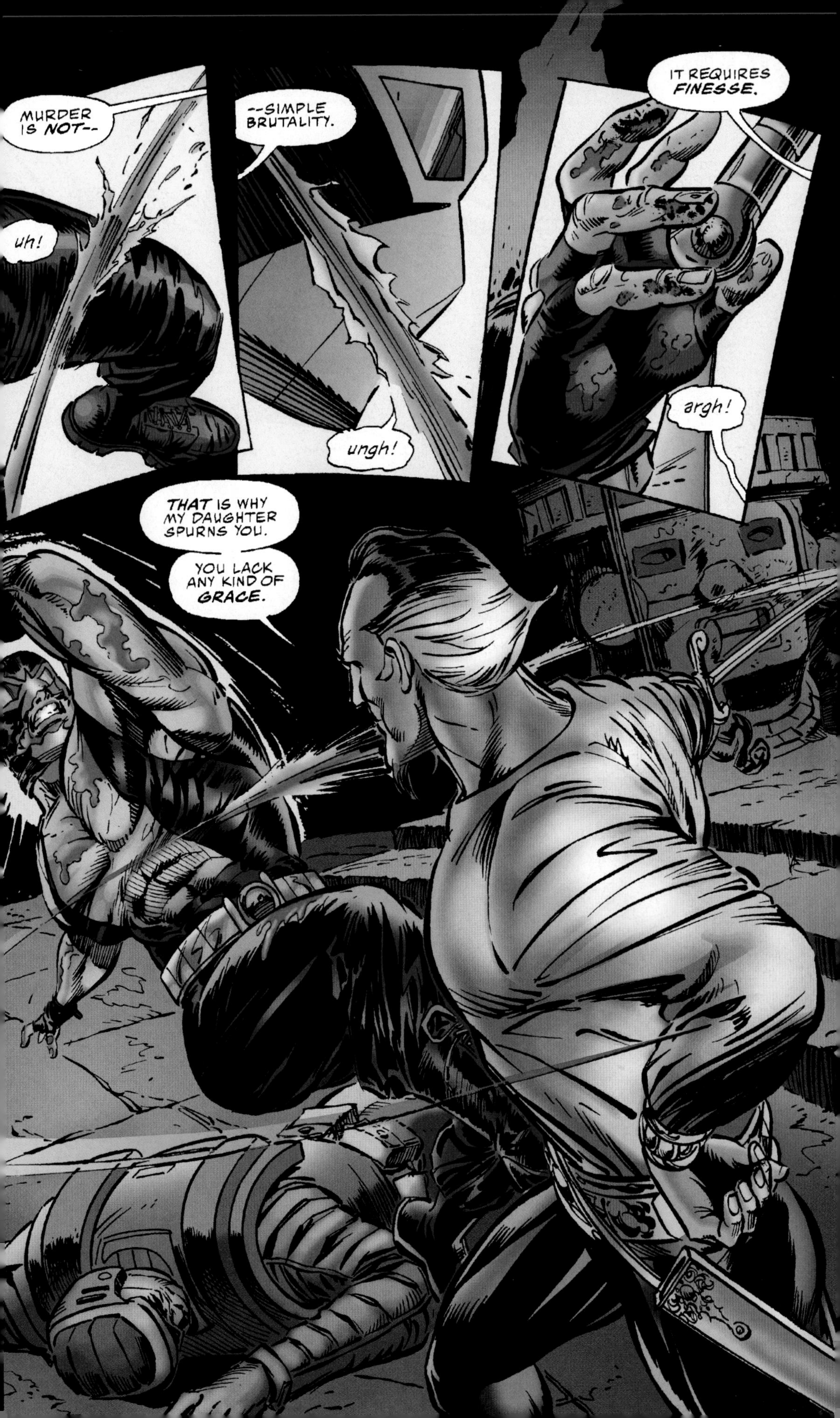
MURDER IS NOT--
uh!
--SIMPLE BRUTALITY.
ungh!
IT REQUIRES FINESSE.
argh!
THAT IS WHY MY DAUGHTER SPURNS YOU.
YOU LACK ANY KIND OF GRACE.

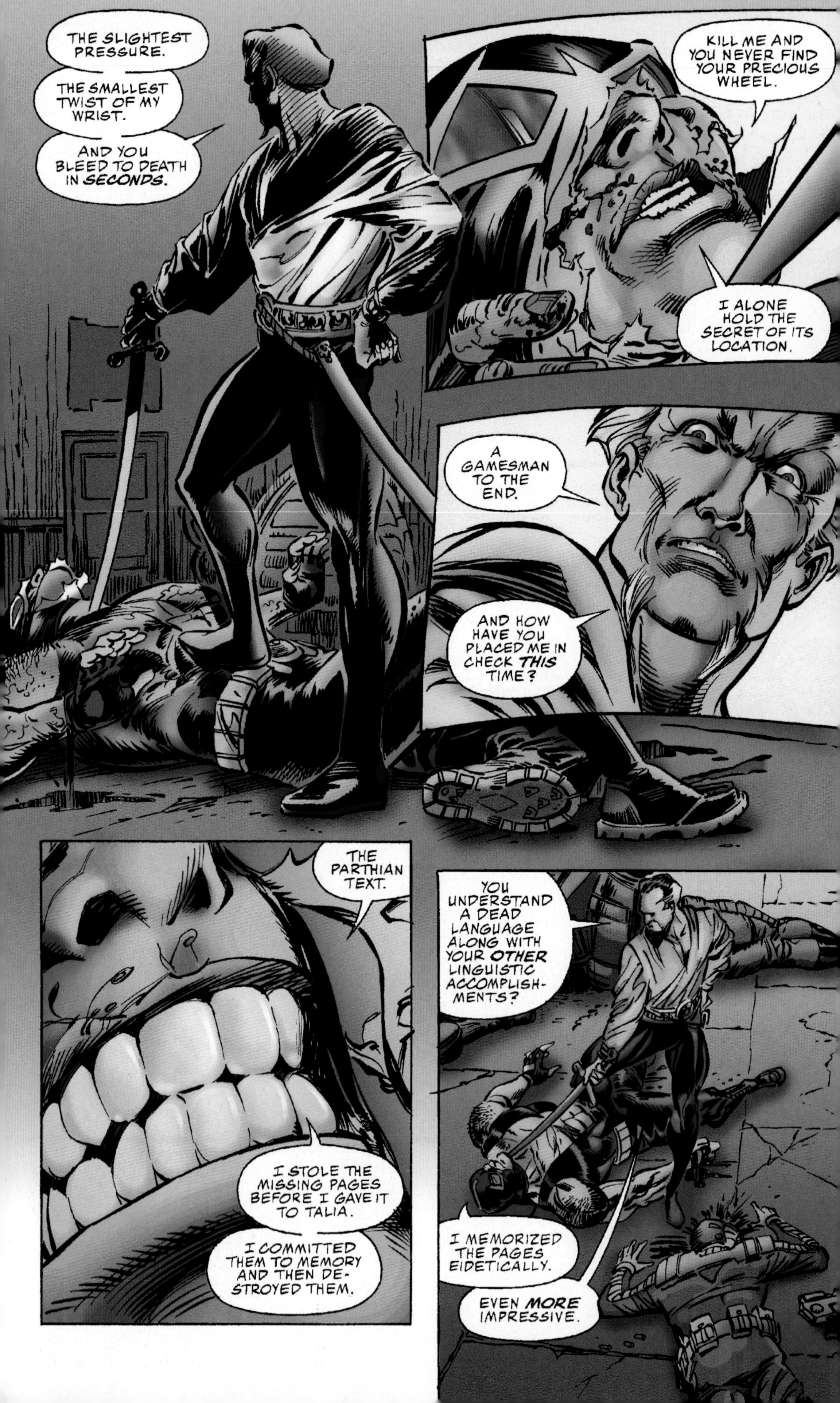
THE SLIGHTEST PRESSURE.
THE SMALLEST TWIST OF MY WRIST.
AND YOU BLEED TO DEATH IN *SECONDS*.
KILL ME AND YOU NEVER FIND YOUR PRECIOUS WHEEL.
I ALONE HOLD THE SECRET OF ITS LOCATION.
A GAMESMAN TO THE END.
AND HOW HAVE YOU PLACED ME IN CHECK *THIS* TIME?
THE PARTHIAN TEXT.
I STOLE THE MISSING PAGES BEFORE I GAVE IT TO TALIA.
I COMMITTED THEM TO MEMORY AND THEN DE-STROYED THEM.
YOU UNDERSTAND A DEAD LANGUAGE ALONG WITH YOUR *OTHER* LINGUISTIC ACCOMPLISH-MENTS?
I MEMORIZED THE PAGES EIDETICALLY.
EVEN *MORE* IMPRESSIVE.

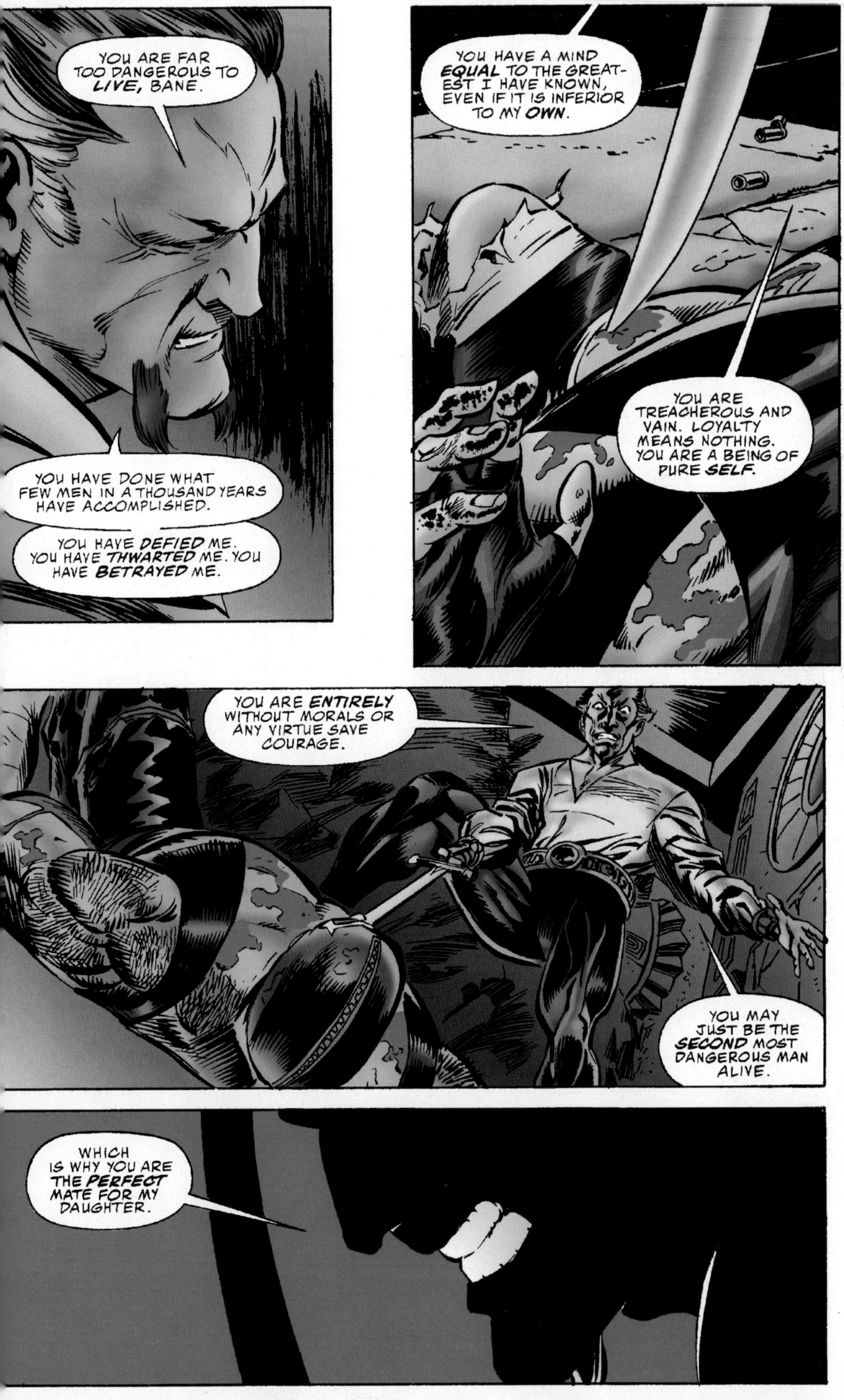
YOU ARE FAR TOO DANGEROUS TO LIVE, BANE.
YOU HAVE DONE WHAT FEW MEN IN A THOUSAND YEARS HAVE ACCOMPLISHED.
YOU HAVE DEFIED ME. YOU HAVE THWARTED ME. YOU HAVE BETRAYED ME.
YOU HAVE A MIND EQUAL TO THE GREATEST I HAVE KNOWN, EVEN IF IT IS INFERIOR TO MY OWN.
YOU ARE TREACHEROUS AND VAIN. LOYALTY MEANS NOTHING. YOU ARE A BEING OF PURE SELF.
YOU ARE ENTIRELY WITHOUT MORALS OR ANY VIRTUE SAVE COURAGE.
YOU MAY JUST BE THE SECOND MOST DANGEROUS MAN ALIVE.
WHICH IS WHY YOU ARE THE PERFECT MATE FOR MY DAUGHTER.

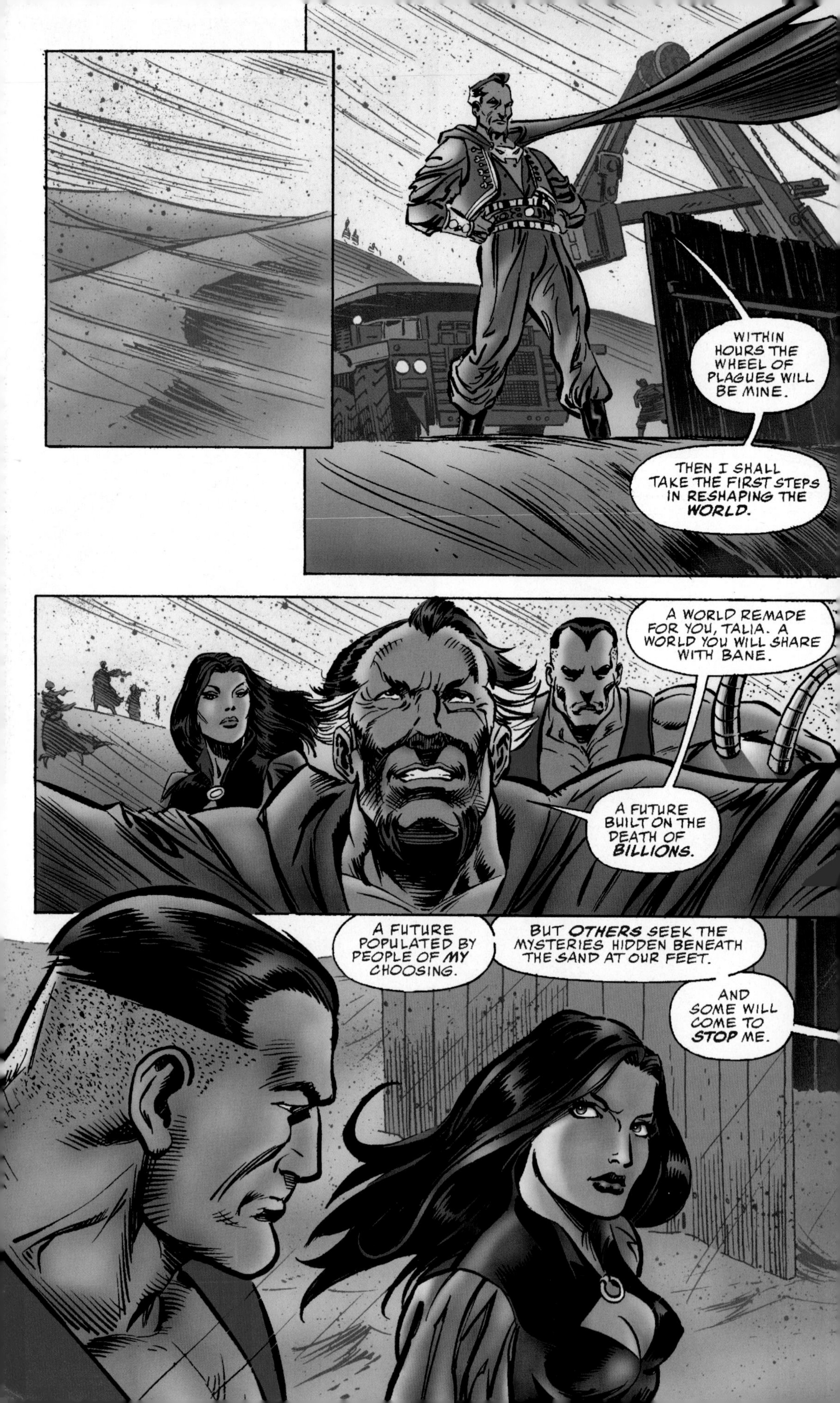
WITHIN HOURS THE WHEEL OF PLAGUES WILL BE MINE.
THEN I SHALL TAKE THE FIRST STEPS IN RESHAPING THE WORLD.
A WORLD REMADE FOR YOU, TALIA. A WORLD YOU WILL SHARE WITH BANE.
A FUTURE BUILT ON THE DEATH OF BILLIONS.
A FUTURE POPULATED BY PEOPLE OF MY CHOOSING.
BUT OTHERS SEEK THE MYSTERIES HIDDEN BENEATH THE SAND AT OUR FEET.
AND SOME WILL COME TO STOP ME.

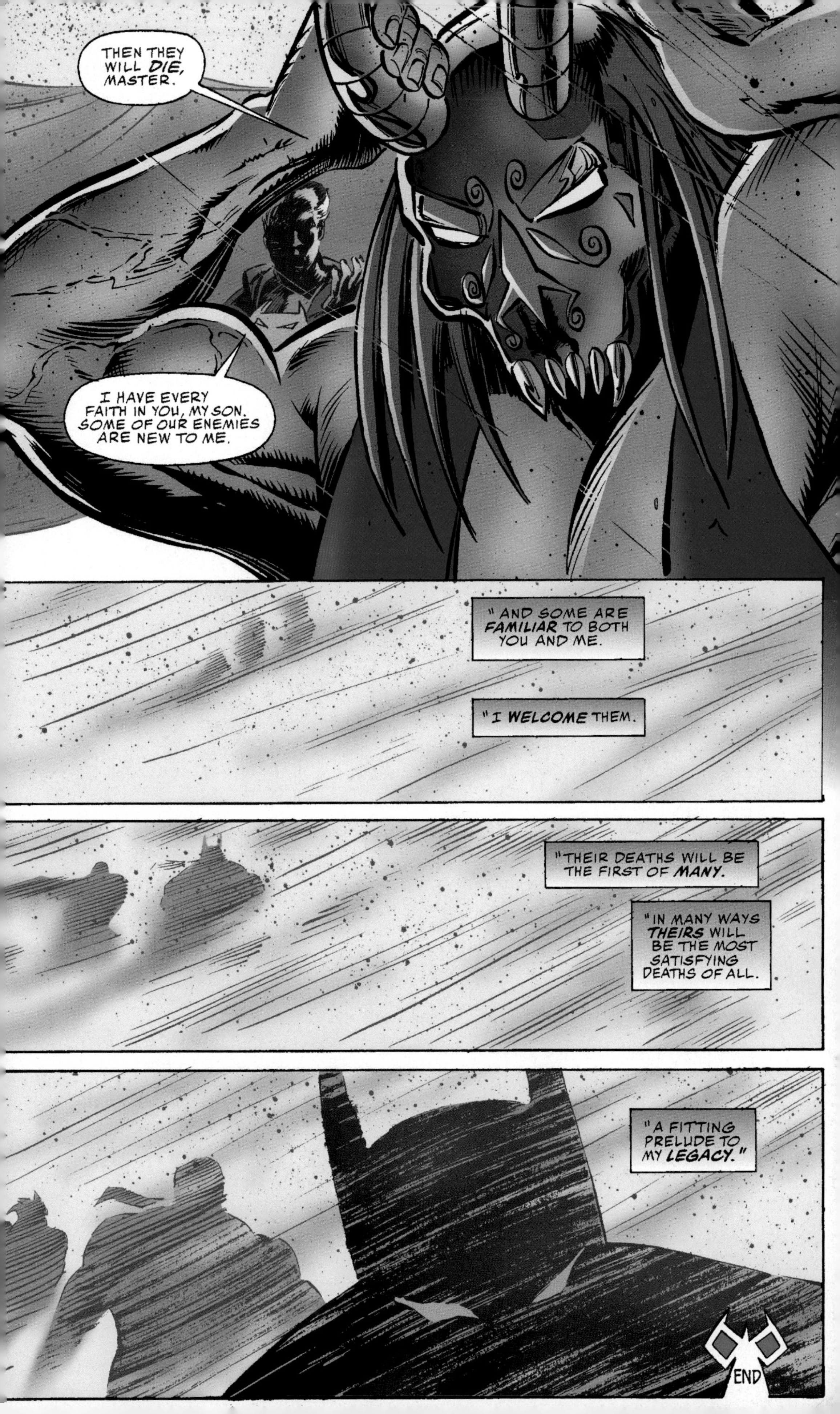
THEN THEY WILL DIE, MASTER.
I HAVE EVERY FAITH IN YOU, MY SON. SOME OF OUR ENEMIES ARE NEW TO ME.
"AND SOME ARE FAMILIAR TO BOTH YOU AND ME.
"I WELCOME THEM.
"THEIR DEATHS WILL BE THE FIRST OF MANY.
"IN MANY WAYS THEIRS WILL BE THE MOST SATISFYING DEATHS OF ALL.
"A FITTING PRELUDE TO MY LEGACY."
END

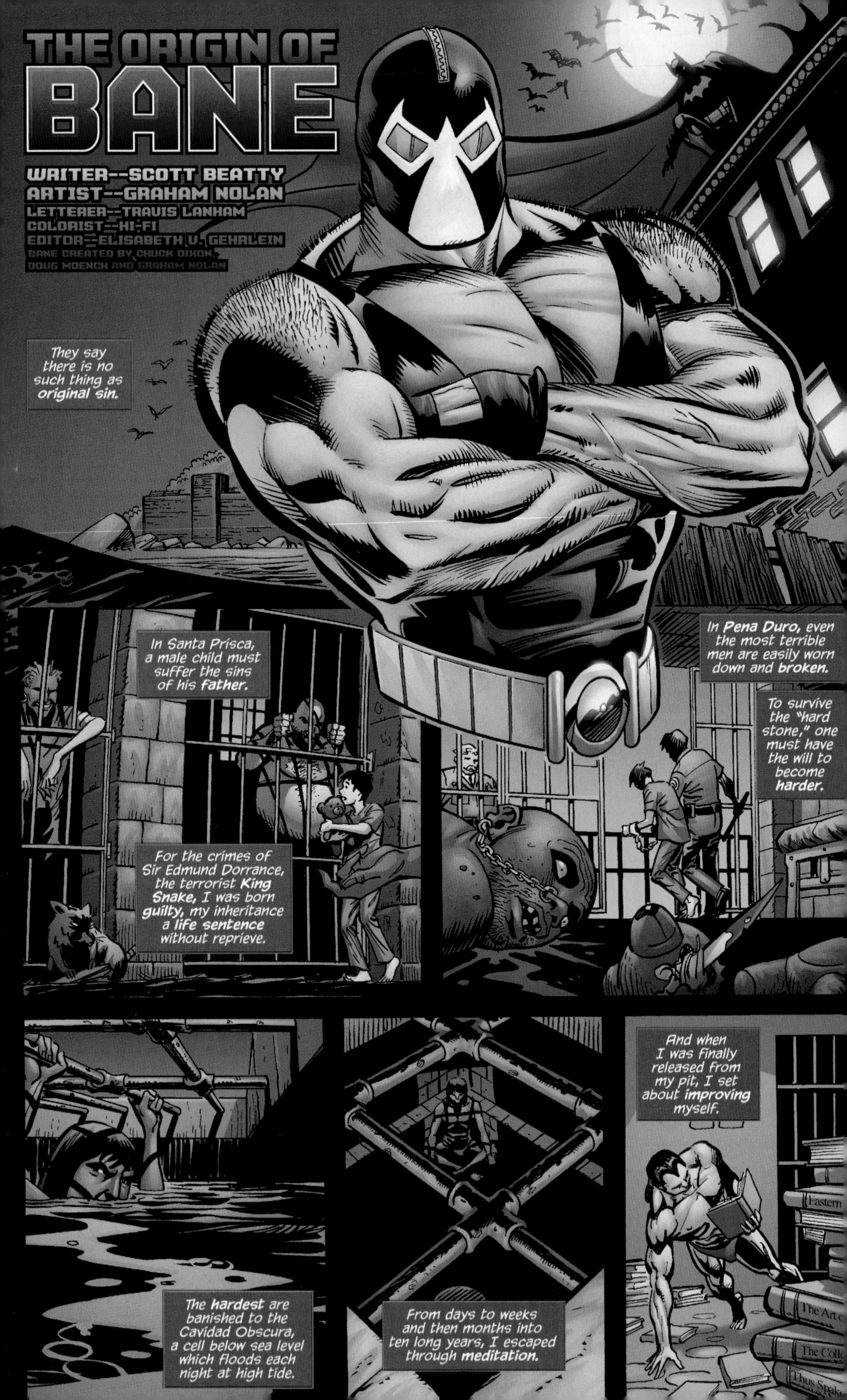
THE ORIGIN OF
BANE
WRITER--SCOTT BEATTY
ARTIST--GRAHAM NOLAN
LETTERER--TRAVIS LANHAM
COLORIST--HI-FI
EDITOR--ELISABETH V. GEHRLEIN
BANE CREATED BY CHUCK DIXON, DOUG MOENCH AND GRAHAM NOLAN
They say there is no such thing as original sin.
In Santa Prisca, a male child must suffer the sins of his father.
For the crimes of Sir Edmund Dorrance, the terrorist King Snake, I was born guilty, my inheritance a life sentence without reprieve.
In Pena Duro, even the most terrible men are easily worn down and broken.
To survive the "hard stone," one must have the will to become harder.
The hardest are banished to the Cavidad Obscura, a cell below sea level which floods each night at high tide.
From days to weeks and then months into ten long years, I escaped through meditation.
And when I was finally released from my pit, I set about improving myself.
Eastern

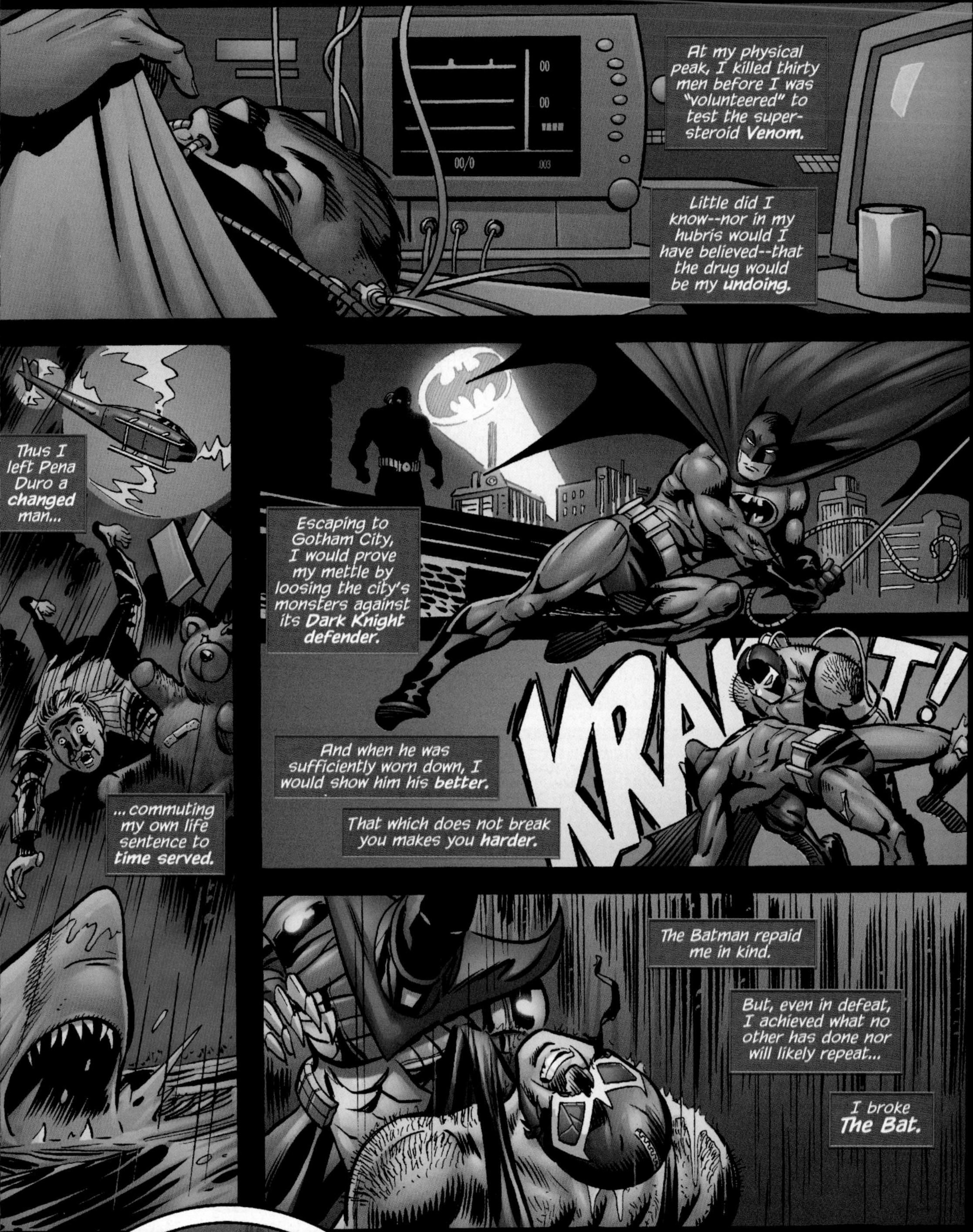
At my physical peak, I killed thirty men before I was "volunteered" to test the super-steroid **Venom.**
Little did I know--nor in my hubris would I have believed--that the drug would be my **undoing.**
Thus I left Pena Duro a **changed** man...
...commuting my own life sentence to **time served.**
Escaping to Gotham City, I would prove my mettle by loosing the city's monsters against its **Dark Knight defender.**
And when he was sufficiently worn down, I would show him his **better.**
That which does not break you makes you **harder.**
The Batman repaid me in kind.
But, even in defeat, I achieved what no other has done nor will likely repeat...
I broke **The Bat.**

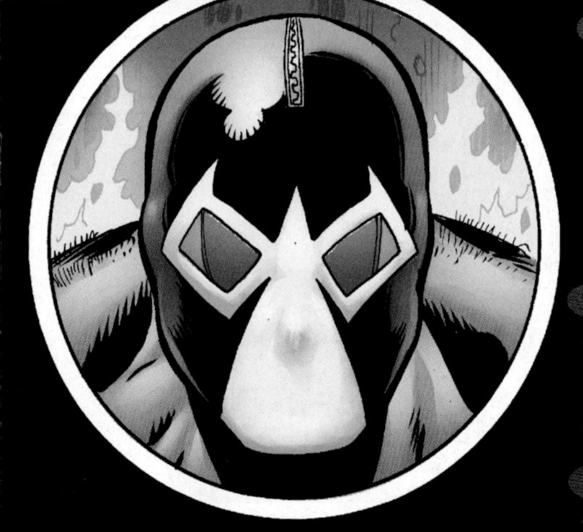

POWERS AND WEAPONS:

In Pena Duro, Bane came to believe that knowledge held true power. A voracious reader, he mastered six languages and studied philosophy and military strategy. Meditation furthered his mental growth, while a vigorous exercise regimen forged his body into a lethal weapon. The adrenocortico steroid Venom increased his strength and stamina tenfold. Bane beat his Venom addiction after the "replacement" Batman, Jean Paul Valley (A.K.A. Azrael), beat him into a coma. Upon waking, the withered Bane rebuilt his broken body to new levels of physical perfection.

ESSENTIAL STORYLINES:

- Batman: Knightfall Volumes 1-3
- Batman: Vengeance of Bane
- Batman: Vengeance of Bane II: The Redemption
- Batman: Bane
- Gotham Knights 33, 47-49

AFFILIATIONS:

- Suicide Squad

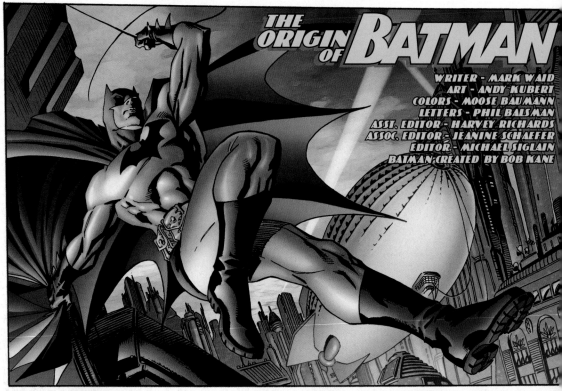

THE ORIGIN OF BATMAN

WRITER - MARK WAID
ART - ANDY KUBERT
COLORS - MOOSE BAUMANN
LETTERS - PHIL BALSMAN
ASST. EDITOR - HARVEY RICHARDS
ASSOC. EDITOR - JEANINE SCHAEFER
EDITOR - MICHAEL SIGLAIN
BATMAN CREATED BY BOB KANE

BRUCE WAYNE LEARNED THE POWER OF FEAR AS A BOY--

--WATCHING IN FROZEN HORROR AS HIS PARENTS, TWO OF GOTHAM CITY'S LEADING CITIZENS, WERE ROBBED AND MURDERED BY A COMMON THUG.

AT THEIR GRAVES, BRUCE SWORE A SOLEMN VOW TO AVENGE THEIR DEATHS.

RELYING LESS UPON HIS BILLION-DOLLAR INHERITANCE THAN ON HIS IRON WILL, BRUCE TRAVELED THE GLOBE--

--GRADUALLY TRAINING HIS MIND AND BODY TO THE PEAK OF HUMAN PERFECTION--

--WHILE STUDYING UNDER THE BEST CRIMINOLOGISTS, DETECTIVES AND FIGHTERS THE WORLD HAD TO OFFER.

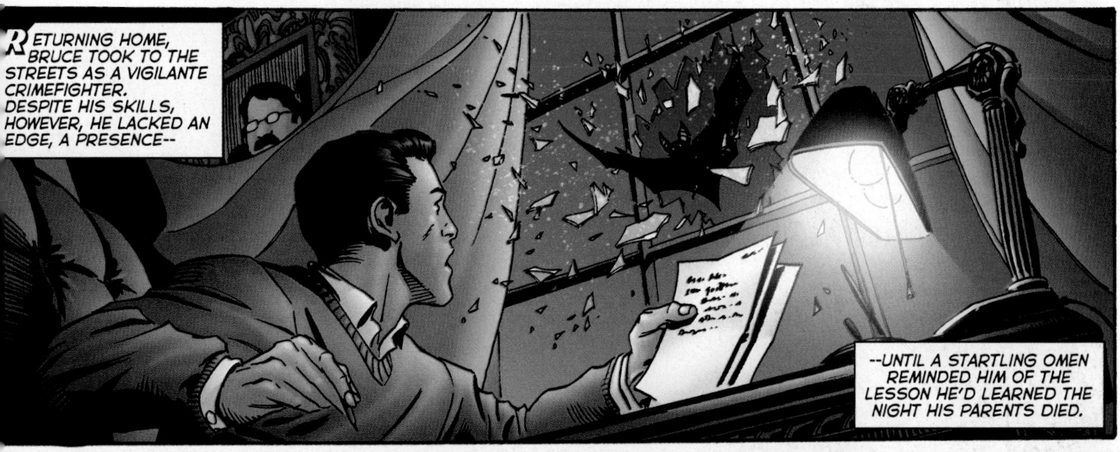
RETURNING HOME, BRUCE TOOK TO THE STREETS AS A VIGILANTE CRIMEFIGHTER. DESPITE HIS SKILLS, HOWEVER, HE LACKED AN EDGE, A PRESENCE--
--UNTIL A STARTLING OMEN REMINDED HIM OF THE LESSON HE'D LEARNED THE NIGHT HIS PARENTS DIED.

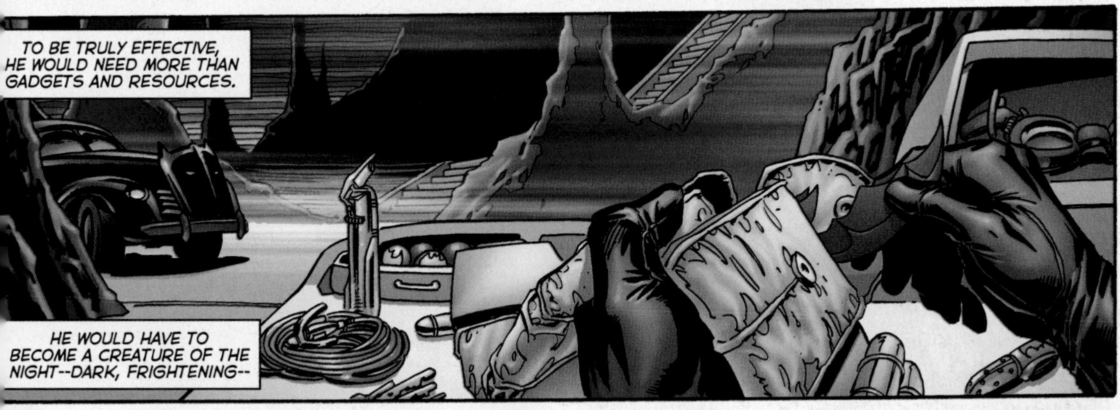
TO BE TRULY EFFECTIVE, HE WOULD NEED MORE THAN GADGETS AND RESOURCES.
HE WOULD HAVE TO BECOME A CREATURE OF THE NIGHT--DARK, FRIGHTENING--

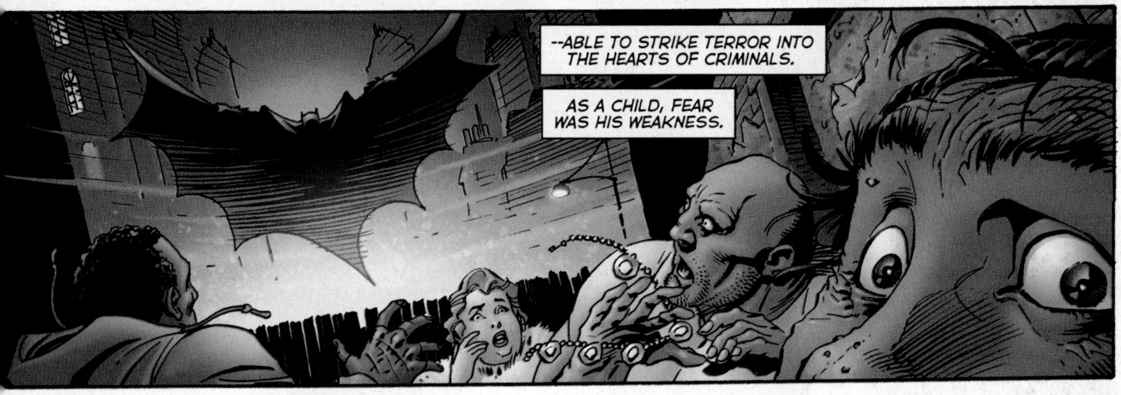
--ABLE TO STRIKE TERROR INTO THE HEARTS OF CRIMINALS.
AS A CHILD, FEAR WAS HIS WEAKNESS.

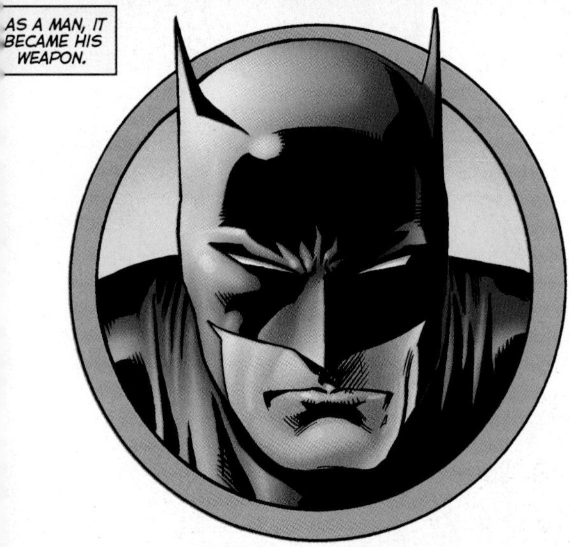
AS A MAN, IT BECAME HIS WEAPON.

POWERS AND WEAPONS:

Besides being a master of fighting styles, the Batman is a legendary escape artist and the world's greatest detective. His utility belt is stocked with a wide array of tools and armaments, including batarangs, grapnels and zip-lines, gas and smoke capsules, and remote controls for his fleet of Batmobiles.

ESSENTIAL STORYLINES:

THE BATMAN CHRONICLES
BATMAN: YEAR ONE
THE DARK KNIGHT RETURNS
BATMAN: THE GREATEST STORIES EVER TOLD

ALLIANCES:

Justice League of America

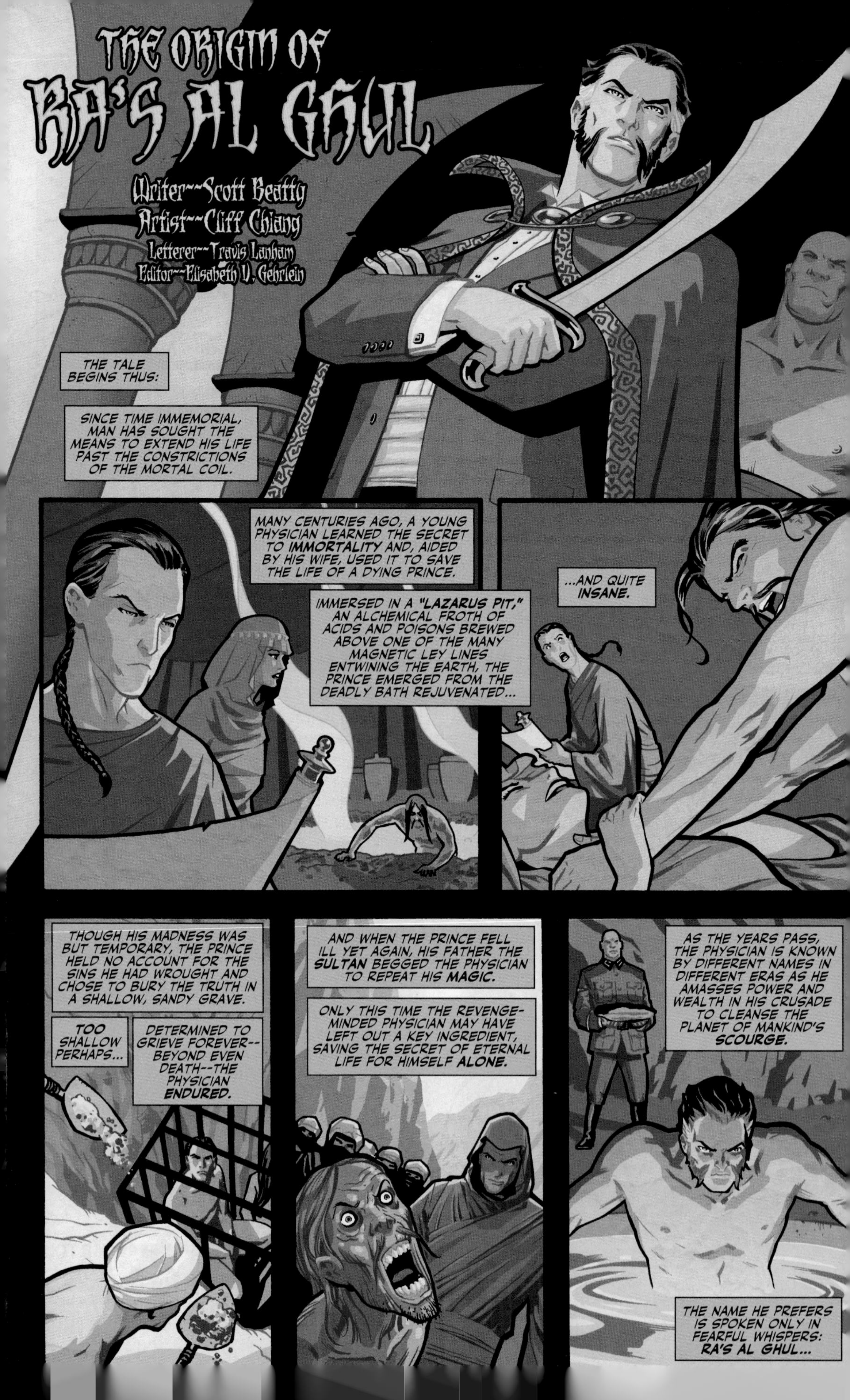
THE ORIGIN OF
RA'S AL GHUL
Writer~~Scott Beatty
Artist~~Cliff Chiang
Letterer~~Travis Lanham
Editor~~Elisabeth V. Gehrlein
THE TALE BEGINS THUS:
SINCE TIME IMMEMORIAL, MAN HAS SOUGHT THE MEANS TO EXTEND HIS LIFE PAST THE CONSTRICTIONS OF THE MORTAL COIL.
MANY CENTURIES AGO, A YOUNG PHYSICIAN LEARNED THE SECRET TO IMMORTALITY AND, AIDED BY HIS WIFE, USED IT TO SAVE THE LIFE OF A DYING PRINCE.
IMMERSED IN A "LAZARUS PIT," AN ALCHEMICAL FROTH OF ACIDS AND POISONS BREWED ABOVE ONE OF THE MANY MAGNETIC LEY LINES ENTWINING THE EARTH, THE PRINCE EMERGED FROM THE DEADLY BATH REJUVENATED...
...AND QUITE INSANE.
THOUGH HIS MADNESS WAS BUT TEMPORARY, THE PRINCE HELD NO ACCOUNT FOR THE SINS HE HAD WROUGHT AND CHOSE TO BURY THE TRUTH IN A SHALLOW, SANDY GRAVE.
TOO SHALLOW PERHAPS...
DETERMINED TO GRIEVE FOREVER--BEYOND EVEN DEATH--THE PHYSICIAN ENDURED.
AND WHEN THE PRINCE FELL ILL YET AGAIN, HIS FATHER THE SULTAN BEGGED THE PHYSICIAN TO REPEAT HIS MAGIC.
ONLY THIS TIME THE REVENGE-MINDED PHYSICIAN MAY HAVE LEFT OUT A KEY INGREDIENT, SAVING THE SECRET OF ETERNAL LIFE FOR HIMSELF ALONE.
AS THE YEARS PASS, THE PHYSICIAN IS KNOWN BY DIFFERENT NAMES IN DIFFERENT ERAS AS HE AMASSES POWER AND WEALTH IN HIS CRUSADE TO CLEANSE THE PLANET OF MANKIND'S SCOURGE.
THE NAME HE PREFERS IS SPOKEN ONLY IN FEARFUL WHISPERS: RA'S AL GHUL...

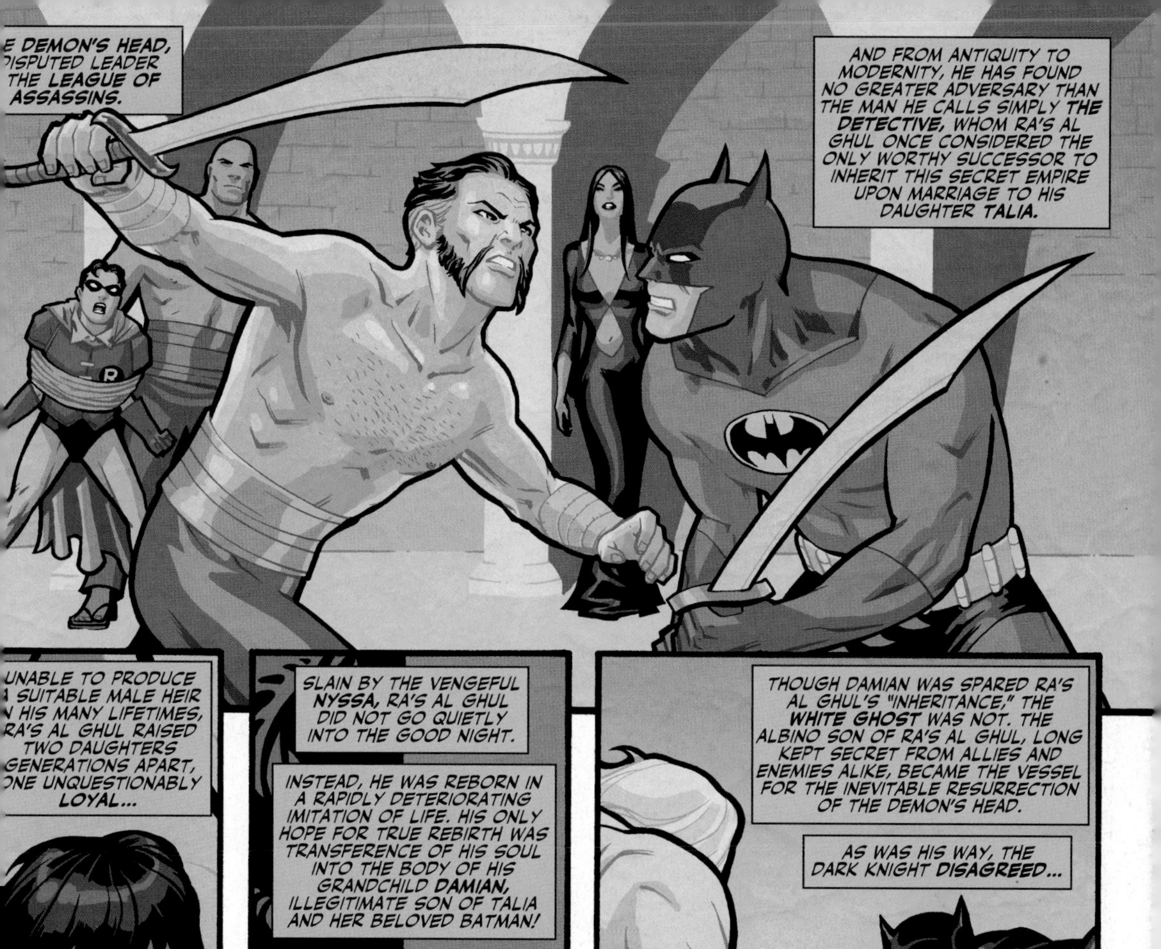
E DEMON'S HEAD, DISPUTED LEADER THE LEAGUE OF ASSASSINS.
AND FROM ANTIQUITY TO MODERNITY, HE HAS FOUND NO GREATER ADVERSARY THAN THE MAN HE CALLS SIMPLY THE DETECTIVE, WHOM RA'S AL GHUL ONCE CONSIDERED THE ONLY WORTHY SUCCESSOR TO INHERIT THIS SECRET EMPIRE UPON MARRIAGE TO HIS DAUGHTER TALIA.
UNABLE TO PRODUCE A SUITABLE MALE HEIR N HIS MANY LIFETIMES, RA'S AL GHUL RAISED TWO DAUGHTERS GENERATIONS APART, ONE UNQUESTIONABLY LOYAL...
...THE OTHER TREACHEROUS.
SLAIN BY THE VENGEFUL NYSSA, RA'S AL GHUL DID NOT GO QUIETLY INTO THE GOOD NIGHT.
INSTEAD, HE WAS REBORN IN A RAPIDLY DETERIORATING IMITATION OF LIFE. HIS ONLY HOPE FOR TRUE REBIRTH WAS TRANSFERENCE OF HIS SOUL INTO THE BODY OF HIS GRANDCHILD DAMIAN, ILLEGITIMATE SON OF TALIA AND HER BELOVED BATMAN!
THOUGH DAMIAN WAS SPARED RA'S AL GHUL'S "INHERITANCE," THE WHITE GHOST WAS NOT. THE ALBINO SON OF RA'S AL GHUL, LONG KEPT SECRET FROM ALLIES AND ENEMIES ALIKE, BECAME THE VESSEL FOR THE INEVITABLE RESURRECTION OF THE DEMON'S HEAD.
AS WAS HIS WAY, THE DARK KNIGHT DISAGREED...
...AND NOW RA'S AL GHUL SERVES A LIFE-SENTENCE IN ARKHAM ASYLUM, KEPT SILENT AND IMMOBILE BY PRESENT-DAY MEDICINE.
BUT FOR A MAN WHO HAS ESCAPED DEATH'S CLUTCHES TIME AND AGAIN, SURELY STONE WALLS AND IRON BARS WILL NOT HOLD HIM FOR LONG.

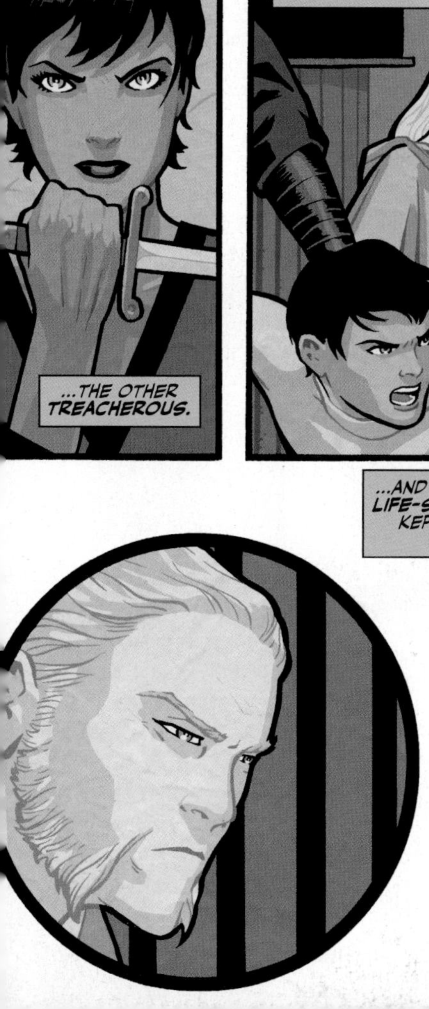

POWERS AND WEAPONS:

In the centuries he has lived, Ra's al Ghul has become a master swordsman and ruthless fighter. He wields even greater power as leader of countless minions willing to go to their death in the name of the Demon's Head. His private bodyguard, always called Ubu, is chosen in a deathmatch between rival combatants vying for the position. Only Ra's al Ghul knows the alchemical formula to create a Lazarus Pit, a secret he jealously guards. He is a brilliant and cunning strategist and perhaps the greatest threat to human life on earth.

ESSENTIAL STORYLINES:

- Batman 232
- Batman: Son of the Demon
- Batman: Birth of the Demon
- Batman: Legacy
- Batman: Death and the Maidens
- The Resurrection of Ra's al Ghul

AFFILIATIONS:

- The League of Assassins

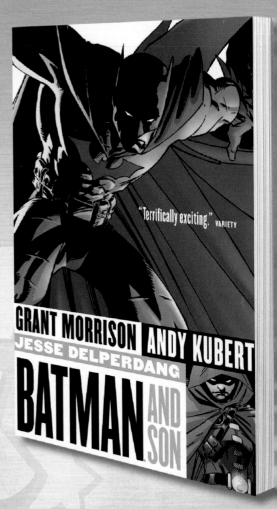
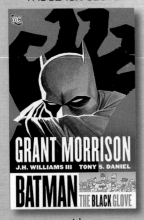